EUROPEAN SOCIETY OF INTERNATIONAL LAW SERIES

Migration and the European Convention on Human Rights

EUROPEAN SOCIETY OF INTERNATIONAL LAW SERIES

The ESIL Book Series publishes high-quality volumes on the themes of ESIL Annual Conferences and ESIL joint events primarily. The volumes include chapters that are based on selected papers presented at ESIL events, revised to fit the theme and focus of the volume, and complemented by additional chapters that address topics that were not fully explored at the events but that are essential for a full coverage of the theme.

Migration and the European Convention on Human Rights

Edited by

BAŞAK ÇALI
LEDI BIANKU
IULIA MOTOC

OXFORD
UNIVERSITY PRESS

OXFORD
UNIVERSITY PRESS

Great Clarendon Street, Oxford, OX2 6DP,
United Kingdom

Oxford University Press is a department of the University of Oxford.
It furthers the University's objective of excellence in research, scholarship,
and education by publishing worldwide. Oxford is a registered trade mark of
Oxford University Press in the UK and in certain other countries

First Edition published in 2021

Impression: 3

Published in the United States of America by Oxford University Press
198 Madison Avenue, New York, NY 10016, United States of America

British Library Cataloguing in Publication Data

Data available

Library of Congress Control Number: 2020947858

ISBN 978–0–19–289519–6

DOI: 10.1093/oso/9780192895196.001.0001

Printed and bound by
CPI Group (UK) Ltd, Croydon, CR0 4YY

Acknowledgements

The editors wish to thank all the contributors for their chapters, which were initially discussed at a conference jointly organised by the European Society of International Law and the European Court of Human Rights at the premises of the Court in October 2017. We believe that this conference which brought together academics and judges of the European Court of Human Rights, alongside a very engaged audience, was a learning experience for all of us. It provided important exchanges as to how the judges of the European Court of Human Rights and academics studying the case law of the Court evaluate the case law of the European Convention on Human Rights on multi-dimensional human rights questions that the phenomenon of migration brings to the fore.

The European Court of Human Rights deserves special credit for hosting the original conference. We thank the then President of the Court, Guido Raimodi, for hosting the event. We also thank Judges Julia Laffranque, Krzysztof Wojtyczek, and Ganna Yudkivska of the European Court of Human Rights, as well as Judge Simona-Maya Teodoroiu of the Constitutional Court of Romania, for their contributions to the conference, and to Mariam Aghavelyan of the Registry of the Court for her assistance in the organisation of the conference.

From the European Society of International Law, Joyce Davies provided, as always, invaluable administrative support. We are also thankful to the Society's then president, Luis Miguel Hinojosa Martînez, and board for continuous support for this project.

The editor of the European Society of International Law book series, Anne van Aaken, and the editor responsible for this book, Yuval Shany, were extremely supportive throughout and provided invaluable feedback and comments. We express our gratitude to them.

From the Hertie School, Stewart Cunningham and Kristina Hatas participated in the editing of the book manuscript and played crucial roles bringing the volume to completion.

From Oxford University Press, we thank Merel Alstein, Jack McNichol, and their team.

Başak Çalı, Berlin
Ledi Bianku, Strasbourg
Iulia Motoc, Strasbourg

Table of Contents

PART IV STAGES OF MIGRATION AND THE EUROPEAN COURT OF HUMAN RIGHTS

List of Contributors

Ledi Bianku is an Associate Professor at the University of Strasbourg and a former Judge of the European Court of Human Rights.

Eva Brems is a Senior Full Professor and Head of the Human Rights Centre at Ghent University, Belgium.

Başak Çalı is Co-director of the Centre for Fundamental Rights and Professor of International Law at the Hertie School, Berlin.

Stewart Cunningham is an independent researcher.

Marie-Bénédicte Dembour is Professor of Law and Anthropology at the Human Rights Centre of Ghent University and the PI on the ERC Advanced Grant 'DISSECT: Evidence in International Human Rights Adjudication'.

Carmen Pérez González is Associate Professor of Public International Law, Universidad Carlos III de Madrid.

Kristina Hatas is Research Associate at the Hertie School, Berlin.

Francesca Ippolito is Associate Professor of International Law at the University of Cagliari.

Violeta Moreno-Lax is Reader in Law, founder of the Immigration Law programme, and Co-Founder and former Co-Director of the Centre for European and International Legal Affairs (CEILA) at Queen Mary University of London.

Iulia Motoc is Judge at the European Court on Human Rights and Professor at the University of Bucharest.

Bianca Selejan-Gutan is Professor of Constitutional Law and Human Rights Law at Lucian Blaga University of Sibiu, Romania, Faculty of Law.

Ksenija Turković is Vice-President of the European Court of Human Rights.

PART I

SITUATING MIGRATION IN THE EUROPEAN CONVENTION ON HUMAN RIGHTS

This part sets out how the European Convention on Human Rights is situated in the broader context of the regulation of migration and the rights of migrants in international law and how the European Court of Human Rights has addressed the textual silence of the European Convention on Human Rights on the question of migration or the rights of migrants in its case law, in particular in comparison to the Inter-American Court of Human Rights.

1
Migration and the European Convention on Human Rights

Başak Çalı, Ledi Bianku, and Iulia Motoc

1. Introduction

"[. . .] Étranges étrangers

vous êtes de la ville
vous êtes de sa vie
même si mal en vivez
même si vous mourez'

Jacques Prévert
Grand bal du printemps"

Migration, voluntary or involuntary, is a phenomenon that was born at the outset of human society.[1] The regulation of migration and asylum through law, however, has a more recent history.[2] It is closely connected with the rise of the nation-state in Europe in the early 20th century.[3] In this period, states in Europe abandoned a permissive view of migration and began to see borders as important sites for reifying homogenous nation-states. This is also when we see law starting to exert its authority on migration. Law has since become the key site for demarcating the rules of inclusion and exclusion of migrants[4] based on multiple underlying logics, namely those of population control and labour market needs.

[1] Robert J Kleiner, *Migration: Immigration and Emigration in International Perspective* (Greenwood Publishing Group 2003) 3–4; Michael H Fisher, *Migration: A World History* (OUP, USA 2014) 2; Dirk Hoerder, *Cultures in Contact: World Migrations in the Second Millennium* (Duke University Press 2002); Linda Rabben, *Sanctuary and Asylum : A Social and Political History* (University of Washington Press 2016) 31ff.
[2] Matthew E Price, *Rethinking Asylum: History, Purpose, and Limits* (Cambridge University Press 2009) 52ff. Vincent Chetail, International Migration Law (OUP 2019) 38–52.
[3] John Torpey, *The Invention of the Passport: Surveillance, Citizenship and the State* (Cambridge University Press 2000); Guy Goodwin-Gill and Jane McAdam, *The Refugee in International Law* (3rd edn, OUP 2007) 1; Thomas Gammeltoft-Hansen, *Access to Asylum: International Refugee Law and the Globalisation of Migration Control* (Cambridge University Press 2011) 12.
[4] Phillip Cole, *Philosophies of Exclusion: Liberal Political Theory and Immigration* (Edinburgh University Press 2000).

Başak Çalı, Ledi Biancu, and Iulia Motoc, *Migration and the European Convention on Human Rights* In: *Migration and the European Convention on Human Rights*. Edited by: Başak Çali, Ledi Bianku, and Iulia Motoc, Oxford University Press (2021).
 DOI: 10.1093/oso/9780192895196.003.0001

International law's relationship with migration law has been deeply affected by the historical shifts in viewing migration primarily as a domestic matter and viewing it also as a matter regulated by international law. When states held a broadly permissive view of migration, international law too reflected the principle of freedom of migration.[5] As the domestic laws' regulatory grip on migration has tightened in the 20th century and onwards, international law has become structurally deferential to domestic law in the field of migration control. In due course, efforts have turned to focus on using international law to tame the regulatory grip of domestic law through an emphasis on recovering rights and justice-based concerns, a common thread that was prevalent in the earlier natural law approaches to international law.[6] Yet, these efforts have been, and continue to persist as piecemeal efforts. Contemporary international law governs neither migration nor those who migrate in a holistic manner.[7] There is no international law of migration, only a patchwork of fragmented international legal regimes, alongside regional and sub regional systems.[8] This is despite recent calls to consolidate a new branch of international law, under the heading of international migration law.[9]

Contemporary international law addresses migration first and foremost in a *particular* form under international refugee law. This regime operates primarily by distinguishing those who migrate due to persecution in their home countries, and those who migrate for reasons that do not fall within the realm of persecution.[10] Currently crystallised under the 1951 Convention on the Status of Refugees and its 1967 Protocol, this regime seeks to offer protection to those who fall in the first category by protecting them from *non-refoulement*[11] and criminalisation due to illegal entry.[12] If their claims for asylum are warranted, the Refugee Convention then regularises their domestic status and assigns them a comprehensive set of civil, political, economic, and social rights in the receiving country.[13] Yet, he or she who falls within the scope of the legal category of a 'refugee' as defined by the

[5] Chetail (n 2) 40–41.

[6] Georg Cavallar, *The Rights of Strangers: Theories of International Hospitality, the Global Community and Political Justice since Vitoria* (Routledge 2002).

[7] Jillyanne Redpath-Cross, Richard Perruchoud, and Brian R Opeskin, 'Conceptualizing International Migration Law' in Jillyanne Redpath-Cross, Richard Perruchoud, and Brian R Opeskin (eds), *Foundations of International Migration Law* (Cambridge University Press 2012) 1–16, 6.

[8] Ibrahim Awad, 'The Multiple Levels of Governance of International Migration: Understanding Disparities and Disorder' (2017) 111 AJIL Unbound 153–58.

[9] Jaya Ramji-Nogales, 'Migration Emergencies' (2017) 68 Hastings Law Journal 609–56; Chetail (n 2).

[10] Jane McAdam, 'The Refugee Convention as a Rights Blueprint for Persons in Need of International Protection' in Jane McAdam (ed), *Forced Migration, Human Rights and Security* (Hart Publishing 2008) 263–82.

[11] Convention Relating to the Status of Refugees (adopted 28 July 1951, entered into force 22 April 1954) 189 UNTS 137, Article 33.

[12] ibid, Article 31.

[13] Andreas Zimmermann, *The 1951 Convention Relating to the Status of Refugees and its 1967 Protocol: A Commentary* (OUP 2011).

Refugee Convention has been the subject of much debate in scholarship[14] and has seen diverging forms of interpretation and comparative domestic practice.[15]

Alongside international refugee law, other fields of international law, too, address questions of migration in a piecemeal way. The international law of statelessness seeks to govern migration by encouraging states to ensure that those who are present in their territories are not rendered stateless due to their migration status.[16] In that respect, the law of statelessness focuses only on those who have already migrated to another country and their descendants and who are at risk of not having any legal status, due to the uncoordinated domestic citizenship laws of each country, which may lead to a situation, due to particular migration flows, where the migrant loses citizenship in both the home state and receiving state. International criminal law focuses on migration by way of its prohibition on extreme forms of forced migration of peoples. The legal definition of crimes against humanity categorises forced displacement of persons as an element of this crime and the forcible transfer of children is an element of the crime of genocide. Forcible displacement or transfer of civilians can also constitute war crimes.[17] In international criminal law, the focus, therefore, is on criminalising those who cause the forced migration of individuals, vulnerable groups such as children, or protected persons such as civilians in armed conflict. International criminal law, as such, cannot restore the rights of those who are forcefully displaced. More recently, international law concerning trafficking in persons focusses on the criminal activities of organized criminal groups and seeks to prevent and combat trafficking in persons and to protect and assist victims of trafficking.[18]

A key site of international law's attempts to regulate migration has been in the field of international labour law. Significantly, the Migration for Employment Convention of 1949 and the Migrant Workers Convention of 1975, under the auspices of the International Labour Organisation, provide a common and broad definition of a migrant worker as a person who is already employed or seeks

[14] See generally, James Hathaway and Michelle Foster, *The Law of Refugee Status* (2nd edn, Cambridge University Press 2014) 105–06, 123; Gregor Noll, 'Evidentiary Assessment under the Refugee Convention: Risk, Pain and the Intersubjectivity of Fear' in Gregor Noll (ed), *Proof, Evidentiary Assessment and Credibility in Asylum Procedures* (Martinus Nijhoff 2005) 141–60; Andreas Zimmermann and Claudia Mahler, 'Article 1 A, Para 2 1951 Convention' in Zimmermann (n 13) 281–465, 341.

[15] Hélène Lambert, Francesco Messineo, and Paul Tiedemann, 'Comparative Perspectives of Constitutional Asylum in France, Italy, and Germany: *Requiescat in Pace*?' (2008) 27(3) Refugee Survey Quarterly 16–32; Zimmermann and Mahler (n 14) 341.

[16] See Ivan Shearer and Brian Opeskin, 'Nationality and Statelessness' in Redpath-Cross et al (n 7) 93–122, 102–14.

[17] Rome Statute of the International Criminal Court (adopted 17 July 1998, entered into force 1 July 2002) 2187 UNTS 3, Arts 7(d) and 8(2)(e)(viii); International Criminal Court, Elements of Crimes (International Criminal Court 2011) 6; 39.

[18] United Nations Protocol to Prevent, Suppress and Punish Trafficking in Persons Especially Women and Children, supplementing the United Nations Convention against Transnational Organised Crime (adopted 15 November 2000, entered into force 25 December 2003) 2237 UNTS 319.

employment in the state in which he/she resides regardless of the type or duration of work and, furthermore, requires respect for their basic rights.[19] However, neither of these conventions provide for a duty to admit migrant workers. Instead, they instruct states parties to co-operate in the fields of regular and irregular migration.[20]

International law's piecemeal efforts to introduce baselines and common and co-operative frameworks to regulate migration are constantly under pressure and the discretion left to states under their duty of co-operation in the field of migration remains vast. As seen in the *en masse* movements of nearly one million Syrians crossing to Greece and beyond from Turkey (in particular in 2015),[21] the ongoing attempts of thousands seeking to cross the Mediterranean from Libya to the shores of Italy,[22] or the attempts to scale the border fences between Morocco and Spain,[23] most of those who may qualify as refugees, or are in need of protection, are not capable of reaching states through safe routes of migration. Instead, many states, in particular in the Global North, are effectively blocking safe routes of migration as well as the right to seek asylum by preventing individuals from crossing borders.[24]

Internal migration within the European Union (EU) is often seen as a successful model for a return to the permissibility of migration paradigm[25] and for expanding the logic of inclusion through supranational regulation of asylum.[26] However, the EU has also reified the logic of exclusion through creating fine-grained rules such as the requirement to claim asylum in the first country of entry[27] and the safe

[19] ILO Convention 97, Convention concerning Migration for Employment (Revised) (adopted 8 June 1949, entered into force 22 January 1952) 120 UNTS 71, Article 11(1) and ILO Convention 143, Convention concerning Migrations on Abusive Condition and Promotion of Equality and Opportunity of Treatment of Migrant Workers (adopted 24 June 1975, entered into force 9 December 1978) 2220 UNTS 3.

[20] Article 1 of ILO Convention 97 and Article 2 of ILO Convention 143 (n 19).

[21] In 2015, 885,386 migrants arrived in the EU via the Eastern Mediterranean route, most of whom were from Syria, with numbers going down since the EU-Turkey statement. Frontex, 'Migratory Routes' available at https://frontex.europa.eu/along-eu-borders/migratory-routes/eastern-mediterranean-route/ (accessed 2 December 2019).

[22] According to the United Nations High Commissioner on Human Rights and European Union Agency Frontex, 119,000 arrivals were recorded in 2017 and about 23,000 in 2018 via the central Mediterranean route. UNHCR, 'Mediterranean Situation' available at https://data2.unhcr.org/en/situations/mediterranean/location/5205 (accessed 2 December 2019): Frontex, 'Migratory Routes' available at https://frontex.europa.eu/along-eu-borders/migratory-routes/central-mediterranean-route/ (accessed 2 December 20119). The International Office for Migration records 17,000 crossings in 2019. IOM, 'Mediterranean Migrant Arrivals Reach 17,000 in 2019; Deaths Reach 493' (5 October 2019) https://www.iom.int/news/mediterranean-migrant-arrivals-reach-17000-2019-deaths-reach-493 (accessed 2 December 2019).

[23] Council of Europe, 'Report of the fact-finding mission by Ambassador Tomáš Boček, Special Representative of the Secretary General on migration and refugees, to Spain, 18–24 March 2018' (3 September 2018) SG/Inf(2018)25.

[24] Daniel Ghezelbash, *Refugee Lost: Asylum Law in an Interdependent World* (Cambridge University Press 2018).

[25] Sara Iglesias Sánchez, 'Free Movement Law within the European Union: Workers, Citizens and Third-Country Nationals' in Marion Panizzon, Gottfried Zürcher, and Elisa Fornalé (eds), *The Palgrave Handbook of International Labour Migration* (Palgrave Macmillan 2015) 361–81.

[26] Cathryn Costello, *The Human Rights of Migrants and Refugees in European Law* (OUP 2016).

[27] Regulation (EU) No 604/2013 of the European Parliament and of the Council of 26 June 2013 establishing the criteria and mechanisms for determining the Member State responsible for examining

third-country policy,[28] through granting financial and other forms of assistance to non-EU member states who share common borders[29] or seas[30] with the EU (with the aim of reducing or preventing migration), and deference to EU member states concerning the regulation of migration of non-EU citizens.

2. International Human Rights Law and Migration

The birth and development of international human rights law is often seen as a key progressive site in efforts to tame states' regulatory grip on migration. [31] This is primarily because international human rights law does not operate by focusing on the *de jure* legal status of individuals, but by shifting attention to the rights of individuals *qua* humans and the consequent duties that states owe individuals. The Universal Declaration of Human Rights, the normative bedrock of international human rights law, does not limit the rights recognised in the Declaration only to the citizens of particular states. In that vein, freedom from torture and inhuman or degrading treatment, equality before the law, or the right to education, for example, must apply equally to non-citizens (with or without a legal status). Furthermore, states do not have only negative, but also positive, obligations to non-citizens and migrants, again regardless of their legal status. What is more, the Universal Declaration of Human Rights in its Article 14 recognised the right to seek asylum and there is a specialised convention that comprehensively lists, and is fully dedicated to protect, the rights of migrants on a global scale: the International Convention on the Protection of All Migrant Workers and Members of their Families.

Yet, in the words of Hannah Arendt, whilst international human rights law has a cosmopolitan premise and promise, it does not fully recognise an unqualified 'right to have rights' for everyone.[32] More crucially, there is no right to migrate in

an application for international protection lodged in one of the Member States by a third-country national or a stateless person [2013] OJ L180/31.

[28] Directive 2013/32/EU of the European Parliament and of the Council of 26 June 2013 on common procedures for granting and withdrawing international protection [2013] OJ L180/60, Art 38.

[29] European Union: Council of the European Union, 'EU-Turkey statement' (18 March 2016) http://www.consilium.europa.eu/en/press/press-releases/2016/03/18-eu-turkey-statement/ (accessed 2 December 2019).

[30] Operation Sophia, established by Council Decision (CFSP) 2015/778 of 18 May 2015 on a European Union military operation in the Southern Central Mediterranean (EUNAVFOR MED) [2015] OJ L122/31, and in its mandate the training of the Libyan coast guard and navy since Council Decision (CFSP) 2016/993 of 20 June 2016 amending Decision (CFSP) 2015/778 on a European Union military operation in the Southern Central Mediterranean (EUNAVFOR MED operation SOPHIA) [2016] OJ L162/18.

[31] On the potential of international human rights law to address questions of migration, see for example Hélène Lambert, 'Protection against Refoulement from Europe: Human Rights Law Comes to the Rescue' (1999) 48(3) International & Comparative Law Quarterly 515–44.

[32] Hannah Arendt, *The Origins of Totalitarianism* (Schocken Books 2004).

international human rights law. Whilst the right to seek and enjoy asylum from persecution (Article 14) and the right to nationality (Article 15) were included in the Universal Declaration of Human Rights in 1948,[33] neither survived the negotiation process of the International Covenant on Civil and Political Rights and are not part of states' legal obligations under the Covenant.[34]

A second limitation of international human rights law with regard to migration is related to the jurisdictional requirements of this body of law. Those who are on the move, voluntarily or involuntarily, must first fall within the jurisdiction of a state to claim rights from that state under international human rights law.[35] This jurisdictional requirement, in particular, imposes significant obstacles for challenging the limits that are placed on migration and asylum through the heightened restrictions that are put in place, including erecting walls and punitive regulations for private carriers. Even when a person crosses an international boundary, only a few of her rights attract absolute duties on the part of states at the moment of entry, namely the right to be free from torture, inhuman and degrading treatment, and protection from *non-refoulement* to another country where the person may suffer from irreparable harm. International human rights law allows for restrictions on many of the rights that are part of its corpus, be they for migrants or citizens. Yet, in the case of migrants, these legitimate restrictions may be more extensive. For example, international human rights law does not categorically prohibit the detention of migrants at the point of entry to a country in order to carry out legal status determinations.[36] Long-term migrants who spend most of their time in a host country can be subject to deportation on the grounds that they have committed a serious crime.[37] Long-term migrants do not enjoy the status of a national minority on account of their lack of historical presence in a country.[38]

In terms of specific treaty based international human rights law standards that apply to migrants, international human rights law has yet to produce a truly global

[33] Universal Declaration of Human Rights (adopted 10 December 1948) UNGA Res 217 A(III).

[34] International Covenant on Civil and Political Rights (adopted 16 December 1966, entered into force 23 March 1976) 999 UNTS 17. Katherine Yon Ebright 'Nationality and Defining "The Right to Have Rights"' 56 Columbia Journal Of Transnational Law 875; Marc Bossuyt, *Guide to the 'travaux Préparatoires' of the International Covenant on Civil and Political Rights* (Martinus Nijhoff Publishers 1987) 463–68.

[35] Maarten den Heijer, *Europe and Extraterritorial Asylum* (Hart Publishing 2012) 15–56.

[36] Kay Hailbronner, 'Detention of Asylum Seekers' (2007) 9 European Journal of Migration and Law 159–72; Guy Goodwin-Gill, 'International Law and the Detention of Refugees and Asylum Seekers' (1986) 20(2) International Migration Review 193–219; Cathryn Costello, 'Immigration Detention: The Grounds Beneath Our Feet' (2015) 68(1) Current Legal Problems 143–77.

[37] Marie-Bénédicte Dembour, *When Humans Become Migrants: Study of the European Court of Human Rights with an Inter-American Counterpoint* (OUP 2015) 172–87.

[38] See eg declarations to the Framework Convention for the Protection of National Minorities ETS 157 <https://www.coe.int/en/web/conventions/search-on-treaties/-/conventions/treaty/157/declarations> (accessed 2 December 2019). See also Ryszard Cholewinski, 'Migrants as Minorities: Integration and Inclusion in the Enlarged European Union' (2005) 43(4) Journal of Common Market Studies 695–716.

solution. The United Nations Convention on the Rights of Migrant Workers[39] is the most detailed legal provision to date. It seeks to progressively ensure that migrants receive equal treatment with host communities in all walks of life. With its explicit recognition that undocumented migrant workers, too, should enjoy rights in the receiving state, it seeks to pierce the veil of state sovereignty in the field of immigration control. Yet, the UN Convention on the Rights of Migrant Workers has received underwhelming international support, and remains the UN treaty with the lowest number of ratifications to date.[40] The low levels of support that the United Nations Convention on the Rights of Migrant Workers enjoys demonstrates the difficulties in codifying comprehensive protections in the field of migration under international law. The most recent attempt to bring coherency and a holistic vision to the regulation of migration in international law, the New York Declaration,[41] has also not succeeded in resolving the tension between states' regulatory autonomy and a comprehensive bill for regulation of migration.[42] It has received significant pushback from many states across the world, despite its non-binding character.[43]

Yet, despite the piecemeal treatment of migration in international human rights law, and the wide discretion that the law allows for states to deny entry, to restrict the rights of migrants or not positively afford them rights on par with host communities, international human rights law continues to offer an important site for holding states to account on their migration practices. The shortcomings identified above are real, yet the pro-person interpretations of international human rights law also continue to offer direction to states in how to develop rights-based domestic approaches to matters of migration as well as to identify and correct the excesses of domestic regulation. In this respect, doctrinal developments at the level of the United Nations Human Rights Treaty Bodies[44] have represented important

[39] International Convention on the Protection of the Rights of All Migrant Workers and Members of their Families (adopted 18 December 1990, entered into force 1 July 2003) 2220 UNTS 3.

[40] As of December 2019, the treaty had only 55 ratifications; United Nations Treaty Collections, 'Status of Treaties' https://treaties.un.org (accessed 2 December 2019).

[41] UNGA Res 71/1 'New York Declaration for Refugees and Migrants' (19 September 2016) UN Doc A/RES/71/1.

[42] ibid, Annex I: Comprehensive refugee response framework leading to the Global Compact on Refugees, affirmed by UNGA Res 73/151 (17 December 2018) UN Doc A/RES/73/151 and Annex II: Towards a global compact for safe, orderly and regular migration leading to the Global Compact for Safe, Orderly and Regular Migration (adopted 11 December 2018).

[43] *The New York Times*, 'Bolsonaro Pulls Brazil From U.N. Migration Accord' (9 January 2019) https://www.nytimes.com/2019/01/09/world/americas/bolsonaro-brazil-migration-accord.html (accessed 2 December 2019); Politico, 'Under far-right pressure, Europe retreats from UN migration pact' (30 November 2018) https://www.politico.eu/article/migration-un-viktor-orban-sebastian-kurz-far-right-pressure-europe-retreats-from-pact/ (accessed 2 December 2019); Euractiv, 'Belgian PM announces resignation in crisis started by migrant row' (19 December 2018) https://www.euractiv.com/section/elections/news/belgian-pm-announces-resignation-in-crisis-started-by-migrant-row/ (accessed 2 December 2019).

[44] See eg UN HRC, 'CCPR General Comment No 20: Article 7 (Prohibition of Torture, or Other Cruel, Inhuman or Degrading Treatment or Punishment' (1992) UN Doc HRI/GEN/1/Rev.9 (vol I); UN HRC, 'General comment No 31 [80], The nature of the general legal obligation imposed on States Parties to the Covenant' (2004) UN Doc CCPR/C/21/Rev.1/Add.13, para 12.

legal-normative attempts to close the regulation gap as well as to hold domestic migration control practices to account. UN Human Rights Treaty Bodies have made specific contributions to migration, in particular in the field of protection against *non-refoulement* through hearing individual cases and through the issuing of General Comments and periodic review of state reports. The Committee against Torture has been instrumental in interpreting and enforcing the *non-refoulement* duties of states in cases when there is a risk of torture in the country of removal.[45] The United Nations Human Rights Committee has extended discussions of non-*refoulement* based on risks to the right to life alongside torture, inhuman and degrading treatment,[46] and has also scrutinised states' use of detention for migrants through an analysis of states' responsibilities towards persons in detention.[47] The Committee on the Elimination of Discrimination against Women has focused on how women who migrate due to risks to their life and bodily integrity should receive special protection that recognises the gendered dimensions of their migration experiences.[48] The Committee on the Rights of the Child, on the other hand, has increased the formulation of absolute obligations on the part of states when they address the migration of unaccompanied migrant children.[49] Regional human rights courts and commissions have also developed case law and principles to address the protection of human rights in the context of migration.[50]

3. Migration and the European Convention on Human Rights

In Europe, the European Convention on Human Rights (ECHR) and its judicial protection system has been at the core of the regional development of the protection of human rights. Whilst the EU also has a Charter of Fundamental Rights with specific protections for the right to asylum, the ECHR not only addresses a larger pan-European space of forty-seven member states, the Treaty of the European

[45] Committee Against Torture, 'General Comment No 4 (2017) on the Implementation of Article 3 of the Convention in the Context of Article 22' (2017) Un Doc CAT/C/GC/4.

[46] UN HRC, 'General Comment No 36 Article 6: right to life' (2019) UN Doc CCPR/C/GC/36, para 31; *F.J. et al v Australia*, CCPR/C/116/D/2233/2013 (22 March 2016).

[47] HRC General Comment 36 (n 46), para 25

[48] Committee on the Elimination of Discrimination against Women, 'General recommendation No 32 on the gender-related dimensions of refugee status, asylum, nationality and statelessness of women' (2014) UN Doc CEDAW/C/GC/32.

[49] Committee on the Rights of the Child, 'General Comment No 6 on the Treatment of Unaccompanied and Separated Children Outside Their Country of Origin' (2005) UN Doc CRC/GC/2005/6.

[50] See eg *Rights and guarantees of children in the context of migration and/or in need of international protection*, Advisory Opinion OC-21/14, Inter-American Court of Human Right Series A No 21 (19 August 2014); *The institution of asylum, and its recognition as a human right under the Inter-American System of Protection (interpretation and scope of Articles 5, 22(7) and 22(8) in relation to Article 1(1) of the American Convention on Human Rights)*, Advisory Opinion OC-25/18, Inter-American Court of Human Right Series A No 25 (30 May 2018); *Good v Republic of Botswana* Communication No 313/05, African Commission on Human and Peoples' Rights, 47th Ordinary Session (26 May 2010).

Union and European Union Law rests on the assumption that the ECHR plays a significant role in guiding the EU and its member states in the field of human rights protection. [51]

Where does the ECHR stand on migration? The starting point in responding to this query is to note its textual silence on the issue. Neither the 1950 text of the Convention nor any of the additional protocols that came after address the general question of migration, or provide specific protections for those that seek asylum in Europe. It is well documented that migration was not in the minds of the drafters of the Convention.[52] Historically, the Convention came about primarily to address other concerns, namely the protection of democratic rights respecting political regimes in Europe and to act as a warning mechanism against them slipping into totalitarian regimes.[53] Protocol No 4 to the Convention of 1963 has partially addressed this silence,[54] in particular, by prohibiting collective expulsion of aliens under its Article 4 and becoming the first ever treaty for doing so. The explanatory report of the Protocol refers to the 'collective expulsions of aliens of the kind which was a matter of recent history' as a rationale for this prohibition.[55] Protocol No 4 Article 2 also recognises the right to movement of non-nationals, but in so doing, underlines that this right is limited only to those who are lawful residents.

Despite the significant silences of the Convention on migration, the European Court of Human Rights (ECtHR), and the former Commission, through the right of individual petition, has traditionally received a significant portion of applications concerning migration from individuals seeking access to Europe,[56] and from non-nationals living in Europe, wishing not to be returned back to their countries.[57] What is more, many long-term migrants in Europe have petitioned the Court demanding equal treatment with members of their host communities.[58]

[51] Vasiliki Costa and Bruno de Witte, 'Human Rights Norms in the Court of Justice of the European Union' in Martin Scheinin (ed), *Human Rights Norms in 'Other' International Courts* (Cambridge University Press 2019) 263–86.

[52] Marco Duranti, *The Conservative Human Rights Revolution: European Identity, Transnational Politics, and the Origins of the European Convention* (Cambridge University Press 2017).

[53] Ed Bates, *The Evolution of the European Convention on Human Rights. From its Inception to the Creation of a Permanent Court of Human Rights* (OUP 2010) 44.

[54] Protocol No 4 to the Convention for the Protection of Human Rights and Fundamental Freedoms, securing certain rights and freedoms other than those already included in the Convention and in the first Protocol thereto, as amended by Protocol No 11, 16 September 1963, ETS 46.

[55] *Guide on Article 4 of Protocol No. 4 to the European Convention on Human Rights: Prohibition of collective expulsions of aliens* (Council of Europe 2020) 5.

[56] Cathryn Costello, 'Courting Access to Asylum in Europe: Recent Supranational Jurisprudence Explored' (2012) 12(2) Human Rights Law Review 287–339.

[57] Dembour (n 37) 161–249; Sonia Morano-Foadi and Stelios Andreadakis, 'The Convergence of the European Legal System in the Treatment of Third Country Nationals in Europe: The ECJ and ECtHR Jurisprudence' (2011) 22(4) European Journal of International Law 1071–88, 1081–82.

[58] Marie-Bénédicte Dembour, 'Still Silencing the Racism Suffered by Migrants ... The Limits of Current Developments under Article 14 ECHR' (2009) 11 European Journal of Migration and Law 221–34; Dembour (n 37) 250–81. Evelien Brouwer and Karin de Vries, 'Third-country Nationals and Discrimination on the Ground of Nationality: Article 18 TFEU in the Context of Article 14 ECHR and EU Migration Law: Time for a New Approach' in Marjolein van den Brink, Susanne Burri, and Jenny Goldschmidt (eds), *Equality and Human Rights: Nothing but Trouble?* (SIM 2015) 123–46, 126–35.

Even though the Convention is silent on migration, the ECtHR has thus been perceived by those who have recourse to it as a last resort court for migrants, where demands for entry, dignified stay, and equal rights with citizens have been at the forefront of migration litigation before it.[59]

The discrepancy between the textual silence of the Convention and the significant number of cases the Court has received concerning the human rights of migrants has given way to three way interpretive dynamics in the case law of the ECtHR when addressing multi-faceted questions related to migration.

First, because the Convention's textual premise on migration is that of silence, the ECtHR has had to interpret what that silence means in light of the overall object and the purpose of the treaty. Whilst in some cases the Court has interpreted the Convention as a 'constitutional instrument of European public order' and transformed the Convention into a convention for migrants in Europe,[60] in other cases it has bowed to the Convention's silence in the field of migration, deferring to the domestic laws of the Council of Europe member states[61] or the duties of those seeking to migrate.[62] The textual silences of the Convention have thus acted both as allowing interpretive creativity and interpretive restraint. In some respects, the ECtHR has been a vanguard institution. Its *Soering* judgment of 1989 on *non-refoulement*, for example, substantively lead to the development of the prohibition of *non refoulement* in international law.[63] It has also provided path-breaking critiques of the EU asylum policy with a focus on deficiencies in conditions of detention in EU member states for asylum seekers.[64] The ECtHR, however, is also very well known for its margin of appreciation doctrine and gives weight to the determinations of state authorities when there is an effective system in place or when it finds that migration control, asylum, or deportation proceedings are not flawed.[65]

Second, because there is no dedicated, special protection for migrants in the Convention, their cases have had to fit within the text of the Convention and were brought under multiple articles ranging from the right to life (Article 2),[66] freedom

[59] Dembour (n 37) 2.

[60] On the characterisation of the Convention by the Court as a 'constitutionalist instrument of European public order, see among others, *Al-Dulimi and Montana Management Inc v Switzerland* [GC] App no 5809/08 (ECtHR, 21 June 2016), para 145.

[61] *Ilias and Ahmed v Hungary* [GC] App no 47287/15 (ECtHR, 21 November 2019). See also Dembour (n 37) 507.

[62] *N.D. and N.T. v Spain* (n 63) § 241–43.

[63] *Soering v United Kingdom* 11 EHRR 439 (1989). Also see, Başak Çalı, Cathryn Costello, and Stewart Cunningham 'Hard Protection through Soft Courts? Non-Refoulement before the United Nations Treaty Bodies' (2020) 21 German Law Journal 355–84

[64] *M.S.S. v Belgium and Greece* [GC] 53 EHRR 2 (2011).

[65] *F.G. v Sweden* App No 43611/11, para 118 (ECtHR, 23 March 2016), *A.J. and F.B. v Sweden* App No 36384/16 (ECtHR, 13 December 2016)

[66] *Bader and Kanbor v Sweden* App no 13284/04 (ECtHR, 8 November 2005); *Al-Saadoon and Mufdhi v United Kingdom* App no 61498/08 (ECtHR, 2 March 2010); *Al Nashiri v Poland* App no 28761/11 (ECtHR, 24 July 2014); *F.G. v Sweden* [GC] App no 43611/11 (ECtHR, 23 March 2016).

from torture, inhuman and degrading treatment (Article 3),[67] the right to a private and family life (Article 8),[68] the right to an effective remedy,[69] the right not to be discriminated against (Article 14),[70] the right to freedom of religion (Article 9),[71] and the prohibition of collective expulsion.[72] In turn, the ECtHR has produced a migration case law coloured by the text of each of the articles set against the diverse facts of migrants' cases: treatment of migrants and asylum seekers when they first enter Europe, protecting the *non-refoulement* rights of migrants and asylum seekers, protecting the right to family life of migrants against deportation or extradition, as well as the treatment of long-term migrants in terms of their social, civil, political, and cultural rights. It is through its interpretation of these rights in varied factual contexts that the European Convention has become a convention in the making for migrants in Europe over time. Yet, the specific protection afforded to migrants in the Convention has also meant that the Court has read its substantive rights protections for migrants through a sovereignty bias, limiting the scope of application of these rights in the case of migrants,[73] or allowing wider margin of appreciation to states in distinguishing infringements of Convention rights from violations.[74]

Third, the ECtHR has shown that the Convention does not exist in a vacuum and that it forms part of international human rights law more generally and international human rights law focusing on migration more specifically. This has been particularly the case when the Court has been brought cases concerning rights of migrant children. Despite specific emphasis on children's rights in the Convention, for example, the Court has aimed to closely align itself with the Convention on the Rights of the Child.[75]

[67] See, generally, *Khlaifia and others v Italy* [GC] App no 16483/12 (ECtHR, 15 December 2016); *J.K. and others v Sweden* [GC] App no 59166/12 (ECtHR, 23 August 2016); *F.G. v Sweden* [GC] App no 43611/11 (ECtHR, 23 March 2016); *N.A. v United Kingdom* App no 25904/07 (ECtHR, 17 July 2008); *Saadi v United Kingdom* [GC] App No 13229/03 (ECtHR, 29 January 2008); *N.A. v United Kingdom* App no 25904/07 (ECtHR, 17 July 2008).

[68] See representatively, *Biao v Denmark* [GC] App no 38590/10 (ECtHR, 24 May 2016); *Şen v the Netherlands* App no 31465/96 (ECtHR, 21 December 2001); *Berrehab v the Netherlands* App no 10730/84 (ECtHR, 21 June 1988); *Abdulaziz v United Kingdom* App nos 9214/80, 9473/81, and 9474/81 (ECtHR, 28 May 1985).

[69] *N D and N T v Spain* [GC] App nos 8675/15 and 8697/15 (ECtHR, 13 February 2020).

[70] *Novruk and others v Russia* App nos 31039/11 and 4 others (ECtHR, 15 March 2016); *Pajic v Croatia* App no 68453/13 (ECtHR, 23 February 2016); *Timishev v Russia* App nos 55762/00 and 55974/00 (ECtHR, 13 December 2005); *Gaygusuz v Austria* App no 17371/90 (ECtHR, 16 September 1996).

[71] *Osmanoğlu v Switzerland* App no 29086/12 (ECtHR, 10 January 2017); *Belkacemi v Belgium* App no 37798/13 (ECtHR, 11 July 2017); *Dakir v Belgium* App no 4619/12 (ECtHR, 11 July 2017); *Ebrahimian v France* App no 64846/11 (ECtHR, 26 November 2015); *S.A.S. v France* [GC] App no 43835/11 (ECtHR, 1 July 2014).

[72] See *Hirsi Jamaa and others v Italy* [GC] App no 27765/09 (ECtHR, 23 February 2012); *Khalifa and others v Italy* (n 61).

[73] See Chapter 3 in this volume.

[74] See Chapters 2, 4, and 9 in this volume

[75] See also Chapter 5 in this volume.

4. Migration and the European Convention on Human Rights: The Approach of the Book

This volume departs from the three-way interpretative dynamics identified above: the limitations (and potentials) that exist in the case law due to the silences in the Convention text, adaptation of the rights of migrants to the rights provided by the Convention, and the embeddedness of European human rights law in international human rights law. The chapters collected in this volume point to how the interpretation of the Convention as a living instrument is still a work in progress and put forward proposals of how to better improve the Convention for the protection of rights of migrants in Europe. Whilst some of the contributors focus on how the sovereignty bias and limited catalogue of rights for migrants operate in the case law of the Court and expose the different ways in which this manifests itself, others place more emphasis on how, in particular through intersectional and comparative readings of the Convention text, the ECtHR can develop its case law.

The book takes a decidedly broad view on migration and the ECHR temporally and thematically with a view to surveying the responses of the ECtHR to the diversity of cases it examines concerning migration. The chapters included in this volume focus not only on questions of who is entitled to enter and remain in Europe, but also what treatment is owed to them when they come within the jurisdiction of a Council of Europe member state. As to the latter, chapters focus both on the obligations owed to those who have just arrived in Europe and as well as to those who have been living in Europe for much lengthier periods of time. This widely canvassed temporal focus allows the book to cover different categories of migrants including asylum seekers, irregular migrants, those who have migrated through domestically lawful routes and those who are currently second- or third-generation migrants in Europe. Thematically, the contributions to this book address a number of cross-cutting themes in the case law of the ECtHR, including the scope of the *non-refoulement* obligation, children as migrants, economic and social rights of migrants, family rights of migrants, freedom of liberty and security of migrants, and cultural rights of migrants. As such, the book showcases the flexibility of the Convention text in addressing migrants' rights regardless of the length of time they spend in Europe and the lack of explicit protections offered to migrants in the Convention text.

The central focus of the chapters in the book is the interpretation of the ECHR in the field of migration broadly conceived. Contributors both analyse the existing case law of the Court and point to new interpretive horizons and doctrinal means at the disposal of the Court to develop its case law. As for the latter, they point to the centrality of pro-person and comparative interpretive techniques to protect rights of migrants. The pro person techniques underlined include reversing the presumption of state sovereignty in the field of migration[76] and intersectional analysis of

[76] See Chapters 2, 4, and 7 in this volume.

rights provided for in the Convention.[77] Whilst some of the contributors compare the case law of the ECtHR to those of other international courts and quasi judicial bodies, such as the Inter-American Court of Human Rights (IACtHR),[78] the Committee on the Rights of the Child,[79] and the European Social Charter Committee,[80] others focus on comparative analysis of migrants case law with non-migrant case law of the Court, asking crucially whether the Court treats migrants differently compared to its decisions in cases that come from non-migrants.[81]

The main finding of the book, as a whole, is twofold.

First is that the interpretation of the ECHR concerning matters of migration continues to be unfinished business. Not only are the multiple dimensions of migration firmly on the agenda of the ECtHR—and we would submit that this will continue to be so in the foreseeable future[82] —most of the case law on migration is open to further development. The contributions to this book converge on the proposition that the ECtHR can indeed do more in the field of migration through legal interpretation and doctrinal development. Indeed, many of the chapters provide doctrinal suggestions for ways out of the broader textual silence in the Convention by reference to what the Court has done in other parts of its jurisprudence, by using comparative methods to demonstrate how other human rights courts have addressed the same issue and by pointing to more effective use of the pro person and living instrument doctrines.

Second, the individual chapters of the book also show that the Court has highly diversified approaches to the migration-related questions that come before it and there is variation as to how concerns of migrants are addressed in the case law. Whilst in some areas, for example the protection of individuals from the right to *non-refoulement*[83] and the protection of migrant children,[84] the Court, over time, has shown a concerted effort to develop a migrant-rights friendly case law, in cases such as fair trial safeguards in asylum proceedings,[85] deportation of long-term migrants,[86] and the cultural rights of long-term migrants,[87] the interest in developing a 'Strasbourg based approach' is largely absent and deference to states in matters of decision-making is more pronounced. Whilst some of the authors praise

[77] See Chapters 2, 5, and 6 in this volume.
[78] See Chapter 2 in this volume.
[79] See Chapter 5 in this volume.
[80] See Chapter 6 in this volume.
[81] See Chapter 9 in this volume.
[82] At the time of writing, the Grand Chamber of the ECtHR has accepted to review four cases in the field of migration, *M.N. and others v Belgium* App no 3599/18 (Grand Chamber hearing on 24 April 2019), *Muhammad v Romania* App no 80982/12 (Grand Chamber hearing on 25 September 2019); *Savran v Denmark* App no 57467/15 (accepted by Grand Chamber Panel on 27 January 2020), *M.A. v Denmark* App no 6697/18 (Grand Chamber hearing scheduled for 18 March 2020).
[83] See Chapter 4 in this volume.
[84] See Chapter 5 in this volume.
[85] See Chapter 2 in this volume.
[86] See Chapter 7 in this volume.
[87] Chapters 8 and 9 in this volume.

the Court's approach in developing migrant-friendly doctrines in the absence of guiding textual standards and propose new ways to deepen this case law, others are more critical and seek to expose the persistent pockets of deferential modes of reasoning in the Court's case law. Amongst these progressive developments and critical assessments emerges a picture of a Court with multiple attitudes on migration as a whole.

5. Contributions to the Volume

Contributions to this volume are organised in four parts. Part I sets the scene, situates the ECHR and its approach to migration in the broader field of international migration law and international human rights law. In Chapter 2, Dembour offers a 'balance sheet' of how migrant rights have been treated by the Court since the inception of this line of case law, arguing that the ECtHR case law generally favours state sovereignty over migrant rights. She proposes that this is because the Court approaches the states' rights to control their borders as the rule, and the protection of migrants as a potential exception to this rule. Dembour proposes that an alternative jurisprudential path is possible, demonstrating that this has been pursued by the IACtHR.

In Part II on right to flee, right to asylum, and right to humane and dignified treatment, authors focus on the first stages of migration and the Convention rights that are engaged in this stage.[88] Chapter 3 starts with those fleeing their home countries who seek to enter Europe, Chapter 4 focuses on the right to asylum, and Chapters 5 and 6 focus on those who are in Europe but under precarious legal and personal conditions.

In Chapter 3, Violeta Moreno-Lax, starts her analysis from the basic premise that the ECHR does not provide a right to asylum, nor to migrate. By theorising an intersectional right to flee in the Convention, Moreno-Lax builds the case for a composite entitlement to leave to escape irreversible harm. Central to her argument is the centrality of substantive equality, and not only formal equality, to the interpretive practices of the ECtHR. Moreno-Lax further lays out two intersecting routes for attaining such substantive justice for those who flee. The first is the canon of evolutive interpretation employed by the Court. The second concerns comparative constitutionalism. Both of these elements can support the Court in further developing its case law for the effective protection of asylum seekers.

Ledi Bianku's focus in Chapter 4 is on the context of asylum and the standards developed by the Court in assessing cases where applicants argue that their return to another country would breach the prohibition on torture, inhuman and

[88] This is inspired by Stopler's analytical framework of 'stages of migration'. Gila Stopler, 'Rights in Immigration: The Veil as a Test Case' (2010) 43 Israel Law Review 183.

degrading treatment. For Bianku, the central doctrinal challenge in these cases has been to take into account two competing principles simultaneously: the discretionary right of states to accept foreigners in their territories and the absolute nature of Article 3 of the Convention. With a focus on the Grand Chamber ruling in *J.K. and others v Sweden*, Bianku argues that there has been a shift in the way the Strasbourg Court approaches its analysis in asylum cases, by recognising first the primary nature of the right to be protected from torture and inhuman and degrading treatment, as an absolute right under Article 3 of the Convention.

In Chapter 5, Ksenija Turković surveys how the Court has addressed the detention of migrant children when they enter a country. Turković shows that the notions of the 'vulnerability of children' and the 'best interests of the child' play an important role in shaping the case law of the Court. The author deals first with the definition of a much-discussed concept in the Court's case law: the vulnerability of asylum seekers.[89] Then her analysis focuses on the vulnerability of children and further to the particular vulnerability of migrant children. After setting out this conceptual frame the author discusses the obligations of national authorities towards migrant children, especially in relation to their detention, under Articles 3 and 8 of the Convention, and how these obligations have developed in close normative relationship with the UN Convention on the Rights of the Child.

In Chapter 6, Francesca Ippolito and Carmen Pérez González turn to a different form of vulnerability—that of undocumented migrants and the question of their entitlement to a minimum degree of socio-economic rights. Their contribution argues that limitations on the rights of migrants are not only placed on the right to stay but cover other rights guaranteed by the ECHR. Starting their analysis from the vulnerable position of migrants the article argues that the right to education, the right to adequate housing, the right to appropriate medical treatment, and protection from exploitation, forced labour, and trafficking are all rights that should be protected for migrants under the ECHR. Their claim is that the dignity of migrants, especially in view of their vulnerable position, requires that these rights be respected in practice in order to have meaningful protection of migrants' right under the Convention.

Part III of the book focuses on rights of long-term migrants and their protection by the ECtHR. In Chapter 7, Başak Çalı and Stewart Cunningham focus on the removal of long-term migrants, in many cases migrants who entered Europe while they were children or even second-generation migrants. In all these cases, the Court is required to conduct a balancing exercise in cases where the state seeks to remove long-term migrants, mostly because of their criminal activities. The chapter analyses the different factors the Court takes into account in conducting this balancing exercise and shows that the current state of the case law does not

[89] See on this point the partly concurring opinion of Judge Sajo in the case of *M.S.S. v Belgium and Greece*, quoted by Judge Turković in Chapter 5.

adequately take into account the length of time migrants workers spend in their host countries, making the review of deportation decisions casuistic.

Bianca Selejan-Gutan focuses on the cultural rights of migrants and the related issue of their acceptance by the host societies in Chapter 8. The question raised is whether the Strasbourg case-law on religious symbols, especially, constitutes a barrier to the acceptance and integration into European societies of migrants belonging to specific cultural and religious groups. The chapter focuses on the notion of 'living together', as interpreted by the Court in the case of *S.A.S. v France*, and its possible repercussions on the integration of migrants.

In Chapter 9, Eva Brems, building on the same case-law on religious freedoms, and also on *S.A.S. v France*, raises the question of whether the Court treats the cases from long term migrants differently from cases that are brought by 'authentic' citizens. Brems shows, in particular, that the methodology used by the Court in burqa cases is different from the one used by the Court on 'gay propaganda'. The difference in the Court's approach to handling these cases, the author argues, reifies the 'otherness' of migrants, and, more specifically, the 'otherness' of Muslim migrants in Europe. Brems proposes that the Court should revisit the messages it is sending to national authorities regarding their approaches to multicultural conflicts over Islamic migrant minority practices. This is situated in the framework of 'positive subsidiarity'. It is argued that even when the margin of appreciation is a wide one, the Court has a responsibility to offer guidance to states parties on three levels: substantive, procedural, and discursive. The paper then explores the messages sent by the Court to states parties in the field of the restriction of Islamic minority practices. First it does so by comparing what is widely considered the Court's 'worst practice' in this field—the face veil cases—with its 'best practice' in a different, but comparable field—the 'gay propaganda' cases.

Part VI of the book offers a comprehensive case guide to the migration case law of the ECtHR by organising the cases with respect to the stages of migration they deal with. The cases are organised to cover issues relevant to the early stages of migration, such as entering the destination country, *non-refoulement*, and the asylum procedure, followed by case law speaking to the treatment of migrants once present in the territory of a state, including asylum detention and family reunification, and lastly the rights of migrants once forming part of the destination state, such as their access to social, economic, and cultural rights as well as freedom of religion.

2

The Migrant Case Law of the European Court of Human Rights

Critique and Way Forward

Marie-Bénédicte Dembour

1. Introduction

On the basis of a close review of six decades of Strasbourg jurisprudence, my book *When Humans Become Migrants*[1] demonstrates that the European Court of Human Rights (ECtHR) generally privileges state sovereignty over migrants' rights. It shows that the ECtHR rarely finds for the migrant—a word used to denote anybody outside their country of origin, including refugees and asylum seekers. Granted, the Strasbourg case law contains resounding judgments which establish protective standards for migrants. However, a comprehensive examination of the case law must include rulings of non-violation and the multitude of decisions of inadmissibility. When this is done, the protective edifice supposedly represented by the European Convention on Human Rights (ECHR) reveals itself to be full of cracks, if not having entire walls missing.[2]

At a time when Europe faces a grave crisis of protection of migrants, it bears repeating that nothing in international human rights law inherently prevents the ECtHR from adopting more progressive interpretations of the ECHR, as shown by the jurisprudence adopted by other human rights adjudicatory bodies. The ECtHR should find the courage to veer in a direction that is more protective of the migrant applicant, thereby ensuring that the expression 'human rights of migrants' does not increasingly become nothing more than empty words in its jurisprudence—a particularly disturbing result for a court established to defend human rights.

In order to illustrate these points, the first section of this chapter starts by tracing the origins of the deficit in protection of migrants which I argue characterises the ECHR system. The second section proceeds with an examination of a largely

[1] Marie-Bénédicte Dembour, *When Humans Become Migrants: Study of the European Court of Human Rights with an Inter-American Counterpoint* (OUP 2015).

[2] See also: Cathryn Costello, *The Human Rights of Migrants and Refugees in European Law* (OUP 2015), describing the Strasbourg Court at 'too timid' at 325.

Marie-Bénédicte Dembour, *The Migrant Case Law of the European Court of Human Rights* In: *Migration and the European Convention on Human Rights*. Edited by: Başak Çali, Ledi Bianku, and Iulia Motoc, Oxford University Press (2021).
 DOI: 10.1093/oso/9780192895196.003.0002

unknown case law related to refused residence permits, which can be said to epitomise this deficit. The jurisprudential paths, long treaded at Strasbourg, which led to these specific cases being declared inadmissible, are explored in section 3. Section 4 outlines the way the ECtHR's Inter-American sister court—the Inter-American Court of Human Rights (IACtHR)—tends to reason. This is followed in section 5 by a brief comparative exercise, which sketches the way immigration detention is viewed by the two courts. Section 6 highlights how other jurisprudential paths could be developed at Strasbourg, were there a strong political will in Europe to nudge the judges in this direction.

2. The (Long) Starting Point: No Migration Case Law at Strasbourg

The ECHR was signed in 1950 and it then took seven years before it came into force (after the tenth ratification required for this to happen was reached).[3] Migrants' legal representatives immediately understood the protection potential which the Convention represented for their clients. Right from the outset, in the 1950s, they started to lodge applications with the European Commission of Human Rights (Commission)—the body which filtered the cases that went to the ECtHR until Protocol 11 came into force in 1998. They did so in surprisingly high numbers.[4]

History has not recorded their complaints as the Commission systematically declared their applications inadmissible—and did so for decades. Admittedly, to begin with, it was not just migrants' applications but virtually all applications that the Commission was rejecting.[5] This earned the Convention system the description of having been, for its first twenty-five years, a 'sleeping beauty'.[6] The system 'awakened' in the late 1970s, with landmark judgments such as *Tyrer v United Kingdom* (about corporal punishment of children),[7] *Marckx v Belgium* (about the discriminatory treatment of children born out of wedlock),[8] and *Airey v Ireland* (about lack of access to justice due to lack of legal aid). Importantly, it then took another decade for the system to awaken to migrant issues. The first judgment in a migrant case was decided by the Court in 1985, and it was not even a victory for migrant rights, as we shall see below. For this to happen, one had to await *Berrehad v the Netherlands* (expulsion violating the applicants' family life) in 1988,[9] which

[3] Ed Bates, *The Evolution of the European Convention on Human Rights: From its Inception to the Creation of a Permanent Court of Human Rights* (OUP 2010).

[4] For some figures, see Dembour 2015 (n 1) 62, 96, 158, 164, 166, 167, 199–201.

[5] Laurens Lavrysen, '"Strasbourg was Something New, it Was an Adventure": A History of the Belgian Cases before the European Court of Human Rights in the 1960s, 1970s and 1980s' (2018) 86 (3–4) Legal History Review482–547..

[6] Bates (n 3) 10 and 257 (quoting Jochen Frowein).

[7] *Tyrer v United Kingdom* App no 5856/72 (ECtHR, 25 April 1978).

[8] *Marckx v Belgium* App no 6833/74 (ECtHR, 13 June 1979).

[9] *Berrehab v the Netherlands* App no 10730/84 (ECtHR, 21 June 1988).

was followed one year later by *Soering v United Kingdom* (extradition putting the applicant at risk of inhuman and degrading treatment).[10]

To explain why the migrant case law encountered an additional delay in its development, it is worth bearing in mind that the fathers of the Convention were seeking to create an instrument which would prove effective at protecting Europeans against a repeat of World War II, the possible arbitrariness of national governments, and the spread of communism.[11] Addressing the plight of migrants was not uppermost in their mind. In fact, it was not at all one of their concerns. This is not to suggest that the negotiators thought the Convention would apply to European citizens exclusively. On the contrary, it was always accepted that it would apply to anyone who found themselves under the jurisdiction of a Contracting State, and this could include foreigners (but not the colonial subjects of four of the signatory states).[12] The point is that European citizens were conceived as the Convention's natural beneficiaries.[13] As a result, the negotiators had no time for guarantees that would have been of particular benefit to migrants such as rights to nationality, asylum, and expulsion only after due process. Commentators who expressed regret about this omission at the time, including most prominently Hersch Lauterpacht,[14] were not listened to.[15]

This context was not propitious for the assertion of migrants' rights under the ECHR. Indeed, getting migrants to be protected under the Convention for issues having to do with their immigration status has proved to be, and continues to be, an uphill battle.[16] The first migrant case which the Commission brought to the Court, *Abdulaziz, Cabales and Balkandali*,[17] concerned 'immigration widows' in the UK. In a huge disappointment for migrant rights' groups, the Court ruled in 1985 that legally settled women had no right under the Convention to be joined by their husband.[18] Six years later, despite the opening that *Soering* might have been

[10] *Soering v United Kingdom* App no 14038/88 (ECtHR, 7 July 1989).

[11] Marco Duranti, *The Conservative Human Rights Revolution: European Identity, Transnational Politics, and the Origins of the European Convention* (OUP 2017).

[12] To the virulent objection of figures such as Léopold Senghor, the colonial subjects were left outside the ambit of the Convention. This was at a time when no one could have imagined that the world would soon witness a vast movement for independence, including from the colonial powers which were signatories to the ECHR, namely, Belgium, France, the Netherlands, and the United Kingdom: Dembour 2015 (n 1), Chapter 3. See also Dembour's inaugural lecture, 'Human rights can save lives, but whose?', University of Brighton (6 May 2015) <https://www.youtube.com/watch?v=8pFXAPOZrz8> accessed 15 December 2019.

[13] Andrew Moravcsil, 'The Origins of Human Rights Regimes: Democratic Delegation on Postwar Europe' (2000) 54(2) International Organisation 21752.

[14] Hersch Lauterpacht, *An International Bill of the Rights of Man* (Columbia University Press 1945).

[15] Dembour 2015 (n 1) 57; Brian Simpson, *Human Rights and the End of Empire: Britain and the Genesis of the European Convention* (OUP 2001) 690.

[16] Moritz Baumgartel, *Europe's Supranational Courts and the Dilemma of Migrants' Vulnerability* (Cambridge University Press 2019).

[17] *Abdulaziz, Cabales and Balkandali v United Kingdom* App nos 9214/80, 9473/81, and 9474/81 (ECtHR, 28 May 1985).

[18] Jacqueline Bhabha and Sue Shutter, *Women's Movement: Women under Immigration, Nationality and Refugee Law* (Trentham Books 1994) 73.

expected to represent for subsequent Article 3 return claims, the Court failed to condemn the deportation to Sri Lanka of Tamil applicants who had been ill-treated upon their return, as their legal representatives unequivocally substantiated.[19] In 2000, the ECtHR ruled in *Maaouia v France*[20] that Article 6, which provides for fair trial guarantees, did not apply to immigration proceedings. As a Grand Chamber judgment, *Maaouia* represented a categorical ruling which closed the possibility of having fair trial guarantees recognised to have to apply to any proceeding deciding the status and fate of a migrant.[21] To give yet another example, in 2008, the removal of a person to a place where lack of medical treatment meant a certain death was found not to breach Article 3 (prohibiting inhuman and degrading treatment).[22]

Of course, the Strasbourg case law also contains victories for migrants. As Nadine El-Enany has observed, the contrary would be near impossible, as it would reveal the ECtHR as an illiberal court.[23] *Soering* and *Berrehab*, already introduced, opened up jurisprudential paths for subsequent successful claims to the effect that return to a country of origin would be contrary to respectively Article 3 and Article 8 (though this would not happen in all such cases, in fact very far from that). Recent significant victories include Grand Chamber judgments in *MSS v Belgium and Greece* (transfer of the applicant under the EU 'Dublin regulation' to Greece, entailing inhuman conditions and lack of domestic remedy) and *Hirsi Jamaa v Italy* (push-back operation to Libya amounting to collective expulsion and making it impossible for asylum seekers to claim asylum).[24]

The ECtHR is thus rightly renowned for judgments that have established important protective standards for migrants. It is nonetheless concerning that the less promising Strasbourg jurisprudence often escapes attention. A striking example is *Maaouia*. Despite its devastating consequences for migrants' rights, which are enduring given its status as a precedent-setting ruling in the Strasbourg case law, it is hardly ever mentioned in academic studies.[25] From a human rights perspective, these gaps in commentary are problematic because they risk inducing complacency. Studies must focus not only on the promising openings but also the

[19] *Vilvarajah and others v United Kingdom* App no 13163/87 (ECtHR, 30 October 1991).

[20] *Maaouia v France* App no 39652/98 (ECtHR, 5 October 2000).

[21] Amanda Spalding, 'Reconceptualising Immigration Measures as Punitive', paper given at the Society of Legal Scholars Conference, University of Central Lancashire, 4 September 2019.

[22] *N. v United Kingdom* App no 26565/05 (ECtHR, 27 May 2008).

[23] Nadine El-Enany, 'Refugee Law in the United Kingdom and the European Union: The Constitutive and Subversive Effects of Immigration and Border Control' (PhD, European University Institute 2012).

[24] *M.S.S. v Belgium and Greece* App no 30696/09, (ECtHR GC 21 January 2011); *Hirsi Jamaa and others v Italy* App no 27765/09 (ECtHR, 23 February 2012). Mariagiulia Giuffré, 'Watered-Down Rights on the High Seas: *Hirsi Jamaa and Others v Italy*' (2012) 61(3) International and Comparative Law Quarterly 728–50; Fernando Arlettaz, 'Expulsions collectives: definition et portée de leur interdiction dans la jurisprudence de la Cour européenne des droits de l'homme' (2019) 56 Canadian Yearbook of International Law 58–97..

[25] For an exception, see Ian Bryan and Peter Langford, 'Impediments to the Expulsion of Non-Nationals: Substance and Coherence in Procedural Protection under the European Convention on Human Rights' (2010) 79 Nordic Journal of International Law 457–79.

implacable closures,[26] so that failures in human rights protection can be identified, debated, and hopefully redressed.

3. *Bonger*, or the Condoning of Rightlessness by the ECtHR

In the sea of Strasbourg case law concerning migrants, I would argue that the little-known *Bonger* case deserves special attention, as it epitomises what is wrong with the ECtHR's approach to migrant cases as well as demonstrating the unacceptable outcomes to which these jurisprudential paths lead. The applicant in *Bonger* had been living in the Netherlands for almost ten years without a residence permit. This meant that he could neither work legally nor access social benefits. It was not in dispute that he could not be returned to his country of origin. He claimed that the limbo situation in which he found himself, with no prospect of this ever ending, was a violation of the ECHR. The Court ruled that the issue at stake was merely one of denial of a residence permit, which fell outside the ambit of Article 3 ECHR or any other provision of the Convention; it declared the case inadmissible.[27] This ruling, dating from 2005, was subsequently confirmed in a series of cases brought by individuals who were likewise denied residence permits in the Netherlands while not being, and unlikely ever to be, returnable to their country of origin.[28]

On a limited and literal examination of what the Convention covers, the *Bonger* case law (that is, both the original decision and those that followed it) makes sense: the ECHR contains no reference to a right to a residence permit per se. However, on a broad understanding of what human rights should be about, it does not make sense at all. One wonders what could be more objectionable, from a legal perspective, than leaving some individuals without any means to live legally. This outcome is surely diametrically opposed to the values of the rule of law and the equality of human beings before the law.

In the wake of World War II, Hannah Arendt produced a masterpiece on *The Origins of Totalitarianism*.[29] In this work, she identified 'the right to have rights' as being central to the protection of the human being in a world of states.[30] She warned that it was entirely possible for governments to deny this ground right

[26] A victory for the applicant before the ECtHR creates an opening, which is promising but never automatic since factual circumstances always differ from case to case and the Court generally rules a violation has happened 'in [all] the circumstances of this [particular] case'. By contrast, closures that rule that a certain practice does not entail a violation tend to be categorical and thus implacable: once the Strasbourg doors are shut (such as in *Maaouia*), it is very difficult to open them again, whatever the circumstances of the case.

[27] *Teshome Goraga Bonger v the Netherlands* App no 10154/04 (ECtHR, 15 September 2005).

[28] Dembour 2015 (n 1) 442.

[29] Hannah Arendt, *The Origins of Totalitarianism* (The World Publishing Company 1951).

[30] See also Alison Kesby, *The Right to Have Rights: Citizenship, Humanity, and International Law* (OUP 2015); Ayten Gundogdu, *Rightlessness in an Age of Rights: Hannah Arendt and the Contemporary Struggles of Migrants* (OUP 2015).

simply by leaving or purposely putting people in a situation of 'rightlessness'. This is exactly the fate meted out to *Bonger* applicants.[31]

Their situation is Kafkaesque. This is well illustrated by a factual detail mentioned in one of the cases, which records that the applicant's wife was penalised for harbouring an 'illegal alien', leading her to lose various fiscal facilities and benefits towards meeting medical insurance, rent, and childcare costs.[32] One wonders where this illegal alien—her husband—was supposed to live. Was he expected to disappear not just from view but also from the surface of the earth?

Some might wish to object that the applicants in the *Bonger* case law were not angels. They had been excluded from the ambit of the Refugee Convention under its Article 1F, due to serious suspicions that they had carried out military or security operations that amounted to crimes against humanity.[33] However, they have not been given the opportunity to have these suspicions properly judged in any kind of legal or judicial process. Human rights law is clear that everyone benefits from the presumption of innocence until tried in a court of law. In a case called *Naibzay*, the ECtHR was specifically challenged on this point. Sitting as a Committee of Three, the Court responded that the complaint was incompatible *ratione materiae* with the Convention since it related to Article 6, which *Maaouia* has established does not extend to proceedings and decisions concerning the entry, stay, and removal of aliens.[34] Interestingly the Court of Justice of the European Union (CJEU) has recently been more circumspect when dealing with refusals of residence and free movement within the EU following an Article 1F application,[35] which may again serve to highlight the comparative timidity of the ECtHR in defending the rights of migrants.[36]

A lesson which can be drawn from this is that a Strasbourg verdict of non-violation, especially adopted by a Grand Chamber, as *Maaouia* was, typically has far-reaching effects: it can be invoked in order to shut the Strasbourg doors over and over again, in a summary fashion, as it were automatically. This is because

[31] And many others: Benedita Menezes Queiroz, *Illegally Staying in the EU: An Analysis of Illegality in EU Migration Law* (Hart 2018).

[32] *I. v the Netherlands* App no 24147/11, partial decision as to admissibility, 18 October 2011, para 33; final decision as to admissibility, 10 July 2012, para 40.

[33] Sandesh Sivakumaran, 'Exclusion from Refugee Status: The Purposes and Principles of the United Nations and Article 1F(c) of the Refugee Convention' (2014) 26(3) International Journal of Refugee Law 350–81. The Netherlands invoke Article 1F of the Refugee Convention more often than other states. They did so 920 times between 1992 and 2014: Maarten Bolhuis and Joris van Wijk, 'Study on the Exchange of Information between European Countries Regarding Persons Excluded from Refugee Status in Accordance with Article 1F Refugee Convention' (Vrije Universiteit Amsterdam 2015) <https://emnbelgium.be/sites/default/files/publications/study-exchange-information-1f-exclusion.pdf> accessed 16 December 2020.

[34] *Mohammed Rafiq Naibzay v the Netherlands* App no 68564/12, decision as to admissibility, 22 October 2012.

[35] Judgment in Joined Cases C-331/16 *K. v Staatssecretaris van Veiligheid en Justitie* and C-366/16 *H.F. v Belgische Staat (Right of residence and alleged war crimes)*, 2 May 2018.

[36] See also how the UN Human Rights Committee stated in its General Comment no 32 that core due process protections apply to immigration hearings: CCPR/C/GC/32, 23 August 2007, para 62.

whoever is in charge of the next case (a Chamber, a Committee of Three, or a single judge formation) need do no more than repeat the original ruling according to which the Convention does not apply (or is not violated), even in circumstances which are vastly different from the situation in relation to which this original verdict was adopted. It is worth pondering the fact that, by contrast, a Strasbourg verdict of violation has a far more limited impact, given the casuistic jurisprudence of the ECtHR, whereby the Court is careful to stress that it finds a violation of the Convention in all the circumstances of the case. Such a formulation makes it impossible to predict what might be decided in a subsequent case, where the circumstances are bound not to be exactly the same. Openings happen incrementally, almost haphazardly. Closures are more categorical (except if the opportunity arises for the Court to reverse its jurisprudence, and it takes it).

The concept of human rights is generally accepted to rest on the belief that every human being without any exception is entitled to be treated with dignity. Upholding an individual's dignity requires recognition, including recognition before the law.[37] It is difficult to resist the conclusion that the applicants of the *Bonger* case law were denied this recognition. For ever illegalised, they are told they cannot work, they cannot access social benefits, they cannot open a bank account, they cannot drive, they cannot travel, and they cannot do all kinds of other things which are critical to a life of dignity, if not survival, in contemporary societies.[38] How this can be considered to be compatible with human rights law defies the imagination. The question then arises: how could the *Bonger* case law ever surface?

4. Locating *Bonger* in the Strasbourg Case Law

How did it become possible for a human rights court to adopt a decision which is arguably the very antithesis of what human rights should be about? The short answer to this question is that *Bonger* was the logical development of earlier Strasbourg case law. Since the mid-1980s, the ECtHR had adopted a number of principles regarding migrants' rights, or rather non-rights. In particular, following even earlier case law by the erstwhile Commission, the Court had established that non-nationals have no right to choose the country where they wish to live, no right not to be separated from their families, no right to be able to rely on social protection systems, and no right to be granted a particular residence permit. These

[37] Myres S McDougal, Harold D Lasswell, and Lung-Chu Chen, *Human Rights and World Public Order: The Basic Policies of an International Law of Human Dignity* (OUP 2019); Terresa Iglesias, 'Bedrock Truths and the Dignity of the Individual' (2001) 4(1) Logos 114–34; Christopher McCrudden, 'Human Dignity and Judicial Interpretation of Human Rights' (2008) 19(4) European Journal of International Law 655–724.

[38] For an account of the reality of life under statelessness, see Mariangela Velkou, 'Back to Basics: Stateless Women and Children in Greece' (2017) 19 Journal of Balkan and Near Eastern Studies 557–70.

provocative statements would ideally require long and detailed consideration to be fully substantiated. In the context of this chapter, however, only a brief overview of these 'non-rights' can be offered.[39]

The very first case involving an immigration issue which came before the Court, namely, *Abdulaziz, Cabales and Balkandali* v *United Kingdom*, was decided in 1985. In its judgment, the Court proclaimed that there was no right for migrants to settle where they wish. The case concerned three women legally settled in the UK who wished to be joined by their husbands. Thankfully, the Court did not accept the Government's claim that the applications fell outside the Convention. But while the Court decided that Article 8 (respect for family and private life) did apply in the case, it found that this provision had not been violated. This was because the positive duties entailed by Article 8 'cannot be considered as extending to a general obligation on the part of a Contracting State to respect the choice by married couples of the country of their matrimonial residence and to accept the non-national spouses for settlement in that country'.[40] In this particular case, the Court continued, the applicants had not shown there were obstacles to establishing life in their own or their husbands' home countries.[41] This judgment paved the way for an interpretation of Article 8 which, to this day, imposes few duties on states regarding migrants' claims to family reunion.[42] It also led to the principle, repeated over and over again in different contexts by the ECtHR, that migrants have no right to choose where they should live.

A second 'non-right' established in the Strasbourg case law is that, with few exceptions, migrants can be separated from their families and/or removed from the environment in which they have established their life without this being a violation of Article 8 of the Convention. Admittedly, the principle is generally enunciated the other way around, namely, it is stressed that the removal of a non-national to their country of origin may entail a violation of Article 8 ECHR. Given the high number of people who are deported each year from states party to the European Convention,[43] and the small number of Strasbourg verdicts finding this to be a violation of the Convention,[44] one must nonetheless conclude that deportability is the norm, non-deportability due to family or private life circumstances the exception. In the mid-1990s some commentators predicted that being separated from one's family or social space might become something that the Convention would regard

[39] But see Dembour 2015 (n 1) for ampler demonstrations.

[40] *Abdulaziz, Cabales and Balkandali*, para 68, emphasis added.

[41] ibid, para 69. This had huge implications on national policy. See eg Helena Wray, *Regulating Marriage Migration into the UK: A Stranger in the Home* (Ashgate 2011).

[42] There are some exceptions. See Dembour 2015 (n 1), Chapter 4, section XIII.

[43] Exact figures are difficult to find but for some statistics see Myriam Cherti and Miklos Szilard, 'Returning Irregular Migrants: How Effective Is the EU Response?' (IPPR 2013) 5 <https://www.ippr.org/publications/returning-irregular-migrants-how-effective-is-the-eus-response> accessed 16 December 2020.

[44] Dembour 2015 (n 1), Chapter 6.

in principle as abhorrent, ie, as something which should only be allowed to happen in truly exceptional circumstances.[45] However, subsequent case law did not confirm this prediction. As things stand, migrants do not have a secure right under the ECHR to be allowed to live where they have developed or are developing family ties, or where they have grown or are growing roots.[46]

A third right which the European Convention does not grant migrants is the right to be given access to social services. Again, this is not how the Strasbourg case law is generally pictured. The most well-known case in this field is probably *Gaygusuz v Austria*, decided in 1996, where the Court found that denying the applicant a social security benefit on the sole ground that he had not been a national of the state where he had worked legally for over ten years breached Article 14 ECHR (prohibiting discrimination and used here in conjunction with Article 1 of Protocol no 1). *Gaygusuz* is often heralded as a victory for equality and non-discrimination.[47] However, by the time the judgment was adopted, nationality rarely constituted a prerequisite for awarding social security benefits. As a commentator observed when the judgment was released, *Gaygusuz* could, and would, have been revolutionary if it had become instrumental in giving migrants access to social security or assistance they had been denied for lack of a work permit or because their residence was deemed 'illegal'.[48] However, the Court did not venture down this path.[49]

[45] Ryszard Cholewinski, 'Strasbourg's "Hidden Agenda"? The Protection of Second-Generation Migrants from Expulsion under Article 8 of the European Convention on Human Rights' (1994) 12(3) Netherlands Quarterly of Human Rights 287–306.

[46] These become mere elements to be taken into account in a balancing exercise which also considers a host of other factors: Dembour 2015 (n 1) 181–82. For a recent judgment concluding on the non-violation of the Convention, see *Ndidi v United Kingdom* App no 41215/14, judgment of 14 September 2017. This case law has been extensively studied. See eg Daniel Thym, 'Residence as De Facto Citizenship? Protection of Long-Term Residence under Article 8 ECHR' in Ruth Rubio-Marin (ed), *Human Rights and Immigration* (OUP 2014) 106–44; Ciara Smyth, 'The Best Interests of the Child in the Expulsion and First-Entry Jurisprudence of the European Court of Human Rights: How Principled Is the Court's Use of Principles?' (2015) 17(1) European Journal of Migration and Law 70–103; Mario Savino, 'The Right to Stay as a Fundamental Freedom? The Demise of Automatic Expulsion in Europe' (2016) 7(1) Transnational Legal Theory 70–94; Sylvie de Lomba, 'Vulnerability and the Right to Respect for Private Life as an Autonomous Source of Protection against Expulsion under Article 8 ECHR' (2017) 6(4) *Laws* 32; Basak Çalı, 'All You Need is Time? Discrepancies between the European Court of Human Rights Case Law and Liberal Normative Theory on Long-Term Migrants' (2017) 50 Israel Law Review 447–97; Eva Hillbrink, 'Adjudicating the Public Interest in Immigration Law: A Systematic Content Analysis of Strasbourg and Luxembourg Case Law on Legal Restrictions to Immigration and Free Movement' (PhD Thesis, Vrije Universiteit Amsterdam 2017).

[47] See eg Daniel Moeckli, 'Immigration Law Enforcement after 9/11 and Human Rights' in Alice Edwards and Carla Ferstman (eds), *Human Security and Non-Citizens: Law, Policy and International Affairs* (Cambridge University Press 2010) 484; Françoise Tulkens, 'L'évolution du principe de non-discrimination à la lumière de la jurisprudence de la Cour européenne des droits de l'homme', in Jean-Yves Carlier (ed) *L'étranger face au droit* (Bruylant 2010) 193–210 at 202.

[48] Bernd von Maydell, 'Discrimination in Domestic Social Security Law of the Member States of the European Union' in Stefaan Van den Bogaert (ed), *Social Security, Non-Discrimination and Property* (Maklu 1997) 93.

[49] Dembour 2015 (n 1), Chapter 8. See also Marie-Benedicte Dembour, '*Gaygusuz* Revisited: The Limits of the European Court of Human Rights' Equality Agenda' (2012) Human Rights Law Review 12,

A fourth 'non right' which exists in the Strasbourg jurisprudence is that migrants do not have a right to a particular residence permit. This is a crucial omission as without such a document, non-nationals can barely build a secure working and/or private life (as EU citizens in the UK are coming to understand in the uncertain context of Brexit). Admittedly, from the mid-1990s, there have been occasional cases where the Court has found the denial of a residence permit in violation of the Convention. This, however, has been the exception rather than the rule.[50] These exceptional verdicts cannot be said to have transformed the general rule, which is that there is no right to a residence permit under the Convention, as the Court has repeated over and over again.[51]

In addition, the Strasbourg institutions have repeatedly found state measures that leave applicants destitute—whether or not they are migrants—not to be a problem under the Convention. An early example of this was a Commission decision of 1990 regarding a family who was living in social housing provided by the state, where heating was electric only, and thus costly to run. The single mother predictably became unable to pay the electricity bill, power supply was cut off, leaving the (non-migrant) family without heating, lighting, or cooking facilities. Their application to Strasbourg was declared inadmissible.[52] To cite a more recent example, *Müslim v Turkey* from 2005 saw the Court referring to previous case law from the Commission in order to reaffirm that Article 8 does not go so far as imposing on states a general obligation to assist refugees in order to provide a certain standard of living and that there is no right to work provided for in the Convention.[53]

Taken separately, each of these 'non-rights' may appear sensible in that converting them into rights would bestow on the state extensive responsibilities and duties, which one may expect many politicians and citizens to resist.[54] However, denying these rights is also extremely problematic in that each 'non-right'

689–721; Ruth Rubio-Marin, 'Integration in Immigrant Europe: Human Rights at a Crossroads' in Ruth Rubio-Marin (ed), *Human Rights and Immigration* (OUP 2014) 90–96.

[50] One of the earliest cases where this happened involved an applicant who was entitled to a residence permit under European Union law: *Aristimuno Mendizabal v France* App no 51431/99, judgment of 3 November 2011. There had also been three verdicts of violation involving applicants of Russian origin living in Latvia, but one of these judgments was overturned by the Grand Chamber, putting an end to the Latvian residence permit case law: *Sisojeva and others v Latvia* App no 60654/00, GC judgment of 15 January 2007. Other cases have seen applicants arguing that they needed a residence permit in order to be able to stay with their child (who may share their nationality or have that of the host state). In such cases, the Court has occasionally accepted that denying the parent a residence permit breaches the Convention. See Dembour 2015 (n 1), Chapter 13, section IX.

[51] Dembour 2015 (n 1), Chapter 13.

[52] *Van Volsem v Belgium* App no 1464/89, decision of the European Commission of Human Rights of 9 May 1990.

[53] *Müslim v Turkey* App no 53566 (ECtHR, 26 April 2005). See Lieneke Slingenberg, 'The Right Not to Be Dominated: The Case Law of the European Court of Human Rights on Migrants' Destitution' (2019) 19 (2) Human Rights Law *Review* 291–314.

[54] Virginie Guiraudon and Gallya Lahar, 'A Reappraisal of the State Sovereignty Debate: The Case of Migrant Control' (2000) 33(2) Comparative Political Studies163–195..

inevitably chips away at the protection that migrants should be entitled to—like everybody else—in an affluent world of equal human beings. The accumulation of a protection deficit, which these cases triggered is what ultimately made it possible for the *Bonger* case law to emerge, as if it was the most logical and natural conclusion to reach.

5. The Strasbourg Reversal

Bonger was the logical extension of previous pronouncements by the ECtHR: it was by referring to the fact that the applicant had no right to choose where he would live, no right not to be separated from his family, no right to a residence permit, and no right to work or receive social benefits that the *Bonger* application could be declared inadmissible without this apparently appearing problematic to the Strasbourg judges. Now these judicial edicts were themselves the product of previous statements originally made by the European Commission of Human Rights. As already mentioned, one of the reasons why it might have appeared sensible to the members of the Commission to reject applications by migrants is that migrants were not the intended beneficiaries of the Convention.[55] When the Convention was drafted, the possibility of including specific guarantees for migrants, such as rights to nationality, asylum, or not to be removed without due process, was specifically rejected. As a result, when migrants started to achieve some victories before the Court in the late 1980s and early 1990s, this was celebrated as an extraordinary and welcome extension of the Convention rather than something which should have gone without saying and should have been present right from the beginning of the system of European human rights protection. French commentators approvingly spoke of migrants' rights happening 'par ricochet', ie, indirectly.[56]

This context allowed what I call 'the Strasbourg reversal' to take place.[57] The reversal entails a reasoning on the part of the ECtHR that—to quote the *Üner* case where the applicant faced expulsion following criminal convictions—takes the following form:

> The Court reaffirms at the outset that a State is entitled, as a matter of international law and subject to its treaty obligations, to control the entry of aliens into its territory and their residence there […]. The Convention does not guarantee the right of an alien to enter or to reside in a particular country and, in pursuance of maintaining public order, Contracting States have the power to expel an alien

55 An amendment suggested by the Italian government regarding the ambit of the Convention as expressed in Article 1 ensured migrants would not be excluded: Dembour 2015 (n 1), Chapter 2, section III.
56 ibid, 106.
57 Dembour 2015 (n 1), Chapter 1, section 1; Chapter 4.

> convicted of criminal offences. However, their decisions in this field must, in so far as they may interfere with a right protected under paragraph 1 of Article 8, be in accordance with the law and necessary in a democratic society, that is to say justified by a pressing social need and, in particular, proportionate to the legitimate aim pursued.[58]

The oddness of this reasoning is best highlighted by comparing the quoted passage with the reasoning that would be followed in a non-migrant case, for example involving the fairness of criminal proceedings under Article 6. In such a case, the reasoning would not open with a statement to the effect that the state has the power to punish criminal offenders. This is not because such a statement would be incorrect, but because it would seem out of place. In turn, this is because the ECtHR's raison d'être is to defend human rights, to ensure the guarantees given by the Convention are respected and to act as the final arbiter of the Convention. Given this mission, it makes sense for it to start its reasoning with the provision to be interpreted—eg, Article 6 as in this imaginary case or Article 8 in a case like *Üner*.

That the Court did not do this in *Üner* is disturbing. What it chose to do is first to refer to the principle according to which the state is entitled to control the entry and residence of aliens. This principle appeared in the Strasbourg jurisprudence right from its first migrant judgment of *Abdulaziz, Cabales and Balkandali*. In this case, however, the principle was not used to open the reasoning of the Court. It was simply presented as one important consideration to bear in mind amongst others. To quote:

> The Court recalls that, although the essential object of Article 8 is to protect the individual against arbitrary interference by the public authorities, there may in addition be positive obligations inherent in an affective 'respect' for family life. However, ... the notion's requirements will vary considerably from case to case. Accordingly, this is an area in which the Contracting Parties enjoy a wide margin of appreciation ... [I]n the area now under consideration, the extent of a State's obligation to admit to its territory relatives of settled migrants will vary according to the particular circumstances of the persons involved. Moreover, the Court cannot ignore that the present case is concerned not only with family life but also with immigration and that, as a matter of well-established international law and subject to its treaty obligations, a State has the right to control the entry of non-nationals into its territory.[59]

In other words, the principle of state control did not take centre stage. The focus remained on how Article 8 works and what it entails.[60]

[58] *Üner v the Netherlands* App no 47410/99, GC judgment of 18 October 2006, para 54, references to previous case law omitted.

[59] *Abdulaziz, Cabales and Balkandali*, para 67, references to previous case law omitted.

[60] On how the reasoning could have developed differently, see Dembour 2015 (n 1), Chapter 4, section III.

However, later on, this principle often became the opening statement of the Court, as for example happened in *Üner*. When state control is implicitly presented as the master principle governing a migrant case, it does not mean that the state will necessarily win against the applicant. The exception providing for individual rights (eg Article 8) may overrule the principle of state sovereignty. Nonetheless, the reversal in reasoning, whereby state control comes before human rights provisions, shifts the default position of the Court slightly towards the state and away from the claimant. The Court commonly describes the principle of state control as 'well-established in international law'.

This claim is spurious, both on historical and on legal grounds.[61] It has encountered fierce opposition, including from within the Court. Judge Francoise Tulkens, Vice-President of the Court from 2011 to 2013, spoke publicly of her efforts to get the principle deleted from the reasoning of judgments in which she participated.[62] That someone in her position did so makes it very clear that the ECtHR is not an entirely homogeneous body. Rather, it is an institution where undercurrents run against the mainstream. When the ECtHR does not mention the state control principle,[63] it is in a position to start its reasoning from the idea that migrants are first of all human beings with human rights and, incidentally, they are also, in a legal sense, aliens over whom the state has powers of exclusion (when these remain acceptable under human rights principles). From a human rights perspective, this is how things should be.

The first abiding principle should be the requirement that human rights are respected; state sovereignty should only come as a secondary consideration. By contrast, when the Court considers the right of the state first, Convention rights seem to be relegated to the status of exceptions which serve to limit the principle of state sovereignty, the latter being the default position. This cannot but undermine the human rights cause.[64]

Talking of a Strasbourg reversal points to the incongruous nature of the logic that is followed when prominence is given to a state prerogative, which neither

[61] The principle had appeared in *one* US Supreme Court judgment, which itself referred to *one* classical writer of international law. For a critique, see Dembour 2015 (n 1), at 117–18; Bas Schotel, *On the Right of Exclusion: Law, Ethics and Immigration Policy* (Routledge 2012); Satvinder Juss, 'Free Movement and the World Order' in Vincent Chétail (ed), *International Law and Migration* (Edgar Elgar 2016).

[62] Judge Tulkens was prompted to do this by a scholarly article that denounced the Strasbourg reversal (without calling it as such), namely: Sylvie Saroléa, 'Quelles vies privée et familiale pour l'étranger? Pour une protection non discriminatoire de ces vies par l'article 8 de la Convention européenne des droits de l'homme (C.E.D.H.)' (2000) 19 Revue Québecoise de droit international 247–85 (Tulkens, personal communication, March 2014). For another denunciation of the reversal, see Olivier Delas, 'Le principe de non-refoulement dans la jurisprudence international des droits de l'homme: De la consécration à la contestation' (PhD thesis, Paris 2 Panthéon-Assas University 2010).

[63] See eg *M.S.S. v Belgium and Greece*, where it is nowhere to be found.

[64] That this is problematic is reflected in the way commentators generally write about human rights. For example, Çalı states that 'the regional institutions in the Americas, Europe and Africa all ... give priority to the effective interpretation of the rights of individuals over the sovereign rights of states' (Çalı. 'Regional Protection', in Moeckli et al. (eds.), *International Human Rights Law*, (OUp, 2017) 411–424 at 419–20). Clearly the Strasbourg reversal does the opposite.

serves to affirm human rights nor is inscribed in the text which the adjudicating court's task is to interpret and apply. The Strasbourg reversal is just one particularly striking pointer that indicates that the Strasbourg case law is not resolutely on the side of migrants' human rights, but there are others, including an interpretation of substantive rights that makes it difficult for violations to be declared and procesual choices that tend to let states off the hook.[65]

6. The *Pro-homine* Approach of the IACtHR

The IACtHR is often presented as the sister institution of the ECtHR. Set up in 1979 and based in San José, Costa Rica, this mainly Latin American court (in which neither the USA nor Canada participate) is often implicitly described in human rights law textbooks as a less effective emulation of its Strasbourg big sister. Students thus seem invited to assume that the IACtHR is a weaker replicate than the model which inspired it. Such an assumption is, in my view, contestable.

For a seasoned observer of the European Convention system, one of the most striking features of the Inter-American case law is its resolutely *pro-homine* orientation. The label '*pro-homine*', meaning pro-human being in Latin, is used by the IACtHR to describe its own approach. The latter can be summarised as entailing a bias towards the human being—rather than towards the other party which appears before the Court, ie the state, as in the European system.[66]

Had it not resolutely adopted this *pro homine* approach, the IACtHR might easily have been deprived of any raison d'être, for the first generation of cases which came before it involved serious human rights violations committed during the brutal dictatorships which had engulfed Latin America in the 1970s. Allegations of, for example, forced disappearance, torture, and massacres were contested by the defendant states. Normal legal practice requests the party who brings a complaint before a judge to prove the veracity and pertinence of their complaint. Adherence to this principle would have made it almost impossible for the IACtHR to reach verdicts of violations. But, in its first judgment on the merits regarding forced disappearances, the IACtHR did not hesitate to shift the burden of proof onto the defendant state as the victims' allegations corresponded to practices described in reports authored by reliable sources.[67] This crucial step was accompanied by other procedural and substantive moves on the part of the Court.

65 For my summary of these, see Dembour 2015 (n 1) 505–08.

66 Yota Negishi, 'The *Pro Homine* Principle's Role in Regulating the Relationship between Conventionality Control and Constitutionality Control' (2017) 28(2) European Journal of International Law 457–81.

67 *Velasquez-Rodriguez v Honduras*, Merits, Judgment of 29 July 1988.

Judge Antonio Cancado-Trindade, who presided over the IACtHR from 1999 to 2003, could never sufficiently explain that the foundations and validity of international law needed to be displaced from the will of states to what he called 'the universal juridical conscience'.[68] He repeatedly scorned 'the excesses of a degenerated legal positivism'.[69] The IACtHR became renowned for the boldness of its determination to push the development of human rights standards, which some commentators feared would damage the effectiveness of the Court.[70] Whatever one's views on this, what is clear is that the Court does not hesitate to take imaginative steps in order to identify human rights abuses and to have them repaired.

Whilst its docket is not large (no more than two dozen new cases a year), it has acquired a reputation for making the most of the cases before it, striving in each case to examine human rights issues from a variety of angles, to identify standards, and, last but not least, to impose on violating states precise and demanding remedial measures, going in all kinds of relevant directions.[71] The result of this determined approach is a jurisprudence which is more inclined to put the human being at its centre.

7. Immigration Detention Case Law

Migrants have benefited from this approach almost from the very beginning of the Inter-American Court.[72] *Vélez Loor v Panama*,[73] decided in 2010, is a case in

[68] *The Right to Information on Consular Assistance in the Framework of the Guarantees of the Due Process of Law*, Advisory opinion O/C-16/99 of 1 October 1999, concurring opinion of Judge AA Cancado-Trindade, paras 13–14.

[69] ibid, para 12.

[70] Gerald L Neuman, 'Import, Export, and Regional Consent in the Inter-American Court of Human Rights' (2008) 19 European Journal of International Law 101–23.

[71] This may be changing. See Clara Sandoval, 'Two Steps Forward, One Step Back: Reflections on the Jurisprudential Turn of the Inter-American Court of Human Rights on Domestic Reparation Programmes (2017) 22 (9) International Journal of Human Rights 1192–1208; Geneviève Lessard, 'Preventive Reparations at a Crossroads: The Inter-America Court of Human Rights and Colombia's Search for Peace' (2017)22 (9) International Journal of Human Rights 1209–1228 .

[72] The fourth ruling of the Court concerned the right to nationality: *Proposed Amendments to the Naturalisation Provision of the Constitution of Costa Rica*, Advisory opinion OA-4/84, 19 January 1984. Worth noting is the fact that migrants receive special protection in the American Convention on Human Rights. See Article 20 ACHR (on nationality) and paras 6–9 of Article 22 ACHR (on expulsion and asylum), which are in line with a Latin American tradition which may well have been responsible for the insertion of migrants' rights in the Universal Declaration of Human Rights: Dembour 2015 (n 1), Chapter 2, section IX. For developments since then see David James Cantor and Stefania Eugenia Barichello, 'The Inter-American Human Rights System: A New Model for Integrating Refugee and Complementary Protection' (2013) 17(5-6) The International Journal of Human Rights 689–706; Ana Beduschi, 'The Contribution of the Inter-American Court of Human Rights to the Protection of Irregular Migrants' Rights: Opportunities and Challenges' (2015) 34 (4) Refugee Survey Quarterly 45–74; Belen Olmos Giupponi, 'Assessing the Evolution of the Inter-American Court of Human Rights in the Protection of Migrants' Rights: Past, Present and Future' (2017) 17(4) The International Journal of Human Rights 1477–1503.

[73] *Vélez Loor v Panama*, Preliminary Objections, Merits, Reparations and Costs, judgment of 23 November 2010.

point. The victim was an Ecuadorian national who had been caught by the police in the Republic of Panama without a valid visa and put in detention, where he endured terrible conditions until his release ten months later. The IACtHR did not find the acts of torture he alleged were sufficiently proven to be ruled upon. However, complaints regarding overcrowding, lack of water, absence of contact with the external world, and lack of medical treatment, were not disputed and indeed were specifically recognised by the defendant state, even prior to the public hearing which the Court held in this case. This acknowledgement by the state did not lead the IACtHR to close the case, for it found that a number of factual issues and points of principle remained in dispute, which accordingly in its view required adjudication.[74] The IACtHR ended up detailing a number of safeguards that must be in place when state authorities resort to immigration detention. These can be summarised as follows:

(a) the state can never use detention as a punitive measure for an immigration offence;
(b) alternatives to immigration detention must be sought. Given the inherent 'sacrifice' detention entails for the right to liberty and the requirement that its disadvantages remain strictly proportionate to its advantages, these alternatives must be used whenever possible. Detention can never become routine;
(c) any immigrant who is arrested and detained must be promptly brought before an officer authorised by law to exercise judicial power; this officer must hear the detainee and motivates the detention by reference to their particular circumstances;
(d) judicial remedies must subsequently be available to the detained migrant; they cannot just exist in the abstract but must be readily accessible in practice by any immigration detainee; they must involve judges;
(e) the immigration detainee must be put in a position to exercise their right to defence. This necessarily entails that they are offered free legal representation by a qualified lawyer. Assistance by organisations which defend the rights of migrants is not sufficient;
(f) the immigrant detainee must be informed of their right to possible consular assistance;
(g) immigration detainees cannot be placed in a prison which hosts criminals and/or people on remand;
(h) special attention must be given to the position of families.

[74] The ECtHR would be unlikely to act in the same way. It regularly strikes cases off. Dembour 2015 (n 1) 325.

This is a far cry from what the ECtHR has decided in complaints related to immigration detention. In *Saadi v United Kingdom*, decided in 2008, the practice of detaining an asylum seeker for the sole purpose of administrative convenience, namely having the person on site and thus available for interview at any time, thereby facilitating the determination of asylum claims, was found to be acceptable under Article 5 ECHR (right to liberty and security).[75] Admittedly, the detention had been short (seven days) and in conditions that were described as relatively relaxed. The minority judges were nonetheless outraged. They closed their dissenting opinion by asking:

> Are we now also to accept that Article 5 of the Convention [on liberty], which has played a major role in ensuring controls of arbitrary detention, should afford a lower level of protection as regards asylum and immigration which, in social and human terms, are the most crucial issues facing us in the years to come? Is it a crime to be a foreigner? We do not think so.

Further cases were subsequently lodged at Strasbourg which continued to question the immigration detention system of the United Kingdom, especially its absence of time limits. In *J.N.*, decided in 2016, the ECtHR ruled that the absence of fixed time-limits and automatic judicial review did not in itself breach the requirements of Article 5 ECHR.[76] *S.M.M.* confirmed this ruling one year later.[77]

In this latter case, the ECtHR found a violation of Article 5 ECHR, but only because the domestic decision about the applicant's asylum claim had not been timely, as a result of which the applicant had not been able to challenge the determination outcome until she had spent two and a half years in detention. This was especially inappropriate given that she was a victim of torture and suffered from serious mental illness. The Court stated: 'Where an applicant is subject to an indeterminate period of detention [as in the system chosen by the UK government], the necessity of procedural safeguards becomes decisive.'[78] Nonetheless it awarded the applicant no damages. This was on the ground that she had requested additional time for submitting documents in support of her asylum claim, which seems to have been taken by the Court to mean that she should have expected her detention to last longer.

The dehumanising effect of immigration detention on detainees is well documented—the sudden feeling that life is taken away from you, the sheer uncertainty about the future, the absolute sense of powerlessness, the utter loss of dignity.[79] One might have thought the ECtHR would have wanted to affirm the

75 *Saadi v United Kingdom* App no 13229/03 (ECtHR, 29 January 2008).
76 *J.N. v United Kingdom* App no 37289/12 (ECtHR, 19 May 2016).
77 *S.M.M. v United Kingdom* App no 77450/12 (ECtHR, 22 June 2017).
78 ibid, para 84.
79 This is particularly well captured in the 'Refugee Tales' commissioned by the organisation of the same name: David Herd and Anna Pincus (eds), *Refugee Tales* (Comma Press 2016); *Refugee Tales II* (Comma Press 2017).

principle that asylum seekers should not be detained, certainly not as a matter of course, as their asylum claim is being determined. But this is not the path the ECtHR has decided to follow.[80]

It is difficult to imagine the IACtHR endorsing the Strasbourg approach. The IACtHR has said, and repeated, that detention can only be a last resort; it has also sought to impose procedural guarantees. This has happened not only in *Vélez Loor*, as we have seen, but also in other cases. For example, in *Pacheco Tineo* which, without involving detention, concerned the right to seek and be granted asylum, the IACtHR insisted that an asylum seeker must be given access to legal counsel and representation as well as interpretation services.[81]

8. The Way Out of the *Bonger* Aporia

This chapter has proposed that the ECtHR's record in protecting migrants' rights is not as positive as one might have hoped, given that protecting human rights is the raison d'être of the Court. It has been careful to explain that this mixed record is the fruit of a long jurisprudential history, which itself can be seen as having emerged from the ECHR having been devised with the aim of protecting the European citizen (rather than anyone and everybody) against European destructive forces. Over the years, relatively small deficits in protection were accepted, which the majority felt were justified by the need to pay due regard to the proclaimed interests of the state. The problem is that a logic was triggered which has induced bigger and bigger deficits in protection. The outcome is, from a staunch human rights perspective, an incomprehensible case law, particularly well epitomised by the *Bonger* case law but also illustrated by other decisions such as *S.M.M.*

The question arises: will it always be like this? It does not have to be. Reassuringly, there are examples in the Strasbourg case law where a seemingly unstoppable logic has been brought to an abrupt stop. I am, for example, thinking of *M.S.S. v Belgium and Greece*.[82] This case, decided in 2011, famously found the transfer of an asylum seeker from Belgium to Greece, in accordance with EU legislation, to be in breach of multiple provisions of the ECHR. The ECtHR said that Belgium should have known that the asylum determination system in Greece was utterly defective and that the applicant would be subjected to inhuman conditions upon his transfer there. The Court recognised the difficulties Greece faced due to its geographical position at the door of Europe, but said this could not absolve it from responsibility for its serious shortcomings. The ECtHR ended up finding each defendant state in

[80] Anita Sinha, 'Defining Detention: The Intervention of the European Court of Human Rights in the Detention of Involuntary Migrants' (2019) 50(3) Columbian Human Rights Law Review 176–227.

[81] *Family Pacheco Tineo v Plurinational State of Bolivia*, Preliminary Objections, Merits, Reparations and Costs, Judgment of the IACtHR of 25 November 2013.

[82] *M.S.S. v Belgium and Greece* App no 30696/09 (ECtHR, 21 January 2011).

violation of Article 3 (inhuman and degrading treatment), and this on two counts (conditions of detention on the one hand and living conditions when not in detention on the other hand), as well as of Article 13 (access to a domestic remedy).[83] These conclusions were the most startling since, in a previous lead case called *K.R.S.* dating from 2008, the Court had specifically decided that the transfer of an asylum seeker to Greece could not be presumed to be against the Convention.[84] After *K.R.S.*, the legitimacy of such a transfer was ingrained in the Strasbourg system. This is so much so that when the applicant in *M.S.S.* made a Rule 39 request to the Court for an interim measure ordering Belgium to refrain from transferring him to Greece during the time of the Strasbourg proceedings, this was refused. As Judge Bratza commented in his dissenting opinion in the *M.S.S.* judgment, how could the Belgian authorities have been expected to know that transferring *M.S.S.* to Greece was to be considered a breach of the Convention? All the signs coming from the Court itself was that such a transfer was an entirely legitimate course of action and perfectly lawful under the Convention.

The Court nonetheless decided to condemn Belgium (most forcefully) and Greece. This is not the place to go into the details of how this was achieved.[85] Suffice it to say that within the logic of its own case law until then, *M.S.S.* made no sense: both *K.R.S.* and the subsequent practice of the Court of systematically declaring similar cases inadmissible, not to mention refusing Rule 39 requests, clearly pointed to the lawfulness of transfers to Greece. One can only surmise that the abysmal conditions suffered by asylum seekers in Greece, denounced in stark terms and with plenty of evidence by numerous organisations, persuaded the Court that it could no longer condone transfers to Greece. The *M.S.S.* judgment made jurisprudential leaps which had never been made before, such as pronouncing that a situation of extreme poverty could entail a breach of Article 3.[86]

What the Court has done with *M.S.S.*, it can do with the *Bonger* or any other objectionable case law. The Court is not bound by its previous judgments. Although it is generally considered good practice to seek legal consistency, and this is for wise reasons, established jurisprudential lines must be abandoned or at least given a different inflexion if this is what human rights require.[87]

[83] This can then be used to build reasoning in favour of migrants' rights. See eg Violeta Moreno-Lax, *Accessing Asylum in Europe: Extraterritorial Border Controls and Refugee Rights under EU Law* (OUP 2017).

[84] *K.R.S. v United Kingdom* App no 32733/08 (ECtHR, 2 December 2008).

[85] See Dembour 2015 (n 1), Chapter 12.

[86] Veronika Flegar, 'Vulnerability and the Principle of Non-Refoulement in the European Court of Human Rights: Towards an Increased Scope of Protection for Persons Fleeing from Extreme Poverty' (2016) 2 Contemporary Readings in Law and Social Justice 148–69; Laurens Lavrysen, 'Human Rights and Poverty: A European Perspective' in Eva Brems, Christophe Van der Beken, and Solomon Abay Yimer (eds), *Human Rights and Development: Legal Perspectives from and for Ethiopia* (Brill Nijhoff 2015) 303–28..

[87] It might be argued that this is what the Court did in the recent case of *Hoti v Croatia* App no 63311/14 (ECtHR, 26 April 2018), where Croatia was found in violation of Article 8 due to the impossibility in which the stateless applicant had been to regularise his residence status. However, the Court made it

In *When Humans Become Migrants*, I put forward a number of substantive and procedural avenues which the ECtHR could consider taking in order to deliver effective human rights guarantees to migrants and thus overturn decisions such as *Bonger*.[88] Most directly relevant to the present discussion is the suggestion that the Court approaches the prohibition of inhuman and degrading treatment contained in Article 3 ECHR with more imagination and compassion for the experience of the applicants, whom it tends not to believe and to blame for their circumstances.[89] Sensitivity to the humane dimension of the cases before it should allow the Court to see more often than it does now that the high threshold of severity in the treatment inflicted, required for Article 3 to apply, is actually met. The resulting more generous and compassionate approach could then 'naturally' come to inflect other areas of the case law, including Article 8.

I would also wish to invite the Court to develop an awareness of the inherent discrimination that the organisation of the world along national lines entails, with some people able to move more or less as they wish and others more or less locked into place. The assumptions underlying the current regime of 'managed migration' must be questioned. At the very least, it must be recognised that classifying human beings by reference to nationality law and various immigration statuses generates differences in treatment. These can only be deemed acceptable if they are justified by truly 'very weighty reasons', as the case law on Article 14 (prohibition of discrimination) suggests. The Court could start insisting that the state actually substantiates its reasons for establishing differences in treatment on grounds of nationality/immigration law.[90]

A third area in need of transformation concerns Article 6 (fair trial guarantees). Migrants' lives are constantly impacted, in a drastic and decisive manner, by administrative decisions regarding their status, right of residence, right to work, right to be joined by family members, etc. These are taken within the context of procedures which do not have to conform with the protections offered by Article 6, given *Maaouia's* conclusion in 2000 that Article 6 does not apply to immigration issues. One hears in the corridors of Strasbourg that the time may be ripe to reverse this Grand Chamber judgment. One must hope that the Court will find an

very clear that the case concerned a 'complex and very specific factual and legal situation' which arose following the break-up of the Socialist Federal Republic of Yugoslavia (para 109). The Court stressed that the stay of the applicant in Croatia had lasted almost forty years and had at times been regular and constantly tolerated (para 117). It is difficult to think on the basis of *Hoti* that the ECtHR might have changed its mind about its *Bonger* case law.

[88] Dembour 2015 (n 1), Chapter 15, section II.

[89] My book is peppered with examples of this. See eg ibid, 2017–11, 278–80, 428–33, 465, 478–79. See also Lourdes Peroni, 'The Borders that Disadvantage Migrant Women in Enjoying Human Rights' (2018) 36(2) Netherlands Quarterly of Human Rights 93–110.

[90] Interestingly, some recommendations and/or resolutions of the Parliamentary Assembly of the Council of Europe (PACE) go further than the ECtHR in setting up norms that protect migrants. See eg Resolution 2243 (2018): Family reunification of refugees and migrants in the Council of Europe member States.

early opportunity to heed these calls. If not, an alternative way to secure procedural justice would entail giving more attention to guarantees under Article 13.

9. Conclusion

As has been stressed throughout this chapter, and however much this may appear paradoxical, the ECHR was not designed with the aim of protecting every human being. The colonial subject—still very much an actual figure when the Convention was signed in 1950—was not automatically covered and the specific plight of migrants was ignored. These intended limitations have carried on in the case law which was developed by the erstwhile European Commission of Human Rights and the European Court of Human Rights. As a result, when times have become tough for migrants, as they are now, far from offering robust protection, the European system of human rights protection—commonly described as the most effective in the world—has faltered. The ECtHR has ended up endorsing treatment by states which sits at the opposite of what respect for the dignity of each human being would command. Examples of this phenomenon include the denial of legal status to individuals who have no prospect of being able to live anywhere else than where they are and the failure to condemn even indefinite detention.

This does not mean that the Strasbourg case law is bound to remain on the track it is currently following. A different jurisprudential approach is possible which would give the migrant person his or her due place in the high ethical framework which human rights law promises to provide. Dormant resources laying in ECHR provisions, including but going beyond Articles 3, 6, and 14, can be harnessed. The Strasbourg reversal can be redressed. It is entirely possible, within the confines of the ECHR, to bestow on migrants the comprehensive protection they deserve.

The human rights logic advocated in this chapter is simple. Encouragingly, it appears to be very much at the heart of the jurisprudence of other human rights adjudicatory bodies, including the IACtHR. Admittedly, this is an ethos which edges towards an intuition for open borders, rather than with the idea that the world is safer when borders are kept closed for a large part of humanity. This optimism in the possibility of constructing a largely open world goes against what many politicians and a great part of the public are currently ready to countenance. In response, it is important to stress that an ethos of equality, freedom, and openness is likely to be to the ultimate advantage of all citizens.

In our era where the excesses of neoliberalism have generated politics of austerity and an erosion of the social democratic principles that the post-war generation started to take for granted, standing together, re-imagining distributive practices, and developing a sustainable society in a spirit of solidarity need to be political and moral imperatives. Human fulfilment is not best measured in terms of capital accumulation, but by reference to humane values. Lest this be forgotten, migrants are human beings too. If we allow ourselves to forget this, we all stand to lose our humanity.

PART II

RIGHT TO FLEE, RIGHT TO SEEK ASYLUM, AND THE RIGHT TO HUMANE AND DIGNIFIED TREATMENT

This part critically analyses the general interpretative outlook of the European Court of Human Rights on the right to flee, the right to seek asylum and the right to humane and dignified treatment of migrants when they reach the territories of Council of Europe member states.

3

Intersectionality, Forced Migration, and the Jus-generation of the Right to *Flee*

Theorising a Composite Entitlement to Leave to Escape Irreversible Harm

*Violeta Moreno-Lax**

1. Introduction

My main preoccupation in this chapter is with the piecemeal approach adopted by the European Court of Human Rights (ECtHR) to the question of access to asylum of those in need of international protection and how intersectionality theory can help facilitate a principled shift towards an analysis that apprehends the complexity of the position of refugees and recovers the indivisibility of human rights.[1] Intersectionality theory, as section 3 of this chapter will elaborate, encapsulates the multi-faceted appreciation of human experience in a way that captures the whole ontological breadth of lived realities, away from categorizations that arbitrarily segment identity and social relations. I advocate the adoption of a similar approach to the construal of the law so that intersectional thinking guides not only the appraisal of factual constellations, but also the interpretation of the applicable norms.[2] The proposal is to 'look at rights and their violations from a persons-centred rather

* This research was completed in Heidelberg, thanks to the generous support of the Max Planck Institute for Comparative Public Law and International Law's Visiting Fellows scheme in July 2018. I am grateful to Prof Christina Binder (Vienna/Munich), for very stimulating conversations during this period, and to Prof Lizzie Barmes (Queen Mary), Prof Başak Çali (Hertie/Koç), Prof Penny Green (Queen Mary), Prof Rosemary Hunter (Kent), Prof Kate Malleson (Queen Mary), and Judge Ledi Bianku (ECtHR) for their invaluable feedback. I also thank the participants in the Refugee and Migration Law Workshop, hosted by Berkeley Law School in December 2019, for their comments on a previous draft. This is a deliverable of the MAPS Project, funded by the Jean Monnet Programme, Grant decision 2018-1606/001-001. The chapter was finalized before the inadmissibility decision in *M.N. v Belgium* [GC] App no 3599/18 (ECtHR, 5 March 2020).

1 The terms 'refugee', 'asylum seeker', and 'protection seeker' are used interchangeably to encompass all persons in need to flee a country, including their own, to escape persecution or serious harm.

2 For a similar approach, speaking of 'modifiers' or 'interstitial norms' as resulting from the intersection of conflicting primary rules of international law, but without relying on intersectionality or identifying any other theoretical framework to justify their emergence, see Vaughan Lowe, 'Sustainable Development and Unsustainable Arguments' in Alan Boyle and David Freestone, *International Law and Sustainable Development* (OUP 1999) 19, 35.

Violeta Moreno-Lax, *Intersectionality, Forced Migration, and the Jus-generation of the Right to* Flee In: *Migration and the European Convention on Human Rights.* Edited by: Başak Çali, Ledi Bianku, and Iulia Motoc, Oxford University Press (2021).
 DOI: 10.1093/oso/9780192895196.003.0003

than a formula-based position, and analysing them contextually rather than abstractly'.[3] This requires embracing a holistic understanding that penetrates the full depth of individual situations, as traversed by the plethora of legal provisions that accumulate, interact, and apply at the same time, so that 'rights ... fit people' rather than the other way around.[4]

It has long been recognised that the European Convention on Human Rights (ECHR)[5] does not include a right to asylum,[6] let alone a freedom to enter any country except for one's own.[7] Notwithstanding the historical importance of the right to leave, as a chief indicator of the democratic nature of states,[8] and as 'the foundation for *any* individual to *escape* power structures with which he disagrees',[9] attempts at codifying a dedicated Protocol on asylum regulating the right to leave of refugees have failed.[10]

Neither has the right to leave been explicitly incorporated in the text of the 1951 Convention on Refugees, despite the very definition of a refugee depending on the person being 'outside the country of ... nationality',[11] with the effect that the denial of the right to leave implies the negation of the right to seek international protection.[12] Only the Universal Declaration of Human Rights incorporates the right to leave in search of asylum in an instrument of global remit, but in non-legally binding form.[13] And, although regional systems of human rights protection

[3] *National Coalition for Gay and Lesbian Equality v Ministry of Justice* 1998 (12) BCLR 1517 (CC) 112 (per Sachs, concurring).

[4] ibid.

[5] Convention for the Protection of Human Rights and Fundamental Freedoms (European Convention on Human Rights, as amended) ETS 5 (ECHR).

[6] *N.D. and N.T. v Spain* [GC] App nos 8675/15 and 8697/15 (ECtHR, 13 February 2020), para 188 and references therein.

[7] For a discussion on the *travaux préparatoires* of Prot 4 ECHR, see William Schabas, *The European Convention on Human Rights* (OUP 2015) 1054–56.

[8] Note that the right is included in key human rights conventions: Art 12(2), International Covenant on Civil and Political Rights (adopted 16 December 1966, entered into force 23 March 1976) 999 UNTS 171 (ICCPR); Art 5(2), Convention on the Elimination of All Forms of Racial Discrimination (adopted 21 December 1965, entered into force 4 January 1969) 660 UNTS 195 (CERD); Arts 37(c) and 10(2), Convention on the Rights of the Child (adopted 20 November 1989, entered into force 2 September 1990) 1577 UNTS 3 (CRC).

[9] VG Stuttgart, A 11 K5036/13, Judgment of 25 March 2014 (emphasis added). On the links between the right to leave and the right to asylum, see Peter Jagerskiold, 'The Freedom of Movement' in Louis Henkin (ed), *The International Bill of Rights* (Columbia University Press 1981) 166, 167. See also Violeta Moreno-Lax, *Accessing Asylum in Europe* (OUP 2017) 337ff.

[10] Parliamentary Assembly of the Council of Europe (PACE), Recommendation 293 (1961) on the right of asylum (26 September 1961). See also Committee of Ministers of the Council of Europe, Resolution (67) 14 on asylum to persons in danger of persecution (29 June 1967); and Committee of Ministers, Declaration on Territorial Asylum (18 November 1977).

[11] Art 1(A)(2), Convention Relating to the Status of Refugees (adopted 28 July 1951, entered into force 22 April 1954) 189 UNTS 150 (CSR).

[12] Many consider, also in light of the *travaux préparatoires*, that the right to leave is implicit in the Convention, 'for the very existence of refugees depend[s] on it'. See Guy S Goodwin-Gill, *The Refugee in International Law* (2nd edn, OUP 1996), 175 and references therein.

[13] Art 14, Universal Declaration on Human Rights (adopted 10 December 1948) UNGA Res 217 A(III) (UDHR).

in America, Africa, and at EU level have codified a right to asylum,[14] the question of access remains ambiguous. What we see instead is the erection of barriers by countries of destination that preclude access to international protection,[15] impeding travel from countries of origin through safe and legal means, such as visa requirements, carrier sanctions, and other measures of extraterritorial border control.[16] Against this background, this chapter proposes an intersectional reading of Strasbourg case law to address this situation, overcoming the limitations of the current sectoral understanding of the rights applicable to refugees' plight, as disconnected from each other and from the realities to which they apply.

As section 2 will show, the approach under the Convention has been fragmented so far. While the Court has recognised a '*right* to gain effective access to the procedure for determining refugee status',[17] and even established its applicability in an extraterritorial setting,[18] it has subsequently denied that these approaches 'imply a *general duty* for a Contracting State ... to bring persons ... within its own jurisdiction' to facilitate its realisation.[19] Jurisprudential developments have occurred without an integrative framework or a comprehensive approach in mind. The relevant legal bases of these findings, whether the prohibition of collective expulsion, the principle of *non-refoulement*, the right to leave, or a combination of the three simultaneously, have not been systematically identified, nor has the rationale for the different conclusions been elucidated or their full implications established.

Typically, what the ECtHR does, when several Convention provisions seem to concurrently apply, is to consider them separately and concentrate the analysis on the one that appears most significant to the resolution of the case, obviating the normative input from related provisions,[20] let alone the potential jus-generative effects of their intersection.[21] This disintegrates justice and leaves real needs unmet.

14 See the 'right to seek and be granted asylum', in Art 22(7) of the American Convention on Human Rights (1969) 1144 UNTS 123; the 'right to seek and obtain asylum', in Art 12(3) of the African Charter on Human and Peoples Rights (1982) 21 ILM 58; and the 'right to asylum' in Art 18 of the Charter of Fundamental Rights of the European Union [2007] OJ C303/17.

15 Council of Europe Commissioner on Human Rights, *The Right to Leave a Country* (Council of Europe 2013) 11. Note, however, that this practice is not constitutive of a customary norm and that efforts to formally codify a duty to combat irregular emigration have never succeeded. Tracing these attempts, see Andrew Wolman, 'The Role of Departure States in Combating Irregular Emigration in International Law: An Historical [sic] Perspective' (2019) 20 International Journal of Refugee Law 1.

16 See further Moreno-Lax (n 9) chs 2–6.

17 *Amuur v France* App no 19776/92 (ECtHR, 25 June 1996), para 43 (emphasis added).

18 *Hirsi Jamaa and others v Italy* [GC] App no 27765/09 (ECtHR, 23 February 2012).

19 *N.D. and N.T.* (n 6), para 221 (emphasis added).

20 A notable exception is represented by the Court's approach to housing rights of vulnerable groups. See section 6 below for an elaboration.

21 The term of 'jus generation' is used in sociological approaches to law and normally associated to sociological processes (*outside* the law and within which the law is deemed embedded) leading to the generation of new norms. See eg Paul Blokker and Chris Thornhill, 'Sociological Constitutionalism: An Introduction' in Paul Blokker and Chris Thornhill (eds), *Sociological Constitutionalism* (Cambridge University Press 2017) 1, 16, speaking of 'the jus-generative potential of social practices'. For a diagram of processes of what the author calls 'constitutional opening' of legal regimes to societal practices, see Riccardo Prandini, 'Morphogenesis of Constitutionalism' in Dobner and Loughlin (eds), *The Twilight of Constitutionalism* (OUP 2010) 309, 318. Here, by contrast, the term is employed without

By contrast, what is suggested here is that the key insight from intersectionality theory be applied to an intersectional reading of the Convention, not only to the assessment of the factual circumstances surrounding claims, but crucially also to the interpretation of legal provisions. This means acknowledging that, at the point of intersection between two relevant rights clauses, say A and B, it is not just A or B, or even A+B that becomes discernible, but something unique (C) that results from their intercourse, the normative content of which is to be taken in consideration. Applied to refugees, the intersectional reading of the relationship between the right to leave and the right to protection against ill-treatment, rather than relying on only one of them in isolation, would consider the ensuing 'right to leave to escape ill-treatment' as the relevant standard.

The following sections will show how the absence of a right to enter any country excluding one's own may be remedied, in so far as refugees are concerned, through the interactive combination of *existing* entitlements already positivised in the Convention, without the need for 'new law'. The chapter will take the disorderly pathway started by the Strasbourg Court in past decisions and propose a method of principled systematisation, using intersectionality as a framework for the reconciliation of the different elements under consideration. Through an intersectional interpretation, the existing entitlements to leave and enjoy protection from irreversible harm,[22] instead of producing disparate and unpredictable results, will consolidate in what I call the (composite) 'right to flee', understood as a right to run away 'to find a solution to a situation ... contrary to Article 3 [ECHR]',[23] with legally binding effect.[24] The American debate will be used, in section 6, to illustrate the concrete operationalisation of the intersectional approach that this chapter advocates, relying on the rich scholarship that has developed therein on jus-generative interactions between constitutional norms.

that sociological connotation to signify the means (*within* the law) through which legal systems self-reproduce and sustain themselves. For an example, see Jurgen Habermas, discussing the jus-generative force of human dignity as 'mother' principle of universal human rights, in 'The Concept of Human Dignity and the Realistic Utopia of Human Rights' in Claudio Corradetti (ed), *Philosophical Dimensions of Human Rights* (Springer 2012) 63.

[22] 'Irreversible harm' refers to that taking 'the form of a violation of Articles 2 [right to life] or 3 [prohibition of torture] of the Convention', as per *Khlaifia and others v Italy* App no 16483/12 (ECtHR, 15 December 2016), para 279. In *refoulement* scenarios, however, the Strasbourg Court has typically interpreted 'the words "inhuman or degrading treatment or punishment" in Art 3 as including the death penalty', thereby subsuming Art 2 ECHR risks within the remit of Art 3 ECHR. See *Al-Saadoon v United Kingdom* App no 61498/08 (ECtHR, 2 March 2010), para 120; and *Soering v United Kingdom* App no 14038/88 (ECtHR, 7 July 1989), paras 102–04. Here, 'irreversible harm' will accordingly be used as a shorthand of both types of risks and deemed covered by Art 3 ECHR.

[23] *M.S.S. v Belgium* App no 30696/09 (ECtHR, 21 January 2011), para 315.

[24] Using the term 'right to escape' in a non-legal, but political perspective, see Sandro Mezzadra, 'The Right to Escape' (2004) 4 Ephemera 267; and Sandro Mezzadra, 'The Proliferation of Borders and the Right to Escape' in Yolande Jansen, Robin Celikates, and Joost de Bloois (eds), *The Irregularization of Migration in Contemporary Europe* (Rowman & Littlefield 2015) 121.

If embraced within the Convention system, this interpretation, while not pursuing an 'open borders' overhaul, will imply that *non-entrée* regimes[25] implemented without consideration of the specific position of refugees are not only '*morally* wrong',[26] but *legally* indefensible too. The intersectional interpretation will palliate this 'wrong' by relying on the legal tools *already* available *within* the system, continuing the trajectory of the Court, but through a value-based approach, rendering ECHR refugee protection actionable, accessible, and predictable on the ground.

The purchase of this method is wider than this chapter will elaborate. It can be adopted across the board to read the Convention 'as a whole', promoting 'internal consistency and harmony between its various provisions'.[27] This would enhance cohesion, legal certainty, fairness, and legitimacy overall, supporting the development of the Convention as 'a constitutional instrument of European public order'.[28]

The reasoning in relation to the 'right to flee' will proceed in seven steps. Section 2 will expand on the Court's piecemeal approach to the question of access to asylum, exposing the need for a principled shift. Section 3 will introduce intersectionality theory, explaining its emancipatory potential and distilling its main insights for the purposes of legal interpretation. The limits of non-discrimination and equality-based reasoning, as the main legal tools employed so far for intersectional adjudication, will be set out in section 4. Section 5 will propose an alternative grounding for the implementation of intersectional reasoning, theorising an (intersectional) 'comprehensive dignity' paradigm to anchor the (intersectional) legal interpretation of rights provisions, giving rise to a whole-of-legal-system approach that matches the whole-of-person analysis called for by the theory. Section 6 will then map out the utilisation of intersectional thinking in American constitutionalism, as an elaborate example of a regime that has long considered formulas, similar to the one advanced in this chapter, to tackle complex realities, complex claims, and complex decision-making puzzles. Section 7 will consolidate findings and apply the lessons learnt to the ECHR context. Conclusions on the resulting (intersectional) 'right to flee' will be summarised in Section 8. Overall, the main proposition will be that, to fully apprehend the compounded nature of the rights and realities of asylum seekers attempting to leave a country in search of international protection, the adoption of an intersectional approach is key in addressing the totality of their plight. Only a whole-of-person approach, matched by a whole-of-legal

[25] See, generally, Moreno-Lax (n 9); Thomas Gammeltoft-Hansen, *Access to Asylum* (Cambridge University Press 2011); and Marten den Heijer, *Europe and Extraterritorial Asylum* (Hart 2012).

[26] Joseph Carens, 'How Should We Think about the Ethics of International Migration?' European University Institute Forum (17–18 November 2014), 5 (emphasis added) <https://www.eui.eu/Documents/RSCAS/PapersLampedusa/FORUM-Carensfinal.pdf> (accessed 5 March 2020).

[27] *N.D. and N.T.* (n 6) para 172.

[28] *Al-Skeini v United Kingdom* App no 55721/07 (ECtHR, 7 July 2011), para 141.

system interpretation of the entitlements concerned, is capable of realising substantive justice in practice.

2. Access to Asylum and the Piecemeal Approach of the Strasbourg Court

The ECtHR has, in recent years, developed a somewhat contradictory approach to the plight of protection seekers blocked without access to asylum and without the possibility of leaving their countries of origin through legal and safe means. While there have been some encouraging pronouncements in cases regarding the principle of *non-refoulement* and the prohibition of collective expulsion, there has been, on the whole, little cognisance of the importance of the right to leave and no systematic treatment of the legal provisions regarding their specific situation.

Amuur,[29] *Hirsi*,[30] and even (parts of) *N.D. and N.T.*[31] can be classified as appreciative of the difficulties facing asylum seekers in extraterritorial situations and of the obstacles placed by states of destination in their way to access ECHR protection. In *Amuur*, the Court engaged in the analysis of the applicants' circumstances, placed in administrative detention in the so-called 'international zone' of Paris-Orly airport, concluding that such confinement prevented them from seeking asylum. The Court opened by recognizing that 'Contracting States have the undeniable sovereign right to control aliens' entry into and residence in their territory', but it emphasised that 'this right must be exercised in accordance with the provisions of the Convention'.[32] Integrating considerations regarding the specific position of the applicants, as persons presumably in need of international protection, it went on to establish that it was acceptable for Contracting Parties to prevent irregular immigration, provided that compliance 'with their international obligations, particularly under the 1951 Geneva Convention and the [ECHR]' was guaranteed.[33] The Court insisted that 'States' legitimate concern to foil the increasingly frequent attempts to circumvent immigration restrictions must not deprive asylum-seekers of the protection afforded by these conventions'.[34] The reasoning continued and went on to ascertain the existence of a (*new*) 'right to gain effective access to the procedure for determining refugee status'.[35]

However, the Court did not explain the origin of such a right or the grounds on which it reached its conclusion, especially taking into account that neither the

[29] *Amuur* (n 17).
[30] *Hirsi Jamaa and others* (n 18).
[31] *N.D. and N.T.* (n 6).
[32] *Amuur* (n 17), para 41.
[33] ibid, para 43.
[34] ibid.
[35] ibid.

1951 Geneva Convention nor the ECHR contain a right to asylum. Its decision was grounded in Article 5 ECHR on detention, but acknowledging that 'account should be taken of the fact that the measure is applicable ... to aliens who, often fearing for their lives, have fled from their own country'.[36] A connection with the right to leave was also invoked to deny the validity of France's allegation that, since confinement in the 'international zone' could be terminated with the claimants' voluntary departure to another country, it should not be considered a deprivation of liberty. The Court deemed such possibility as 'theoretical' when 'no other country offering protection comparable to the protection they expect to find in the country where they are seeking asylum is inclined or prepared to take them in'.[37] But it did not dwell on whether this amounts to a general 'right to flee'.

Hirsi applied a similar reasoning, transposing the *Amuur* rationale to the extraterritorial setting of the high seas, in the context of the 2009 pushback campaign undertaken by Italy in cooperation with Libya, leading to the collective expulsion of (presumed) asylum seekers from Somalia and Eritrea. The Court concluded that the aim and underlying motives of Italy's actions were irrelevant. The focus was instead placed on the *effects* of Italy's conduct on the applicants' 'enjoyment of the rights and guarantees protected by the Convention',[38] preventing the maritime environment from becoming 'an area outside the law'.[39] To ensure the *effet utile* of the Convention,[40] the Court ruled accordingly that 'interceptions ... the *effect* of which is to prevent migrants from reaching the borders of the State ... constitute an exercise of jurisdiction ... which engages the responsibility of the State ... under Article 4 of Protocol 4'.[41] Because the interceptions in question exposed the applicants to (direct and indirect) *refoulement*, they were also (separately) forbidden under Article 3 ECHR.[42] But the Court did not explicitly acknowledge the link between the two provisions or elaborate upon the impact of their interplay.

The intersection between the prohibition of collective expulsion and the principle of *non-refoulement* has been explicitly recognised in *N.D. and N.T.*, but with an exclusionary effect. The case concerned the 'hot expulsion' of two sub-Saharan nationals attempting to enter Spain irregularly by climbing the border fence of Melilla as part of a large group of aliens 'attempt[ing] ... to cross that border in an unauthorised manner and *en masse*'.[43] The measure in dispute entailed their immediate handover to the Moroccan police by the Spanish authorities on descent from the fence, without any formal procedure. There, the Court 'emphasised ... the link between ... Article 4 of Protocol 4 ... and ... the principle of *non-refoulement*'.[44]

36 ibid.
37 ibid, para 48.
38 *Hirsi Jamaa and others* (n 18), paras 80–81 and 178.
39 ibid, para 178.
40 ibid, para 166ff.
41 ibid, para 180 (emphasis added).
42 ibid, para 113–57.
43 *N.D. and N.T.* (n 6), para 166.
44 ibid, para 171.

However, rather than taking that link as mutually reinforcing the two provisions, it was used to subordinate the applicability of the prohibition of collective expulsion to situations where Article 3 ECHR applies as well, with the former serving as the procedural vehicle of the latter, thus reducing the separate scope and independent significance of Article 4 of Protocol 4. The provision was seen as a means to 'maintaining the possibility, for each of the aliens concerned, to assert a risk of treatment ... incompatible with ... Article 3'.[45] But because their situation had been appraised as not entailing a risk of *refoulement*,[46] the combined effect of the prohibition of ill-treatment with the prohibition of collective expulsion was of no help to the applicants. The Court considered, instead, that their 'own conduct'—a factor immaterial in Article 3 cases[47]—had become relevant.[48]

The fact that the applicants had 'cross[ed] a land border in an unauthorised manner, deliberately tak[ing] advantage of the[] large numbers [in the group of which they were part] and us[ing] force',[49] was considered to justify the Spanish response.[50] Having a priori excluded the risk of *refoulement*, the Court deemed the course of action by N.D. and N.T. as a matter of choice. This is probably why it turned to assess whether Spain had otherwise 'provided genuine and effective access to means of legal entry'.[51] According to the (cursory) assessment by the Court,[52] that had been the case. And, since the applicants had apparently failed to submit 'cogent reasons' for not having had recourse to them,[53] the lack of an individualised examination became imputable to their behaviour.[54] The prohibition of collective expulsion—read through the prism of the prohibition of *refoulement*—was hence declared not to have been violated.[55]

What remains unclear is how the Court would have proceeded in a case regarding a real risk of irreversible harm. Had an Article 3 claim been arguable, the pronouncements of the Court could acquire a new dimension. Conceivably, the provision of 'genuine and effective access to means of legal entry'[56] would be required to 'allow *all persons who face persecution* to submit an application for protection ... under conditions which ensure that the application is processed in a manner consistent with ... international norms'.[57] Arguments regarding the

[45] ibid, para 198.
[46] ibid, para 206 and *N.D. and N.T.* [Chamber] App nos 8675/15 and 8697/15 (ECtHR, 3 October 2017).
[47] See eg *Saadi v Italy* [GC] App no 37201/06 (ECtHR, 28 February 2008), para 127.
[48] *N.D. and N.T.* (n 6), para 200.
[49] ibid, para 201.
[50] ibid, paras 221–22 and 229.
[51] ibid, paras 201 and 208.
[52] ibid, para 211ff.
[53] ibid, paras 201 and 210.
[54] ibid, paras 230–31.
[55] ibid, paras 231–32.
[56] ibid, para 201.
[57] ibid, para 209 (emphasis added).

'effectiveness of Convention rights' would support this interpretation.[58] The Court could follow the same reasoning as in *Hirsi*. Otherwise, '[i]n the absence of appropriate arrangements, the resulting possibility for States to refuse entry to their territory [would] render ineffective all the Convention provisions designed to protect individuals who face a genuine risk of persecution'.[59]

Yet, the remit of the obligation to make available legal pathways for potential refugees and whether it applies to all countries of destination that are parties to the Convention is uncertain. Although the Court took account in *N.D. and N.T.* of the possibility for the applicants to 'apply[] for a visa ... at Spain's diplomatic and consular representations in their countries of origin'[60] to reach its conclusion, it refused to take a position on whether embassies and consulates would be under an obligation to accept asylum claims or issue visas for the purposes of seeking refuge through safe and legal avenues.[61] A narrow reading would deem the obligation as limited to the context of 'border procedures' at issue in the case,[62] which normally cater for claimants who have *already* reached the territory of the country of destination and are awaiting official admittance at the frontier.[63] This is in line with the Court's proposition that the Convention 'does not ... imply a general duty ... to bring persons who are under the jurisdiction of another State within its own jurisdiction'.[64] However, that approach appears to differentiate the scope of the ECHR protections on account of the mode of arrival to the country of destination—a consideration that should have no bearing on the absolute character of *non-refoulement* and that may amount to discrimination amongst refugees.[65] Such a stance ultimately implies that only those risking their lives to reach ECHR countries are covered by the Convention, disregarding that it is the absence of legal pathways to access protection in those same countries which propels asylum seekers into unsafe routes.[66] The end effect is to entrench unauthorised travel through

58 ibid.

59 ibid.

60 ibid, para 212.

61 ibid, para 222.

62 ibid, para 209, although note the wording 'in particular', which should exclude an exhaustive reading.

63 Daniel Thym, 'A Restrictionist Revolution? A Counter-Intuitive Reading of the ECtHR's N.D. and N.T.-Judgement on "Hot Expulsions"', EU Migration Law Blog, 17 February 2020 <http://eumigrationlawblog.eu/a-restrictionist-revolution-a-counter-intuitive-reading-of-the-ecthrs-n-d-n-t-judgment-on-hot-expulsions/> (accessed 10 March 2020).

64 *N.D. and N.T.* (n 6), para 221.

65 This is explicitly forbidden by Art 3 CSR. For an elaboration on visas and refugees, see Moreno-Lax, 'Must EU Borders Have Doors for Refugees?' (2008) 10 European Journal of Migration and Law 315. See also Moreno-Lax (n 9) chs 4 and 8.

66 Up to 90% of all those seeking asylum in EU Member States who are subsequently recognised as refugees or granted subsidiary protection reached the Union through irregular means. See European Parliament Resolution of 11 December 2018 with recommendations to the Commission on Humanitarian Visas (2018/2271(INL)), para E. See also Moreno-Lax, *European Added Value Assessment accompanying the European Parliament's legislative own-initiative report (Rapp. Lopez Aguilar) on Humanitarian Visas, Annex I: Legal Aspects* (Brussels: European Parliament, 2018), 23–125 <https://www.europarl.europa.eu/RegData/etudes/STUD/2018/621823/EPRS_STU(2018)621823_EN.pdf> (accessed 5 March 2020).

dangerous channels (that compound the harm fled from) as a pre-condition for ECHR protection—with human rights violations along the way becoming not only tolerated, but structuralised as part of the forced migrant's journey.

In *Sharifi*,[67] similarly concerning 'hot expulsions', but from Italy to Greece, the Court had adopted the opposite view. The main difference between the two cases is the type of border, it being a maritime border in *Sharifi*, rather than a land border, as in *N.D. and N.T.*[68] Otherwise, as in *N.D. and N.T.*, *Sharifi* regards the implementation of summary rejections without any formalities, before the applicants could file an asylum application. The Court considered that the rejections in question 'deprive[d] the persons concerned of any effective opportunity to submit an application for international protection and of any other procedural and material guarantee'.[69] Instead, protection against expulsion, the Court continued, requires 'an examination of the personal circumstances of the applicant, *including his protection needs*'.[70] The 'automatic *refoulement*' to which Italian action amounted,[71] immediately transferring applicants to the custody of captains of ferry boats operating the commercial route between Patras and Bari/Ancona/Venice for their direct return to Greece, impeded access to the asylum procedure in Italy, to which the Court implied they were entitled by virtue of Article 3 (combined with Article 4 Protocol 4) ECHR.[72] So, it is not clear why the legal principles at land and sea borders should differ. And it is also obscure why the Court has never explicitly relied on the right to leave in any of these cases.

The Court's interpretation of Article 2 of Protocol 4 ECHR has been especially restrictive. When applied to non-nationals, the Court has concluded that the provision must be understood as entailing 'a right to leave for such country of the person's choice *to which he may be admitted*',[73] thereby virtually denying any practical effect vis-à-vis the country of destination. Such qualification may result from the interpolation of the absence of a right to enter no other country but one's own, but it has no literal basis in the text of the Convention and it ignores its interconnection with the principle of *non-refoulement*.

Xhavara--the first case in which the argument was put forward that extraterritorial measures of immigration control by countries of destination may violate the right to leave, including for the purpose of seeking ECHR protection--exemplifies this approach.[74] Therein the Court adopted a particularly deferential position

[67] *Sharifi v Italy* App no 16643/09 (ECtHR, 21 October 2014).
[68] Partly Dissenting Opinion of Judge Koskelo in *N.D. and N.T.* (n 6), para 38.
[69] *Sharifi* (n 67), para 215 (own translation from French original).
[70] ibid, para 219 (own translation from French original) (emphasis added).
[71] ibid. The exact words used are 'renvois automatiques' and 'refoulements immédiats'.
[72] ibid, paras 233 and 242–43.
[73] *Baumann v France* App no 33592/96 (ECtHR, 22 May 2001), para 61 (emphasis added), reiterated in *Battista v Italy* App no 43978/09 (ECtHR, 2 December 2014), para 37. For recent commentary and further references, see Elspeth Guild and Vladislava Stoyanova, 'The Human Right to Leave Any Country: A Right to Be Delivered' (2018) European Yearbook on Human Rights 373. See also Moreno-Lax (n 9) ch 9.
[74] *Xhavara v Italy* App no 39473/98 (ECtHR, 11 January 2001).

towards the country of destination. The case concerned an Italian maritime blockade performed with Albanian authorization, leading the Albanian-flagged *Kater I Rades* to sink and cause the death of 58 persons. The Court considered that the measure, however, was not aimed at hindering the right to leave Albania, but at preventing irregular entry in Italy. Without going into considerations of legality, necessity, or proportionality of the measure, or its linkage with Article 3 ECHR, the applicants' claim was declared incompatible *ratione materiae* with the Convention—as if the right to leave had no bearing on Italy, as country of intended destination. Unlike in *Hirsi*, *Amuur*, or *Sharifi*, the impact of the measure on the protection needs of the applicants was ignored.

From the foregoing the conclusion can only be that the stance of the Court has been fragmentary and unreliable so far. The current chapter proposes, instead, that the Court embraces a principled position that favours legal certainty and predictability, contributing to the coherent interpretation of the Convention overall.[75] The suggestion implies the adoption of an intersectional reading of the Convention, 'mindful of [its] special character as a human rights instrument',[76] and on consideration of the particular needs of refugees.[77]

Under this approach, when confronted with persons in need to escape a country to avoid persecution or serious harm, decisions would take account not only of the prohibition of (extraterritorial) *refoulement* and/or the prohibition of collective expulsion, but also of the right to leave. Taken together, these provisions would be capable of sustaining the new compound 'right to leave *in order to* avoid ill-treatment', akin to the right to seek asylum found in Article 14 of the Universal Declaration on Human Rights, but, crucially, in legally-binding form. The interplay would be particularly fruitful, in that it would neutralize the non-absolute character of the right to leave in the specific situation of persons in need of international protection. Indeed, while the right to leave can be subjected to the limitations contemplated in Article 2(3) of Protocol 4 ECHR, in line with the principles of legality, legitimacy, and proportionality, the prohibition of *refoulement* entails a non-derogable, unconditional protection.[78] Intersectionality, as expounded in the next sections, supplies the theoretical substrate to explain the jus-generative force of the encounter between the two when applied to refugees, overcoming the limitations of compartmentalised interpretations of the different rights clauses when taken in isolation, and resolving the problem of access to asylum through safe and legal pathways in a consistent and principled way.

75 *N.D. and N.T.* (n 6), para 172.

76 *Al-Adsani v United Kingdom* [GC] Appl no 35763/97 (ECtHR, 21 November 2001), para 55.

77 For a recent acknowledgement, see *Transforming our world: the 2030 Agenda for Sustainable Development*, (adopted 21 October 2015), A/RES/70/1, paras 23 and 29. See also the *Global Compact for Migration* and the *Global Compact on Refugees* in UN Refugees and Migrants, undated <https://refugeesmigrants.un.org/> (accessed 10 March 2020).

78 Art 15 ECHR.

3. Intersectionality and Injustice: Insights from Feminist Theory

Intersectionality is one of the most important cross-disciplinary contributions of feminist theory to the construction of social problems and related forms of oppression.[79] In essence, it draws attention to 'how multiple social forces, such as race, class, gender, age, sexuality, culture [or migration status], shape individual experiences'.[80] It captures both the different identity constituents of the person and the systemic power relations underpinning institutions and human interactions.[81] Historically, these two elements (identity and structure) had been dealt with separately.[82] But the contemporary account of intersectionality considers both in tandem.

When the theory first emerged in the US in the 1970s and 1980s, it was intended as a critique of mainstream feminism, a reaction against the stifling oversimplification of the (white, middle-class, heterosexual) 'woman', and as a call to look behind given conceptualisations to take account of the complex, overlapping layers that make up a person's identity.[83] The initial drive was to facilitate an understanding of the race-gender dyad as interrelated loci of dominance affecting black women in a very particularised (and insidious) manner. Intersectionality, under its original conceptualisation, was a metaphor, articulated as a way to mediate 'the tension between assertions of multiple identity and the ongoing necessity of group politics'.[84]

A second wave of intersectionality studies, in the 1990s and 2000s, followed, transcending identity politics and emphasising the importance of context; of the cultural, spatio-temporal 'interlocking systems of domination' at play in the

[79] On the 'travels' of intersectionality, see Gudrun-Axeli Knapp, 'Race, Class, Gender: Reclaiming Baggage in Fast Travelling Theories' (2005) 12 European Journal on Women Studies [EJWS] 249.

[80] Maneesha Deckha, 'Is Culture Taboo? Feminism, Intersectionality, and Culture Talk in Law' (2004) 16 Canadian Journal of Women and the Law [CJWL] 14, 16.

[81] Anastasia Vakulenko, '"Islamic Headscarves" and the European Convention on Human Rights: An Intersectional Perspective' (2007) 16 Social and Legal Studies 183, 185.

[82] There are different 'schools' of intersectionality. Phoenix and Pattynama, in their Editorial to the (2006) EJWS Special Issue on intersectionality, separate the 'systemic' (predominantly US-based) from the 'constructionist' (essentially UK-based) families, at 188. Within these groups, others have distinguished between 'liberal', 'postcolonial', and 'deliberative' trends. See eg Beverly Baines, 'Gender and Constitution: Is Constitutionalism Bad for Intersectional Feminists?' (2010) 28 Penn State International Law Review 427, 442–47. So, the above is a very rough simplification of an extremely rich body of literature spanning multiple fields of research. For a recent comprehensive compendium of different approaches to intersectionality, see Emily Grabham and others (eds), *Intersectionality and Beyond* (Routledge-Cavendish 2009).

[83] The first to use the term 'intersectionality' was Kimberlé Crenshaw in 'Demarginalizing the Intersection of Race and Sex: A Black Feminist Critique of Anti-Discrimination Doctrine, Feminist Theory and Anti-Racist Politics' [1989] University of Chicago Legal Forum 139. See also Wendy Brown, 'The Impossibility of Women's Studies' (1997) 9 Differences: A Journal of Feminist Cultural Studies [Differences] 79.

[84] Kimberlé Crenshaw, 'Mapping the Margins: Intersectionality, Identity Politics, and Violence against Women of Colour' (1991) 43 Stanford Law Review 1241, 1296.

configuration of gender, race, and class as social formations.[85] Rather than naturally occurring, identity traits were instead seen as being defined by 'large-scale historically constructed and hierarchical power systems'.[86]

My understanding of the theory consolidates insights from these two streams of intersectionality to generate a multi-dimensional, holistic account of subjectivity that considers identity composition as reflective of, and traversed by, the broader power relations in society, at any given point in time. Identities and power relations interact to produce intricate webs of advantage and disadvantage.[87] Through this prism, the theory takes a whole-of-person/whole-of-world approach that is of interest to the apprehension of forced migration. It offers a nuanced appreciation of the various identity components of the individual as co-constituted by the various structures and social forces that shape them into a constantly and mutually adjusting integrated whole.[88]

As a method, intersectionality thus resists essentialising categorisations, making visible the multiple positionings of individuals and their inter-relations.[89] As McCall posits, it serves to 'deconstruct' categories and look 'behind' their specific rationality; to unpack *anti*-categorical, *intra*-categorical, and *inter*-categorical links that simultaneously interconnect, separate, and minoritise groups and persons along multiple axes of inequality (*within*, *between*, and *beyond* classifications).[90] Intersectionality's main concern is with asymmetrically distributed power and its impact on different historical and contextual systems, forms of governance,

[85] Sherene Razack, 'Speaking for Ourselves: Feminist Jurisprudence and Minority Women' (1991) 4 CJWL 400, 454.

[86] Bonnie Dill, Sandra Nettles, and Lynn Weber, 'What Do We Mean by Intersections?' (Spring 2001) Connections: Newsletter of Consortium for Research on Race, Gender, and Ethnicity, 4<http://crge.umd.edu/wp-content/uploads/2017/07/RC2001_spring.pdf> (accessed 5 March 2020). See also Davina Cooper, '"And You Can't Find Me Nowhere": Relocating Identity and Structure within Equality Jurisprudence' (2000) 27 Journal of Law and Society 249.

[87] See eg the Feminists@Law <https://journals.kent.ac.uk/index.php/feministsatlaw> and the Feminist Judgments projects <http://ukscblog.com/the-feminist-judgments-project/> (accessed 10 March 2020). For a book-length elaboration, see Rosemary Hunter, Claire McGlynn, and Erica Rackley (eds), *Feminist Judgments: From Theory to Practice* (Hart 2010).

[88] This understanding has penetrated international human rights law, especially in regards to gender mainstreaming and policies of protection of women and girls. For an overview, see Dianne Otto, 'Women's Rights' in Daniel Moeckli, Sangeeta Shah, and Sandesh Sivakumaran (eds), *International Human Rights Law* (3rd edn, OUP 2018) 309. See also Anastasia Vakulenko, 'Gender and International Human Rights Law: The Intersectionality Agenda' in Sarah Joseph and Adam McBeth (eds), *Research Handbook on International Human Rights Law* (Edward Elgar 2010) 196. cf Mieke Verloo, 'Multiple Inequalities, Intersectionality and the European Union' (2006) 13 EJWS 211, critiquing the distortion of the approach in the EU context.

[89] Developing intersectionality as an approach to empirical research, see Ange-Marie Hancock, 'When Multiplication Doesn't Equal Quick Addition: Examining Intersectionality as a Research Paradigm' (2007) 5 Perspectives on Politics 63. cf Gabriele Winker and Nina Degele, 'Intersectionality as Multi-Level Analysis: Dealing with Social Inequality' (2011) 18 EJWS 51, 56–64, propounding a praxeological model in eight steps. And proposing the use of systems and complexity theory in the study of intersecting inequalities, see Sylvia Walby, 'Complexity Theory, Systems Theory, and Multiple Intersecting Social Inequalities' (2007) 37 Philosophy of the Social Sciences 449.

[90] Leslie McCall, 'The Complexity of Intersectionality' (2005) 30 Signs: Journal of Women in Culture and Society 1771.

personal interactions, and symbolic processes of meaning creation and representation. Whether in the social, the political, the economic, or the cultural sphere, processes of exclusion and differentiation (and their interplay) remain the key interest.

In this guise, intersectionality goes beyond a mere recognition of the multiplicity of the mechanisms of oppression emerging from, and functioning through, given categorisations. It separates the several analytical levels at which social divisions occur, refuting pre-determined hierarchisation and compartmentalisation between them, instead postulating their concurrent interaction in the production and reproduction of marginalisation. The intersectional method looks at how categories are constructed and intermeshed in concrete spatio-temporal conditions, and considers the dynamic connections between positionings, identities, and values, as a way to interrogate and challenge them in a comprehensive way.

Against this background, Yuval-Davis proposes four levels of analysis: experiential/individual, inter-subjective, organisational/institutional, and symbolic/representational—adding a meta-level that theorises links and intersections between them.[91] Law, as a political artefact, intervenes at all these levels, in legal texts and processes that organise power, and that penetrate public administration, inter-personal relations, and the lived experiences of individuals. It works to 'homogenise' and 'naturalise' meanings, categories, and practices of centring and relegation, constructing *the* legal standard, and establishing the boundary between what the 'norm' is and what lies 'outside the norm'. In the most literal of senses, law is the primary tool of 'normalisation'. It is the maker and marker of structures of domination, entrenching hierarchies of legal recognition and stratified access to legal protection. As much as there can be (*de facto*) discrimination *outside* the law, there can also be (*de jure*) discrimination *through* law, in processes of 'othering' and minoritisation of certain individuals.[92] To remedy legally-created or legally-perpetuated (unfair) distinctions, remedial (legal) intervention is required to ensure (legal *and* real) equality, empowerment, and redress.[93]

With this in mind, an intersectional analysis of the law seeks to implement *substantive* (rather than *formal*) justice, attaining equitable outcomes.[94] It is concerned

[91] Nira Yuval-Davis, 'Intersectionality and Feminist Politics' (2006) 13 EJWS 193, 198, 205. See also Marcel Stoetzler and Nira Yuval-Davis, 'Standpoint Theory, Situated Knowledge and the Situated Imagination' (2002) 3 Feminist Theory 315. cf Bilge, instead, arranging the analytical ranks at the micro-social and macro-social level, along the four key domains of power distinguished by Collins: structural, disciplinary, hegemonic, and interpersonal, in Sirma Bilge, 'Recent Feminist Outlooks on Intersectionality' (2010) 225 Diogenes 58, 60, 65. See also Patricia Collins, *Black Feminist Thought* (rev 10th Anniversary edn, Routledge 2000) 277–90.

[92] See generally Susan Stabile, 'Othering and the Law' (2016) 12 University of St Thomas Law Journal 381.

[93] Other authors are not convinced that law can 'absorb' intersectionality adequately to produce an 'intersectional remedy' based on historical experience. See eg Joanne Conaghan, 'Intersectionality and the Feminist Project in Law' in Grabham and others (n 82) 21; and Rosemary Hunter and Tracey De Simone, 'Identifying Disadvantage: Beyond Intersectionality' in Grabham and others (n 82) 159.

[94] Speaking of 'parité', see Joan Scott, 'French Universalism in the Nineties' (2004) 15 Differences 32. Introducing the notion of 'equality of condition', see John Baker and others, *Equality: From Theory to Action* (Palgrave Macmillan 2004).

with *ends*, rather than only with *means*. Instead of focusing on equality *qua* sameness of treatment or opportunity, as (simply) entailing the 'absence of discrimination', it aspires to realise equality of result,[95] aiming for the comprehensive fulfilment of human dignity.[96] And this insight—I argue—should be taken into account when interpreting the ECHR. Its provisions should be construed in light of the complete set of circumstances of applicants, adopting a whole-of-person approach that addresses rights claims holistically and delivers protection that is not 'theoretical or illusory', but 'practical and effective' in the individual case,[97] to meet the justice needs of real-life subjects—including forced migrants.

4. Intersectional Legal Thinking: The Limits of Comparisons, Equivalence, and Discrimination-based Reasoning

The implementation of the whole-of-person approach is not without difficulties. While intersectionality includes a call for heightened attention to the individual (subjective, objective, contextual, and structural) circumstances of claimants, to detect particular needs and address them in a comprehensive manner, (equality) law has typically responded through the medium of comparisons.[98] Yet, comparisons are inadequate to capture the wholeness of individuality. They tabulate experience and characteristics, fostering a categorical approach that compartmentalises equality.

A paradigmatic example of the shortcomings of discrimination-based reasoning is provided by *Rogers v. American Airlines*,[99] where a black woman filed a claim for indirect discrimination, denouncing her employer's policy banning the cornrow hairstyle for flight attendants. The problem was proving that she had been discriminated against on grounds of gender *and/or* on grounds of race. But neither *white* women, nor black *men* were impacted upon by the measure. Her distinct position, concurrently engaging gender and racial discrimination—not separately, but in combination—was not taken into consideration. As a member of a 'dual minority', her case fell through the cracks of the intersection between sex and colour, as protected characteristics, and she received no protection, leaving her in a position not only lesser than the majority of the population, but also lesser than her 'single minority' counterparts. She was differently positioned to both groups,

[95] Vanessa Sauls Avolio, 'Rewriting Reproductive Rights: Applying Feminist Methodology to the European Court of Human Rights' Abortion Jurisprudence' (2017) 6 feminists@law 1, 2.

[96] For a debate on human flourishing and its conditions, see Martha Nussbaum and Amartya Sen (eds), *The Quality of Life* (Clarendon Press 1993). And on dignity as 'self-realisation', see Jill Marshall, *Personal Freedom through Human Rights Law?* (Brill 2009) 15ff.

[97] *Artico v Italy* App no 6694/ 74 (ECtHR, 13 May 1980), para 33.

[98] For a critique of 'strict comparison', 'flexible comparison', and 'contextual comparison' approaches, see Shreya Atrey, 'Comparison in Intersectional Discrimination' (2018) 38 Legal Studies 379.

[99] *Rogers v American Airlines*, 527 F Supp 229 (SDNY 1981).

simultaneously situated *within* and *at the crossroads* of the different race/gender categories. The question was not one of disadvantage based on gender *or* colour, or on gender *and* colour, but one resulting from the *interaction* between the two. A binary approach was, therefore, not enough; neither was the mere *addition* of the relevant causes. 'Intersectional minorities' are in a (real *and* legal) position that requires heightened attention. They can be harmed in very specific ways, drawing on their several identities and the power structures that compose them, which exacerbate their disadvantage. An intersectional approach is, therefore, necessary to fully apprehend their plight in its complete factual and legal scale.

However, the deeper problem is that a pure non-discrimination-based reasoning neglects the innate flaws of the comparisons required. As discrimination specialists have highlighted, comparisons 'build[] on an essentially "relative" idea of equality',[100] so that any harm suffered only counts if based upon discretely defined (protected) grounds, demonstrating that the (otherwise similarly positioned) claimant is (unjustifiably) worse off than a real or hypothetical referent group without good cause.[101] But not every case of injustice yields itself to the comparator test.

Denial of dignity transcends group boundaries. For instance, in *Abdulaziz*—one of the first immigration-related cases that came before the Strasbourg Court—a group of UK-based Pakistani women, requesting to be joined by their husbands in Britain, alleged discrimination on the grounds of race *and* gender. UK family reunification rules for long-term residents maintained a stereotypical understanding of male and female roles, establishing stricter conditions for permission to be granted for husbands to join their wives than the other way around, thus distinctively disadvantaging women of Asian descent, who came from archetypically patriarchal societies. The Court, however, focused only on gender as the sole basis for discrimination, relying on Articles 8 and 14 ECHR, opining that the UK immigration provisions did not distinguish on the basis of race or ethnicity at large.[102] It thus had no regard, in the particular case of the claimants, for the specific role played by national origin at the intersection with gender.

Nevertheless, one wonders whether a different result would have been achieved, in terms of final redress, if also race (and the way it interacts with gender) had been taken into account. Would that have captured the complex positioning of the claimants and their plight before the law? Would that have contested its underlying bias? Is it (only) because of the blindness of the Strasbourg Court to

[100] Päivi Johanna Neuvonen, 'From a "Relative" to a "Relational" Equality: Rethinking Comparability in the Light of Relational Accounts of Social Justice' in Daniel Cuypers and Jogchum Vrielink (eds), *Equal is not Enough* (Intersentia 2016) 135, 136. See also Kenneth Simons, 'Equality as a Comparative Right' (1985) 65 Boston University Law Review 387; Suzanne Goldberg, 'Discrimination by Comparison' (2010–2011) 120 Yale Law Journal 728; and Aileen McColgan, 'Cracking the Comparator Problem: Discrimination, "Equal" Treatment and the Role of Comparisons' (2006) 6 EHRLR 650.

[101] Tarunabh Khaitan, *A Theory of Discrimination Law* (OUP 2015) 165–71 and references therein.

[102] *Abdulaziz v United Kingdom* App nos 9214/80, 9473/81, and 9474/81(ECtHR, 28 May 1985).

intersectionality that such a narrow understanding of equality was endorsed? Or is it rather due to the failings of the discrimination-based analysis *itself*? What if UK law had banned spousal reunification for *all* settled migrants? The comparative pool would have disappeared. All foreign claimants of whatever gender and ethnic origin would have been affected. Would the Court, then, have been able to single out the applicants in the instant case and reach a finding of discrimination to address their situation?

The shortcomings of the comparator test, including the unprincipled approach to the selection of *the* appropriate comparator and the inconsistences in its conceptual framing and operationalisation, reveal the limits of equality-based reasoning. Feminist scholars have long pointed to the need for replacements and complementary principles to enshrine the whole-of-person approach underpinning intersectionality theory.[103] Some have proposed a needs-led methodology,[104] or a 'disadvantage analysis'.[105] Others have advanced a dominance/subordination approach,[106] while still others propound a vulnerability-based model to overcome the relativism of comparisons and the fragmentation effects of categorisations.[107] They serve the same end—the achievement of material equality and substantive justice—but with different foci and through different pathways, calling for a contextual understanding.

The Strasbourg Court has participated in this process, relying precisely on the concept of 'vulnerability' to mobilise tailored responses in certain situations. But it has done so in a manner that latches onto categorical thinking.[108] Rather than adopting a contextual, whole-of-person approach, identifying circumstances that could render anyone vulnerable, it has used the notion to construct new categories and single out particular groups. In this guise, HIV/AIDS patients, considering that they have 'historically [been] subject to prejudice with lasting consequences, resulting in their social exclusion',[109] and on account of the 'considerable discrimination' they have 'suffered … in the past', have been construed as a 'particularly

[103] Claiming that 'equality' may be reaching its rhetorical or strategic 'use-by-date', see Rosemary Hunter, 'Alternatives to Equality' in Rosemary Hunter (ed), *Rethinking Equality Projects in Law* (Hart 2008) 81, 83.

[104] Nancy Fraser, 'Talking about Needs: Imperative Contests as Political Conflicts in Welfare-State Societies' (1989) 99 Ethics 291.

[105] Deborah Rhode, *Justice and Gender: Sex Discrimination and the Law* (Harvard University Press 1989).

[106] Catharine MacKinnon, *Feminism Unmodified: Discourses on Life and Law* (Harvard University Press 1987).

[107] Martha Feinman, 'The Vulnerable Subject: Anchoring Equality in the Human Condition' (2008) 20 Yale Journal of Law and Feminism 1. See also Martha Feinman, *The Illusion of Equality* (University of Chicago Press 1991).

[108] For an elaboration, see Alexandra Timmer, 'A Quiet Revolution: Vulnerability in the European Court of Human Rights' in Martha Fineman and Anna Grear (eds), *Vulnerability: Reflections on a New Ethical Foundation for Law and Politics* (Routledge 2014) 111; and Lourdes Peroni and Alexandra Timmer, 'Vulnerable Groups: The Promise of an Emerging Concept in European Human Rights Convention Law' (2013) 11 International Journal of Constitutional Law 1056.

[109] *Kiyutin v Russia* App no 2700/10 (ECtHR, 10 March 2011), para 63.

vulnerable *group* in society'.[110] The same applies to Roma,[111] persons with mental disabilities,[112] minor children,[113] or women affected by domestic violence.[114] Asylum seekers, too, have been described as 'a particularly underprivileged and vulnerable *population group*',[115] considering vulnerability as 'inherent' in their status[116]—as if naturally occurring or necessarily implied—and explicitly 'irrespective of other ... factors'.[117]

The consequence in these cases is usually the recognition of positive (if minimal) obligations to provide for the special needs of those considered to belong to 'particularly',[118] 'specially',[119] 'highly',[120] or 'extremely'[121]—ie *relatively* more—vulnerable groups, *as compared to* the rest of the population.[122] While the notion of vulnerability has served to recognise the specific needs of certain groups, it has also worked as an exclusionary tool, denying heightened protection to other similarly situated individuals. For example, in *Khlaifia*, non-asylum-seeking migrants were disqualified 'as not hav[ing] the specific vulnerability inherent in [the asylum seeker] status'.[123] The applicants had survived the journey to reach Italy and, as the Grand Chamber recognised, 'were weakened physically and psychologically because they had just made the dangerous crossing of the Mediterranean'.[124] Nonetheless, they had not formally filed an asylum application and 'they belonged neither to the *category* of elderly persons nor to that of minors'.[125] They also 'did not claim to be suffering from any particular medical condition'.[126] The trauma of the shipwreck and its after-effects were not accorded any significance, neither was the

[110] *Alajos Kiss v Hungary* App no 38832/06 (ECtHR, 20 May 2010), para 42 (emphasis added).

[111] *Chapman v United Kingdom*, App no 27238/95 (ECtHR, 18 January 2001), para 96. See also *Connors v United Kingdom* App no 66746/01 (ECtHR, 27 May 2004), para 84; *Oršuš and others v Croatia* App no 15766/03 (ECtHR, 16 March 2010), para 147; *Winterstein and others v France* App no 27013/07 (ECtHR, 17 October 2013), para 88.

[112] *Renolde v France* App no 5608/05 (ECtHR, 16 October 2008), para 84.

[113] *Okkali v Turkey* App no 52067/99 (ECtHR, 17 October 2006), para 70.

[114] *Yordanova and others v Bulgaria* App no 25446/06 (ECtHR, 24 April 2012), para 130.

[115] *M.S.S.* (n 23), para 251 (emphasis added). Confirmed in *S.H.H. v United Kingdom* App no 60367/10 (ECtHR, 29 January 2013), para 76; *A.S. v Switzerland* App no 39350/13 (ECtHR, 30 June 2015), para 29; *Jama v Malta*, App no 10290/13 (ECtHR, 26 November 2015), para 137.

[116] *M.S.S.* (n 23), para 233.

[117] *Jama* (n 115), para 100.

[118] *Dudgeon v United Kingdom* App no 7525/76 (ECtHR, 22 October 1981), para 62.

[119] *Valiuliene v Lithuania* App no 33234/07 (ECtHR, 26 March 2013), para 51.

[120] *Campeanu v Romania* App no 47848/08 (ECtHR, 17 July 2014), para 104

[121] *Mayeka v Belgium* App no 13178/03 (ECtHR, 12 October 2006), para 55; *Tarakhel v Switzerland* App no 29217/12 (ECtHR, 4 November 2015), para 119. See also *V.M. and others v Belgium*, App no 60125/11 (ECtHR, 7 July 2015).

[122] Ana Beduschi, 'Vulnerability on Trial: Protection of Migrant Children's Rights in the Jurisprudence of International Human Rights Courts' (2018) 36 Boston University Law Journal 55, 85, speaking of vulnerability as 'a magnifying glass, exposing a greater duty to protect and care imposed upon States'.

[123] *Khlaifia* (n 22), para 194.

[124] ibid.

[125] ibid (emphasis added).

[126] ibid.

lawless detention they endured upon arrival—for which Italy was condemned.[127] Despite the ordeal of the deadly voyage by sea and the subsequent suffering experienced when deprived of liberty, the fact that they did not claim to have faced persecution or other serious harm '*in their country of origin*'[128] was sufficient to categorically exclude their vulnerability and concomitant entitlement to 'special protection'.[129] The Court used the applicants' non-membership of a pre-recognised vulnerable sub-population group to deny them both. The result, as Hudson has pointed out, 'is an unduly rigid, essentializing conceptualisation of vulnerability that is ill-equipped to respond effectively to the reality of [claimants]'.[130]

Against this background, my proposal is to abandon comparisons and arbitrary categorisations altogether, discarding equality-only based reasoning. As the next section elaborates, I propose to instead adopt a 'comprehensive dignity' standard that relies also on other relevant principles, harnessing their combined normative input through an intersectional interpretation. The underpinning rationale is a whole-of-legal system approach that mirrors, and caters for, the whole-of-person model at the heart of the intersectionality paradigm. Rather than applying intersectional reasoning only to the (contextual) description of the facts, identities, and realities of claimants, what I suggest is that it also be employed in the (contextual) interpretation of their rights; not just in the *selection* of the appropriate legal bases in the ECHR,[131] but in their *construal* as well. The purpose is to attain substantive justice, drawing from the normative force of a comprehensive understanding of human dignity that goes beyond non-discrimination and equality-based discourse.

5. Comprehensive Dignity: The 'Equal Liberty' Standard as Alternative Frame

If it is true that there are, at least, two ways to approach disadvantage in law and the encroachment on human dignity that comes with it: as a violation of equality or as a violation of liberty,[132] my suggestion is to unite the two approaches intersectionally, in a comprehensive and productive relation, taking them as complementary, rather than as (mutually exclusive) alternatives to remedy injustice. Both principles underpin human dignity and the entire system of human rights

[127] ibid, paras 108, 122, 163, declaring violations of Arts 5(1), 5(2), and 5(4) ECHR for lack of a legal basis.

[128] ibid, para 194 (emphasis added). cf *M.S.S.* (n 23), para 232, attaching relevance to 'everything [the applicant] had been through during his migration', without geographical limitation, 'and the traumatic experiences he was likely to have endured previously', without further specification.

[129] *M.S.S.* (n 23), para 251.

[130] Ben Hudson 'Migration in the Mediterranean: Exposing the Limits of Vulnerability in the European Court of Human Rights' (2018) 4 Maritime Safety and Security Law Journal 26, 43.

[131] cf Vakulenko (n 81) 183.

[132] Deborah Hellman, 'Equality and Unconstitutional Discrimination' in Deborah Hellman and Sophia Moreau (eds), *Philosophical Foundations of Discrimination Law* (OUP 2013) 51, 51–53.

protection, substantiating the ECHR regime,[133] based on the premise that '[a]ll human beings are born *free* and *equal* in dignity and rights'.[134] Both principles, in conjunction, are therefore better placed to articulate narratives of emancipation, positive action, and real protection in a more systematic way, as the two complementary pillars of human dignity.[135] The 'equal liberty' paradigm that emerges from their interaction—as advocated here—is thus *pro*-active, rather than *re*-active. It can (and should) be mobilised *before* and *independently from* any discrimination occurring.

If all human beings—including forced migrants—are by nature not only equal, but also free and endowed with the same 'inherent dignity and ... inalienable rights',[136] then both equality and liberty should inform the analysis of related entitlements. The resulting 'equal liberty' standard encapsulates a comprehensive conceptualisation of dignity that serves as a single overarching commitment, bearing on the properties of the two disaggregated rationales simultaneously.[137] There are therefore two gravitational loci—not one deriving from the other—that reciprocally converge, engage, and interact, not only reinforcing the separate bases of equality and freedom, but producing a *new* principle to be assessed from the two perspectives at the same time. What is proposed is not an amalgam, but an 'integrated understanding' of reciprocal in-formation between liberty and equality; not a mere encounter or static merger, but one with 'synergistic effects' that captures the full extent of human dignity.[138]

Such an understanding seems to be at work, for example, in the jurisprudence of the Committee on Economic, Social and Cultural Rights (CESCR),[139] (implicitly) taking the comprehensive dignity standard as a framework of analysis in its decisions on the right to food and the right to health. In its configuration of the *new* (intersectional) 'right to nutrition security', the Committee considers the different normative attributes of the right to food, on the one hand, and the right to health, on the other, and takes account of how they intersect, creating specific

[133] See Preamble, Recital 1, ECHR referring to the UDHR. See also Preamble and Art 1 UDHR.

[134] Art 1 UDHR.

[135] cf On the insufficiency of equality as a source of human rights and defending the notion of liberty as 'high-level right', see James Griffin, *On Human Rights* (OUP 2008) 40ff and 160ff.

[136] Preamble, Recital 1, UDHR.

[137] Other authors have also relied on the conjunction of equality and liberty, but for other purposes. See eg Etienne Balibar, 'Is a Philosophy of Human Civic Rights Possible? New Reflections on Equaliberty' (2004) 103 The South Atlantic Quarterly 311, 316, using the compound to explain the dual 'democratic foundation of the rights of citizen' in both the 'liberal' and the 'civic republican' traditions. See further Etienne Balibar, *Equaliberty* (Duke University Press 2014).

[138] Similarly, see Pamela Karlan 'Equal Protection, Due Process, and the Stereoscopic Fourteenth Amendment' (2002) 33 McGeorge Law Review 473. According to her, this form of 'stereoscopic' interaction is to be distinguished from instances of fungibility, where liberty and equality values are used interchangeably through different linguistic formulations but producing basically the same effects. These are cases in which '[t]he two clauses *become*, rather than *inform*, one another', 474–75 (emphasis added).

[139] The committee oversees the application of the International Covenant on Economic, Social and Cultural Rights (adopted 16 December 1966, entered into force 3 January 1976) 993 UNTS 3 (ICESCR).

state obligations to address food insecurity as both a matter of adequate nutrition *and* public health. So, in its General Comment No 12 on the right to food, it declared the existence of an (individual) 'right to adequate food', defining it as a right to 'essential food which is sufficient, nutritionally adequate and safe, to ensure ... freedom from hunger'.[140] In parallel, the Committee has also recognised the value of 'proper nutrition' under the right to health, coupling the quantity and quality of food necessary for 'the highest attainable standard of health', so as 'to ensure freedom from hunger to everyone'.[141] The newly emerging human right rests on an intersectional conceptualisation that emphasises underlying determinants of health, requiring the provision of proper food and nutrition security for physical and mental development and well-being, as a central component of human dignity.[142] The resulting right highlights the interdependency of the 'mother' rights to food and to health. It emerges from the intersection between the two, with none of the clauses in isolation being deemed sufficient to generate the entitlement on their own, and regardless of any consideration of comparisons and discrimination, relying on a comprehensive view of dignity.[143]

In its jurisprudence on vulnerable groups, the Strasbourg Court has also adopted a variant of intersectional legal thinking. Under, for instance, the 'home' limb of Article 8 ECHR, it has recognised a duty to provide alternative shelter, where housing deprivation is state-caused or aggravated by a lack of provision that has rendered the home unsafe or unsanitary,[144] especially when there are risks to life that are known to the state.[145] As a result, a 'minimum core of housing protection' emerges as an irreducible state obligation.[146] In this line of case law, the demolition of an elderly claimant's home, in *Selçuk*,[147] was considered inhuman treatment, engaging the normative force of the intersection between Articles 8 and 3 ECHR. The

[140] CESCR, 'General Comment No 12: The Right to Adequate Food (Art. 11)' (1999) UN Doc E/C.12/1999/5.

[141] CESCR, 'General Comment No 14: The Right to the Highest Attainable Standard of Health (Art. 12)' (2000) UN Doc E/C.12/2000/4.

[142] Ana Ayala and Benjamin Meier, 'A Human Rights Approach to the Health Implications of Food and Nutrition Insecurity' (2017) 38 Public Health Reviews 1, 9–12.

[143] In this vein, see also Benjamin Meier and Yuna Kim, 'Human Rights Accountability through Treaty Bodies: Examining Human Rights Treaty Monitoring for Water and Sanitation' (2015) 26 Duke Journal of Comparative & International Law 141, commenting on the right to water, as emerging out of the intersection between the right to health and the right to an adequate standard of living.

[144] *Fadeyeva v Russia* App no 55723/00 (ECtHR, 9 June 2007); *Moreno Gómez v Spain* App no 4143/02 (ECtHR, 16 November 2004).

[145] *Öneryildiz v Turkey* App no 48939/99 (ECtHR, 30 November 2004), para 71; *Budayeva v Russia* App no 15339/02 (ECtHR, 20 March 2008), para 111. For commentary, see Colm O'Cinneide, 'A Modest Proposal: Destitution, State Responsibility, and the European Convention on Human Rights' (2008) 5 European Human Rights Law Review 583. See also Scott Leckie, 'The Right to Housing' in Asbjorn Eide, Catarina Krause, and Allan Rosas (eds), *Economic, Social and Cultural Rights* (2nd edn, Brill 2001) 149.

[146] Ingrid Leijten, *Core Socio-Economic Rights and the European Court of Human Rights* (Cambridge University Press 2018) 239.

[147] *Selçuk v Turkey* App nos 23184/94 and 23185/94 (ECtHR, 24 April 1998).

dismantling of a Roma settlement by a police-instigated mob, in *Moldovan*,[148] rendering entire families homeless and forcing them to live in miserable conditions, amounted to degrading treatment. The denial of housing assistance to a severely ill and disabled applicant, in *Marzari*,[149] also raised a prima facie issue under Articles 8 and 3 ECHR taken together. And, although the applicant's living standards and housing rights in *M.S.S.* were channelled through Article 3 ECHR only, the Court arguably deduced a right to 'accommodation and decent material conditions' out of the intersection between the Convention and the explicit housing provisions of the EU Reception Conditions Directive[150]—conferring Article 8 ECHR rights onto asylum applicants within the Common European Asylum System.[151] However, the pivotal element in all these cases was the '*particular* vulnerability' of claimants,[152] rather than a genuine intersectional understanding of their rights and of the state's related obligations.

By contrast, the argument here is that a holistic approach must be adopted by default and vis-à-vis all claims under the ECHR, considering individual circumstances contextually, comprehensively, and in detail, avoiding speculation about the a priori 'special' or 'relative' vulnerability of applicants—which leads back into the trap of comparisons and categorical thinking once again. Following this approach, the call is to surpass discrimination-based compartmentalisation, and instead to examine norms, values, and principles holistically, as mutually constitutive, and underpinned by the 'equal liberty' standard. The call is to embrace the comprehensive dignity model as substantiating the whole of the legal system and as requiring a whole-of-legal system approach to the law, delivering solutions that respond to a whole-of-person understanding of applicants' claims in a meaningful way.

Based on this premise, the next section explores the workings of the intersectionality-inspired trends emerging in US legal theory on the adjudication of constitutional rights, as an illustration of the route available to the Strasbourg Court to deliver substantive justice as a real, Convention-wide resource. Comprehensive dignity and 'equal liberty' themes will be highlighted as the underlying basis of the jus-generative processes at play.

148 *Moldovan v Romania (No 2)* App nos 41138/98 and 64320/01 (ECtHR, 12 July 2005). For analysis, see Roberta Medda-Windischer, 'Housing Rights and the Inclusion of Roma and Travellers: Towards Positive Action Measures from the Rulings of the European Court of Human Rights?' in Cuypers and Vrielink (n 100) 27; and Christina Binder and Thomas Schobesberger, 'The European Court of Human Rights and Social Rights—Emerging Trends in Jurisprudence?' (2015) 201 Hungarian Yearbook of International Law and European Law 51.

149 *Marzari v Italy* App no 36448/97 (ECtHR, 4 May 1999).

150 Parliament and Council Directive 2013/33/EU of 26 June 2013 laying down standards for the reception of applicants for international protection [2013] OJ L180/96.

151 *M.S.S.* (n 23), para 250.

152 Concurring, see Jessie Hohmann, *The Right to Housing: Law, Concepts, Possibilities* (Hart 2013) 74.

6. Lessons from Comparative Constitutionalism

Debates on legal aggregation,[153] concerning relations between different normative systems and/or sources of law, are not new. They have a long pedigree on both sides of the Atlantic. In the European context, they have principally centred around the question of systemic integration and the fragmentation of public international law,[154] using Article 31(3)(c) of the Vienna Convention on the Law of Treaties as a main point of reference.[155] This provision has played a key role in the development of the 'effectiveness' doctrine within the ECHR system.[156]

However, the emphasis in this literature has mostly been on *inter*-systemic relations (at regime level), between different parts of general international law, including international human rights law as enshrined in the ECHR. The reception of international law within the Convention has actually prompted thorough discussion,[157] as has the issue of norm conflicts and, particularly, the interplay between international human rights law and international humanitarian law in war situations.[158] The Strasbourg Court has, indeed, recognised on numerous occasions that the '[ECHR] should be interpreted as far as possible in harmony with other principles of international law of which it forms part'.[159] The other aspect the debate has covered is the interaction (at rule level) between ECHR provisions and exogenous norms, sometimes for explanatory purposes of undefined terms,[160] other times as a means to expand the remit of individual rights and/or

[153] Ariel Porat and Eric Posner, 'Aggregation and Law' (2012) 122 Yale Law Journal 2, explaining the distinction between factual and normative aggregation and their effects in different areas of private and public law.

[154] For an elaboration, see Violeta Moreno-Lax, 'Systematising Systemic Integration' (2014) 12 Journal of International Criminal Justice 907.

[155] Vienna Convention on the Law of Treaties (adopted 23 May 1969, entered into force 27 January 1980) 1155 UNTS 331 (VCLT). See, generally, Panos Merkouris, *Article 31(3)(c) VCLT and the Principle of Systemic Integration* (Brill 2015).

[156] Vassilis Tzevelekos, 'The Use of Article 31(3)(c) of the VCLT in the Case-law of the ECtHR: An Effective Anti-Fragmentation Tool or a Selective Loophole for the Reinforcement of the Teleology of Human Rights? Between Evolution and Systemic Integration' (2010) 31 Michigan Journal of International Law 621.

[157] See eg Magdalena Forowicz, *The Reception of International Law in the European Court of Human Rights* (OUP 2010); and Cesare Pitea, 'Interpreting the ECHR in the Light of "Other" International Instruments: Systemic Integration or Fragmentation of Rules on Treaty Interpretation?' in Boschiero and others (eds), *International Courts and the Development of International Law* (TMC Asser Press 2013) 545.

[158] Alexander Orakhelashvili, 'The Interaction between Human Rights and Humanitarian Law: Fragmentation, Conflict, Parallelism, or Convergence?' (2008) 19 European Journal of International Law 161; Andrea Gioia, 'The Role of the European Court of Human Rights in Monitoring Compliance with Humanitarian Law in Armed Conflict' in Orna Ben-Naftali (ed), *International Humanitarian Law and International Human Rights Law* (OUP 2011) 201; and, generally, Gerd Oberleitner, *Human Rights in Armed Conflicts* (Cambridge University Press 2015).

[159] eg *Al-Adsani* (n 76), para 55; *Bosphorus v Ireland* App no 45036/98 (ECtHR, 30 June 2005), para 150; *Al-Saadoon* (n 22), para 126.

[160] For a theorisation, see Akhil Reed Amar, 'Intratextualism' (1999) 112 Harvard Law Review 747.

state obligations.[161] American constitutionalism, on the other hand, has spent time dissecting *intra*-systemic encounters between different parts of their foundational text, describing and cataloguing mechanisms of 'constitutional borrowing'.[162]

This is not to say that ECHR scholarship has ignored in its analyses the tools employed by the Strasbourg Court to interpret and advance Convention rights *from within*. Works on the 'autonomous concepts', the 'living instrument', the 'margin of appreciation', or the 'European consensus' doctrines are rich and abundant.[163] But—with a few exceptions—there has been less attention being paid to the theorising of *how* the 'coupling' of different ECHR rights functions and with what effects.

Several authors have concentrated on jus-generative techniques, including via implicit rights,[164] positive obligations,[165] procedural safeguards attached to substantive clauses,[166] or the role of the non-discrimination protection under Article 14 ECHR in the reading of other Convention provisions.[167] Yet, the analysis is, generally, conducted by focusing on a *single* gravitational centre around *one* particular clause from which a wider scope or ancillary protections are derived. This is why a look at the American debate on synergies between different substantive provisions (of equal rank) may be illuminative, in order to demonstrate how the process of rights-production from an intersectional perspective could work when transposed to the ECHR.

The taxonomy discussed in the next sub-sections does not attempt to be exhaustive, but representative of the different approaches to the explication of *intra*-systemic interfaces between rights claims of a constitutional nature in US constitutional theory. The objective is to explore the diversity of methods available to judges (in America and elsewhere) to deal with complex constellations of harms and remedies in a rationalised way that favours substantive justice and the rule of

161 With illustrations of the two trends, see Jarlath Clifford, 'The UN Disability Convention and its Impact on European Equality Law' (2011) 6 Equal Rights Review 11; Ursula Kilkelly, 'The CRC in Litigation Under the ECHR' in Ton Liefaard and Jaap Doek (eds), *Litigating the Rights of the Child* (Springer 2015) 193.

162 Nelson Tebbe and Robert Tsai, 'Constitutional Borrowing' (2010) 108 Michigan Law Review 459.

163 See eg George Letsas, *A Theory of Interpretation of the European Convention on Human Rights* (OUP 2007); Yutaka Arai, *The Margin of Appreciation Doctrine and the Principle of Proportionality in the Jurisprudence of the ECHR* (Intersentia 2002); Kanstantsin Dzehtsiarou, *European Consensus and the Legitimacy of the European Court of Human Rights* (Cambridge University Press 2015); Christian Djeffal, *Static and Evolutive Treaty Interpretation* (Cambridge University Press 2016) 272.

164 Maris Burbergs, 'How the Right to Respect for Private and Family Life, Home and Correspondence became the Nursery in which New Rights are Born: Article 8 ECHR' in Eva Brems and Janneke Gerards (eds), *Shaping Rights in the ECHR* (Cambridge University Press 2013) 315.

165 Alastair Mowbray, *The Development of Positive Obligations under the European Convention on Human Rights by the European Court of Human Rights* (Hart 2004); Dimitris Xenos, *The Positive Obligations of the State under the European Convention of Human Rights* (Routledge 2012).

166 Eva Brems, 'Procedural Protection: An Examination of Procedural Safeguards Read into Substantive Convention Rights' in Brems and Gerards (n 164) 137.

167 Oddný Mjöll Arnardóttir, *Equality and Non-Discrimination Under the European Convention on Human Rights* (Brill 2003); Janneke Gerards, 'The Discrimination Grounds of Article 14 of the European Convention on Human Rights' (2013) 13 European Human Rights Law Review 99.

law. The sequence below follows a funnel-like structure, ranging from the intersection with/between principles and good faith reasoning to concrete rule-level combinations, and up to the intersectional conceptualisation of norm-to-norm interactions, showing how they work in detail in the generation of *new* substantive rights from which the ECtHR could take inspiration. The following section will then apply these insights to the conceptualisation of the 'right to flee' under the ECHR.

6.1 Constitutional Borrowing

For Tebbe and Tsai, constitutional borrowing, in a very wide sense, captures the ages-old practice of the jurist of reproducing, adjusting, and recycling heuristics, frameworks, ideas, and tropes from different realms to argue cases and substantiate legal conclusions.[168] The technique is broad and encompasses methods beyond mere intra-textualism,[169] involving relations between textual and non-textual sources of constitutional knowledge, with varying degrees of intensity, from wholesale to piecemeal incorporations. Any element from which authoritative strength can be obtained that 'trades between' two or more constitutional fields, be it a statute, a principle, a doctrinal test, or an overarching rationale, is of relevance to this definition. The practice, however, cannot be random. To be categorised as an instance of 'borrowing' it needs to be deliberate, purposive, and performed in good faith, being the product of a conscious calculation of 'principled synthesising' undertaken for the benefit of the constitution as a whole.

For the authors, cross-area interpretation (including between different clauses of the Bill of Rights) constitutes a main tool of borrowing.[170] The exercise shall be performed with a view to enlightening or bolstering the 'receiving' domain, through input from another 'sending' domain, in an effort to bridge them both for persuasive ends.[171] This process, then, results in the unifying import of substance or underlying notions from one to the other norm/framework/doctrine in a mutually reinforcing way, for example, introducing freedom-based reasoning into equality-based claims. The recognition that both 'are linked in important respects',[172] and that liberty simultaneously protects essential equality values, serves to make conceptual space for the *new* 'equal liberty' principle this chapter advocates, thenceforth relevant to the adjudication of subsequent cases.[173] Such inter-change allows

168 Tebbe and Tsai (n 162) 461.

169 Amar (n 160).

170 Tebbe and Tsai (n 162) 463.

171 According to the authors the interpretative exercise can take different shapes, distinguished by its underlying motives or its ultimate results, which they describe as instances of 'transplantation', 'hedging', 'displacement', and 'corruption'. See ibid, 472–83.

172 *Lawrence v Texas* 539 US 558 (2003) 575.

173 cf Laurence Tribe, speaking of 'equal dignity' instead, in 'Equal Dignity: Speaking Its Name' (2015) 129 Harvard Law Review Forum 16, 20.

for a re-framing of future non-discrimination claims in the language of shared freedom and 'equal citizenship',[174] obviating the need for comparators and relative advantage/disadvantage assessments—equality and liberty (together) underpinning the ideal of comprehensive dignity.

There are several justifications for engaging in borrowing strategies, all of which should, ultimately, be rule-of-law enhancing. The operation is to improve coherence and realise commitments to generality, accountability, and systematization through its transparency boosting and rationalization effects on legal argumentation. Constitutional borrowing holds the promise of overarching gains at systemic level, hindering hyper-specialisation and promoting consistency across constitutional domains, unearthing commonalities of purpose and structure, and reinforcing synergies between them. This, in turn, improves predictability and legal certainty, fostering a sense of fairness and objectivity overarching the constitution as a whole. As Tebbe and Tsai put it, borrowing 'rewards syntheses of different areas of [constitutional] law, thereby advancing holistic thinking . . . making connections between policy objectives and long-term interests'.[175]

6.2 Interlocking Method

A way of 'holistic thinking' that can be classified as a particular mode of constitutional borrowing is Gerken's interlocking method.[176] The focus in this case is on two specific sources of constitutional knowledge of a different kind that work together as 'interlocking gears' moving the constitutional project forward. The sources in question are individual rights provisions, on one hand, and structural principles, on the other, such as subsidiarity, separation of powers, or competence allocation between distinct territorial and/or administrative units within the state.

The decision the author uses to illustrate the interplay between federalism (*qua* federal integration) and the First Amendment of the American constitution is one of same-sex marriage rights, where structural arguments of power distribution between the federal and state levels of government in the US are mobilised to palliate the shortcomings of the substantive clause to thereby achieve justice.[177] What the interlocking reasoning does in *Windsor*, for example, is to 'blend' the federalism principle and the First Amendment together into a new compound that promotes integration, liberty, and equality, all at once. Such technique served to strike down as unconstitutional the federal interpretation of 'spouse' and 'marriage', enshrined

[174] For the coinage of this term, see Kenneth Karst, 'The Liberties of Equal Citizens' (2007–2008) 55 UCLA Law Review 99, commenting on *Lawrence v Texas* (n 172).

[175] Tebbe and Tsai (n 162) 488.

[176] Heather Gerken, 'Windsor's Mad Genius: The Interlocking Gears of Rights and Structure' (2015) 95 Boston Law Review 587.

[177] *Windsor v The United States* 133 S Ct 2675 (2013).

in Section 3 of the Defence of Marriage Act (DOMA), covering only opposite-sex unions. Justice Kennedy, pronouncing the majority opinion, concluded that the federal statute was invalid because it entailed 'a deprivation of the *liberty* [rather than equality] of the person'; it lacked a defensible purpose, since its effect was 'to disparage and to injure those whom the State, by its marriage laws, sought to protect in personhood and dignity'.[178] The federal government was, therefore, barred from treating *state*-level-sanctioned heterosexual marriages differently from *state*-level-sanctioned same-sex marriages for the purposes of *federal*-level recognition. The ends of equality were thus defended on liberty-inspired grounds—rather than non-discrimination reasoning—delivering justice through a comprehensive-dignity based rationale.

6.3 Transactional Approach

A method that looks into relations between *same*-type norms of constitutional relevance is the 'transactional' perspective advocated by Faigman.[179] The approach here proposes a mechanism to assess combined wrongs of constitutional worth, again, in a holistic manner. The premise is that people do not suffer harm in clause-specific, compartmentalised form. Accordingly, an approach to adjudication that is clause-specific miscalculates the totality of the injury undergone. Dignity is indivisible. It cannot be tabulated and pigeonholed. This would amount to 'something like calculating damages in torts one arm and one leg at a time . . [ignoring] the fact that the plaintiff is completely disabled'.[180] For this reason, rights ought to be aggregated, so as to consider the full effect of the damage endured *in toto*.

However, the aggregation exercise is not just a matter of arithmetical addition of different rights clauses aligned in a sequence, but rather an (intersectional) process of transformation. The cost in dignity, Faigman posits, is not measurable by reference to the many rights clauses implicated, but rather by the 'depth of liberty' they represent when taken together.[181] It is a *qualitative*, rather than *quantitative* question, that accounts for the 'full liberty value' impacted upon. Rights aggregation, in this way, acts as an 'inclusive lens' that corrects the blindness of clause-specific analysis and surpasses equality-only characterisations.[182] Since rights enumeration can never be complete or exhaustive, aggregation provides a rational and justifiable way to deal with the richness and complexity of dignity, as

[178] ibid, 2696 (emphasis added).
[179] David Faigman, 'Measuring Constitutionality Transactionally' (1994) 45 Hastings Law Journal 753.
[180] ibid, 773.
[181] ibid, 775. Faigman bases his reasoning on liberty, rather than dignity. I have, therefore, adapted the original argumentation, based on my 'equal liberty'/comprehensive dignity rationale.
[182] ibid, 783–84.

inspired by liberty-based thinking too. Because dignity is not 'a series of isolated points', it manifests in unenumerated form as well, which must be apprehended in its entirety.[183]

What Faigman does not explain is *how* exactly the aggregation operates *in concreto*. But he distinguishes it from the doctrine of 'incorporation'. Incorporation, in the way used by Justice Cardozo in *Palko v. Connecticut*, for instance, implies a process of abstraction, 'dictated by a study and appreciation of the meaning, the essential implications, of liberty itself'[184] that leads to the articulation of implied, unenumerated rights as *necessarily* flowing from enumerated clauses—as in the ECHR doctrine of 'inherent' or 'implicit' protections.[185] Drawing on this logic, Faigman proposes that the 'same wisdom' requires acceptance of the aggregation technique.[186]

A hint of what aggregation may demand in individual cases is provided by two judgments Faigman cites.[187] In *Smith*, the combination of freedom of religion (or the Free Exercise clause) with freedom of expression (or Freedom of Speech) warranted a heightened standard of scrutiny of state action, thereby changing the nature of the review on account of the compound harm sustained by the victim, cutting across and engaging more than one right at a time.[188] By contrast, in *Griswold*, the juxtaposition of several constitutional Amendments led to the recognition of the 'right of privacy' as a separate entitlement, located 'in the penumbras' of the several clauses taken together.[189] The jus-generative force of the conjunction between the different substantive rights provisions went thus a step further in this instance, identifying not simply a need for enhanced policing of multiplex violations, but—in line with the intersectional reading proposed herein—actually 'creating' a *new* right.

6.4 Combination Analysis

Coenen has shed light onto the inner workings of aggregation in his defence of 'combination analysis' for constitutional adjudication, which is relevant to the intersectional construction of the ECHR.[190] In his view, when multiple, overlapping

[183] ibid, 782.
[184] *Palko v Connecticut* 302 US 319 (1937) 326.
[185] *Golder v United Kingdom* App no 4451/70 (ECtHR, 21 February 1975), para 36, on the right of access to a court as being 'inherent' in Art 6 ECHR; and *Soering* (n 22), para 88, deducing a duty not to extradite anyone to a country where there is a 'real risk' of exposure to irreversible harm, as 'implicit' in Art 3 ECHR.
[186] Faigman (n 179) 777.
[187] ibid, 775.
[188] *Employment Division, Department of Human Resources v Smith* 494 US 872 (1990).
[189] *Griswold v Connecticut* 381 US 479 (1965) 484.
[190] Michael Coenen, 'Combining Constitutional Clauses' (2016) 164 University of Pennsylvania Law Review 1067.

provisions are implicated in a constitutional puzzle, the clauses concerned shall be looked at in combination, rather than disjointedly or in consecutive fashion. He adds an extra layer of nuance, when compared to Faigman's 'transactional aggregation' formula, asserting that there may be situations in which several rights provisions may mandate the invalidation of state action 'even where no single provision would do so on its own'.[191]

Under this optic, the process of jus-generation gives rise to novel multifold claim-based rights that are *independent* from the 'mother' rights from which they derive. The point is not to aver that two or more constitutional provisions *separately* support a specific finding, but that the finding can only be reached if the clauses are taken *together*, in coordination, providing a single compound rationale with decisional force. The end result is a newly constituted freedom, which may be breached without the underlying clauses having to be individually infringed as well—similarly to the ESCR rights to adequate food and nutrition security referred to above.

However, the ultimate effect of right/right combinations should not only be to yield more stringent limits to state action, as Coenen explicitly acknowledges,[192] but arguably also to generate new and *autonomous* individual entitlements of constitutional standing—as two complementary sides of the same coin. Rights combinations—if the theory is taken to its logical extent—should be deemed to act both as a 'shield' against arbitrary interferences and as a 'sword' to vindicate yet-unrecognised (aspects of) human dignity,[193] like the 'right to flee' proposed below.

The imposition of stronger restrictions on state intervention as a result of rights combinations is visible in the *Smith* judgment mentioned earlier,[194] while the new-rights outcome is exemplified by *Obergefell v. Hodges*.[195] In this later decision the US Supreme Court declared a *new* constitutional right to same-sex marriage, relying on the '[r]ights implicit in liberty [ie the Due Process clause] and rights secured by equal protection [ie the Equal Protection clause] ... [which] *converge[d]* in the identification and definition of the right'.[196] According to Justice Kennedy, writing for the Court, 'though they set forth independent principles', the two clauses, jointly inspired by equality and liberty in combination, 'are connected in a profound way'.[197] 'This *interrelation of the two principles* furthers our understanding of what freedom is and must become',[198] capturing the dynamic, contextually-sensitive, and open-ended texture of human dignity.

[191] ibid.
[192] ibid, 1078.
[193] cf Porat and Posner (n 153) 63, using the metaphor in a different way.
[194] Coenen (n 190) 1071; and *Smith* (n 188).
[195] *Obergefell v Hodges* 135 S Ct 2584 (2015), cited by Coenen (n 190) 1079.
[196] *Obergefell* (n 195) 2603 (emphasis added).
[197] ibid, 2602.
[198] ibid, 2603 (emphasis added).

Whether or not rights combinations are called for depends on the specific circumstances of the case. The 'ultimate normative payoff' is to be evaluated on a case-by-case basis, taking account of all the relevant factors taken together,[199] mediated—it should be added—by a holistic, whole-of-person approach, underpinned by the comprehensive dignity principle proposed in this chapter. What is understood by this holistic consideration and whether it entails the 'amalgam' of substantive rationales,[200] the 'hybridization' of perspectives,[201] the 'stereoscopical' reading of rights,[202] or an operation of 'intersectional' thinking,[203] has been further explored by other authors.

6.5 Hybridisation

An example of 'hybridisation' is presented by Chen, referring to water, as resulting from the combination of two molecules of hydrogen with one of oxygen making the new chemical compound, and to the colour green, resulting from the physical integration of two equal parts of blue and yellow.[204] Just as water is *qualitatively* different from both hydrogen and oxygen and green is not reducible to a 'shade' of either blue or yellow, for Chen, 'hybrid claims'—using the *Smith* formula[205]—result from a similar process, where several constitutional claims join together into something distinct from their component parts.[206]

What she adds to the theoretical debate reconstructed above is a normative justification for 'hybridisation', by focusing not only on the resulting new rights, but also paying attention to 'the cumulative and distinctive effects' of composite claims that affect the new rights at stake.[207] She looks at the structure of 'hybrid claims' as a logical prior step to properly analysing the substance of 'hybrid rights', relying, precisely, on 'intersectionality' to explain hybridity.[208]

This allows for a rational response as to why heightened protection may be required in certain situations. As with my proposal for a whole-of-legal system approach to adjudication to match a whole-of-person analysis of ECHR applications, in Chen's understanding, there are particular circumstances that warrant both the hybridisation of claims, as a point of departure in the legal examination of complex

[199] Coenen (n 190) 1120.
[200] *Richmond Newspapers Inc v Virginia* 448 US 555 (1980) 577.
[201] *Smith* (n 188).
[202] Karlan (n 138).
[203] *Griffin v Illinois* 351 US 12 (1956).
[204] Ming Hsu Chen, 'Two Wrongs Make a Right: Hybrid Claims of Discrimination' (2004) 79 NYU Law Review 685, 695.
[205] *Smith* (n 188) 882.
[206] Chen (n 204) 701.
[207] ibid, 709.
[208] ibid, 687.

factual configurations, and the hybridisation of rights, as an appropriate remedy for damage that would otherwise go unaccounted for.

6.6 Cumulative Constitutionalism

Abrams and Garrett's work on 'cumulative' constitutional rights provides the final element to complete this theoretical exploration.[209] They look, exactly, at the multiple facets and potential uses of intersectionality, arguing for the adoption of the theory on a more general basis than Chen does. They come back to the division between multiplex harm and composite rights, that Chen uses, and propose the extension of intersectionality to cover both, regardless of whether they occur together in the same case or not. Unlike Chen, they distinguish 'hybrid claims' from 'intersectional rights'. For them, while the former are constituted when plaintiffs denounce a single act by the state as violating several rights provisions, which, if taken individually, would not result in redress—contrary to Chen's proposition—the latter occur when state action does violate more than one rights provision, which are to be read together, as mutually informing and bolstering one another. While the first category emphasises the *process* or invocation of intersection, the second category represents the success of the intersectional *result*. For Abrams and Garrett, hybrid claims are, so to speak, intersectional rights 'in the making'.[210]

But the key point to incorporate in the whole-of-legal system approach advocated in this chapter is the way in which they emancipate intersectionality from its 'multiple discrimination' claims origin. They propose to import its essential rationale to instances where the need for intersectional analysis flows not from harm based on multiple intertwined identities, but from the logical interaction of multiple intertwined rights clauses that combine and augment each other, requiring a distinct examination, co-informed by the two (or more) rights concerned.[211] On this basis, they suggest three different functions for intersectional rights to play: *evidentiary*, assisting judges in the determination of the correct level of scrutiny; *unifying*, leading to the generation of new substantive rights; and *limiting*, undercutting state defences for interferences with existing or new rights.[212] This triad of roles is of particular relevance to the identification and definition of new (independent) constitutional standards,[213] when transposing the technique to the ECHR to give meaning to the Convention as a whole.

[209] Kerry Abrams and Brendon Garrett, 'Cumulative Constitutional Rights' (2017) 97 Boston University Law Review 1309.
[210] ibid, 1313.
[211] ibid, 1331 and 1354.
[212] ibid, 1331 and 1341.
[213] ibid, 1347.

What transpires from this brief investigation of US constitutionalism is that for the Strasbourg Court to continue channelling analysis through one provision, however pertinent, is not always warranted and can lead to incorrect findings and inconsistent interpretations, leaving deserving applicants with no protection. The proposal is to, instead, appreciate and respond to complexity on, at least, four distinguishable levels, considering: (1) intersectional factual configurations (in the real world) that give rise to (2) intersectional claims (in the courtroom), which require for (3) intersectional reasoning to be adopted, so as to secure (4) intersectional rights that procure adequate redress. Such a holistic understanding will integrate equality-based with liberty-based perspectives, apprehending human dignity in its totality, and conferring greater meaning to the assertion that the Convention represents the basic 'constitutional instrument of European public order'.[214]

7. Forced Migration and the Intersectional Interpretation of the ECHR

The application of an 'equal liberty'/comprehensive dignity approach to the interpretation of the right to leave any country as it applies to refugees constitutes the focus of this section. Having regard to the insights above from American constitutionalism, the emphasis will be on the synergistic interaction between complementary protections as they play out against a background of compound harm, catering for the complex plight of asylum seekers, especially in extraterritorial situations, when they are trying to reach safety in a country different from their own. As announced, it will be posited that the interplay between the right to leave and the (extraterritorial) prohibition of *refoulement* gives rise to an intersectional 'right to flee to avoid irreversible harm', generating a duty on the part of the state exercising effective control/jurisdiction abroad not to impede access to asylum procedures, as a matter of legally-binding obligation under the Convention.[215]

7.1 The Right to Leave

The starting point is Article 2 of Protocol 4 ECHR, which recognises the right of freedom of movement and the right to leave any country, but without any explicit

[214] See eg *Bosphorus* (n 159), para 156, citing *Loizidou v Turkey* App no 15318/89 (ECtHR, 18 December 1996), para 75. See also Stephen Gardbaum, 'Human Rights as International Constitutional Rights' (2008) 19 EJIL 749, 752; and Alec Stone Sweet, 'On the Constitutionalisation of the Convention' (2009) 71 Yale Law School: Faculty Scholarship Series.

[215] For a detailed argumentation, including from the perspective of EU law, see Moreno-Lax (n 9) 337ff.

references to asylum.[216] Pursuant to its wording, while freedom of movement is reserved to those 'lawfully within the territory' of a Contracting Party, the right to leave any country belongs to 'everyone' without qualification, comprising nationals and non-nationals alike. Interferences with the enjoyment of these rights by public authorities are admissible, but they must be construed narrowly and according to the express terms of the Convention.[217] According to Article 2(3), worded similarly to other limitation clauses in the ECHR,[218] restrictions must, therefore, be stipulated by law, pursue one of the legitimate aims enumerated therein, and be proportionate.

The denial or seizure of a passport, the confiscation of travel documents, or a ban on exit have been considered direct interferences with the right to leave.[219] Indirect restrictions, such as the imposition of taxes to obtain permission to leave or limitations on the export of foreign currency linked to that right, may also fall within its scope of application.[220] And their legality, legitimacy, and proportionality cannot be presumed, but must instead be measured on a case-by-case basis.[221] According to the Strasbourg Court, national authorities must 'take appropriate care to ensure that any interference with the right to leave one's country remains justified and proportionate *throughout its duration* in the individual circumstances of the case'.[222] Automatic restrictions, for indeterminate reasons or for an indefinite period of time,[223] amount to *de facto* punishment and are incompatible with the Convention.[224] General prohibitions, 'preventing almost the entire population

216 The right to enter one's own country is regulated in Art 3 Prot 4 ECHR, whereas protection from expulsion of aliens 'lawfully resident' in the territory of a contracting party is provided for in Art 1 of Prot 7 ECHR. On the other hand, collective expulsions are banned without qualification with regard to all foreigners under Art 4 Prot 4 ECHR. And *refoulement* is prohibited in absolute terms under Art 3 ECHR, as interpreted in the case law of the Strasbourg organs, starting with *Soering* (n 22).

217 Supporting this reading, see Antonio Cassese, 'International Protection of the Right to Leave and Return' in *Studi in Onore di Manlio Udina* (Giuffrè 1975) 221.

218 See Arts 8(2) to 11(2) ECHR.

219 *M. v Germany* App no 10307/83 (ECtHR, 6 March 1984); *Schmid v Austria* App no 10670/83 (ECtHR, 9 July 1985); *Baumann* (n 73); *Napijalo v Croatia* App no 66485/01 (ECtHR, 13 November 2003); *Ignatov v Bulgaria* App no 50/02 (ECtHR, 2 July 2009); *Dzhaksybergenov v Ukraine* App no 12343/10 (ECtHR, 10 February 2011).

220 *Sissanis v Romania* App no 23468/02 (ECtHR, 25 January 2007) (on an arbitrary entry in a passport that prohibited the individual to leave the country).

221 *Riener v Bulgaria* App no 46343/99 (ECtHR, 23 May 2006); *Bartik v Russia* App no 55565/00 (ECtHR, 21 December 2006).

222 *A.E. v Poland* App no 14480/04 (ECtHR, 31 March 2009), para 49; *Bessenyei v Hungary* App no 37509/06 (ECtHR, 31 October 2008), para 24; *Hajlik v Hungary* App no 41463/02 (ECtHR, 31 October 2006), para 36.

223 *Gochev v Bulgaria* App no 34383/03 (ECtHR, 26 November 2009), para 50 (automatic and *de facto* unlimited ban).

224 *Luordo v Italy* App no 32190/96 (ECtHR, 17 July 2003) (restriction of movement of a bankrupt beyond the period necessary to secure assets for creditors); *Federov v Russia* App no 31008/02 (ECtHR, 13 October 2005) (charge of fraud without prosecution for a prolonged period during which the applicants' freedom of movement was restricted). See also *Ciaramella v Italy* App no 6597/03 (ECtHR, 23 September 2004); and *Ivanov v Ukraine* App no 15007/02 (ECtHR, 7 December 2006). For a similar conclusion, see Harris and others, *Law of the European Convention on Human Rights* (3rd edn, OUP 2014) 958–59.

of a State from leaving', are also inadmissible.[225] Against this background, '[t]he Court cannot consider ... blanket and indiscriminate measure[s] as being proportionate'; 'the automatic imposition of such ... measure[s] without any regard to the individual circumstances of the person concerned [cannot] be characterised as necessary in a democratic society'.[226] '*[A]ll* the factors involved' must be taken into account.[227] And there must be 'concrete elements which are *truly* indicative of the continued existence of the risk that such measures seek to forestall'[228]--a suitability test is thus necessary, requiring that there be some empirical basis to conclude that the measure imposed is such as to realise the objective pursued, not in the abstract, but in the concrete individual case.

When applied to refugees, their specific circumstances and their need to leave in search of asylum should, accordingly, be a consideration when devising instruments that may interfere with their exercise of the right. But this implies that the right be understood as being opposable to *any* ECHR Party, not only to the country of which the applicant may be a national,[229] and without considering the absence of a complementary right to enter any other country but one's own to annul the legal strength of this provision. This interpretation would align with the principle of effectiveness and the related presumption against redundancy, according to which every single clause of an international treaty has to be construed as possessing its own independent meaning and effect.[230] Yet, as pointed out earlier, the Strasbourg Court has not been consistent in its evaluation and has considered that Article 2 Protocol 4 ECHR entails 'a right to leave for such country of the person's choice *to which he may be admitted*'.[231]

Such an approach reduces the scope of beneficiaries to those legally permitted to travel—as authorised both by the state of origin and the one of destination[232]—against the express wording of the provision, which benefits 'everyone' without qualification. It renders the right to leave into an 'imperfect' entitlement with respect to 'each particular country [of destination]',[233] seemingly based on an understanding that a prior system of coordination or allocation of the burden to allow

225 *Streletz v Germany* App nos 34044/96, 35532/97, and 44801/98 (ECtHR, 22 March 2001), para 100. On whether visas and carrier sanctions should be understood as meeting this definition, see extensively Moreno-Lax (n 9) 357ff.

226 *Stamose v Bulgaria* App no 29713/05 (ECtHR, 27 November 2012), paras 34 and 36.

227 *Gochev* (n 223), para 50 (emphasis added).

228 *Nalbantski v Bulgaria* App no 30943/04 (ECtHR, 10 February 2011), para 65 (emphasis added). See also *Hajibeyli v Azerbaijan* App no 16528/05 (ECtHR, 10 July 2008), para 63.

229 cf *Miażdżyk v Poland* App no 23592/07 (ECtHR, 24 January 2012) (French applicant in Poland).

230 See eg Alexander Orakhelashvili, *The Interpretation of Acts and Rules in Public International Law* (OUP 2008), 422 and references cited.

231 *Baumann* (n 73), para 61 (emphasis added), reiterated in *Battista* (n 73), para 37.

232 cf *Stamose* (n 226), paras 34 and 36, concerning a two-year travel ban imposed by Bulgaria on one of its citizens, who had been deported from the US, to prevent him from re-attempting an irregular entry into other countries. The measure was automatically imposed as a deterrent on anybody in this same situation 'without any regard to the individual circumstances of the person concerned'.

233 Emmerich de Vattel, *The Law of Nations*, Bk 1, ch XIX [1797] (Liberty Fund 2008), para 230.

entry into a state different from the one of nationality needs to be in place among all Parties to the Convention, especially to cater for any foreigners requiring protection. This construction sees not the individual member state of potential destination, but the entire membership of the ECHR—if not the international community 'as a whole'[234]—to be the bearer of the related obligation. However, without specific wording to this effect, such a collectivisation of the duties attached to the right to leave contradicts the principle of independent responsibility, which 'reflects the position under general international law'.[235] The principle applies by default and involves that each and every individual state be responsible for each and every of its freely contracted obligations. The *pacta sunt servanda* rule, whereby '[e]very treaty in force is binding upon the parties to it', comes in support of this interpretation in so far as it requires that international obligations 'be performed *by them* in good faith'.[236] As a result, ECHR Parties should not be able to hide behind a 'collectivised' reading of the right to leave in order to negate its effects in their regard. Each contracting state should instead be deemed to remain 'the guarantor of individual rights and freedoms .... within its jurisdiction'[237] and be bound to guarantee them to 'everyone' in that situation. The determination of when and how a potential asylum seeker in an extraterritorial situation may come within its authority and control constitutes a separate question to be answered from the perspective of Article 1 of the Convention.

Insisting on the 'imperfect' nature of the right to leave, as 'half a right' that other states need to complete—if they will,[238] is systematically unwarranted too. The interpretation seems to concern only one section of one provision of Protocol 4 ECHR, whereas all other clauses in the same Protocol, and in the rest of the Convention, follow the general rule of independent state responsibility under international law. Such an approach results, precisely, in the 'discrepancy' that the Court's pronouncements in *Hirsi* attempted to avoid 'between the scope of application of the Convention as such and that of... Protocol 4', upsetting 'the principle that the Convention must be interpreted as a whole'.[239] Therefore, the right to leave should be treated as all the other rights in the Convention, its scope of application following the general design of Article 1 ECHR. The right should hence be understood to be opposable to any state Party to the Convention, including the state of destination, which will need to justify interferences with it according to the relevant rules. If this can be accepted, then its conduct, including in the form of

234 Den Heijer (n 25), 148–50.

235 ILC, 'Commentary to the Articles on the Responsibility of States for Internationally Wrongful Acts' (2001) YILC vol II, part 2, 124.

236 Art 26 VCLT (emphasis added).

237 *Refah Partisi v Turkey* [GC] App no 41340/98 (ECtHR, 13 February 2003), para 119.

238 Satvinder Juss, 'Free Movement and the World Order' (2004) 16 International Journal of Refugee Law 289, 293.

239 *Hirsi Jamaa and others* (n 18) para 178.

measures of extraterritorial border control, becomes justiciable under the right to leave, including vis-à-vis potential refugees.

7.2 The Right to Leave (to Escape Irreversible Harm)

The findings of the Court in *Amuur* appear to go in the direction of recognising the opposability of the right to leave to the country of destination, when it underlined that 'the mere fact that it is possible for asylum seekers to leave voluntarily the country where they wish to take refuge cannot exclude a restriction on ... the right to leave any country, including one's own'.[240] The Court further remarked the connection with the search for international protection, requiring France to give special consideration to the motives of the claimants on account of the fact that the possibility of leaving again and seeking asylum elsewhere 'becomes theoretical if no other country offering protection comparable to the protection they expect to find in [France as country of intended destination] is inclined or prepared to take them in'.[241] In so far as the claimants are 'aliens who ... fearing for their lives, have fled from their own country',[242] their motives crisscross into Article 3 ECHR and become an overriding factor.

The Court appears to have followed this approach in *M.S.S.* to a certain extent. In that case, an Afghan national escaping persecution in his country of origin, entered Belgium from Greece to seek asylum. Belgian authorities transferred him back, against the advice of UNHCR and in complete disregard of the situation prevailing in Greece at the material time. Both countries were condemned precisely for their failure to consider the individual situation of the applicant in all its complexity.[243] In particular, the transfer to Greece had exposed him to degrading treatment and to a risk of onward removal in breach of Article 3 ECHR. The Court noted in this connection that '[t]he fact that ... the applicant had been trying to leave Greece [irregularly] [could not] be held against him'.[244] This was so, in particular, because 'the applicant was attempting to find a solution to a situation the Court consider[ed] contrary to Article 3 [ECHR]'.[245] Although indirectly, the intersection between the right to leave and the right to protection against ill-treatment was thereby explicitly acknowledged, on account of the fact that the applicant was 'a *potential* asylum seeker'.[246] The Court arguably adopted an intersectional approach to consider his

[240] *Amuur* (n 17) para 48.
[241] ibid.
[242] ibid, para 43.
[243] *M.S.S.* (n 23), para 217.
[244] ibid, para 315. cf the general approach by the Committee on the Rights of Migrant Workers, speaking out against the criminalisation of unauthorised emigration, in 'Concluding Observations on Morocco' (8 October 2013) UN Doc CMW/C/MAR/CO/1, paras 23–26.
[245] *M.S.S.* (n 23), para 315.
[246] ibid, para 225 (emphasis added). See also para 231: '... such conditions, which are found in other detention centres in Greece, amounted to degrading treatment within the meaning of Article 3 of the

'need of special protection'[247] and implicitly embraced the intersectional 'right to flee' a situation of exposure to irreversible harm.

The same reasoning seems to underpin *Hirsi*, where the Court extends the Convention's protection to 'migrants having taken to the sea [and] risking their lives'.[248] Therein, 'expulsion' is not interpreted in the technical, legal sense but 'in the generic meaning' to denote the action 'to drive away from a place'.[249] This covers multiple ways of conduct by the ECHR states, taking into account that 'the interdiction of migrants on the high seas and their removal to countries of transit or origin are now a means of migratory control'.[250] It follows a purposive interpretation of the prohibition of collective expulsion 'in the light of present day conditions' and with a view to guaranteeing 'concrete and effective' protection.[251] The opposite would have allowed 'a significant component of contemporary migratory patterns' to fall outside the ambit of this provision, 'notwithstanding the fact that the conduct it is intended to prohibit can occur outside national territory [including] on the high seas', rendering the prohibition it enshrines 'ineffective in practice'.[252]

If this is true, as a matter of coherence, the same wisdom should apply to measures that impede flight imposed further afield, including right inside the countries in which refugees may face Article 3 ECHR risks. Otherwise, as noted in *N.D. and N.T.*, '[i]n the absence of appropriate arrangements, the resulting possibility for States to refuse entry to their territory [would] render ineffective all the Convention provisions designed to protect individuals who face a genuine risk of persecution'.[253] A 'comprehensive dignity' reading of the right to leave would take account of its intersection with the prohibition of *refoulement*, so as to 'maintain[] the possibility . . . to assert a risk of treatment . . . incompatible with . . . Article 3'.[254] Following the Resolution on Asylum of the Committee of Ministers of the Council of Europe, that intersection should be deemed to prevent that anyone 'be subjected [not only] to refusal of admission at the frontier' or to individual or collective expulsion, but also to 'any other measure which would have the result of compelling him to ... *remain* in a territory where he would be in danger of persecution'.[255] Any measure that 'constitutes an exercise of jurisdiction within the meaning of

Convention. In reaching that conclusion, it took into account the fact that *the applicants were asylum seekers*' (emphasis added).

[247] ibid, para 251.
[248] *Hirsi Jamaa and others* (n 18), para 177.
[249] ibid, para 174. See also *N.D. and N.T.* (n 6), para 185.
[250] *Hirsi Jamaa and others* (n 18), para 176.
[251] ibid, para 175.
[252] ibid, para 177.
[253] *N.D. and N.T.* (n 6), para 209.
[254] ibid, para 198.
[255] Committee of Ministers of the Council of Europe, Resolution (67) 14 on asylum to persons in danger of persecution (29 June 1967), para 2 (emphasis added).

Article 1 of the Convention' and 'the effect of which is to prevent migrants from reaching the borders of the State [of destination]' should be considered to 'engage[] the responsibility of the State in question',[256] including in situations 'where the authorities ... ha[ve] not yet examined the existence of grounds entitling the persons concerned to claim protection'.[257]

This means that there is no principled reason to exclude eg visa issuing procedures or embassy scenarios from this equation.[258] The rule according to which 'acts of diplomatic or consular agents ... may amount to an exercise of jurisdiction when these agents exert authority and control over others' remains valid.[259] And it is also unquestionable that visa issuing powers are an attribute of state sovereignty. Under international diplomatic law, the issuance of visas 'to persons wishing to travel to the sending State' pertains to its exclusive competence and constitutes a manifestation of its *de jure* jurisdiction long recognised under international law, falling within its sole authority and control.[260] It is part and parcel of explicitly recognised and accepted consular functions according to customary and conventional norms governing consular relations,[261] over which the territorial state has no power to interfere. After all, visas simply advance to the pre-entry stage the checks that foreign applicants undergo on arrival at the physical border of the state concerned—the conditions for obtaining a visa normally coinciding with the conditions for being allowed admission.[262] Therefore, the grant or denial of a visa, on which the exercise of the right to leave may be dependent, cannot but be considered an act of jurisdiction, with the potential to expose the applicant to a violation of Article 3 ECHR. Whether a visa rejection may result in the exposure of the individual to a risk of *refoulement* needs to be assessed against all the relevant elements of the case, adopting a whole-of-person/whole-of-legal-system approach to their characterisation. But, in situations in which it is well-known through reliable reports that there is a pattern of grave human rights violations by or in the territorial state,[263] wilful ignorance of such information should be deemed to amount to a breach of the 'right to flee'. This assertion 'does not ... imply a *general* duty ... to bring persons who are under the jurisdiction of another State within its own jurisdiction'.[264] The focus is not on *all* persons, but on refugees. It enjoins ECHR parties to consider the

[256] *Hirsi Jamaa and others* (n 18), para 174.
[257] *N.D. and N.T.* (n 6), para 186.
[258] cf ibid, para 222. See further Moreno-Lax (n 9) ch 8.
[259] *Al-Skeini* (n 28), para 134.
[260] Art 5(d) Vienna Convention on Consular Relations (adopted 24 April 1963, entered into force 19 March 1967) 596 UNTS 261 (VCCR). cf *M.N. v Belgium* [GC] App no 3599/18 (ECtHR, 5 March 2020).
[261] On the "functional" approach to jurisdiction, see Moreno-Lax, 'The Architecture of Functional Jurisdiction: Unpacking Contactless Control – On Public Powers, S.S. and Others v. Italy, and the "Operational Model"' (2020) 21 German Law Journal 385.
[262] See further Moreno-Lax (n 9) ch 4.
[263] *Hirsi Jamaa and others* (n 18), paras 118, 123, 125–26, and 156–57. See also *M.S.S.* (n 23), paras 258–59, 263, 358–59, and 366–67.
[264] *N.D. and N.T.* (n 6), para 221 (emphasis added).

specific effects of their policies of *non-entrée* on persons with no other option but to escape unsafe countries in search of protection on the basis of an intersectional interpretation of the provisions of the Convention.

8. Conclusion

Intersectionality, as a deliberate choice for a whole-of-person/whole-of-legal system interpretation that serves and furthers the ECHR constitutional project in its entirety, would require the Court to consciously develop the *Amuur-M.S.S.-Hirsi* reasoning into a fully-fledged (pronounced) right, based on the 'comprehensive dignity' methodology, drawing from American constitutionalism, and as expounded in the preceding sections. Pulling the pieces together, the conclusion should accordingly be that, where '*potential* asylum seekers' are concerned,[265] their specific circumstances lead to the conclusion that a departure in order to avoid irreversible damage--whether via regular or irregular channels--should be considered a sufficient and incontestable ground for one to escape any country, including one's own, which states of destination should take in consideration, especially when implementing migration policies and mechanisms of pre-border control.[266] And if the measure concerned exposes the potential asylum applicant to a real risk of treatment contrary to Article 3 ECHR, the jus-generative intersection between the right to leave and the right to protection against *refoulement* should be deemed to prohibit it.[267] The two provisions are co-constitutive—each transforming and strengthening the other—and are to work in tandem in relevant situations, achieving results that neither could attain in isolation,[268] both similarly embedded in the principles of liberty *and* equality underpinning the whole of the Convention.[269]

Most importantly, considering the declaratory nature of refugee status,[270] a previous formal filing for international protection should be considered irrelevant

[265] *M.S.S.* (n 23), para 225 (emphasis added).
[266] In this line, see HRC, 'General Comment No 27: Freedom of Movement (Art. 12)' (1999) UN Doc CCPR/ C/ 21/ Rev.1/Add.9.
[267] Such a risk may materialise extraterritorially, even while within the country of origin of the person concerned, as eg *Al-Skeini* (n 28) or *Al-Saadoon* (n 22). For an elaboration, see Moreno-Lax (n 9), 272ff. cf Nora Markard, 'The Right to Leave by Sea' (2016) 27 European Journal of International Law 591, 616, concluding that '[n]on-refoulement only applies once the refugee has left their home state[]'.
[268] Similarly, see Karlan (n 138), 474.
[269] Preamble, ECHR, referring to the UDHR. See also Preamble and Art 1 UDHR.
[270] Parliament and Council Directive 2011/95/EU of 13 December 2011 on standards for the qualification of third-country nationals or Stateless persons as beneficiaries of international protection, for a uniform status for refugees or for persons eligible for subsidiary protection, and for the content of the protection granted [2011] OJ L337/9, Recital 21, confirming UNHCR, 'Handbook on Procedures and Criteria for Determining Refugee Status' (January 1992) HCR/IP/4/Eng/REV.1, para 28: 'A person is a refugee within the meaning of the 1951 Convention as soon as he fulfils the criteria contained in the definition ... Recognition of his refugee status does not therefore make him a refugee but declares him to be one. He does not become a refugee because of recognition, but is recognized because he is a refugee.'

for the imposition of an obligation on the state of destination. As accepted by the Court, 'the wish to apply for asylum does not have to be expressed in a particular form'. It can be articulated 'by means of a formal application, but also by means of any conduct which signals clearly the wish ... for protection'.[271] What is more, when 'faced with a situation in which human rights [are] being systematically violated', it would be for the national authorities of the Convention Party concerned 'to [proactively] find out about the treatment to which the applicants would be exposed',[272] if denied a visa, permission to board a plane, or any other means to escape ill-treatment. The fact that the 'potential asylum seeker' may 'fail[] to expressly request asylum' would not exonerate the state in question 'from fulfilling *its obligations* under Article 3 [ECHR]'[273]—and it is worth recalling that the rights to leave and to protection from *refoulement* concern *everyone* without exception. The knowledge of such circumstance should, moreover, be imputed, where the 'situation [is] well-known and easy to verify on the basis of multiple sources'.[274]

Through the synergistic encounter between the two provisions, the non-derogability of *non-refoulement* would be understood to neutralize the limitable character of the right to leave in circumstances in which both intersect, as applied to refugees. The intersection would, then, give rise to a (*new*) particularised prohibition, enjoining contracting states (of departure, transit, or destination) from adopting measures—via territorial or extraterritorial action—that impede one's flight in the face of persecution or a real risk of irreversible harm. As a result, the current state of affairs, whereby *all* irregular migrants are indistinctly prevented from reaching European shores, whatever their rights and circumstances, without destination countries simultaneously putting in place concrete guarantees for those entitled to ECHR protection,[275] becomes incompatible with the Convention. The intersectional reading of the right to leave with the prohibition of *refoulement* generates a new (intersectional) 'right to flee' that engenders new (intersectional) obligations for state parties to fulfil. Ultimately, the key requirement would be that they re-design their pre-entry schemes in a way that allows them to respect and protect the 'right to flee', permitting 'persons who face persecution to submit an application for protection, based in particular on Article 3 of the Convention'.[276]

Denial of the right to leave can have particularly devastating effects when it ignores or compounds a real risk of irreversible harm from which a refugee is trying to escape. The accent, in this regard, should not be on discrimination or comparative disadvantage in relation to other persons, but on the specific justice

[271] *N.D. and N.T.* (n 6), para 180.
[272] *Hirsi Jamaa and others* (n 18), para 133.
[273] ibid, para 133 (emphasis added). See also para 157.
[274] ibid, para 131. See also paras 121 and 157.
[275] See eg UNHCR, 'As States Increase Border Controls, UNHCR Calls for Sensitivity for Those Fleeing Persecution' (7 January 2011) <https://www.unhcr.org/print/4d2713c19.html> (accessed 10 March 2020).
[276] *N.D. and N.T.* (n 6), para 209.

needs of (prospective) asylum claimants. If 'equal liberty', as a hybrid rationale, is to achieve its intended effects, the jus-generative force of interactions between related rights must be recognised. It is only the intersection between equality-based and freedom-based claims that may yield a complete vision of dignity and provide meaningful reparation. In the concrete situation of would-be asylum applicants, the sole recognition of a (limitable) right to leave *or* of an (inchoate) right to *non-refoulement* is not enough; neither is the sequencing of the right to leave *and* the protection against *refoulement* in compartmentalised fashion. In circumstances in which persons have no alternative but to flee situations of persecution and ill-treatment, the intersection between the two provisions requires an intersectional interpretation. They must apply jointly, cumulatively, and inter-actively to produce the intersectional entitlement to escape abuse and oppression.

Intersectionality holds the promise of an emancipatory reading of the Convention, but it requires a shift towards an understanding that apprehends facts and norms in their totality. The Strasbourg Court has the tools at its disposal to embrace this shift and provide for holistic justice, especially to those with nowhere else to go for redress and recognition of their most basic freedoms. The path is to develop the Court's findings in *Amuur*, *Hirsi*, and *M.S.S.* in systematic fashion, rendering explicit the 'right to flee' incipient in existing case law, in order for the specific positionings of claimants to duly translate into effective legal protection, particularly in extraterritorial situations. If it is true that ECHR rights apply 'even in the context of a migration crisis',[277] and that 'an increasing influx of migrants cannot absolve a State of its obligations under [Article 3 ECHR]',[278] then the 'access to rights' question needs to be reckoned with. Regarding refugees, this means that the full acknowledgement of the 'right to flee' becomes the necessary corollary to guarantee that 'States' legitimate concern to [control migration] [does] not deprive asylum-seekers of the protection afforded by the[] [C]onvention[]'.[279] Like the rest of claimants, they, too, are entitled to rights that are 'practical and effective' rather than 'theoretical or illusory'.[280]

This approach starts from the premise that judicial reasoning is not fixed or pre-determined; that Strasbourg judges enjoy a margin of discretion in their adjudicatory functions to promote the goals of certainty and predictability, serving the ends of substantive justice.[281] It provides them with a framework to deal with complex claims of claimants trapped in complex situations and invites them to consider the entire normative and factual constellations. Intersectionality

[277] *Khlaifia* (n 22), para 106.
[278] ibid, para 184. See also *M.S.S.* (n 23), para 223; and *Hirsi Jamaa and others* (n 18), paras 122 and 176.
[279] *Amuur* (n 17), para 43.
[280] *Artico* (n 97), para 33.
[281] Starting from a similar perspective, see Vaughan Lowe, 'The Politics of Law-Making: Are the Method and Character of Norm Creation Changing?' in Michael Byers (ed), *The Role of Law in International Politics: Essays in International Relations and International Law* (OUP 2000) 207.

as a technique of legal interpretation provides a more adequate template than discrimination-based or vulnerability-inspired reasoning that lends legitimacy to judicial conclusions. The broader significance of my whole-of-person/whole-of-legal-system proposal requires further investigation, to identify the limits of this approach and tease out the full methodological, substantive, and theoretical implications. For the time being, the intersectional 'right to flee' constitutes an example of how intersectionality can modulate legal thinking, establishing priorities and accommodations between competing understandings on the reconciliation of simultaneously applicable norms in a manner that advances the rights of refugees and the overarching aims of the Convention.

4

The *J.K.* Decalogue

A Paradigm Shift in Dealing with Asylum Cases in Strasbourg?

Ledi Bianku

1. Introduction

The productivity of the European Court of Human Rights (ECtHR or the Court) in asylum and migration matters has reached a very high level in recent years with several judgments and decisions delivered by the Grand Chamber[1] and a few more in the Grand Chamber's pipeline at the moment of writing.[2] The focus of the analysis of this chapter will be the judgment delivered on 23 August 2016 in the case of *J.K. and others v Sweden*,[3] and it will be examined from the perspective of the past and future case law of the ECtHR in asylum matters. While the author of this chapter was part of the Grand Chamber formation in the *J.K.* case, it is hoped that these additional views and considerations might contribute to the doctrinal debate on the Court's approach to asylum matters generally.

The case concerned three Iraqi nationals, J.K., his wife, and his son, who had sought asylum in Sweden. National administrative and judicial authorities had ordered their deportation to Iraq. Accepting that the general security situation in Iraq, per se, did not prevent the removal of J.K. and his wife and son, the Court had to assess whether their personal circumstances were such that they would face a real risk of treatment

[1] *F.G. v Sweden* [GC] App no 43611/11 (ECtHR, 23 March 2016); *Biao v Denmark* [GC] App no 38590/10 (ECtHR, 24 May 2016); *J.K. and others v Sweden* [GC] App no 59166/12 (ECtHR, 23 August 2016); *V.M. and others v Belgium* [GC] (Striking out) App no 60125/11 (ECtHR, 7 July 2016); *Khlaifia and others v Italy* [GC] App no 16483/12 (ECtHR, 15 December 2016); *Paposhvili v Belgium* [GC] App no 41738/10 (ECtHR, 13 December 2016); *Khan v Germany* [GC] (striking out) App no 38030/12 (ECtHR, 21 September 2016); *Harkins v United Kingdom* [GC] (dec) App no 71537/14 (ECtHR, 15 June 2017).

[2] *Ilias and Ahmed v Hungary* App no 47287/15 (ECtHR, 14 March 2017); *Z.A. and others v Russia* App nos 61411/15, 61420/15, 61427/15, and 3028/16 Grand Chamber hearing on 18 April 2018; *N.D. and N.T. v Spain* App nos 8675/15 and 8697/15, Grand Chamber hearing on 26 September 2018. The case of *M.N. and others v Belgium* App no 3599/18 was relinquished to the Grand Chamber on 26 November 2018 and the case of *Muhammad v Romania* was relinquished on 1 March 2019. See also *A.M. v France* App no 12148/18, heard before a Chamber on 22 January 2019.

[3] *J.K. and others* (n 1).

Ledi Bianku, *The* J.K. *Decalogue* In: *Migration and the European Convention on Human Rights.* Edited by: Başak Çali, Ledi Bianku, and Iulia Motoc, Oxford University Press (2021). © The Several Contributors.
DOI: 10.1093/oso/9780192895196.003.0004

contrary to Article 3 of the European Convention if expelled to Iraq. The facts of the case, and the claims brought by the applicants, appear to have much in common with most of the other asylum cases arriving on the desks of Strasbourg judges and lawyers. From this perspective one would have considered the case to be a 'routine' asylum case, where the outcome depends merely on the specific facts of the case and the way the national authorities have discharged their duty under the Convention in assessing the risk faced by the applicants if they were to be returned to their country of origin.

On 4 June 2015 a Chamber of the ECtHR held, by a majority, that the implementation of the deportation order in respect of the applicants would not give rise to a violation of Article 3. It seems that the disagreement within the Chamber on how to assess the particular facts of the case and the national authorities' handling of it provided sufficient grounds for the Grand Chamber Panel to send the case before the Grand Chamber.[4] The Grand Chamber reversed the Chamber judgment and by a majority of ten to seven decided that it would be a violation of Article 3 if the deportation order made against the applicants would be enforced. Such a split, both at the Chamber and at the Grand Chamber level, shows the difficulties and the differences of views amongst the Strasbourg judges in dealing with asylum cases.[5]

Hence, there is an obvious need to establish clear general principles applicable in asylum cases to help guide Strasbourg and national judges in dealing with them. As it will be explained below, unanimity was lacking even in relation to the general principles applied in asylum cases. In order to better analyse and understand the results of the Court's efforts in the *J.K.* judgment to provide general principles I will first recall how the Court has traditionally approached asylum cases in its case law (section 1), then expose and analyse the contribution of the *J.K.* judgment (section 2) and, at the end, try to offer some concluding remarks.

2. The Traditional Paradigm in Dealing with Asylum Cases in Strasbourg

2.1 Use of the Traditional Paradigm in the Strasbourg Court's Case Law

It is well known that, contrary to the Universal Declaration on Human Rights (UDHR)[6] and the 1951 Convention Relating to the Status of the Refugees,[7] the

[4] See the Chamber judgment of 4 June 2015, and, especially part II and III of the dissenting opinion of Judge Zupančič, with which Judge De Gaetano agrees.

[5] See as well *F.G.* (n 1); *Tarakhel v Switzerland* [GC] App no 29217/12 (ECtHR, 4 November 2014); *M.S.S. v Belgium* App no 30696/09 [GC] (ECtHR, 21 January 2011), none having been decided unanimously.

[6] Art 14 of the Universal Declaration on Human Rights provides: 'Everyone has the right to seek and to enjoy in other countries asylum from persecution', Universal Declaration of Human Rights (adopted 10 December 1948 UNGA Res 217 A(III)).

[7] The 1951 Geneva Convention as amended in 1967 provides:

European Convention of Human Rights (ECHR)[8] does not guarantee the right to obtain asylum or the right to migrate to another country.[9] Under such conditions, the construction of the Strasbourg Court's case law in asylum cases stems from the development of the notion of extraterritorial responsibility by the Court, under Article 1, combined with Articles 2 and 3 of the Convention. Starting with extradition cases under Article 3,[10] such an approach was logically extended quite soon thereafter to asylum cases as well.[11] In its *Cruz Varas and others v Sweden* judgment, the old Court in a Plenary formation found that a state was liable, under the Convention, in cases of expulsion to a third country in the same way as it is in cases of extradition, as found in *Soering*, to which the Court makes a clear reference. In *Cruz Varas* the old Court reasoned in the following terms as far as the applicability of Article 3 in expulsion cases is concerned:

> In its Soering judgment of 7 July 1989 the Court held that the decision by a Contracting State to extradite a fugitive may give rise to an issue under Article 3 (art. 3), and hence engage the responsibility of that State under the Convention, where substantial grounds have been shown for believing that the person concerned, if extradited, faces a real risk of being subjected to torture or to inhuman or degrading treatment or punishment in the requesting country. Although the establishment of such responsibility involves an assessment of conditions in the requesting country against the standards of Article 3 (art. 3), there is no question of adjudicating on or establishing the responsibility of the receiving country, whether under general international law, under the Convention or otherwise. In so far as any liability under the Convention is or may be incurred, it is liability incurred by the extraditing Contracting State by reason of its having taken action which has as a direct consequence the exposure of an individual to proscribed ill-treatment.

> A person who owing to a well-founded fear of being persecuted for reasons of race, religion, nationality, membership of a particular social group or political opinion, is outside the country of his nationality and is unable or, owing to such fear, is unwilling to avail himself of the protection of that country; or who, not having a nationality and being outside the country of his former habitual residence as a result of such events, is unable or, owing to such fear, is unwilling to return to it.

Art 1, A para 2 Convention Relating to the Status of Refugees (adopted 28 July 1951, entered into force 22 April 1954) 189 UNTS 137. Compare as well with Art 22 para 7 of the American Convention on Human Rights (adopted 22 November 1969, entered into force 18 July 1978) 1144 UNTS 123.

[8] Convention for the Protection of Human Rights and Fundamental Freedoms (European Convention on Human Rights, as amended) ETS 5.

[9] See *Vilvarajah and others v United Kingdom* App nos 13163/87, 13164/87, 13165/87, 13447/87, and 13448/87 (ECtHR, 30 October 1991), para 102.

[10] *Soering v United Kingdom* App no 14038/88 (ECtHR, 7 July 1989), paras 90–91.

[11] See *Cruz Varas and others v Sweden* App no 15576/89 (ECtHR, 20 March 1991), paras 69–70; *Vilvarajah and others* (n 9), para 103; *Chahal v United Kingdom* App no 22414/93 (ECtHR, 15 November 1996), para 74. In the latter case the British Government argued in favour of revisiting this principle but accepted its application in their pleadings before the Court.

> Although the present case concerns expulsion as opposed to a decision to extradite, the Court considers that the above principle also applies to expulsion decisions and a fortiori to cases of actual expulsion.[12]

Such protection, by ricochet, has since become the judicial tool used by the Court in all asylum related cases, due to the lack of the right to political asylum under the Convention.[13] The traditional approach adopted by the Court in asylum and migration cases has been to recognise, first, the lack of a right to asylum under the Convention, and then secondly to recall the absolute character of Article 3 of the Convention. Such an approach is easily visible in the Court's asylum and migration cases. For instance, in *Hirsi Jamaa and others v Italy* the Court first says that:

> According to the Court's established case-law, Contracting States have the right, as a matter of well-established international law and subject to their treaty obligations, including the Convention, to control the entry, residence and expulsion of aliens ... The Court also notes that the right to political asylum is not contained in either the Convention or its Protocols.[14]

After setting out this as the starting premise, in the subsequent paragraphs of the same judgment, the Court continues:

> However, expulsion, extradition or any other measure to remove an alien may give rise to an issue under Article 3 of the Convention, and hence engage the responsibility of the expelling State under the Convention, where substantial grounds have been shown for believing that the person in question, if expelled, would face a real risk of being subjected to treatment contrary to Article 3 in the receiving country. In such circumstances, Article 3 implies an obligation not to expel the individual to that country *(see Soering, §§ 90–91; Vilvarajah and Others, § 103; Ahmed, § 39; H.L.R. v. France, 29.04. 1997, § 34; Jabari v. Turkey, no. 40035/98, § 38; and Salah Sheekh v. the Netherlands, no. 1948/04, § 135, 11.01.2007).*
>
> In this type of case, the Court is therefore called upon to assess the situation in the receiving country in the light of the requirements of Article 3. In so far as any liability under the Convention is or may be incurred, it is liability incurred by the Contracting State by reason of its having taken action which has as a direct consequence the exposure of an individual to the risk of proscribed ill-treatment (see *Saadi v Italy* [GC], no 37201/06, § 126, ECHR 2008).[15]

[12] *Cruz-Varas* (n 11), paras 69–70, citing *Soering* (n 10), para 91.

[13] See Nuala Mole and Catherine Meredith, *Asylum and the European Convention on Human Rights*, Human Rights Files no 9 (Council of Europe Publishing 2003) 19ff.

[14] *Hirsi Jamaa and others v Italy* [GC] App no 27765/09 (ECtHR, 23 February 2012), para 113.

[15] ibid, paras 114–15. The same paradigm *Tarakhel* (n 5), para 93; *J.K. and others* (n 1) para 79.

This two-step process in setting out the general principles in asylum cases has been consistent in migration cases since 1985.[16] Initially this approach was used only in migration cases dealt with under Article 8 of the Convention, where the Court was required to conduct a proportionality analysis to consider whether the state's decision to remove the applicant was in violation of the Convention. It must be underlined that in *Cruz Varas* the Court, very curiously, did not use this two-step approach, and no reference is made to the right of states, as a matter of well-established international law and subject to their treaty obligations, including the Convention, to control the entry, residence, and expulsion of aliens. This formulation is to be found for the first time in asylum cases, properly speaking, in 1991[17] and continued with very minor drafting variations until 2016.[18] Such a structure in the Strasbourg Court's approach in asylum cases recognises the right of states to control the entry, residence, and expulsion of aliens as the principle. This principle is considered by the Court's consistent case law as a right based on well-established international law. Then, the human rights obligations, including those under the Convention, are viewed as a caveat, as an exception to the right of states to decide on the fate of asylum seekers, only when certain criteria applicable under articles 2, 3, or 8 of the Convention are met.

2.2 Doctrinal Foundations of the Traditional Approach

The approach adopted by the Court in asylum cases, especially the starting point, finds support in international conventions[19] and in the doctrine of international law over time.[20] The works of Chetail, in particular, shows international legal doctrine has become sovereignty regarding over time in the field of migration, tracing

[16] See *Abdulaziz v United Kingdom* App nos 9214/80, 9473/81, and 9474/81 (ECtHR, 28 May 1985), para 67; and *Berrehab v the Netherlands* App no 10730/84 (ECtHR, 21 June 1988), paras 28–29, where this basic premise was clearly set out in relation to migration examined under Art 8 of the Convention.

[17] The paradigm was also adopted in the asylum cases starting from the above-mentioned *Moustaquim v Belgium* App no 12313/86 (ECtHR, 18 February 1991), para 43, and more clearly in *Vilvarajah and others* (n 9), paras 102–03.

[18] See as the latest GC judgment on these terms *F.G.* (n 1), para 111 and *Paposhvili* (n 1), paras 172–74.

[19] Art 1 para 1 of the 1967 Declaration on Territorial Asylum provides that 'Asylum granted by a State, in the exercise of its sovereignty, to persons entitled to invoke art 14 of the UDHR, including persons struggling against colonialism, shall be respected by all other States.' Para 3 of the same art continues: 'It shall rest with the State granting asylum to evaluate the grounds for the grant of asylum.' UNGA Res 2312 (14 December 1967) UN Doc A/RES/2312(XXII).

[20] See James Crawford, *Brownlie's Principles of Public International Law* (8th edn, OUP 2012) 632, where Judge Crawford asserts that: 'In principle, this is a matter of domestic jurisdiction: a state may choose not to admit aliens or may impose conditions on their admission.' In the French doctrine see Jean Combacau and Serge Sur, *Droit International Public* (8th edn, LGDJ 2018) 370, where it states that 'Dans l'ensemble, le droit international général ne limite qu'a peine, sous réserve bien sûr de conventions contraires, le pouvoir qu'a l'État d'aménager l'entrée, le séjour et la sortie des personnes.'

developments from Vitoria and Vatel.[21] He recalls that Samuel von Pufendorf and Christian von Wolff maintained that controlling the entry of foreigners into a state's territory is as an absolute sovereign right of states. They starkly depart from the earlier positions of Vitoria and Grotius which will be recalled briefly in the second part of this chapter. Chetail quotes Pufendorf as saying:

> [I]t is left in the power of all states, to take such measures about the admission of strangers, as they think convenient; those being ever excepted, who are driven on the coasts by necessity, or by any cause that deserves pity and compassion.[22]

By completely reversing the debate that existed until then, Pufendorf considers sovereignty as the principle and hospitality as an exception. Wolff, too, with his theory of the patrimonial state, retained absolute discretion to establish the reasons for refusing admission of foreigners into territory. This absolute discretion could be nuanced by the need to accept foreigners for special reasons, but the decision remains with each sovereign state.[23]

It would be natural to think that the first and strongest reason for Strasbourg's regard for sovereignty is the fact that the right to asylum or to migrate are not protected as such by the Convention. But one might also think that such doctrinal understanding, based on a long standing Westphalian concept of states rights and obligations, has significantly influenced the way the Convention was drafted in relation to the right to asylum and also the two-step paradigm in the Strasbourg's Court approach to asylum cases. This puts the Court in a delicate situation where it must recall the legislative setting, because it is correct and must do so in order to elucidate the legal basis and legal principles upon which is asked to decide.

3. *J.K.*—A New Paradigm?

3.1 The Decalogue of General Principles Established in the *J.K.* Judgment

The above case law referred to above forms the context in which the *J.K.* Grand Chamber judgment intervened. As mentioned previously, it might be considered as a 'routine' asylum case. However, the Grand Chamber seized the opportunity to establish a comprehensive set of general principles to be applied in prospective asylum cases.

[21] Vincent Chetail, 'Sovereignty and Migration in the Doctrine of the Law of Nations: An Intellectual History of Hospitality from Vitoria to Vattel' (2016) 27(4) European Journal of International Law 901.

[22] ibid, 910.

[23] ibid.

The judgment sets out ten general principles to be applied in asylum cases. A listing of them all seems to me necessary in order to assist the analysis that will follow. The principles are:

(a) General nature of obligations under Article 3;
(b) Principle of *non-refoulement*;
(c) General principles concerning the application of Article 3 in expulsion cases;
(d) Risk of ill-treatment by private groups;
(e) Principle of *ex nunc* evaluation of the circumstances;
(f) Principle of subsidiarity;
(g) Assessment of the existence of a real risk;
(h) Distribution of the burden of proof;
(i) Past ill-treatment as an indication of risk;
(j) Membership of a targeted group.

These ten general principles do not include any innovative principle discovered or elaborated anew by the Court. All the above principles had been elaborated in earlier judgments of the Court and consistently used in many Chamber and Grand Chamber cases. The Court establishes this list by rightly quoting the earlier judgments where each of those principles had been established or recalled. Thus, the Court recalls first the general nature of obligations under Article 3 by recalling the *Labita* judgment[24] with references to the earlier cases therein.[25] Second, it continues with the principle of *non-refoulement* and the importance of this concept in asylum cases by citing *M.S.S. v Belgium*,[26] *M.A. v Cyprus*,[27] and other judgments or decisions.[28] Third, and only third, the Court recalls the general principles concerning the application of Article 3 in expulsion cases, by quoting at length paragraphs from the judgments in *Saadi v Italy* and *F.G. v Sweden*, paragraphs which are almost identical to the excerpt from the *Hirsi Jamaa* judgment which is quoted above. The list is completed with seven other general principles which all stem from the Court's previous case law, most having been recalled only five months earlier by the Grand Chamber in the case of *F.G.*[29] One might then ask why all this fuss about so little?

[24] *Labita v Italy* [GC] App no 26772/95 (ECtHR, 6 April 2000), para 119.

[25] *J.K. and others* (n 1), para 77.

[26] *M.S.S.* (n 5), para 286.

[27] *M.A. v Cyprus* App no 41872/10 (ECtHR, 23 July 2013), para 133 (extracts).

[28] *Müslim v Turkey* App no 53566/99 (ECtHR, 26 April 2005), paras 7276; *T.I. v United Kingdom* (dec) App no 43844/98 (ECtHR, 7 March 2000).

[29] Besides the general principles concerning the application of Art 3 in expulsion cases in para 79, the judgment in *F.G. v Sweden* (n 1) had recalled other principles included in the *J.K.* list such as point (e), on the principle of *ex nunc* evaluation of the circumstances, in para 83, point (f), on principle of subsidiarity, in para 84, point (g), on the assessment of the existence of a real risk, in paras 86, 87, and 90, and point (h), on the distribution of the burden of proof (F.G.), on paras 91 and 93.

The *J.K.* judgment is the first to offer what seems to be a wide-ranging and structured list of principles to be applied in asylum cases. This has been clearly recognised by the Grand Chamber's judgment,[30] some of the dissenting opinions,[31] as well as the legal commentary on the judgment[32]. As Judge O'Leary explains in her concurring opinion, the *J.K.* judgment '... systematizes some of the general principles to be applied by domestic authorities in Article 3 cases'.[33] The judgment dedicates an unprecedented length to setting out a set of general principles which for the most part reiterate, consolidate, and put in order principles already referred to by the Court in previous asylum-related judgments. It is indeed rare, if not unique, to see a judgment of the Court displaying the general principles relevant to a case across almost ten pages.

The Grand Chamber was split ten to seven in this judgment. It is quite evident from the concurring and the dissenting opinions that there is no agreement, not only as to the application of the principles on the concrete circumstances of the case, but also with regard to the identification and establishment of these principles by the majority of the Grand Chamber. While Judge O'Leary, part of the majority, welcomes this systematisation of some general principles, she raises doubts particularly as to the *ex nunc* assessment that the Court engages in in such cases.[34] In his strongly worded dissenting opinion, Judge Ranzoni expresses substantial disagreements with the Grand Chamber majority particularly as far as the identification of the general principles is concerned.[35] Judge Ranzoni's critique of these general principles starts by relativising and limiting their impact when he says that 'these principles are of significance for me when considering the present case and assessing the majority's reasoning'.[36] Then he criticises the way the majority has operated in elaborating these principles by declaring:

> At first sight, it does not seem clear whether the intention is to reflect the principles laid down in the existing case-law or whether new principles are to be established. A thorough assessment of the different criteria and their application later in the judgment makes it plain that the majority have established new principles in this crucial paragraph 102 without providing sufficient reasoning.[37]

Judge Ranzoni at the end of his opinion concludes that:

30 See paras 77–105 of the judgment.
31 Para 2 of the concurring opinion of Judge Bianku, para 3, and especially para 8 of the concurring opinion of Judge O'Leary, and paras 1, 2, and especially 5 of the dissenting opinion of Judge Ranzoni.
32 See for instance Gloria Fernández Arribas 'A European Court of Human Rights' Systematization of Principles Applicable to Expulsion Cases' (2017) 2(3) European Papers: European Forum, Insight 977.
33 At para 8 of the concurring opinion of Judge O'Leary.
34 ibid.
35 At para 5 of the dissenting opinion of Judge Ranzoni.
36 ibid, para 2.
37 ibid, para 4.

> These new general principles are my main concern. First, their development is not explained in the judgment. Secondly, they are in my view an unbalanced and fragmentary mixture of existing case-law and other international sources; they are not clear enough and not persuasive and are therefore not suitable for giving helpful guidance either to the domestic authorities in their difficult task of assessing asylum cases or to the Court itself when it is called upon, pursuant to Article 3, to make its own assessment. Thirdly, under the title 'Past ill-treatment as an indication of risk' these principles mix different elements like the burden of proof, credibility and the consequences of past ill-treatment in an incoherent and, at least for me, unsatisfactory manner. Fourthly, taking into account the existing case-law, the establishment of new principles is not necessary.[38]

One might agree or not on the novelty of these principles, on their consistency, clarity, and usefulness for the Court and national judges in dealing with asylum cases. What I want to stress, however, is a second novelty of the *J.K.* judgment and, to my mind, the most important feature of this new list, which is the ordering of the principles included therein. It has to be noted that this list starts by recalling the general nature of obligations under Article 3 of the Convention. The Court in *J.K.*, therefore, beings its recollection of general principles by evoking a principle which always comes first in Article 3 cases not related to expulsion, which is the absolute character of Article 3. This way of setting out the general principles—to start with the general nature of Article 3 is an absolute novelty in an expulsion case. One might, for example, recall that in the *Chahal* judgment[39] there is a clear reference to the general nature of obligations under Article 3, but this principle is recalled in paragraph 79 of that judgment, only after the principle that states have the right to control the entry, residence, and expulsion of aliens had been recalled clearly in the earlier paragraphs of the judgment.[40] In all other asylum-related cases, any statement with regard to the general nature of the obligations under Article 3 of the Convention comes after the principle that states as a matter of well-established international law and subject to their treaty obligations, including the Convention, have the right to control the entry, residence, and expulsion of aliens. As explained in section 2 of this chapter, this has been the established paradigm since one of the first judgments the Court delivered on an expulsion case, *Vilvarajah and others*,[41] until the very last Grand Chamber judgment delivered only five months earlier, in the case of *F.G.*[42] In *J.K.*, the absolute nature of the obligations under Article 3 finds its ordinary place as the starting point of all analysis under that article in the

[38] ibid, para 5.
[39] *Chahal* (n 11).
[40] ibid, paras 73 and 74.
[41] *Vilvarajah and others* (n 9), para 102.
[42] *F.G.* (n 1), para 111.

cases brought before the Court. What has changed with *J.K.*? Did the Court become aware of a need for such a change?

It seems that with the *J.K.* judgment the Court has decided to move away from its asylum exceptionality analysis under Article 3 and to shift the paradigm by considering asylum cases in the same way it analyses all other cases dealt with under Article 3 of the Convention, which is by recalling first the absolute character of that article and then by dealing with other elements such as burden of proof, threshold, etc.

3.2 Doctrinal Foundations of the New Approach

In his above-mentioned article Chetail recalls that Francisco de Vitoria and Hugo Grotius—commonly referred to as the founding fathers of international law—quite clearly pleaded in favour of migration, considering it as a 'rule of international law through the right of communication between peoples'.[43] Vitoria started his analysis from the premise of hospitality, which he considered to be a principle of international law grounded in the natural sociability of human beings.[44] Vitoria even maintained that hospitality is a truly universal rule binding all nations. Further, Chetail explains that Grotius 'not only endorsed the view of Vitoria, but he also refined and enriched the principle of free movement by delineating its key components: the right to leave one's own country and the right to remain in a foreign country, as the two sides of the same coin'.[45] Chetail quotes Grotius as saying that 'a fixed abode ought not to be refused to strangers, who being expelled from own country, seek a retreat elsewhere: provided they submit to the laws of the state, and refrain from everything that might give occasion to sedition'.[46] Whereas the earlier part of this quotation seems to have been an early inspiration for Article 1 of the 1951 Geneva Convention the latter part shows that Grotius, as well as de Vitoria,

[43] Chetail (n 21) 902.

[44] ibid, 904.

[45] ibid, 907. One might recall at this point Art 13 para 2 of the Universal Declaration of Human Rights (n 6) which provides that 'Everyone has the right to leave any country, including his own, and to return to his country.' Art 12.2 of the International Covenant on Civil and Political Rights (ICCPR) which provides that 'Everyone shall be free to leave any country, including his own.' International Covenant on Civil and Political Rights (adopted 16 December 1966, entered into force 23 March 1976) 999 UNTS 17. And the UN Human Rights Committee, 'CCPR General Comment No 27 Article 12 (Freedom of Movement)' (1999) UN Doc CCPR/C/21/Rev1/Add.9. On the other side, Art 2 para 2 of the Protocol 4 of the ECHR provides that: 'Everyone shall be free to leave any country, including his own.' Art 2.3 continues: 'No restrictions shall be placed on the exercise of these rights other than such as are in accordance with law and are necessary in a democratic society in the interests of national security or public safety, for the maintenance of *ordre public*, for the prevention of crime, for the protection of health or morals, or for the protection of the rights and freedoms of others.' Protocol 4 to the Convention for the Protection of Human Rights and Fundamental Freedoms, securing certain rights and freedoms other than those already included in the Convention and in the first Protocol thereto ETS 46.

[46] See Chetail (n 21) 909, quoting Hugo Grotius, *The Rights of War and Peace* (R Tuck edn, Book II, Liberty Fund 2005) 447, para xvi.

accepted that there should be exceptions to the right to enter a foreign country when the persons benefiting from such a right conduct themselves in ways that are harmful or detrimental to the host country.[47] The reasons Grotius and Vitoria advance for justifying exceptions to the right to enter and to remain in another country sound quite related to the formulation of Article 1, F of the 1951 Geneva Convention.[48] These are the theoretical sources of international law which could be logically seen as the early foundations of the regime of international protection for refugees and which find their articulated expression in the 1951 Geneva Convention.[49]

Chetail, in his article, continues with an analysis of the position of the prominent Swiss diplomat and lawyer Emer de Vattel. Vattel tries to combine the two above-described opposing approaches by declaring that 'necessity prevails over sovereignty if, and only if, irregular entry is the only way to safeguard an essential interest of the foreigner'.[50]

Chetail explains very well the context and the possible sources of inspiration for all the above approaches. What is interesting for the purposes of this chapter is the conclusion drawn by Chetail that the starting premise of many national jurisdictions[51] and international law doctrine[52] is a 'conventional wisdom ... grounded

[47] Chetail (n 31) 905 referring to Vitoria.

[48] Art 1, F of the 1951 Geneva Convention (n 7) provides that:

> The provisions of this Convention shall not apply to any person with respect to whom there are serious reasons for considering that: (a) he has committed a crime against peace, a war crime, or a crime against humanity, as defined in the international instruments drawn up to make provision in respect of such crimes; (b) he has committed a serious non-political crime outside the country of refuge prior to his admission to that country as a refugee; (c) he has been guilty of acts contrary to the purposes and principles of the United Nations.

Whereas Art 2, entitled 'General obligations', provides that 'every refugee has duties to the country in which he finds himself, which require in particular that he conform to its laws and regulations as well as to measures taken for the maintenance of public order'.

[49] See again in this regard Vincent Chetail, 'Théorie et pratique de l'asile en droit international classique: étude sur les origines conceptuelles et normatives du droit international des réfugiés' (2011) 115(3) Revue générale de droit international public 625.

[50] ibid, 921.

[51] *Ekiu v United States* 142 US 651 (1892), where the US Supreme Court, referring to Vattel, held in 1892 that 'It is an accepted maxim of international law, that every sovereign nation has the power, as inherent in sovereignty, and essential to its self-preservation, to forbid the entrance of foreigners within its dominions, or to admit them only in such cases and upon such conditions as it may see fit to prescribe. *Attorney-General for Canada v Cain* [1906] AC 542, 546; *House of Lords European Roma Rights Centre and others v Immigration Officer at Prague Airport* [2004] *UKHL* 55, para 11, in which the Lord Bingham, delivering the main judgment used the following expression: 'like most international conventions, [the Geneva Convention] represented a compromise between competing interests, in this case between the need to ensure humane treatment of the victims of oppression on the one hand and the wish of sovereign states to maintain control over those seeking entry to their territory on the other'. See also *Z.H. (Tanzania) (F.C.) (Appellant) v Secretary of State for the Home Department (Respondent)* [2011] UKSC 4, para 18, Lady Hale. Once again, the starting point is the right of all states to control the entry and residence of aliens.

[52] Chetail refers to Crawford (n 30) 608; Malcolm Shaw, *International Law* (6th edn, Cambridge University Press 2008) 826; Robert Jennings and Arthur Watts (eds), *Oppenheim's International Law*, vol 1 (9th edn, OUP 2008) 897–98.

on false premises for both historical and normative reasons. Indeed, assuming the power to exclude aliens as the earliest prerogative of the state is highly disputable.'[53]

What is especially interesting for our debate is that the conclusion made by Chetail raises the important question as to whether the initial paradigm used by the ECHR to deal with asylum and migration cases is based on a false premise, or, to say the least, on a selective reading of international law doctrine?[54] Of course, in addition to the doctrinal approaches, a court that is called to apply the law in concrete cases also has to take into account, and to a considerable extent, the practice of states in international relations in that regard.[55] It has to be accepted that especially during the twentieth century, the right to control the entry, residence, and removal of foreigners has been considered as the prerogative of many states, if not all. Nevertheless, the question is whether the *J.K.* judgment with its new decalogue of general principles—what I consider an overturning of the traditional paradigm—was established, in turn, on solid ground.

In this point, Professor Goodwin-Gill, a worldwide authority on the subject, makes a reference to Article 1 of the 1967 UN Declaration on Territorial Asylum[56] which notes that 'Asylum granted by a state, in the exercise of its sovereignty, to persons entitled to invoke Article 14 of the Universal Declaration of Human Rights ... shall be respected by all other States.' But it is for 'the State granting asylum to evaluate the grounds for the grant of asylum'.[57]

[53] Chetail (n 31) 922.

[54] Chetail goes further in his article when he says that 'Among the domestic courts of common law countries, this assertion has even become a maxim without any further inquiry into its rationale and justification' and then refers to a series of judgments delivered by national courts, ibid, 902.

[55] The Statute of the ICJ, in its well-known Art 38, identifies following sources:

a) Treaties between States;
b) Customary international law derived from the practice of States;
c) General principles of law recognized by civilised nations; and, as subsidiary means for the determination of rules of international law:
d) Judicial decisions and the writings of 'the most highly qualified publicists of the various nations, as subsidiary means for the determination of rules of law'.

See also *Case concerning military and paramilitary activities in and against Nicaragua (Nicaragua v United States of America)* (Merits) [1986] ICJ Rep 14 where the ICJ says that:

> The Court does not consider that, for a rule to be established as customary, the corresponding practice must be in absolutely rigorous conformity with the rule. In order to deduce the existence of customary rules, the Court deems it sufficient that the conduct of States should, in general, be consistent with such rules, and that instances of State conduct inconsistent with a given rule should generally have been treated as breaches of that rule, not as indications of the recognition of a new rule.

[56] Declaration on Territorial Asylum (n 29).

[57] Guy Goodwin-Gill, 'Introduction to the 1967 United Nations Declaration on Territorial Asylum' (2012) UN Audio-Visual Library of International Law, Historic Archives <http://www.un.org/law/avl/> accessed 11 November 2019.

4. Which Is the Correct Paradigm in Asylum Cases under the Convention?

Asylum seekers come to Strasbourg with allegations that typically fall under Articles 2 and 3 of the Convention which contain absolute and non-derogable rights under the Convention.[58] The absolute nature and fundamental character of the rights claimed mostly by asylum seekers has been clearly and repeatedly recognised by the Court since its early judgments on asylum cases.[59] In addition, and *a fortiori*, the Court had to reject allegations that Article 3, in the asylum context, does not have an absolute character and instead has implied limitations. In that regard, the Court clearly dismissed such a perspective advanced by the British Government in the case of *Chahal*,[60] where it gave a clear answer to the issue in view of the debate between the British Government, the former European Commission on Human Rights, and the Court.[61] The Court cogently states that:

> Article 3 (art. 3) enshrines one of the most fundamental values of democratic society (see the above-mentioned Soering judgment, p. 34, para. 88). The Court is well aware of the immense difficulties faced by States in modern times in protecting their communities from terrorist violence. However, even in these

[58] See from *Ireland v United Kingdom* App no 5310/71 (ECtHR, 18 January 1978), para 163 where the Court says that:

> The Convention prohibits in absolute terms torture and inhuman or degrading treatment or punishment, irrespective of the victim's conduct. Unlike most of the substantive clauses of the Convention and of Protocols Nos. 1 and 4 (P1, P4), Article 3 (art. 3) makes no provision for exceptions and, under Article 15 para. 2 (art. 15-2), there can be no derogation therefrom even in the event of a public emergency threatening the life of the nation.

See as well *Soering* (n 10), para 88; *Labita* (n 39), para 119; and *Svinarenko v Russia* [GC] App nos 32541/08 and 43441/08 (ECtHR, 17 July 2014), para 113 (extracts); *Muršić v Croatia* [GC] App no 7334/13 (ECtHR, 20 October 2016), para 96. See also David Harris, Colin Warbrick, and Michael O'Boyle, *Law of the European Convention on Human Rights* (3rd edn, OUP 2014) 235–36.

[59] Starting with *Vilvarajah and others* (n 9). See also *Selmouni v France* [GC] App no 25803/94 (ECtHR, 28 July 1999), para 95; *Salah Sheekh v the Netherlands* App no 1948/04 (ECtHR, 11 January 2007), para 135 and more recently *FG* (n 1), para 127. See as well UNHCR, 'Note on International Protection' (13 September 2001) A/AC.96/951, para 16.

[60] *Chahal* (n 11).

[61] ibid, see especially paras 76 and 78–80. In that case the British Government alleged that:

> [T]he guarantees afforded by Article 3 (art. 3) were not absolute in cases where a Contracting State proposed to remove an individual from its territory. Instead, in such cases, which required an uncertain prediction of future events in the receiving State, various factors should be taken into account, including the danger posed by the person in question to the security of the host nation. Thus, there was an implied limitation to Article 3 (art. 3) entitling a Contracting State to expel an individual to a receiving State even where a real risk of ill-treatment existed, if such removal was required on national security grounds. The Government based this submission in the first place on the possibility of implied limitations as recognised in the Court's case-law, particularly paras 88 and 89 of its above-mentioned Soering judgment. In support, they furthermore referred to the principle under international law that the right of an alien to asylum is subject to qualifications, as is provided for, inter alia, by Articles 32 and 33 of the United Nations 1951 Convention on the Status of Refugees.

> circumstances, the Convention prohibits in absolute terms torture or inhuman or degrading treatment or punishment, irrespective of the victim's conduct. ....
>
> ... The prohibition provided by Article 3 (art. 3) against ill-treatment is equally absolute in expulsion cases. Thus, whenever substantial grounds have been shown for believing that an individual would face a real risk of being subjected to treatment contrary to Article 3 (art. 3) if removed to another State, the responsibility of the Contracting State to safeguard him or her against such treatment is engaged in the event of expulsion (see the above-mentioned Vilvarajah and Others judgment, p. 34, para. 103). In these circumstances, the activities of the individual in question, however undesirable or dangerous, cannot be a material consideration. The protection afforded by Article 3 (art. 3) is thus wider than that provided by Articles 32 and 33 of the United Nations 1951 Convention on the Status of Refugees (see paragraph 61 above).[62]

It is frequently observed that the Convention system has become one of the most effective systems for the protection of asylum seekers' and migrants' rights, even if compared with dedicated systems such as the 1951 Geneva Convention.[63] But, it is important to underline that this protection to asylum seekers is offered through the extra-territorial operation of Articles 2, 3, or 8 of the Convention and the evolutive interpretation[64] of the Convention protection under those articles. The Court manages to efficiently protect the rights of asylum seekers and migrants, but only indirectly. It has continuously done so under a 'however', which follows from the starting point—the right of states to regulate entry, stay, and removal of aliens from their territories.

Another reason for continually emphasising the state's right to regulate migration into its territory might be to avoid the risk that the Court be called an 'asylum court',[65] which may make it difficult to increase support and legitimacy for the Court in the middle of a migration crisis in Europe.[66] Furthermore, for a Court that

[62] ibid, paras 79–80.

[63] See Mole and Meredith (n 14) 249.

[64] See *Tyrer v United Kingdom*, App no 5856/72 (ECtHR, 25 April 1978) and especially in the subject matter of our interest *Soering* (n 10), para 104, or *Paposhvili* (n 1), para 182, as to the effective protection of asylum seekers rights.

[65] See for example the President of the Belgian Constitutional Court, Marc Bossuyt, 'The Court of Strasbourg Acting as an Asylum Court' (2012) 8(2) European Constitutional Law Review 203. See from the same author *Strasbourg et les demandeurs d'asile: des juges sur un terrain glissant* (Bruylant 2010) 189.

[66] The message is clearly given by the Court in the landmark judgment *MSS* (n 5), and the concurring opinion of Judge Rozakis to that judgment. See the Annual Reports on the Situation of Asylum in the European Union prepared by the European Asylum Support Office. See European Parliament, 'Migration and Asylum: A Challenge for Europe' (2018) PE 600.414. See also Stefano Zirulia and Steve Peers 'A template for protecting human rights during the "refugee crisis"? Immigration detention and the expulsion of migrants in a recent ECtHR Grand Chamber ruling' (*EU Law* Analysis, 5 January 2017) <eulawanalysis.blogspot.com/2017/01/a-template-for-protecting-human-rights.html> accessed 28 February 2018.

has consistently affirmed that the application of the Convention is principally territorial,[67] it might seem logical to argue that the protection given to asylum seekers under Article 3 of the Convention is not construed in the same way, and might not follow the same principles and tests as the other Article 3 cases, where the alleged violation has taken place in the territory of the member states to the Convention.[68]

It seems the Court considers this basic premise so important that in each and every asylum or migration case it starts its legal analysis by recalling it. One might notice a manifest difference with other Article 3-related cases, such as, for example, detention conditions cases. It appears that in all such cases, the Court does not consider it necessary to proclaim or to recall, under the general principles, for instance, that states have the right to determine their penal policies and to sentence and imprison the criminals.[69] Or this statement appears too evident that the Court does not need to restate it? Does this mean in turn that the one mentioned in paragraph

[67] In *Banković v Belgium and other 16 States* [GC] App no 52207/99 (ECtHR, 12 December 2001), paras 59 and 61 the Court said that 'the jurisdictional competence of a State is primarily territorial' and that 'Article 1 of the Convention must be considered to reflect this ordinary and essentially territorial notion of jurisdiction, other bases of jurisdiction being exceptional and requiring special justification in the particular circumstances of each case.' In *Soering* (n 10), para 86 the Court noted that:

> Article 1 (art. 1) of the Convention, which provides that 'the High Contracting Parties shall secure to everyone within their jurisdiction the rights and freedoms defined in Section I', sets a limit, notably territorial, on the reach of the Convention. In particular, the engagement undertaken by a Contracting State is confined to 'securing' ['*reconnaître*' in the French text] the listed rights and freedoms to persons within its own 'jurisdiction'. Further, the Convention does not govern the actions of States not Parties to it, nor does it purport to be a means of requiring the Contracting States to impose Convention standards on other States. Article 1 (art. 1) cannot be read as justifying a general principle to the effect that, notwithstanding its extradition obligations, a Contracting State may not surrender an individual unless satisfied that the conditions awaiting him in the country of destination are in full accord with each of the safeguards of the Convention. Indeed, as the United Kingdom Government stressed, the beneficial purpose of extradition in preventing fugitive offenders from evading justice cannot be ignored in determining the scope of application of the Convention and of Article 3 (art. 3) in particular.

See also Sarah Miller, 'Revisiting Extraterritorial Jurisdiction: A Territorial Justification for Extraterritorial Jurisdiction under the European Convention' (2010) 20(4) European Journal of International Law; and Lord Dyson, 'The extraterritorial application of the European Convention on Human Rights: now on a firmer footing, but is it a sound one?' (Speech at Essex University 30 January 2014) <https://www.judiciary.uk/wp-content/uploads/JCO/Documents/Speeches/lord-dyson-speech-extraterritorial-reach-echr-300114.pdf> accessed 16 March 2019.

[68] See *Bouyid v Belgium* [GC] App no 23380/09 (ECtHR, 28 September 2015) and especially the dissenting opinion of Judges De Gaetano, Lemmens, and Mahoney, who in para 7 of their opinion argue that '... we should avoid trivialising findings of a violation of Article 3. The situation complained of in the present case is far less serious than the treatment inflicted by law-enforcement officers in many other cases that the Court has unfortunately had to deal with. What impact, then, does a finding of a violation of Article 3 still have?'. They continue with the clarification of this issue in footnote [2] by interestingly stating 'A question that has not been discussed in the present case but will no doubt arise in the future is whether the strict standard set by the majority should now also be applied in cases concerning the extradition or expulsion of aliens. Would Article 3 stand in the way of the extradition or deportation of an alien to a country where he or she is at risk of being slapped (once)?'

[69] See for example *Muršić* (n 75), para 96; *Labita* (n 39), para 119; *Svinarenko* (n 75), para 113 (extracts) etc. Compare however with the approach under Art 7 in *Del Río Prada v Spain* [GC] App no 42750/09 (ECtHR, 21 October 2013), paras 84, 117; *Kafkaris v Cyprus* [GC] App no 21906/04 (ECtHR, 12 February 2008), para 151 etc.

113 of the *Hirsi Jamaa* judgment, recalling the rights of states to control the entry, residence, and removal of foreigners, is not so evident that the Court finds it appropriate to remind itself and the readers that it is the starting point of its analysis?

In addition, it has to be recalled that the almost three-decade-old paradigm in asylum cases in Strasbourg has had a peculiar journey. The principle that states as a matter of well-established international law and subject to their treaty obligations, including the Convention, have the right to control the entry, residence, and expulsion of aliens, was first embraced in the case law of the Court in Article 8-related cases. More importantly, in those early cases this principle was recalled in the framework of the 'necessary in a democratic society' question as part of a proportionality analysis. Thus, for example, in *Berrehab*,[70] mentioned above, the Court stated that:

> In determining whether an interference was 'necessary in a democratic society', the Court makes allowance for the margin of appreciation that is left to the Contracting States (see in particular the W v. the United Kingdom judgment of 8 July 1987, Series A no. 121-A, p. 27, § 60 (b) and (d), and the Olsson judgment of 24 March 1988, Series A no. 130, pp. 31–32, § 67).
>
> In this connection, it accepts that the Convention does not in principle prohibit the Contracting States from regulating the entry and length of stay of aliens. According to the Court's established case-law (see, inter alia, the judgments previously cited), however, 'necessity' implies that the interference corresponds to a pressing social need and, in particular, that it is proportionate to the legitimate aim pursued.[71]

Earlier, in the first case in which this principle was referred to, *Abdulaziz*, the Court used it purely as an additional argument. In that judgment, this time when assessing the positive obligation of states under Article 8, the Court held:

> Moreover, the Court cannot ignore that the present case is concerned not only with family life but also with immigration and that, as a matter of well-established international law and subject to its treaty obligations, a State has the right to control the entry of non-nationals into its territory.[72]

It seems that the Court has become aware, almost thirty years later, that the traditional principle recognising the right of states to control the entry, residence, and removal of foreigners in its territory cannot be the starting point in Article 3 asylum cases. It has, therefore, made a significant shift in its asylum case law, as far

[70] *Berrehab* (n 17).
[71] See ibid, para 28. See as well *Moustaquim v Belgium* (n 17).
[72] See para 67, *in fine*.

as general principles are concerned, making clear that it is indeed the absolute nature of Article 3 obligations that is primordial in its adjudication of asylum cases. The *J.K.* ordering of general principles could also be understood as an attempt to make a distinction, indeed as it should be, to my mind, between cases related to the removals of non-nationals dealt with under Article 3 and those dealt with under Article 8. The first category will always undergo a strict analysis test, whereas the second is decided under a proportionality test. One could, in addition, wonder how a public interest aim, used as an *a fortiori* argument in Article 8 expulsion cases was silently converted into 'the general principle' for asylum cases in Strasbourg. It is understandable, then, that there was a need for the Court to define a list of general principles to be applied in Article 3 removal cases.

There is an additional point that warrants mention here. It is curious how the ECtHR, which consistently interprets the Convention in light of international law rules,[73] when dealing with asylum cases has never recalled under its general principles Article 1 A of the 1951 Geneva Convention? The general references the Court makes to the 1951 Geneva Convention are mostly to dissociate the analyses to be conducted under the ECHR from the analysis that can be conducted under the Geneva Convention.[74] From another methodological point of view, it seems rather curious that a Court which often refers to the European or international consensus in its adjudication of Convention protected rights, does not refer to the legal situation faced by asylum seekers in the member states[75] or to European legal codification in this area in its judgments. This is especially curious given the huge extent of legislative and regulatory work in Europe, especially at the EU level, in the field of asylum and migration since 1999. One key example is Article 18 of the EU Charter of Fundamental Rights,[76] which provides that '[t]he right to asylum shall be guaranteed with due respect for the rules of the Geneva Convention of 28 July 1951 and the Protocol of 31 January 1967 relating to the status of refugees and in

[73] See for instance *Al-Adsani v United Kingdom* [GC] App no 35763/97 (ECtHR, 21 November 2001), para 55; *Varnava and others v Turkey* [GC] App nos 16064/90, 16065/90, 16066/90, 16068/90, 16069/90, 16070/90, 16071/90, 16072/90, and 16073/90 (ECtHR, 18 September 2009), para 185; *Hassan v United Kingdom* [GC] App no 29750/09 (ECtHR, 16 September 2014), paras 77, 100, 102, 103, 106, etc.

[74] See for instance *F.G. v Sweden* (n 1), para 117, where the Court states very clearly:

> In cases concerning the expulsion of asylum-seekers, the Court does not itself examine the actual asylum applications or verify how the States honour their obligations under the Geneva Convention relating to the status of refugees. Its main concern is whether effective guarantees exist that protect the applicant against arbitrary refoulement, be it direct or indirect, to the country from which he or she has fled.

[75] See for instance on the right to asylum in many member states: Laure Jeannin and others, *Le droit d'asile en Europe—Etude comparée* (L'Harmattan 1999) 85, as well as Hélène Lambert, Francesco Messineo, and Paul Tiedemann, 'Comparative Perspectives of Constitutional Asylum in France, Italy, and Germany: Requiescat in Pace?' (2008) 27(3) Refugee Survey Quarterly 16.

[76] Charter of Fundamental Rights of the European Union [2012] OC J326/391.

accordance with the Treaty establishing the European Community'.[77] Neither the Charter[78] nor the very specific EU secondary legislative acts have been used by the Court in search of the existence of a consensus at the European level as far as the right to asylum is concerned.[79]

These and other documents at the international and European level,[80] through the recognition of the right to asylum, militate in favour of confirming the absolute nature of the right protected by Article 3 of the Convention, in the asylum context, subject of course to the usual conditions of threshold, burden of proof, etc, as stated in *J.K.* The Court in that judgment finally decided to structure its general principles in Article 3 asylum cases in a way which seems natural and appropriate for an absolute right protected by Article 3.[81] Such presentation of the applicable general principles in asylum cases might not change anything as far as the findings, or not, of violations in specific cases. It is, however, crucial that the Court adopts the correct methodology, by setting out in the right way the principles it uses for the determination of the cases before it.

[77] Referred for other purposes in *M.S.S.* (n 5), para 61, and *F.G.* (n 1), para 50.

[78] See also Art 19 of the Charter which states:

Protection in the event of removal, expulsion or extradition
1. Collective expulsions are prohibited.
2. No one may be removed, expelled or extradited to a State where there is a serious risk that he or she would be subjected to the death penalty, torture or other inhuman or degrading treatment or punishment.

[79] See especially the well-known recast European Parliament and Council Directive 2011/95 of 13 December 2011 on standards for the qualification of third-country nationals or stateless persons as beneficiaries of international protection, for a uniform status for refugees or for persons eligible for subsidiary protection, and for the content of the protection granted [2011] OJ L337/9; Council Directive (EC) 2001/55 of 20 July 2001 on minimum standards for giving temporary protection in the event of a mass influx of displaced persons and on measures promoting a balance of efforts between Member States in receiving such persons and bearing the consequences thereof [200] OJ L212/12; and the recast European Parliament and Council Directive 2013/32 of 26 June 2013 on common procedures for granting and withdrawing international protection [2013] OJ L180/60.

[80] See for an interesting analysis in this regard María-Teresa Gil-Bazo, 'Asylum as a General Principle of International Law' (2015) 27(1) International Journal of Refugee Law 3–28. In that article Gil-Bazo maintains that:

> The practice of states shows largely that domestic legislation has incorporated article 34 of the Refugee Convention. In the European context, the Recast Qualifications Directive(which incorporates the Refugee Convention into a legally binding instrument of EU law for EU member states) does enshrine a right to asylum for refugees and for beneficiaries of subsidiary protection. The Directive does not word it in these terms, but it imposes an obligation on member states to grant refugee status and subsidiary protection status to individuals who meet the criteria (articles 13 and 18), and one of the rights attached to that status is the right of residence (article 24 of the Directive). It is in this sense that this article approaches asylum, as an institution for protection whose contours have been developed over centuries crystalising in today's legal and institutional framework worldwide.

[81] See also the impact the absolute nature of Art 3 of the Convention has had in the case law related to Art 13 when combined with Art 3. See *M.S.S.* (n 5), paras 293, 386–96; *Hirsi Jamaa and others* (n 15), paras 197–207; *Čonka v Belgium* App no 51564/99 (ECtHR, 5 February 2002), paras 81–83; and *Gebremedhin [Geberamadhien] v France* App no 25389/05 (ECtHR, 26 April 2007), para 66.

5. Concluding Remarks

This chapter is intended to intervene in the debate on the methodological approach of the Strasbourg Court in dealing with asylum cases and to provide reasoned justification, as far as possible, for asserting which approach seems to be correct in the Convention setting. It supports the idea that the Court should orientate its methodology and mindset first towards 'protection' of an absolute right provided by the Convention, notwithstanding the source, European or not, of the violation. It is not trying to argue that the Court should introduce the right to seek asylum as such in its case law. I am not even sure that the recognition of the right to seek asylum will offer more protection to asylum seekers in Strasbourg, compared to what is given through a proper application of the absolute nature of Article 3.[82] Whether the methodology elaborated in the *J.K.* judgment offers the appropriate protection and whether this will be applied generally and consistently in asylum cases will only become clear over time. In *Khlaifia and others*, the Grand Chamber continued to assert, at the outset of its analysis under Article 3, the absolute character of that provision in expulsion cases.[83] However, an empirical analysis of post *J.K.* jurisprudence shows that in other cases the Court has demonstrated a tendency to fall back to the old traditional paradigm. In *Paposhvili*,[84] delivered only a few months after *J.K.*, the *J.K.* formulation of general principles was not maintained and the Grand Chamber stepped back to the original paradigm.[85] It remains to be seen which methodology the Court will use in the future and whether it will maintain this position or move back again to the traditional paradigm. The above-referred dissenting opinions in the *J.K.* judgment show that there are judges who find the new paradigm problematic. At this stage it cannot be asserted conclusively whether in Strasbourg the starting point in asylum cases is the right of states to decide on the fate of asylum seekers, or the affirmation of the absolute nature of the protection to be given to the latter in case of risk to life or ill-treatment.

[82] See Hersch Lauterpacht's critique on the way the above quoted Art 14 of the Universal Declaration of Human Rights is drafted, 'The Universal Declaration of Human Rights' (1948) 25 British Yearbook of International Law 354, 373–74.

[83] See Khlaifia (n 1), para 158 (extracts). See also the Chamber decision of *Ilias and Ahmed v Hungary* App no 47287/15 (ECtHR, 14 March 2017). This case is, at the time of writing this chapter, before the Grand Chamber.

[84] *Paposhvili* (n 1), para 172.

[85] See also the way the Court does refer to the *J.K.* judgment only for recalling the third general principle established in that judgment, ie the old paradigm, and 'forgetting' the first two general principles: the absolute nature and the *non-refoulement*. See also *M.O. v Switzerland* App no 41282/16 (ECtHR, 20 June 2017), para 68; *Batyrkhairo v Turkey* App no 69929/12 (ECtHR, 5 June 2018), para 45; and *Amerkhano v Turkey* App no 16026/12 (ECtHR, 5 June 2018). See as well the Committee decisions in *B.U. and others v Russia* App nos 59609/17, 74677/17, and 76379/17 (ECtHR, 22 January 2019); and *U.A. v Russia* App no 12018/16 (ECtHR, 22 January 2019). The reference was maintained, however, without stressing the absolute character of Art 3, in *M.A. v France* App no 9373/15 (ECtHR, 1 February 2018), para 51.

5

Challenges to the Application of the Concept of Vulnerability and the Principle of Best Interests of the Child in the Case Law of the ECtHR Related to Detention of Migrant Children

Ksenija Turković

1. Introduction

The notion of migrant children refers to children who find themselves in a broad range of migrant situations: asylum seekers, refugees, beneficiaries of subsidiary protection, stateless migrants, long-term economic migrants, irregular or undocumented migrants.[1] As migrants, children have specific social and legal needs which present challenges to states and to the international community, especially when there are vast inflows of people and when children make up over half of the world's refugees.[2]

In addressing these issues the European Court of Human Rights ('the Court' or 'the ECtHR') relies on various international instruments (hard[3] and soft[4] law),

[1] For definitions under international and EU law, see generally, IOM, 'Glossary on Migration' (2011) 25 International Migration Law Series <https://www.iom.int/key-migration-terms> accessed 29 April 2019, Council Directive 2004/83/EC of 29 April 2004 on minimum standards for the qualification and status of third-country nationals and stateless persons as refugees or as persons who otherwise need international protection and the content of the protection granted [2004] OJ L304/12, UN Convention Relating to the Status of Stateless Persons (adopted 28 September 1954, entered into force 6 June 1960) 360 UNTS 117, Art 1, Regulation (EU) 2016/399 [2016] OJ L77/1 (Schengen Borders Code) or other conditions for entry, stay or residence in that EU Member State (see European Commission, 'EMN Glossary' (*Migration and Home Affairs*) <https://ec.europa.eu/home-affairs/content/irregular-migrant-0_en> accessed 29 April 2019.

[2] See Global Compact on Refugees, UN Doc. A/73/12 (17 December 2018), para 76.

[3] Convention Relating to the Status of Refugees (adopted 28 July 1951, entered into force 22 April 1954) 189 UNTS 137 (Refugee Convention); Protocol Relating to the Status of Refugees (adopted 31 January 1967, entered into force 4 October 1967) 606 UNTS 267 (Protocol); Convention on the Rights of the Child (adopted 20 November 1989, entered into force 2 September 1990) 1577 UNTS 3 (CRC) art 3 and art 37.

[4] Regional Refugee Instruments & Related, 'Cartagena Declaration on Refugees, Colloquium on the International Protection of Refugees in Central America, Mexico and Panama' (22 November 1984); UNHCR, 'Note on Burden and Standard of Proof in Refugee Claims' (1998); Recommendation

Ksenija Turković, *Challenges to the Application of the Concept of Vulnerability and the Principle of Best Interests of the Child in the Case Law of the ECtHR Related to Detention of Migrant Children* In: *Migration and the European Convention on Human Rights*. Edited by: Başak Çali, Ledi Bianku, and Iulia Motoc, Oxford University Press (2021). © The Several Contributors.
DOI: 10.1093/oso/9780192895196.003.0005

EU law,[5] and consensus built through national laws. The Court has had the opportunity to shape its response to some of these challenges through the prism of human rights in the area of age assessment,[6] access to justice,[7] immigration detention of children,[8] protection from ill-treatment,[9] family reunification,[10] and expulsion,[11] mainly under Articles 3, 5, 8, and 13 of the Convention. The Court's approach to the specific social and legal needs of children, in general, and migrant children, in particular, is, to a great extent, shaped by three concepts: the inherent vulnerability of children, the best interests of the child, and circumscribed children's autonomy. All three concepts are gathering momentum in the Court's jurisprudence.

The present chapter will discuss the concept of vulnerability and the principle of the best interests of the child, and their legal consequences, for the effective respect, protection, and fulfilment of the human rights of migrant children in the context of immigration detention. In doing so, it will give a short overview of the developments in the Court's case law related to detention of migrant children. Using the

Rec(2003)5 of the Committee of Ministers of the Council of European on 'Measures of detention of asylum seekers,' 16 April 2003; Recommendation 1985 (2011) of the Parliamentary Assembly of the Council of Europe on 'Undocumented migrant children in an irregular situation: a real cause of concern,' 7 October 2011; Resolution 1707 (2010) of the Parliamentary Assembly on 'Detention of asylum seekers and irregular migrants in Europe', 28 January 2010; Recommendation CMRec(2019)4 of the Committee of Ministers on 'Supporting young refugees in transition to adulthood,' 24 April 2019; Resolution 2299 (2019) of the Parliamentary Assembly on 'Stop violence against, and exploitation of, migrant children,' 27 June 2019; Resolution 2299 (2019) of the Parliamentary Assembly on 'Pushback policies and practice in Council of Europe member States', 28 June 2019.

[5] *Primary legislation*: Consolidated version of the Treaty on the Functioning of the European Union (TFEU) [2016] OJ C202/1, arts 21, 67, 73, 78, and 79; Consolidated version of the Treaty on European Union (TEU) [2016] OJ C202/1, arts 2, 3, and 6; Charter of Fundamental Rights of the European Union (CFR) [2016] OJ C202/391; Protocols No 24 and No 30 TFEU [2016] OJ C202/304 and 312; *Secondary legislation*: Reception Conditions Directive 2013/33/EU [2013] OJ L180/96; Return Directive 2008/115/EC [2008] OJ L348/98; Asylum Procedures Directive 2013/32/EU [2013] OJ L180/60; Dublin Regulation 604/2013 [2013] OJ L180/31; Qualification Directive 2011/95/EU [2011] OJ L337/9; Freedom of Movement Directive 2004/38/EC [2004] OJ L158/77; Schengen Borders Code Regulation (n 1); Family Reunification Directive 2003/86/EC [2008] OJ L251/1; Temporary Protection Directive 2001/55/EC [2001] OJ L212/1; Long-Term Residents Directives 2003/109/EC, and 2011/51/EU amending Council Directive 2003/109/EC to extend its scope to beneficiaries of international protection [2003] OJ L132/1; Victims' Directive 2012/29/EU [2012] OJ L315/57, art 8.

[6] See *Abdullahi Elmi v Malta* App nos 25794/13 and 28151/13 (ECtHR, 22 February 2017).

[7] See for example on effective remedies to challenge conditions of detention *Rahimi v Greece* App no 8687/08 (ECtHR, 5 July 2011); *H.A. and others v Greece* App no 19951/16 (28 February 2019), paras 177–83; *G.B. and others v Turkey* App no 4633/15 (ECtHR, 17 October 2019), paras 118–37.

[8] On detention in view of expulsion see for example *Mubilanzila Mayeka v Belgium* App no 36369/06 (ECtHR, 12 October 2006); *Popov v France* App nos 39472/07 and 39474/07 (ECtHR, 19 January 2012); *Kanagaratnam v Belgium* App no 15297/09 (ECtHR, 13 March 2012); *H.A. and others* (n 7); *G.B. and others* (n 7).

[9] See *S.F. and others v Bulgaria* App no 8138/16 (ECtHR, 7 December 2017) (ill treatment of minors while in detention).

[10] See *Bajsultanov v Austria* App no 54131/10 (ECtHR, 12 June 2012); *Şen v the Netherlands* App no 31465/96 (ECtHR, 21 December 2001) (balancing rights); *Jeunesse v the Netherlands* [GC] App no 12738/10 (ECtHR, 3 October 2014) (family life, child's best interests).

[11] See *Gül v Switzerland* App no 23218/94 (ECtHR, 19 February 1996); *Boultif v Switzerland* App no 54273/00 (ECtHR, 2 August 2001); *Tarakhel v Switzerland* [GC] App no 29217/12 (ECtHR, 4 November 2014) (deportation of family/children).

Court's concepts of vulnerability, the best interests of the child, and circumscribed child's autonomy, as well as gaining inspiration from other international instruments and EU law, this chapter will attempt to demonstrate where the ECtHR case law on detention of migrant children could grow further, the opportunities for such growth, as well as the hindrances.

2. The Concept of Vulnerability in the ECtHR Jurisprudence

The Court has explored the notion of vulnerability on several occasions and has referred to the vulnerability of certain groups, and categories of persons, in a number of its decisions. So far, the Court has applied the concept towards, *inter alia*, Roma people,[12] children,[13] women,[14] detainees,[15] persons with disabilities,[16] criminal defendants,[17] asylum seekers,[18] people living with HIV,[19] or people with unpopular views.[20] Notwithstanding, the concept of 'vulnerability' and its legal consequences, are still not clearly defined in the Court's jurisprudence.[21]

In the Court's case law one could discern three—to a certain extent overlapping—categories of specifically vulnerable social groups and/or individuals: underprivileged and vulnerable groups that have 'a history of oppression or inequality, or that face deep-rooted prejudices, hostility, and discrimination'[22] including stereotyping[23] (such as Roma[24] or people with mental disabilities[25]); individuals who are inherently vulnerable due to some of their personal features (such as age,[26]

[12] See in particular *D.H. and others v Czech Republic* [GC] App no 57325/00 (ECtHR, 13 November 2007), para 182; *Oršuš and others v Croatia* [GC] App no 15766/03 (ECtHR, 16 March 2010), para 147; *V.C. v Slovakia* App no 18968/07 (ECtHR, 8 November 2011), para 146.

[13] See eg *M.C. v Bulgaria* App no 39272/98 (ECtHR, 4 December 2003); *Juppala v Finland* App no 18620/03 (ECtHR, 2 December 2008), para 41.

[14] See *Opuz v Turkey* App no 33401/02 (ECtHR, 9 June 2009).

[15] See *Salman v Turkey* App no 21986/93 (ECtHR, 27 June 2000).

[16] See *M.B. v Romania* App no 43982/06 (ECtHR, 3 November 2011), para 52; *Keenan v United Kingdom* App no 27229/95 (ECtHR, 4 March 2001), para 111.

[17] *Salduz v Turkey* App no 36391/02 (ECtHR, 27 November 2008), para 54; *Paskal v Ukraine* App no 24652/04 (ECtHR, 15 September 2011), para 76.

[18] *M.S.S. v Belgium* [GC] App no 30696/09 (ECtHR, 21 January 2011), para 236; *Tarakhel* (n 11).

[19] *Kiyutin v Russia* App no 2700/10 (ECtHR, 10 March 2011).

[20] *Bączkowski and others v Poland* App no 1543/06 (ECtHR, 3 May 2007), para 64; *Alekseyev v Russia* App nos 4916/07, 25924/08, and 14599/09 (ECtHR, 21 October 2010), para 70.

[21] See partly concurring and partly dissenting opinion of Judge Sajó in *MSS* (n 18).

[22] *Sava Terentyev v Russia* App no 10692/09 (ECtHR, 28 August 2018), para 76.

[23] *Carvalho Pinto De Sousa Morais v Portugal* App no 17484/15 (ECtHR, 25 July 2017).

[24] For example, Roma people have 'become a specific type of disadvantaged and vulnerable minority due to their turbulent history', see *D.H. and others* (n 12).

[25] They 'have suffered considerable discrimination in the past', according to *Alajos Kiss v Hungary* App no 38832/06 (ECtHR, 20 May 2010), para 42.

[26] For children see, for example, under art 3 (corporal punishment): *A. v United Kingdom* App no 25599/94 (ECtHR, 23 September 1998), para 22; *Z. and others v United Kingdom* [GC] App no 29392/95 (ECtHR, 10 May 2001), para 73; (young children tried by a criminal court): *T. v United Kingdom* [GC] App no 24724/94 (ECtHR, 16 December 1999), para 62; (in the context of art 8): *Fernández Martínez v*

health,[27] disability status, or gender[28]); individuals in a vulnerable position (eg position of inferiority and powerlessness[29]) because of the situation they are exposed to, for example, by virtue of a relationship of dependency, by virtue of being under the control of the authorities,[30] or being wholly dependent on state support[31] (such as victims of domestic violence,[32] persons under exclusive control of agents of the state such as detainees,[33] persons in custody,[34] victims of torture,[35] or asylum seekers[36]).

All of these categories of people are, for different reasons (socio-historical, intrinsic, or situational) particularly susceptible to social exclusion, abuse, manipulation, corrupt influence, intimidation, coercion, exploitation or various other sorts of ill treatment and human rights violations, either by state officials or private individuals, or are dependent on others for realisation of their rights. Consequently, they may face an increased likelihood of being wronged and of incurring physical or psychological harm. For the very same reasons, they have specific needs and, thus, their specific individualised circumstances have to be taken into consideration in order to provide effective protection and a guarantee of their procedural and substantive rights.

2.1 Asylum Seekers—Persons in a Vulnerable Position

In *MSS v. Belgium*, the Court considered asylum seekers to be inherently vulnerable and members of a particularly underprivileged population group in need of special protection because of everything they had been through during their migration and the traumatic experiences they were likely to have endured previously.[37] In *Khlaifia*, the Court considered that the applicants, who had just undergone a

Spain [GC] App no 56030/07 (ECtHR, 12 June 2014), para 87; *K.U. v Finland* App no 2872/02 (ECtHR, 2 March 2009), paras 41, 46.

27 Such as pregnant women, see *Bati and others v Turkey* App nos 33097/96 and 57834/00 (ECtHR, 3 June 2004), persons with mental disorders see *Stanev v Bulgaria* [GC] App no 36760/06 (ECtHR, 17 January 2012) and *Đorđević v Croatia* App no 41526/10 (ECtHR, 24 July 2012), or HIV see *Kiyutin* (n 19) and *I.B. v Greece* App no 552/10 (ECtHR, 3 October 2013).

28 *Abdulaziz v United Kingdom* App nos 9214/80, 9473/81, and 9474/81 (ECtHR, 28 May 1985), para 78.

29 See *M.S. v Croatia (no 2)* App no 75450/12 (ECtHR, 19 February 2015), para 98.

30 See *Bataliny v Russia* App no 10060/07 (ECtHR, 23 July 2015), para 107.

31 *Tarakhel* (n 11), para 98.

32 *Opuz* (n 14); *Volodina v Russia* App no 41261/16, (ECtHR, 9 July 2019), para 72.

33 *Rupa v Romania (no 1)* App no 58478/00 (ECtHR, 16 December 2008).

34 *Anguelova v Bulgaria* App no 38361/97 (ECtHR, 13 June 2002); *Zeynep A.V.C.I. v Turkey* App no 37021/97 (ECtHR, 3 February 2003).

35 *Aksoy v Turkey* App no 21987/93 (ECtHR, 18 December 1996).

36 See *M.S.S.* (n 18), paras 232, 233, 251, 263; *Hirsi Jamaa and others v Italy* [GC] App no 27765/09 (ECtHR, 23 February 2012); *Tarakhel* (n 11) (extracts).

37 *M.S.S.* (n 18).

dangerous journey on the high seas, were in a situation of vulnerability.[38] In *M.S.S.*, the Court implied that all asylum seekers are vulnerable *as such*, regardless of their individual circumstances, and affirmed that the distress caused by the situation of detention was exacerbated by the applicant's inherent vulnerability as an asylum seeker. The Court noted the existence of a broad consensus at the international and European level concerning the need for special protection of asylum seekers, as evidenced by the Geneva Convention, the remit and the activities of the UNHCR, and the standards set out in the Reception Directive.[39]

However, the Court has also acknowledged that some asylum seekers will need specific protection because of personal characteristics, such as their age, gender identity, disability, or health status, that aggravate or heighten their original vulnerability. For example, in *O.M. v. Hungary*[40] the Court found a violation of article 5 § 1 of the Convention because the authorities failed to take into consideration the individual circumstances of the applicant who claimed to be part of a vulnerable group in his country of origin, by virtue of belonging to a sexual minority (LGBT persons) in Iran and, thus, the applicant's detention verged on arbitrariness.[41] However, in *Thimothawes v. Belgium*, the fact that the applicant had mental health problems (his additional or double vulnerability) was, in itself, not sufficient for the Court to find that his detention was unjustified, especially because, in a closed centre, he had received psychological support adapted to his mental health situation. The reports prepared by the psychological support services did not indicate that the detention or its duration was unreasonable.[42]

Judge Sajó in his partial dissenting opinion attached to *M.S.S.*,[43] called into question the qualification of asylum seekers as a vulnerable group because, according to him, asylum seekers do not represent a group that has been historically subjected to prejudice with lasting consequences, resulting in social exclusion. However, he disregarded the fact that the sources of vulnerability may vary for different groups and that the vulnerability of asylum seekers has its basis primarily in the situations they experience, which commonly renders them helpless, hopeless, anxious, and exposed to various kinds of abuses.

Indeed, in a recent judgment, *Ilias and Ahmed*, the Grand Chamber endorsed the view in *M.S.S.*[44] that asylum seekers may be considered vulnerable because of everything they might have been through during their migration and the traumatic experiences they were likely to have endured previously. However, the Court

[38] See *Khlaifia and others v Italy* App no 16483/12 (ECtHR, 15 December 2016), para 135.

[39] *M.S.S.* (n 18), paras 232–33, 251.

[40] *O.M. v Hungary* App no 9912/15 (ECtHR, 5 July 2016).

[41] ibid, paras 53–54.

[42] *Thimothawes v Belgium* App no 39061/11 (ECtHR, 4 April 2017), paras 79–80. Dissenting judges Karakas and Turković criticised lack of individualised approach in that case in imposing a detention to an applicant with double vulnerability.

[43] *M.S.S.* (n 18).

[44] ibid, para 232.

took the position that there is no indication that the applicants in the present case were more vulnerable than any other adult asylum seeker confined to the same transit zone.[45]

Consequently, asylum seekers may face varying degrees of vulnerability according to the type of treatment or persecution they are at risk of or have been subjected to, their age, their family situation, their health, their disability, or the means of subsistence available to them. The Court has directly acknowledged the risks of double vulnerability in its jurisprudence related to minor migrants.

2.2 Children—Inherently Vulnerable Group

Under the Universal Declaration of Human Rights, the international community recognised that childhood is a state of being that is entitled to special care and protection.[46] Childhood is a phase in which a person is undergoing specific physical, emotional, and psychological development. The Convention on the Rights of the Child (CRC) has defined childhood as a separate space from adulthood, thus, what is appropriate for an adult may not be suitable for a child. It also recognised that children are the holders of their own rights and are, therefore, empowered actors in their own development.[47]

However, during such a developmental process, children are more susceptible to harm and the influence of pressure or coercion from others, in comparison to adults. They have less means and capability to deal with violations of their rights and the consequences thereof, and they have greater economic and emotional dependence, or reliance, on others to meet their basic needs.[48] Thus, children are, per se, inherently more vulnerable than adults to abuses of their rights. This was already recognised in 1959, in the Declaration of the Rights of the Child: 'the child, by reason of his physical and mental immaturity, needs special safeguards and care, including appropriate legal protection, before as well as after birth.'[49] The Committee on the Rights of the Child has emphasised, on many occasions, the vulnerability of children in general.[50]

[45] *Ilias and Ahmed v Hungary* App no 47287/15 (ECtHR, 21 November 2019), paras 191–93.

[46] Universal Declaration of Human Rights (adopted 10 December 1948) UNGA Res 217 A(III) (UDHR), art 25. The same was reiterated in the Preamble of the CRC (n 3).

[47] UNICEF, 'Childhood under Threat—The State of the World's Children in 2005' (December 2004) <https://www.unicef.org/sowc05/english/childhooddefined.html> accessed 13 January 2019.

[48] For the summary of different sources of child's vulnerability see, Lois A Weithorn, 'A Constitutional Jurisprudence of Children's Vulnerability' (2018) 69 Hastings Law Journal 179, 189.

[49] Declaration of the Rights of the Child (adopted on 20 November 1959) UNGA A/RES/1386(XIV) Preamble. The same is later reiterated in the CRC Preamble (n 3).

[50] The Committee formulated particular vulnerability of children in the following words: 'At a universal level all children aged 0–18 years are considered vulnerable until the completion of their natural, psychological, social and psychological growth and development.' Committee on the Rights of the Child, 'General Comment No 5 on General Measures of Implementation of the Convention on the Rights of the Child' (2003) UN Doc CRC/GC/2003/5, para 72. See also 'General Comment No 8: The

The ECtHR, unlike the Inter-American Court of Human Rights (IACtHR),[51] has never expressly elaborated its position on the inherent vulnerability of children, yet it is clear from its jurisprudence that the Court considers children as an inherently vulnerable group entitled to state protection owing to their age.[52] As a consequence the Court has developed child-specific human rights approaches to a whole range of issues, relying, to a great extent, on the concept of vulnerability and by using the principle of the best interests of the child.[53] In so doing, the Court is alert to the dangers of paternalism. In *M. and M. v. Croatia*, the Court emphasised that children are subjects of rights, but, in their case, the right to personal autonomy has a different scope—children have 'circumscribed autonomy, which gradually increases with their evolving maturity'.[54] They have progressive capacity to exercise their rights, primarily through the right to be consulted and heard.[55] Consequently, children are simultaneously entitled to protection in accordance with their relative vulnerability deriving from their youth, immaturity, and dependency, and are acknowledged as active agents having increasing autonomy in exercising their rights.

2.3 Migrant Children—An Especially Vulnerable Group

Many international documents and credible reports from various international organisations and non-governmental organisations recognise migrant children, whether or not they are accompanied, as a particularly vulnerable group, combining the special vulnerability of an alien with the general vulnerability of a

Right of the Child to Protection from Corporal Punishment and Other Cruel or Degrading Forms of Punishment' (2006) UN Doc CRC/C/GC/8, para 21.

[51] See eg *Vargas-Areco v Paraguay*, Inter-American Court of Human Rights Series C No 25 (26 September 2006), para 77.

[52] See *Bouyid.Belgium* App no 23380/09 (ECtHR, 28 September 2015), para 110, *A. and B. v Croatia* App no 7144/15 (ECtHR, 20 June 2019), paras 111–12.

[53] See ECtHR, 'Factsheet on Children's Rights' (December, 2019) <https://www.echr.coe.int/Documents/FS_Childrens_ENG.pdf> accessed 15 February 2020, 'Factsheet on Protection of Minors' (January 2020) <https://www.echr.coe.int/Documents/FS_Minors_ENG.pdf> accessed 15 February 2020; 'Factsheet on Accompanied Migrant Children in Detention' (October 2019) <https://www.echr.coe.int/Documents/FS_Accompanied_migrant_minors_detention_ENG.pdf> accessed 15 February 2020, and 'Factsheet on Unaccompanied Migrant Minors in Detention' (June 2019) <https://www.echr.coe.int/Documents/FS_Unaccompanied_migrant_minors_detention_ENG.pdf> accessed 15 February 2020; related 'Factsheet on International Child Abduction' (January 2020) <https://www.echr.coe.int/Documents/FS_Child_abductions_ENG.pdf> accessed 15 February 2020.

[54] The right to personal autonomy in the case of adults means the right to make choices as to how to lead one's own life, provided that this does not unjustifiably interfere with the rights and freedoms of others. See *M. and M. v Croatia* App no 10161/13 (ECtHR, 3 September 2005), para 171.

[55] ibid. In framing this approach the Court relied on the Preamble to the Optional Protocol [of 19 December 2011] to the Convention on the Rights of the Child which came into force on 14 April 2014. CJEU has emphasised that obligation to hear the views of the competent child is not absolute, but it must be assessed in each individual case as to what is in the best interest of the child. See Case C-491/10 *PPU Aguirre Zarraga* [2010] ECR I-14247.

child.[56] They are, thus, especially susceptible to an increased negative impact on their health, development, and well-being, and to experiencing disparities in the enjoyment of their rights. At first, in assessing the vulnerability of migrant children the Court gave the impression that it was distinguishing between unaccompanied and accompanied minors, though the consequences of doing so were not sufficiently clear and elaborated. However, later on, as demonstrated below, the Court abandoned such distinction.

In *Mubilanzila Mayeka*, the Court considered that the second applicant, owing to her very young age (five years old), the fact that she was an illegal alien in a foreign land, that she was not accompanied by her family from whom she had become separated, and that she had been left to her own devices, was in an extremely vulnerable situation.[57] This was confirmed in *Rahimi*, where the Court, in particular, stressed that an unaccompanied foreign minor (fifteen years old) must belong to the 'category of the most vulnerable persons in the society'.[58] In *Abdullahi Elmi*, the Court considered that the applicants, two unaccompanied minors from Somalia, who, at the relevant time, had been sixteen and seventeen years of age, were vulnerable both as asylum seekers[59] and minors, and it considered that they had been more vulnerable than any other adult asylum seeker detained at the time because of their age.[60] Judge Sajó, in his concurring opinion, expressed concerns because the applicants were regarded as vulnerable without any specific information having been provided concerning their traumatic experiences. Also, according to him, case law based on the problems of small children should not be applicable to adolescents.[61] However, recently, in *HA and others* (six applicants between fourteen and seventeen years of age)[62] and *Sh.D. and others* (five applicants

[56] The Committee on the Rights of the Child has identified among groups of children who may be especially vulnerable to experiencing disparities in the enjoyment of their rights: refugee and internally displaced children. See, UNGA, 'Report of the UN Committee of the Rights of the Child' (November 2002) UN Doc A/57/41, para 49 and 'General Comment No 17 on the Right of the Child to Rest, Leisure, Play, Recreational Activities, Cultural Life and the Arts' ((2013) UN Doc CRC/C/GC/17, para 16). Also see, CoE Parliamentary Assembly Recommendation 1985 (2011) 'Undocumented migrant children in an irregular situation: a real cause for concern' (7 October 2011), The Council of Europe Strategy for the Rights of the Child (2016–2021) <https://edoc.coe.int/en/children-s-rights/7207-council-of-europe-strategy-for-the-rights-of-the-child-2016-2021.html> accessed 15 February 2020, Council of Europe Committee for the Prevention of Torture and Inhuman or Degrading Treatment or Punishment (CPT), 'Factsheet: Immigration Detention' (March 2017) CPT/Inf (2017)3. EU Reception Directive (n 5) art 17. See also eg Commission, 'The Protection of Children in Migration' (Communication) COM 2017/211 final; Cordis Bright, 'Defining Child Vulnerability: Definitions, Frameworks and Groups, Technical Paper 2', in *Children's Commissioner Project on Vulnerable Children* (2017) 13–16. Some of these documents have been cited in the Court's case law. See for example *Rahimi* (n 7), para 29; *Abdullahi Elmi* (n 6), para 43.

[57] *Mubilanzila Mayeka* (n 8), para 55.

[58] *Rahimi* (n 7), para 109.

[59] *Abdullahi Elmi* (n 6), para 113.

[60] ibid. cf *Mahamed Jama v Malta* App no 10290/13 (ECtHR, 26 November 2015), para 100.

[61] See concurring opinion of Judge Sajó attached to case of *Abdullahi Elmi* (n 6).

[62] *H.A. and others* (n 7), para 171.

between fourteen and seventeen years of age),[63] the Court once again clearly acknowledged the compounded vulnerability of unaccompanied minors, deriving from their age and their personal circumstances (being illegal aliens in a foreign land, unaccompanied by their family and left to their own devices). The Court, reconfirmed that unaccompanied minors find themselves in a situation of extreme vulnerability and that they belong to a category of the most vulnerable persons in society.[64] For the Court this is an irrefutable presumption (*presumptio iuris et de iure)* requiring no specific information concerning the applicants' actual traumatic experiences,[65] and it applies regardless of their actual age, as long as they are minors.[66] In all of these cases the child's extreme vulnerability was the decisive factor that took precedence over considerations relating to their status as an illegal immigrant.[67]

In *Muskhadzhiyeva and others v. Belgium*, the Court specifically noted that, as opposed to the *Mubilanzila* case, the children were not separated from their mother but that did not suffice to exempt the authorities from their obligation to protect the children.[68] The Court examined the ages of the four children, who were seven months, three and a half, five, and seven years old, at the material time. They also showed serious physical and psychosomatic symptoms related to their experiences back home and during migration. According to the Court, the age of at least two of them was such that it allowed them to be aware of their surroundings. Their mother was in a situation of distress so intense that it intensified that of the children, who felt that their mother was unable to protect them. Thus, for the Court, the children, although accompanied by their mother, were in a state of extreme vulnerability, which was further aggravated by detention.[69]

In *Kanagaratnam v. Belgium*, the Court acknowledged that this case differs from *Muskhazhiyeva and others* since there were no medical certificates attesting to psychological disturbances affecting the children during their detention and the children were older (thirteen, eleven, and eight years old at the material time), however, in the view of the Court these elements were not decisive. The Court started its review from the presumption that the children were vulnerable, both

[63] *S.hD. and others v Greece, Austria, Croatia, Hungary North Macedonia, Serbia and Slovenia* App no 14165/16 (ECtHR, 13 September 2019), para 56.

[64] ibid. See also *Mubilanzila Mayeka* (n 8), paras 55, 103; *Rahimi* (n 7), para 86; *Abdullahi Elmi* (n 6), paras 103, 145.

[65] For the Court, unaccompanied children indisputably come within the class of the most vulnerable persons in society. See *Mubilanzila Mayeka* (n 8), para 55; *Rahimi* (n 7), para 87; *Abdullahi Elmi* (n 6), para 113.

[66] The age of children varied from five years in *Mubilanzila Mayeka* (n 8) to eighteen in *Mohamad v Greece* App no 70586/11 (ECtHR, 11 December 2014).

[67] *Mubilanzila Mayeka* (n 8), para 55. This was reconfirmed in *Rahimi* (n 7), para 109.

[68] *Muskhadzhiyeva and others v Belgium* App no 41442/07 (ECtHR, 19 January 2010), paras 58, 62.

[69] ibid, paras 59–63, 73, 74.

because of their status as children and because of their personal history. However, as opposed to the cases related to unaccompanied children, where the Court took their extreme vulnerability as irrefutable fact, in *Kanagaratnam*, the Court provided rather detailed information concerning the applicants' traumatic experiences. The children had lived through a traumatic situation already before arriving in Belgium. They were separated from their father upon his arrest and they had left their country, with their mother, in the midst of the civil war, afraid of reprisals by local authorities. This vulnerability was recognised by the Belgian authorities who granted them refugee status. The Belgian authorities further exacerbated their vulnerability by putting them into a closed centre (detention) and keeping them there for a relatively long time (four months).[70]

In *Popov v. France*, in which the applicant children were accompanied by their parents throughout the period of detention, the Court explicitly acknowledged that children have specific needs that are related, in particular, to their age and lack of independence, but also to their asylum-seeker status. Furthermore, the Court, relying on the European Union Directive concerning the Reception of Aliens, identified migrant minors, whether or not they are accompanied, as a category of vulnerable persons requiring particular attention from the authorities.[71] However, in analysing the concrete situation of the applicant children, the Court regarded them as belonging to a vulnerable group mainly due to the fact that they were confined in conditions not adapted for children and it failed to recognise the vulnerability resulting from the applicants' migration and irregular residency status.[72]

In *Tarakhel*, the Court confirmed that the requirement of 'special protection' of asylum seekers is particularly important when the persons concerned are children, in view of their specific needs and their extreme vulnerability.[73] The Court, again, emphasised that the requirement of 'special protection' applies even when the children seeking asylum are accompanied by their parents.[74] In a number of recent French cases[75], as well as in *S.F. and others v. Bulgaria*[76] and most recently in *G.B. and others v. Turkey*,[77] the Court has reaffirmed that migrant minors, whether accompanied or not, are extremely vulnerable and that their extreme vulnerability is the decisive factor that takes precedence over considerations relating to their status as illegal immigrant.

[70] See *Kanagaratnam* (n 8), para 67.
[71] *Popov* (n 8), para 91.
[72] ibid, paras 100–03.
[73] *Tarakhel* (n 11), para 99. See also, *Mubilanzila Mayeka* (n 8), para 55; *Abdullahi Elmi* (n 6), para 103.
[74] *Tarakhel* (n 11), para 119.
[75] See among others *A.B. and others v France* App no 11593/12 (ECtHR, 12 July 2016), para 110.
[76] *S.F. and others* (n 9), para 79.
[77] *G.B. and others* (n 7), para 101.

2.4 Vulnerability—Flexible Concept

Vulnerability is a universally shared characteristic—by our very nature we are all capable of being harmed and we all seek protection from harm.[78] The Court, together with the whole Convention system, is one of the institutions created to provide such protection to individuals. As has been demonstrated above, the Court recognises that the concept itself is not monolithic,[79] that certain social groups are more vulnerable than others, and that certain circumstances make certain persons more or less vulnerable than others from within his or her group. Indeed, being a member of vulnerable group does not mean that a particular person will necessarily have poorer life outcomes. Obviously, the notion of vulnerability is a nuanced and flexible phenomenon that exists on a continuum.

The Court has not taken a clear position towards group vulnerability and the individual vulnerability of a person belonging to the group. In cases involving unaccompanied migrant children, the Court has expressly stated that there should be a presumption of their extreme vulnerability regardless of their actual age and stage of development. In relation to accompanied children, however, the Court leaves the impression that such a presumption could be rebutted. The Court has also, several times, reiterated the view that unaccompanied minors fall into 'the category of the most vulnerable individuals in society,[80] and thus gives the impression of making a distinction in the degree of vulnerability between unaccompanied and accompanied children. However, it is not clear what consequences should flow from this distinction. So far, the Court has, in numerous cases, confirmed that the child's extreme vulnerability is the decisive factor that should take precedence over considerations relating to their status as an illegal immigrant and has encouraged states to take appropriate measures to ensure that children seeking refugee status, whether they are accompanied or not, receive appropriate protection and humanitarian assistance.[81]

The relation between, and consequences of, different degrees and layers of vulnerability remain unclear and underexplored, with the notion of vulnerability often used merely as a synonym for specific situations deserving attention. Thus, it is important to reflect on the ways in which vulnerability is, and could be, operationalised, and meaningfully used, in legal reasoning.

[78] Bryan Turner, *Vulnerability and Human Rights* (Penn State University Press 2006); Martha Albertson Fineman, 'Equality Autonomy and the Vulnerable Subject' in Martha Albertson Fineman and Anna Grear (eds), *Law and Politics, in Vulnerability: Reflections on a New Ethical Foundations for Law and Politics* (Ashgate Publishing 2013) 18, 20.

[79] That vulnerability need not be conceived as a monolithic concept was emphasised in literature by Anna Grear, *Redirecting Human Rights: Facing the Challenge of Corporate Legal Humanity* (Palgrave Macmillan 2010) 128.

[80] *Rahimi* (n 7) para 87; *Khan v France* App no 12267/16 (ECtHR, 28 February 2019), para 74.

[81] Most recently in *G.B. and others* (n 7), para 101.

Vulnerability is a relative state with its degree and type varying over time and geography, making it highly contextual. Since it is determined by individual predispositions and external or situational risk factors such as the 'personal, social, political, economic, or environmental situations of individuals or social groups'[82] which can be short-term, intermittent, or enduring, the study of vulnerability should be intersectional.[83] The research and literature in the area of intersectionality could assist the Court in having a more nuanced understanding of applicants' needs, interests, capacities, and experiences, and thus in better identifying appropriate services and protection mechanisms for ensuring their dignity and safety.[84]

3. Overlap and Complementarity between the Principle of the Best Interests of the Child and the Concept of Vulnerability of Migrant Children

In a concrete case, the principle of the best interests of the child may be used as a substantive right, interpretative norm, or rule of procedure.[85] A child's best interests must be taken as a primary consideration and weighed against other interests whenever decisions concerning children are made, regardless of the final result.[86] National authorities are obliged to demonstrate that they have, in fact, taken such interests into account. The right of the child to have his or her best interests taken as a primary consideration means that the child's interests may not be considered

[82] cf Catriona Mackenzie, Wendy Rogers, and Susan Dodds, 'Introduction: What Is Vulnerability and Why Does it Matter for Moral Theory?' in Catriona Mackenzie and others (eds), *Vulnerability: New Essays in Ethics and Feminist Philosophy* (OUP 2014) 1, 7.

[83] See Kimberle Crenshaw, 'Demarginalizing the Intersection of Race and Sex: A Black Feminist Critique of Antidiscrimination Doctrine, Feminist Theory and Antiracist Politics' *University of Chicago Legal Forum*, 1989 (1/8), http://chicagounbound.uchicago.edu/uclf/vol1989/iss1/8 (accessed 15 February 2019).

[84] See eg Citizens for Public Justice, The Most Vulnerable—an intersectional approach to Refugee Policymaking and Advocacy Efforts (report prepared by Serisha Iyar, 2018–2019) <https://cpj.ca/wp-content/uploads/The-Most-Vulnerable-Report-by-Serisha-Iyar.pdf> accessed 20 February 2020; Elena Fiddian-Qasmiyeh, Co-Director of the UCL Migration Research Unit to the UNHCR High Commissioner's Dialogue on Protection Challenges, Panel 1, Session 1 on 'Reception and Admission,' <https://www.unhcr.org/5a745f4f7.pdf> accessed 20 February 2020; Simona Zavratnik, Addressing Intersectional Vulnerabilities in Contemporary Refugee Movements in Europe, (April 2019) <https://www.researchgate.net/publication/326201211_ADDRESSING_INTERSECTIONAL_VULNERABILITIES_IN_CONTEMPORARY_REFUGEE_MOVEMENTS_IN_EUROPE/citation/download> accessed 20 February 2020.

[85] Guidelines of the Committee on the Rights of the Child, published in 'General Comment No 14 on the Right of the Child to have his or her best interests taken as a primary consideration' (2013) UN Doc CRC/C/GC/14, provide the worldwide accepted standard on the best interests of the child concept, its interpretation, and application. See also Ksenija Turković and Aida Grgić, 'Best Interests of the Child in the Context of Article 8 of the ECHR' in Josep Casadevall and others (eds), *Mélanges en l'honneur de Dean Spielmann—Essays in honour of Dean Spielmann: liber amicorum Dean Spielmann* (Wolf Legal Publishers 2015) 629.

[86] This has been confirmed in many cases. See, among many, *Rahim* (n 12), para 108; *Popov* (n 8), para 141; *A.B. and others* (n 77), paras 153–54; *G.B. and others* (n 7) paras 167–68, 186.

on the same level as all other considerations. They have a higher priority and, thus, greater weight must be attached to what serves the child's best interests than to other competing considerations.[87] There are, however, circumstances in which the community, or other parties, might have superior interests (eg religious, economic, security) so that the child's best interests may not prevail. In migration cases, the best interests of the child are generally weighed against the interests and desires of the state to control migration.

Under international law vulnerability is one of a number of specific elements which should be taken into consideration in the assessment of the best interests of the child.[88] This has been acknowledged in the Court's jurisprudence. In *Kanagaratnam and others v. Belgium*,[89] the Court emphasised that in determining the best interests of the child in expulsion cases, one must start from the presumption that children are vulnerable due to their characteristics as children and due to their personal histories. The children, in that case, experienced traumatic situations before arriving in Belgium, escaping together with their mother from a civil war in their country. The Belgian authorities recognised their vulnerability and granted them refugee status. In *Rahimi v. Greece*,[90] taking into account the extreme vulnerability of an unaccompanied migrant boy from Afghanistan, who was detained for two days and subsequently abandoned to live on the streets, the Court held that the automatic application of the legislation in question and failure to apply the principle of the best interests of the child while deciding on his detention, indicated that the Greek authorities could not be deemed to have acted in good faith. In a number of cases, the Court confirmed that the domestic authorities have to give sufficient consideration to the best interests of the child, in compliance with obligations stemming from international law.[91]

Accordingly, in the assessment and determination of the best interests of migrant children when they are involved in different procedures (age determination, asylum procedures, detention, expulsion, family reunification), special attention has to be given to their vulnerabilities and the risk factors associated with the different phases in the migration process that may harm their mental health, well-being, and development. However, to safeguard the best interests of the child, differentiated treatment of vulnerable children may be required, because they might need specific, closely defined protective measures corresponding to their specific physical, emotional, educational, developmental, and other needs. Thus, domestic authorities should first take into account the children's particular

[87] General Comment No 14 (n 85).
[88] ibid. Also see *Y.C. v United Kingdom*, App no 4547/10 (ECtHR, 13 March 2012), para 135.
[89] See *Kanagaratnam* (n 8), para 67.
[90] See *Rahimi* (n 7), para 109.
[91] See for example *A.B. and others* (n 77), paras 153–54; *Bistieva v Poland* App No 75157/14 (ECtHR, 10 April 2018), para 86. *H.A. and others* (n 7), paras 202, 205–08 is a rare example in which the Court has established that the state failed to assess the best interests of the child.

situation of vulnerability and then consider what would be in their best interests in order to adopt the most appropriate measure. The needs, and corresponding measures, should be assessed at the time of the decision, but should also reflect the continuity and stability of the child's present and future situation. Such context-specific assessment is required to ensure both the full and effective enjoyment of all the children's rights—recognised in the CRC as well as the ECHR—and to secure the holistic development of the child. Guided by the principle of subsidiarity, the Court leaves the assessment of the best interests of the child primarily to the national authorities and intervenes only when the decision of those authorities does not appear Convention-compliant.[92]

4. Legal Consequences of the Concept of Vulnerability in the ECtHR Jurisprudence Related to Migrant Children

The concept of vulnerability might appear vague and elusive, and thus difficult to frame in legal terms, but, nevertheless, it brings an added value to the Court's reasoning. The Court has had regard to the vulnerability of the applicants in determining their special needs and, through that, the scope of the positive obligations of the State—both substantive[93] and procedural[94]—in assessing whether the threshold of severity justifying the application of Article 3 of the Convention had been attained;[95] in assessing lawfulness under Articles 5 and 8;[96] in assessing proportionality under Article 8 of the Convention;[97] in determining the burden[98] and standard of proof;[99] in narrowing the margin of appreciation enjoyed by member states; in determining the extent of compensation;[100] and in enhancing the Court's understanding of human dignity.[101]

[92] See for example *Hokkanen v Finland* App no 19823/92 (ECtHR, 23 September 1994), para 55; *Kutzner v Germany* App no 46544/99 (ECtHR, 26 February 2002), paras 65, 66. See also Milka Sormunen (ed), *The Best Interests of the Child—A Dialogue between Theory and Practice* (Council of Europe, 2016).

[93] For example finding Roma children as members particularly vulnerable and disadvantaged led to a substantive positive obligation to 'undo a history of racial segregation in special schools'. *Horvath v Hungary* App no 11146/11 (ECtHR, 29 April 2013), para 127.

[94] States have procedural obligations of criminal prosecution and effective investigation. See for example *M.C.* (n 18), paras 167, 179, 184; *M. & C. v Romania* App no 29032/04 (ECtHR, 27 September 2011), para 112. This procedural obligation extends to the duty to protect rights of children as victims of various abuses. See eg *Siliadin* (n 58), paras 89, 112, 271, 284–87.

[95] *Raninen v Finland* App no 20972/92 (ECtHR, 26 December 1997), para 55.

[96] *Muskhadzhiyeva and others* (n 70); *Kanagaratnam* (n 8); *Rahimi* (n 7).

[97] *Mubilanzila Mayeka* (n 8); Popov (n 8).

[98] See *Nachova and others v Bulgaria* [GC] App nos 43577/98 and 43579/98 (ECtHR, 6 July 2005), para 147.

[99] In cases concerning deportation and expulsion of migrants the Court does not take into consideration only evidence provided by domestic authorities, but compares such information with information from other reliable and objective sources. See for example *Rahimi* (n 7), paras 64, 65, 91–94.

[100] *Mahmundi and others v Greece* App no 14902/2010 (ECtHR, 31 July 2012), paras 104–07.

[101] *M.S. v United Kingdom* App no 24527/08 (ECtHR, 3 May 2012), paras 44–45.

As I have demonstrated above, the Court has identified children as a vulnerable group and migrant children as an extremely vulnerable group. Vulnerability, thus, necessarily plays an important role in the analysis and outcome of cases, and has important legal consequences in the jurisprudence of the Court, in relation to children. This is further reinforced through the application of the principle of the best interests of the child because vulnerability, as elaborated above, is one of a number of specific elements which should be taken into consideration in the assessment of the best interests of the child. The best interests of the child principle, therefore, provides an additional protection for children requiring implementation of special measures adapted for migrant children.

If the age of someone is unknown, authorities may need to conduct an assessment to determine whether the person is a child or an adult.[102] According to the UN Committee on the Rights of the Child there is a presumption of minority.[103] However, if a person refuses to submit to an age assessment procedure the Court may infer adverse consequences.[104]

I will now address the ways in which the concept of vulnerability and the principle of the best interests of the child have influenced the Court's jurisprudence within the context of the detention of migrant children, whether accompanied or not, in determining the scope of the positive obligations of the state, the threshold under Article 3, lawfulness under Article 5, and proportionality under Article 8 of the Convention.

4.1 Particular Obligations of the States towards Migrant Children

The Court has recognised that particularly vulnerable individuals may, in principle, need special and heightened protection from the state, for the equal and effective enjoyment of their human rights.[105] This, in particular, applies to children

[102] Council of Europe has recently published a guide for policy makers on age assessment procedures which is reinforcing child-sensitive and child-responsive rights-based approach to migration. See 'Age assessment for children in migration—A human rights based approach, A guide for policy makers' (December 2019) <https://rm.coe.int/ageassessmentchildrenmigration/168099529f> accessed 21 February 2020.

[103] According to the Committee on the Rights of the Child '[a]nyone claiming to be a child should be treated as such'. See Joint General Comment No 3 of the Committee on the Protection of the Rights of All Migrant Workers (CMW) and Members of Their Families and General Comment No 22 on the general principles regarding the human rights of children in the context of international migration (2017) UN Doc CMW/C/GC/3-CRC/C/GC/22, para 32(h).

[104] *Ahmade v Greece* App no 50520/09 (ECtHR, 25 September 2012), para 78.

[105] See in this respect eg *Opuz* (n 14), para 160; *Hakim Aka v Turkey* App no 62077/08 (ECtHR, 6 November 2018), para 41; *Fortalnov and others v Russia* App no 35973/07 (ECtHR 26 June 2018), para 77; *Oršuš* (n 12), para 147; *MSS* (n 18), para 251; *Bouyid* (n 54), para 83. In *Opuz* (n 14), for example, the Court emphasised that due to the vulnerability of victims of domestic violence, domestic authorities should have been able to pursue the proceedings as a matter of public interest, regardless of the victims' withdrawal of complaints (paras 144–45). In *O'Keeffe v. Ireland* App no 35810/09 (ECtHR 28 January

since they have circumscribed autonomy and to properly develop they need continuity and stability.[106]

Relying on article 22 § 1 of the CRC,[107] and on the EU Directive concerning the Reception of Aliens,[108] the Court has reaffirmed, in a number of cases, that member states have positive obligations under Articles 3, 5, and 8 of the Convention, towards migrant children, whether accompanied or not and regardless of their illegal immigrant status.[109] Member states are obliged to ensure that migrant children, in light of their particular vulnerability, receive special protection and humanitarian assistance corresponding to their specific needs.[110] The authorities should do all that could reasonably be expected of them to meet such obligation.[111] Minors themselves, lawyers representing them, or NGOs supporting them, cannot be criticised for failing to take measures which had manifestly been the responsibility of the state.[112] However, the Court acknowledged that the state's obligations regarding the protection and care of minor migrants can differ depending on whether or not they are accompanied.[113] Furthermore, authorities are expected to take reasonable measures (regulations and practices) to prevent the ill treatment of migrant children of which they have, or ought to have, knowledge,[114] to ensure effective, child-friendly procedures in any proceedings involving migrant children,[115] as well as to provide effective remedies to deal with the substance of arguable complaints related to the detention of migrant minors.[116]

2014), the Court affirmed that as primary education is an 'important public service', school authorities are obliged to protect young children who are especially vulnerable and are under exclusive control of those authorities (paras 145–46, 150).

[106] See General Comment No 14 (n 92), para 84.

[107] The Committee on the Rights of the Child encourages states to take the appropriate measures to ensure that a child seeking refugee status enjoys protection and humanitarian assistance, whether alone or accompanied by parents. See CRC (n 8), art 22. The Committee emphasised that especially vulnerable children require increased attention and that the states have an obligation to ensure adequate access to adequate health, education, and other social services for these groups of children (General Comment No 14 (n 92)). See also Reception Directive (n 10).

[108] The specific situation of children, which combines vulnerability, limited autonomy and potential adulthood, requires states to grant them specific rights, such as those enshrined in the following provisions of the Charter: Right to Shelter (art 31, para 2), Right to Health (arts 8, 11, 7, 19, para 2), Right to Education (arts 9, 10, 15, 17, 19, paras 11–12), Protection of the Family and Right to Family Reunion (arts 16, 27, 19, para 6), Protection against Danger and Abuse (arts 7, para 1, 17), Prohibition of Child Labour under the age of 15 (art 7, paras 1, 3), and specific working conditions between the age of 15 and 18 (art 7).

[109] See *G.B. and others* (n 7) para 101 citing previous case law. See also chapter 4.3 in this volume.

[110] See for example *S.F. and others* (n 9), para 79; *Popov* (n 8), para 91.

[111] For example *Khan* (n 82), para 92, and *Sh.D. and others* (n 65) paras 55, 61 (where the authorities had failed to do what could reasonably be expected from them to fulfil their obligation to provide for protection and care of particularly vulnerable minors in violation of Article 3 of the Convention.

[112] *Khan* (n 82), para 90; *Sh.D. and others* (n 65) paras 58–60.

[113] *Rahimi* (n 7), para 63.

[114] *Mubilanzila Mayeke* (n 8), paras 53–54; *Muskhadzhiyeva* (n 70), para 55.

[115] *G.B. and others* (n 7) paras 167, 177, 179, 185; *H.A. and others* (n 7) paras 209–12.

[116] *G.B. and others* (n 7), paras 125–37; *H.A. and others* (n 7), paras 177–83.

So far, the Court, taking into account the extreme vulnerability of migrant children, has identified a number of concrete measures, substantive and procedural, which states are obliged to take to fulfil their positive obligations towards them once they arrive in their territory.

If in doubt as to the age of a migrant person, the age assessment should be done promptly and the person should be informed about the results of the assessment as soon as possible.[117]

The state should determine beyond a reasonable doubt whether a minor is accompanied, since the state's obligations regarding minor migrants can differ depending on whether or not they are accompanied.[118]

There should be a specific legal framework governing the situation of unaccompanied foreign minors and, if there is none, the authorities should prevent or remedy the situation, if they are in a position to do so.[119] There is an obligation on the state to employ adequate means to identify unaccompanied minors.[120] An unaccompanied minor, as soon as he or she is identified, should be provided with a guardian[121] who should seek the assistance of a lawyer or lodge adequate appeals in the name of the minor, always with a view to protecting his or her best interests.[122] The Court has further held that states have a responsibility to look after unaccompanied minors and not to abandon them when releasing them from detention. A failure to do so amounts to degrading treatment.[123] The authorities should provide secure shelter to unaccompanied minors suited to their status.[124] States are also under an obligation to facilitate the reunification of an unaccompanied foreign minor with their family.[125]

The Court has acknowledged that the deprivation of liberty of migrant children is not, in principle, contrary to domestic law.[126] However, migrant children should not be detained automatically because of their illegal status. In placing a minor in detention, the authorities have to give consideration to his or her individual circumstances, including his or her extreme vulnerability,[127] and they must do everything in their power to avoid detaining children for lengthy periods.[128]

[117] *Abdullahi Elmi* (n 6), paras 144, 146.

[118] *Rahimi* (n 7), para 63.

[119] *Mubilanzila Mayeka* (n 8), paras 56–57.

[120] *Khan* (n 82), para 87.

[121] *Rahimi* (n 7), para 89.

[122] *H.A. and others* (n 7), para 211.

[123] *Rahimi* (n 7), paras 92–93; *Khan* (n 82), para 75.

[124] *Khan* (n 82), para 93. See also *S.S. v Slovenia* App no 40938/16 (ECtHR, 30 October 2018), para 84 (with further references therein). Generally, however, the Court has held that Article 8 of the Convention does not impose a duty on states to guarantee everyone within their jurisdiction the right to be provided with a home (see *Chapman v United Kingdom* [GC] App no 27238/95 (ECtHR, 18 January 2001), para 95.

[125] *Mubilanzila Mayeka* (n 8), paras 82, 85, 90.

[126] *A.B. and others* (n 77), para 121.

[127] *Rahimi* (n 7), paras 61–62.

[128] *Popov* (n 8), paras 144–45 (two weeks' detention very long for children in an environment ill-suited to their age); *Rahimi* (n 7) (two days detention unacceptable because of the conditions of

To be lawful under article 5 § 1 of the Convention, their detention must be used as a measure of last resort and for the shortest possible time as required by Article 37 (b) of the CRC.[129] The domestic authorities have to demonstrate that they have indeed examined whether the detention was used as a measure of last resort, i.e., that they have verified that no less restrictive measure, or solution, could have been applied.[130] The Court has further noted that the move in international law towards adopting alternative measures to the administrative detention of migrants applies not only to children but also to their parents and has affirmed under Article 5 of the Convention the obligation that the authorities have to take all necessary steps to limit, as far as possible, the detention of families accompanied by children,[131] an obligation which had already been confirmed under Article 8 of the Convention.[132]

Children should not be detained in centres intended for adults.[133] Conditions in detention facilities have to be adapted for children and their position of extreme vulnerability.[134] There should be a support mechanism for migrant children in detention,[135] to provide them with counselling and educational assistance from a qualified person specially mandated for that purpose.[136] The authorities must, in addition, take all the necessary steps to enforce the removal as quickly as possible and this way limit the time spent by children in detention.[137]

Recently, in the case *G.B. and others* the Court has noted, citing a number of international documents, that various international bodies, including the Council of Europe, are increasingly calling on states to expeditiously cease or eradicate the immigration detention of children.[138] However, as of yet, the Court itself has not taken such a stand.

detention; *A.B. and others* (n 77) (eighteen days' detention disproportionate in the absence of a particular risk of absconding); *S.F. and others* (n 9) (the conditions of detention were such that the Court found violation even where detention lasted for only thirty-two or forty-one hours).

[129] Art 37 CRC provides *inter alia* that '[t]he arrest, detention or imprisonment of a child shall be in conformity with the law and shall be used only as a measure of last resort and for the shortest appropriate period of time'. See for example *A.M. and others v France* App no 24587/12 (ECtHR, 12 July 2016) and *R.C. v France* App no 76491/14 (ECtHR, 12 July 2016), paras 52, 79, where the Court did not find a violation of Article 5 § 1 of the Convention because the domestic authorities had effectively sought to establish whether the placement of the families in administrative detention was without alternative. See also *Abdullahi Elmi* (n 6), paras 111, 146.

[130] *Rahimi* (n 7); *Popov* (n 8) para 119; *Abdullahi Elmi* (n 6), para 146; *A.B. and others* (n 77) para 123; *G.B. and others* (n 7), para 151. This is also in accordance with the Parliament and Council Directive 2008/115/EC of 16 December 2008 on common standards and procedures in Member States for returning illegally staying third-country nationals [2008] OJ L348/98.

[131] *G.B. and others* (n 7), para 168.

[132] *Popov* (n 8) para 147.

[133] *Rahimi* (n 7), para 86; *Kanagaratnam* (n 8), para 85; *Mahmundi* (n 103), para 72.

[134] *Muskhadzhiyeva* (n 70), paras 57–63; *Mubilanzila Mayeka* (n 8), paras 103–04; *Kanagaratnam* (n 8), para 86. For example *Popov* (n 8), paras 93–96.

[135] *Abdullahi Elmi* (n 6), para 111; *Mahmundi* (n 103), para 72.

[136] *Mubilanzila Mayeka* (n 8), para 150.

[137] See for example *Popov* (n 8), para 146.

[138] *G.B. and others* (n 7) paras 67–79, 151.

In terms of procedural positive obligations, the Court confines itself, in accordance with the subsidiarity principle, to verifying that the domestic procedures were effective and that they safeguarded human rights.[139] The higher the degree of vulnerability, the more prompt and effective the proceedings should be for examining a migrant's detention, asylum application, and enforcement of judgments. Children should not only be provided with effective and speedy remedies but they should also be able to exercise them,[140] and they should be applied effectively in their case.[141] The information brochure outlining some of the remedies available should be written in a language which migrant children understand and interviews should be conducted in their native language in order for them to have effective access to their rights.[142] They should be able, in practice, to contact a lawyer.[143] The excessive length of time in processing asylum applications can be regarded as a lack of sufficient due diligence on the part of authorities.[144] Moreover, when deciding upon detention the states must take into consideration the best interests of the child.[145] A number of procedural obligations derive from the application of the best interests of the child assessment, which must be accompanied by certain procedural guarantees. For example, the child's best interests should be assessed by professionals who have expertise in child and adolescent development and, as far as possible, by a multidisciplinary team of professionals. The child's own views, as well as the views of his or her parents or guardian, on the child's current environment and prospects of remaining in the host country, or returning to the home country, should be taken into account.[146] Children should have appropriate legal representation, and judicial review of the decision should be allowed where it seems that appropriate procedures for establishing the best interests of the child were not followed. Decisions must be reasoned and justified. Many of the procedural guarantees for migrant children reinforced by the Court correspond to the concept of child-friendly justice developed by the Council of Europe.[147]

The Court insists on states having a greater duty to care for, and to protect, migrant children due to their extreme vulnerability, and to take the best interests of the child as a primary consideration in providing such care and protection. Both

[139] See *I.M. v France* App no 9152/09 (ECtHR, 2 February 2012), para 127.

[140] *Abdullahi Elmi* (n 6), para 123; *Mahmundi* (n 103), para 91; *Popov* (n 8), para 124; *G.B. and others* (n 7), paras 125–38. See also *I.M.* (n 142), paras 136–60.

[141] See *H.A. and others* (n 12) paras 177–83; and *G.B. and others* (n 7) paras 125–38.

[142] *Rahimi* (n 7), para 120.

[143] ibid.

[144] cf *Ndikumana v The Netherlands* App no 4714/06 (ECtHR, 6 May 2014), para 47, where the Court rejected as manifestly ill-founded the complaint by an applicant who had spent two days on the streets in front of the reception centre before he was provided with accommodation.

[145] *Rahimi* (n 7), para 109,where the Greek authorities had not examined whether the detention was in the applicant's best interests.

[146] See *mutatis mutandis*, *M. and M.* (n 56), para 171.

[147] See Guidelines of the Committee of Ministers of the Council of Europe on Child Friendly Justice (17 November 2010) <https://rm.coe.int/16804b2cf3> accessed 1 February 2020.

concepts contribute to strengthening and further developing the positive and negative obligations of states towards migrant children. Indeed, relying on various international documents and evolving state practices, the ECtHR has imposed upon states a range of special measures of care and protection of migrant children taking into account their specific needs. For the very same reason, some of the measures are applicable only to unaccompanied minors.

4.2 Assessing the Threshold of Severity Justifying the Application of Article 3

To fall within the scope of Article 3 of the Convention the ill-treatment experienced by an applicant must attain a minimum level of severity. The assessment of this minimum is relative; it depends on all the circumstances of the case, such as the duration of the treatment, its physical or mental effects and, in some instances, the sex, age, and state of health of the victim.[148] The Court ruled that treatment was 'degrading' when it was likely to inspire in victims feelings of fear, anguish, and inferiority that humiliated and degraded them.[149]

Increasingly, vulnerability, although not originally listed by the Court among the relevant circumstances, plays a role in the assessment of whether the threshold of severity justifying the application of Article 3 of the Convention has been attained. A greater degree of vulnerability justifies a lower threshold of tolerance and a higher requirement for due diligence on the part of the authorities.

In *MSS*, the Court held that, in determining whether the threshold of severity required by Article 3 had been attained, particular importance had to be attached to the applicant's status as an asylum seeker.[150] In *Khlaifia*, the Court emphasised that in order to determine whether the threshold of severity has been reached the Court should also take into account that persons deprived of their liberty, including migrants in administrative detention, are considered as being in a vulnerable situation.[151] Since migrant children, accompanied or not, are considered as being extremely vulnerable, the threshold of tolerance related to asylum seeking migrant children in detention should be very low.

In *Mubilanzila,* the Court noted that a five-year-old child was quite clearly dependent on adults and had no ability to look after herself so that, when separated from her parents and left to her own devices, she would be totally disoriented. Thus, the Court did not regard the fact that the five-year-old child received legal assistance, had daily telephone contact with her mother or uncle, and that the staff

[148] See, among many, *Mubilanzila Mayeka* (n 8), para 48.
[149] See, among many, *Khan* (n 82), para 72; *Rahimi* (n 7), para 59, and references therein.
[150] See *M.S.S.* (n 18), paras 219, 251.
[151] *Khlaifia* (n 40), para 160; *Rahimi* (n 7), para 60.

and residents at the centre did their best for her as sufficient to meet all her needs. The Court further considered that the uncoordinated attention she had received had been far from adequate.[152]

In *Muskhadzhiyeva*, the Court found a breach of Article 3 taking into consideration several factors, including the applicants' age (they had been respectively seven months, 3 and a half years, five years, and seven years old), the length of their detention (one month), the fact that the detention facility had not been adapted for minors, and medical evidence indicating that they had undergone serious psychological problems while in custody.[153]

In *Rahimi*[154] and *S.F. and others*,[155] due to the appalling conditions of the detention facility in which migrant children were kept and the way they were treated (eg lack of food, limited access to toilets), the threshold was considered to have been reached, and a violation of Article 3 of the Convention was found even in respect of very short periods of time in detention.

In *Abdullahi*, relying on *Tarakhel*, the Court emphasised that in order not to attain the threshold of severity under Article 3 of the Convention, the reception conditions for children seeking asylum must be adapted to their age, to ensure that those conditions do not 'create ... for them a situation of stress and anxiety, with particularly traumatic consequences'.[156] Furthermore, the conditions complained of, which had involved overcrowding, lack of light and ventilation, no organised activities, and a tense, violent atmosphere, for a period of around eight months, were considered by the Court to be all the more difficult in view of the applicants' vulnerable status as asylum seekers and minors.[157]

In *Kanagaratnam*, although there was no medical evidence of mental distress having been experienced by the applicants (thirteen, eleven, and eight years old) in custody, the Court considered that by placing migrant children accompanied by their mother in a closed centre for four months the Belgian authorities had exposed them to feelings of anxiety and inferiority, and had done so in full knowledge of the fact that this risked compromising their development.[158] In *Popov*, the Court held that the inappropriate conditions in which the applicant children (five months and three years old) had been obliged to live with their parents, for fifteen days, in a situation of their vulnerability, heightened by their detention, were bound to cause them distress and have serious psychological repercussions despite the lack of evidence to that effect.[159]

152 *Mubilanzila Mayeka* (n 8), para 52.
153 *Muskhadzhiyeva* (n 70), paras 57–63. See also *S.F. and others* (n 9), para 80.
154 *Rahimi* (n 7), para 86.
155 *S.F. and others* (n 9), paras 84–89.
156 *Abdullahi Elmi* (n 6), para 104; *Tarakhel* (n 16), para 119.
157 *Abdullahi Elmi* (n 6), para 111.
158 *Kanagaratnam* (n 8), paras 64–69. See also *S.F. and others* (n 9), para 81.
159 *Popov* (n 8), paras 92–103.

In five French cases from 2016, the Court noted that unlike the detention facility at issue in *Popov*, the material conditions in the detention facilities, in those cases, had not been problematic.[160] They had been adapted for families who were kept apart from other detainees and provided with specially fitted rooms and child-care materials. The Court still found that the threshold under Article 3 of the Convention had been reached and that, consequently, there was a violation of the Convention. The Court emphasised that the constraints inherent in a place of detention, and the conditions in which the facilities had been organised, had been a source of stress and anxiety for the young children (they had been between four months and four years old). In addition, one of the centres had been constructed immediately next to an airport runway and, thus, detainees were exposed to excessive levels of noise, while in the other centre, children were permanently subjected to announcements made over the centre's loudspeakers and the interior courtyard of the family area was separated from the 'mens' area by only a metal fence, allowing everything that happened inside to be observed. Lastly, children witnessed the mental distress experienced by their parents in a place of confinement that did not allow them to distance themselves.

Although over a short period of time those factors had not been sufficient to attain the threshold of severity engaging Article 3 of the Convention, the Court found, without having to rely on the medical certificates produced by the applicants, that over a longer period their accumulated effects would necessarily have affected a young child to the point of exceeding that threshold. A period of seven days of detention, in the Court's view, had been long enough to find a breach of Article 3 in such circumstances.[161]

In *HA and others*, the Court found, in particular, that the detention conditions to which the applicants had been subjected, in the various police stations they were held in, represented degrading treatment and explained that detention in those premises was likely to generate feelings of isolation from the outside world with potentially negative consequences for their physical and moral well-being.[162]

There is nothing particularly new in the Court's approach to the application of Article 3 in cases related to the detention of migrant children. The Court is simply taking all the circumstances, which include the applicant's age and particular situation of vulnerability, into account when deciding whether the level of severity of a treatment falls within the scope of Article 3 of the Convention. Yet, the Court makes a presumption with regard to the extreme vulnerability of migrant children, whether accompanied or not. It requires no medical evidence for proving that detained migrant children have experienced feelings of anxiety and inferiority. Actually, the Court took the view that the constraints inherent in closed centres

[160] *R.M. and others v France* App no 33201/11 (ECtHR, 12 July 2016); *A.B. and others* (n 77); *A.M. and others* (n 141); *R.K. and others v France* App no 68264/14 (ECtHR, 12 July 2016); and *R.C.* (n 132).

[161] *R.M. and others* (n 163) paras 72–76; *AB and others* (n 77), paras 111–15; *R.K. and others* (n 163), paras 68–72; *R.C. (n 132)*, paras 36–40.

[162] See *H.A. and others* (n 7) paras 166–70.

for migrants (administrative detention) are, as such, a source of stress and anxiety for children, regardless of their age, even when material conditions are adapted to their needs. This is because such institutions are, in many respects, similar to penal establishments and thus, detention there is likely to generate feelings of anxiety and isolation from the outside world, with potentially negative consequences for young children's physical and moral well-being.

The Court assigns great weight to the compounded extreme vulnerability of migrant children in analysing the threshold of severity under Article 3 of the Convention. If reception conditions have not been adequate and adapted to the needs of migrant children, the Court has considered even a very short period of detention to be contrary to the Convention, regardless of the age of the child.[163] In cases in which the material conditions in migrant detention facilities appeared to have been proper but children were exposed to excessive noise pollution from the nearby airport, the Court took the view that while such places are a source of stress and anxiety for children it would only become inappropriate for children if they were held there for a longer period of time (seven days already qualifying as a long period). In such cases, the Court found the passage of time of paramount importance in assessing whether the threshold under Article 3 had been reached.

Consequently, in assessing the threshold of severity under Article 3 of the Convention regarding administrative detention of migrant children, the Court is mainly concentrated on three elements which are interrelated: the extreme vulnerability of children, the conditions of detention, and the duration of detention. The conditions of detention have to be adapted to the specific needs of migrant children. The less adapted the conditions the shorter the detention should be. The Court recently emphasised that the detention of minor migrants even for a very short period of time in unsuitable conditions gives rise to issues under Article 3.[164]

Furthermore, in *Rahimi* and *Khan*, the Court found that the threshold of gravity required by Article 3 of the Convention had been reached in those cases mainly because the authorities failed to follow up with, and supervise, an unaccompanied minor, who belongs to the most vulnerable group in society.[165] According to the Court, the threshold is reached in situations in which owing to the authorities' indifference, the applicant, left to fend for himself, must have experienced profound anxiety and concern, as, for example, the applicant did in the *Rahimi* case,[166] or where on account of the failure of the state authorities to take the requisite action, the applicant had found himself living for a prolonged time, in a makeshift camp, in a situation tantamount to degrading treatment, despite the support of various NGOs.[167]

[163] Two days in *Rahimi* (n 7), paras 81, 85–86; and thirty-two hours in *S.F. and others* (n 9), paras 84–92.
[164] *G.B. and others* (n 7), para 117.
[165] *Rahimi* (n 7), para 59; *Khan* (n 82), para 75.
[166] *Rahimi* (n 7), para 59.
[167] *Khan* (n 82), paras 92–94. See also *Sh.D. and others* (n 65), paras 52–62.

On the other hand, the Court has considered that open facilities per se do not have such a detrimental effect on migrant children. In *H.A. and others*, the Court held that the living conditions in the Diavata Centre, which had a 'safe zone' set up in order to meet the needs of unaccompanied minors and which was an open facility where the applicants could go in and out as they pleased, had not exceeded the threshold of seriousness required to engage Article 3 of the Convention.[168]

4.3 Determining the (Un)lawfulness of the Detention of Migrant Children under Article 5 of the Convention

In order to meet the requirement of lawfulness, the detention of migrant children under Article 5 § 1 (f) of the Convention must comply with the substantive and procedural rules of the relevant national law.[169] That law must, itself, be in conformity with the Convention, including the general principles expressed, or implied, in it. Article 5 § 1 case law refers to the following principles defining lawfulness: the principle of the rule of law,[170] the principle of necessity and proportionality,[171] and the principle of protection against arbitrariness,[172] which is the very aim of Article 5.[173] Consequently, detention must be lawful in both domestic and Convention terms.[174]

[168] *H.A. and others* (n 7), paras 171–76.

[169] The Convention refers essentially to national law, but also, where appropriate to other applicable legal standards, including international law. See *Medvedyev and others v France* App no 3394/03 (ECtHR, 29 March 2010), para 79. For example, in *Rahimi* (n 7), para 108, the Court found detention to be unlawful because the decision to detain the applicant appeared to be the result of automatic application of domestic rule which did not conform to Articles 3 and 37 of the CRC.

[170] Principle of the rule of law relates to the 'quality of the law' which implies that relevant law regulating deprivation of liberty must be clearly and precisely defined, foreseeable in its application to a degree that is reasonable in the circumstances, and accessible. See *J.N. v United Kingdom* App no 37289/12 (ECtHR, 19 May 2016), para 77; see also *Khlaifia* (n 40), para 92; and *Abdolkhani and Karimnia v Turkey* App no 30471/08 (ECtHR, 22 September 2009), paras 128–35.

[171] All that is required for detention under Art 5 § 1 (f) is that 'action is being taken with a view to deportation or extradition'. See for example *Chahal v United Kingdom* [GC] App no 22414/93 (ECtHR, 15 November 1996), para 112. The only exception in this respect is when the migrant child is involved. If in such cases test of necessity of detention is not satisfied (the detention is a measure of last resort with no alternative and it was applied for the shortest possible time), the Court treats detention as being arbitrary and thus unlawful under Art 5 § 1 (f). See *A.B. and others* (n 77), paras 120, 123.

[172] To avoid being branded as arbitrary, detention under Art 5 § 1 (f) must be carried out in good faith; it must be closely connected to the ground of detention relied on by the Government; the place and conditions of detention should be appropriate; and the length of the detention should not exceed that reasonably required for the purpose pursued. *A. and others v United Kingdom* App no 3455/05 (ECtHR, 19 February 2009), para 164. Consequently, a deprivation of liberty may be lawful in terms of domestic law but still arbitrary and thus contrary to the Convention (ibid). See also *Saadi* (n 98), para 74.

[173] *Simons v Belgium* (dec) App no 71407/10 (ECtHR, 28 August 2012), para 32.

[174] *G.B. and others* (n 7), para 146; *Bilalova and others v Poland* App no 23685/14 (ECtHR, 19 March 2020), para 74.

Both the concept of vulnerability and the principle of the best interests of the child are used as tools to establish whether detention was arbitrary and, thus, unlawful under article 5 § 1 (f) of the Convention. As explained above, the extreme vulnerability of migrant children is an important element in assessing whether the place and conditions of detention have been appropriate, while the extent to which the domestic authorities have taken into consideration the best interests of the child is vital in analysing whether the detention had been carried out in good faith.

Detention of a migrant child, whether accompanied or not, in a closed detention facility in which material conditions are not adapted to the needs of children is considered arbitrary and thus unlawful, regardless of its duration[175] and the age of the child.[176] According to the Court, by keeping children in an inappropriate place and in inappropriate conditions, the respondent state fails to sufficiently protect their right to liberty.[177]

In *Rahimi*, a seventeen-year-old minor at the time was kept for a short period in appalling conditions contrary to human dignity. In finding that his administrative detention was unlawful under Article 5 § 1 of the Convention, the Court, in addition to criticising the conditions in which he was held, reproached the Greek authorities for failing to assess whether the detention was used as a measure of last resort and whether detaining him was in his best interests.[178] This way the Court introduced two procedural duties for states under Article 5 § 1 (f). Such a procedural approach contributes to preventing substantive violations of children's rights and it is in accordance with the increasing 'proceduralisation' of the Court's case law. Thereby, the Court lays primary responsibility for protecting children's rights on the domestic authorities confirming the subsidiary nature of the Convention system.

By establishing these two procedural obligations the Court is also encouraging states to comply with their international obligations.[179] Yet, the Court has never explained the relationship between these two procedural duties. It has never considered whether it would be lawful to detain a migrant child as a measure of last resort for which no alternatives exist, even in cases in which domestic authorities would, through correct procedures, establish that his or her detention would be

[175] *Rahimi* (n 7), para 107. See also *G.B. and others* (n 7), para 117; *S.F. and others* (n 9); and *Bilalova and others* (n 177), para 75.

[176] In cases in which violation of Art 5 §1 (f) was found on the bases of conditions of detention, the age of children ranged from couple of months to seventeen years.

[177] *Mubilanzila Mayeka* (n 8), para 100, (unaccompanied minor); *Muskhadzhiyeva* (n 70), paras 73, 74; and *Kanagaratnam* (n 8), para 80 (accompanied children). In *Rahimi* (n 7), para 110; *Abdullahi Elmi* (n 6), paras 147; *H.A. and others* (n 7), para 196 the Court also considered, besides inappropriate conditions, procedural failures in not searching for alternative measures (in all three cases) or doubts as to the authorities' good faith (*Abdullahi Elmi*).

[178] *Rahimi* (n 7), paras 108–10.

[179] In *Rahimi* (n 7) the Court considered Arts 3 and 37 (b) CRC.

contrary to his or her best interests.[180] In short, the Court should not limit itself to a purely procedural review of these procedural obligations. It would be perverse to conclude that the detention of migrant minors is lawful once the state has assessed the best interests of the child and has effectively sought alternative measures to detention.[181] A proper process does not necessarily guarantee a proper outcome. Thus, even if the procedure under domestic law was compliant with the requirements of the Convention the Court should still check whether the substantive requirements were fulfilled as well.

In cases subsequent to *Rahimi*, the Court has looked at whether detention had been used as a measure of last resort even when it found that the place and conditions of the detention had been inappropriate.[182] Notwithstanding, in light of the previous case law, the two should be seen as independent requirements under Article 5 § 1 (f) and, therefore, a violation of either should make the detention arbitrary and, hence, unlawful.[183] Accordingly, in situations in which a migrant child was held in inappropriate conditions, the fact that the state may have searched for alternative measures should be irrelevant in finding a violation under Article 5 § 1 (f) of the Convention.[184]

The Court has acknowledged that the environment in which migrant children find themselves when detained for expulsion purposes is itself a source of anxiety and tension that may cause children serious harm and further exacerbate their vulnerability.[185] As a result, the Court has taken the position that even when the organisation and material conditions in immigration detention facilities are specifically adapted to the children's situation of vulnerability, their detention would still be considered unlawful if alternative measures had not been effectively sought.[186]

However, the Court did not find detention to be unlawful in cases in which the domestic authorities, under the same circumstances, had effectively searched for alternative, less coercive measures and had dismissed such options.[187] This was so even in cases in which the Court had held that the detention in issue, due to its long duration, had reached the threshold of severity under Article 3 of the

[180] In *A.M. and others* (n 141), paras 48–53, and *R.C.* (n 132), paras 36–40 detention was considered lawful because authorities established that there was no option of resorting to a less coercive measure, and also considered that keeping children with their parents was in their interest.

[181] Examples for that could be found in two French cases in which the Court has held that conditions in detention facility were degrading, but still considered confinement of migrant children in such conditions lawful because authorities were effectively searching for alternatives, albeit unsuccessfully. See nn 197–201 in this volume and accompanying text.

[182] For example in *Popov* (n 8), para 119.

[183] Requirements spelled out in *Saadi* (n 98) and later reiterated in a number of cases were laid down in accumulation.

[184] This could be eventually at most only an aggravating or mitigating element under Art 41 of the Convention. But the Court is usually not making such fine distinctions under Art 41.

[185] *A.B. and others* (n 77), para 122; *S.F. and others* (n 9), para 83.

[186] See in this respect eg *A.B. and others* (n 77), paras 119–25; *R.M. and others* (n 163), paras 72–76; *R.K. and others* (n 163), paras 68–72; and *Bilalova and others* (n 177), paras 79–80.

[187] As for example in *A.M. and others* (n 141), paras 48–53, or *R.C.* (n 132), paras 36–40.

Convention.[188] In short, the Court took a position that detention which is considered degrading under Article 3 of the Convention, due to its duration in places of detention which are inherently a source of anxiety and tension for migrant children, could still be deemed lawful under Article 5 § 1 (f).[189] This is a contradiction, which the Court should rethink. It follows from the case law relating to Article 5 § 1 (f) that, in order not to be regarded as arbitrary and, therefore, unlawful, among other requirements, the places and conditions of detention must be appropriate.[190] If keeping a person under particular conditions after a certain period of time is considered degrading, then, after that period of time keeping a person in such conditions is simply inappropriate and this should also violate Article 5 § 1 (f). This should be so even if the domestic authorities have effectively assessed that there is no other less intrusive measure available to fulfill the aim of deportation or extradition of a child.

Notwithstanding certain deviations, from the majority of cases it follows that, as a matter of principle, merely placement for a short period of time under appropriate conditions could be compatible with the Convention, provided that the authorities establish that they resorted to this measure only after having verified concretely that no other less intrusive measure could be put in place. Otherwise the detention would not be considered necessary and thus it would be arbitrary and unlawful.[191] Furthermore, according to *Rahimi*, failure to actively search for an alternative placement indicates that the authorities could not be deemed to have acted in good faith. Accordingly, their actions are again seen as arbitrary and, thus, unlawful under Article 5 § 1 of the Convention.[192]

Consequently, the Court has gradually established three cumulative elements that are important for establishing the lawfulness of the detention of migrant children: appropriate conditions of detention, short duration of detention, and detaining as a last resort. This was recently confirmed in *G.B. and others* and *Bilalova*.[193]

[188] See (n 190).

[189] The Court has found non-violation of Art 5 § 1 (f) in circumstances in which it has found violation of Article 3 due to bad conditions in detention facility only in three other cases related to migrants, however, without providing any proper explanation. See *Mahmundi and others* (n 103), para 95; *Horshill v Greece* App no 70427/11 (ECtHR, 1 August 2013), paras 54–66; and *E.A. v Greece* App no 74308/10 (ECtHR, 30 July 2015), paras 84–90. Article 5 and Article 3 of the Convention have different aims. Thus, finding a violation of Article 3 on the basis of inappropriate conditions in detention facility should not in itself be used as an excuse for not taking conditions of detention into consideration once again under Article 5 when considering lawfulness of detention. On the contrary, not finding unlawfulness under such circumstances should be carefully justified, if justification is possible at all.

[190] See (n 175).

[191] See for example *A.B. and others* (n 77), para 123; *Popov* (n 8), para 119.

[192] See *Rahimi* (n 7), para 109. See also (n 183) and (n 184). The 'necessary and proportionate' language has been also used by the Human Rights Committee (HRC), Committee against Torture (CAT). For examples see Moriette Grange and Izabelle Mojcher, *When Is Immigration Detention Lawful? The Monitoring Practices of UN Human Rights Mechanisms* (2017) Global Detention Project Working Paper No 21, 5–7 <https://www.globaldetentionproject.org/wp-content/uploads/2017/02/Grange-Majcher-GDP-Working-Paper-Feb-2017.pdf> accessed 13 February 2020.

[193] In *G.B. and others* (n 7), para 151; *Bilalova and others* (n 177), paras 78–82.

4.4 Assessing Proportionality under Article 8 of the Convention in Connection with a Right to Family Life of Migrant Children in Administrative Detention

Under Article 8 of the Convention, states have an obligation to 'act in a manner calculated to allow those concerned to lead a normal family life'.[194] Although mutual enjoyment by parent and child of each other's company constitutes a fundamental element of family life, the sole fact that the family unit is maintained does not necessarily guarantee respect for the right to a family life. Indeed, the Court took a position that the fact of confining the migrant children together with their parent(s) in a detention centre and thereby subjecting them to living conditions typical of a custodial institution, can be regarded as an interference with the effective exercise of their family life.[195] Such an interference entails a violation of Article 8 of the Convention unless it can be justified under paragraph 2 of that article, in other words, unless it is 'in accordance with the law', it pursues one or more of the aims enumerated in that provision, and it is 'necessary in a democratic society' for the fulfilment of said aim or aims.

When the Court is reviewing whether administrative detention of migrant families with children constitutes (dis)proportionate interference with the effective exercise of their family life, the Court takes account of the child's best interests, which according to its well-established case law and international law, in particular the CRC, must be a primary consideration in all decisions concerning children.[196] Contrary to its positions under Articles 3 and 5 of the Convention, the Court has defined relatively precisely, under Article 8, what is considered to be in the best interests of migrant children who are detained, or at risk of being detained, and which criteria to apply in assessing their best interests. Relying on international reports, the Court took the view that the protection of the migrant child's best interests involves keeping the family together, as far as possible. At the same time, the Court emphasised that the child's best interests cannot be confined to that. Furthermore, the authorities have to take all necessary steps to limit, as far as possible, the detention of families accompanied by children. They should consider alternatives to detention so that the detention of minors is a measure of last resort.[197] The Court also insisted that the authorities should keep the duration of detention

[194] *Marckx v Belgium* App no 6833/74 (ECtHR, 13 June 1979), para 31.

[195] See *Bistieva* (n 93), para 73 and cases cited therein. Indeed, whilst mutual enjoyment by parent and child of each other's company constitutes a fundamental element of family life, it cannot be inferred from this that the sole fact that the family unit is maintained necessarily guarantees respect for the right to a family life.

[196] See *Popov* (n 8), paras 139, 140, including further references. See also nn 92–95 above and accompanying text.

[197] ibid, paras 141, 147; see also *Bistieva* (n 93), paras 78, 85. This was recently transposed in discussion under Article 5 § 4 of the Convention. See *G.B. and others* (n 7), para 168.

to a minimum, which calls for promptness and due diligence on the part of the authorities in asylum proceedings.[198]

In *Bistieva*, the Court clarified that, in the absence of a proper justification, administrative detention of families would be considered a disproportionate interference, even if there is a risk of absconding.[199] The Court has already emphasised that the states' interest in foiling attempts to circumvent immigration rules must not deprive aliens of the protection afforded by international conventions or deprive foreign minors, especially if unaccompanied, of the protection their status warrants.[200]

In performing the proportionality assessment, both in *Popov*[201] and in *Bistieva*,[202] the Court limited itself to a procedural review, in line with the 'proceduralisation' trend in the Court's jurisprudence. However, there are significant dangers in conducting an exclusively procedural review, especially if it leads to complete deference in the review of the substantive outcomes at the domestic level.[203] Fulfilment of procedural obligations by the state does not mean that the right could not otherwise be compromised.[204]

Thus, in my view, a two-step assessment of the best interests of the child and the balancing of various interests is needed. First, the assessment of the quality of the domestic procedures (procedural review) should be done. If the quality of the domestic procedure was in compliance with Convention requirements, the Court would still have to confirm that there was no substantive violation.[205] If, on the contrary, the domestic authorities have not properly conducted the proportionality analysis, the Court might already find a violation of Article 8 in that respect. However, even in such circumstances, sidestepping a substantive review could be criticised. For example, rolling over the obligation to protect the substantive rights of children to states might, in certain cases, prolong the duration of proceedings and incur additional expenses for the applicants. This, in itself, could be perceived as being contrary to the best interests of the child when children are applicants

198 *Popov* (n 8), paras 132–48; *Bistieva* (n 93), paras 69–88.

199 *Bistieva* (n 93), para 88.

200 *Mubilanzila Mayeka* (n 8) para 81.

201 *Popov* (n 8), paras 145–46. See also *A.B. and others* (n 77), paras 144–56; and *R.K. and others* (n 163), paras 105–17.

202 *Bistieva* (n 93), para 88.

203 The literature on the procedural review in the case law of the ECtHR is divided on the question of whether positive inferences from due procedural diligence at the national level can go so far as to bar the Court's own normative engagement on the issue in question (complete reference). For the review of the relevant literature and ECtHR's case law see, Oddný Mjöll Arnardóttir, 'The "Procedural Turn" under the ECHR and Presumption of Convention Compliance' (2017) 15 *International Journal of Constitutional Law* 9.

204 On development of the procedural review before the Court and its advantages and disadvantages see more in Jenneke Gerards and Eva Brems (eds), *Procedural Review in European Fundamental Rights Cases* (2017 Cambridge University Press).

205 Such approach to procedural and substantive violations of the Convention is well established under Articles 2 and 3 of the Convention.

before the Court. The Court is not, and should not be, immune from taking the best interests of the child as a primary consideration when it, itself, is making decisions affecting children. Thus, I would argue that the best interests of the child should guide the Court in deciding whether it will conduct merely a procedural review or embark on substantive review in a particular case.

5. Conclusion

Having regard to the extreme vulnerability of migrant children, the Court is constantly enhancing and strengthening the protection of their rights under the Convention taking into consideration their specific needs, adopting additional safeguards with regard to the deprivation of their liberty, and further limiting the circumstances under which their immigration detention is possible. The Court's jurisprudence is gradually evolving towards a child-sensitive and child-responsive rights-based approach to the migration of children.

Taking into consideration the particular vulnerability of migrant children, the Court is slowly, but steadily, lowering the threshold for finding a violation of Article 3 in cases of their detention, regardless of whether they are accompanied or not and regardless of their age.[206] The Court has acknowledged that the constraints inherent in a place of detention and the conditions of organised life in detention facilities are a source of stress and anxiety for migrant children,[207] and that detention was likely to generate feelings of isolation from the outside world with negative consequences for the migrant child's physical and moral well-being.[208] Moreover, the Court has confirmed many times in its rulings that: 'the child's extreme vulnerability is the decisive factor and takes precedence over considerations relating to the status of illegal immigrant'.[209] Under the Article 5 § 1 (f) requirement of lawfulness, the Court has introduced procedural obligations for the states to assess the best interests of the child and to search for less restrictive alternatives. Detention may be imposed only as a measure of last resort, in the least restrictive setting, for the shortest possible period of time, under conditions that respect children's human rights, and in a manner that takes into account, as a primary consideration, the best interests of the child.[210] Under Article 8, the Court has imposed procedural safeguards on the detention of migrant children, which serve to ensure that interference with family life is proportionate. The Court requires states to limit and carefully evaluate the need to detain families accompanied by children, instead prioritising non-custodial solutions for the entire family and securing

[206] See section 2 of this chapter.
[207] *Popov* (n 8), para 102.
[208] *H.A. and others* (n 7), para 168. *Sh.D. and others* (n 65), para 50.
[209] See most recently *G.B. and others* (n 7), para 101, citing a number of previous cases.
[210] See section 3 of this chapter.

prompt consideration of asylum proceedings.[211] Under both Articles 5 and 8 of the Convention, the Court requires member states to provide judicial review as a way of preventing substantive violations of the rights of migrant children placed in administrative detention and to introduce a number of child-friendly procedural guarantees.[212] Nonetheless, the Court is avoiding taking a clear stand on whether the detention of migrant children, as such, is contrary to their best interests. Should the Court continue to do so?

In 2005, in General Comment No 6, the Committee on the Rights of the Child gave substantive guidance for the interpretation of the principle of the best interests of migrant children according to which '[i]n application of Article 37 of the CRC and the principle of the best interests of the child, unaccompanied or separated children should not, as a general rule, be detained. Detention cannot be justified solely on the basis of the child being unaccompanied or separated, or on their migratory or residence status, or lack thereof.'[213] In 2012, the Committee called on states to 'completely cease the detention of children in general on the basis of their immigration status' and 'adopt alternatives to detention that fulfil the best interests of the child.'[214] Furthermore, in 2017 the Committee on the Rights of the Child together with the Committee on the Protection of the Rights of All Migrant Workers released a Joint General Comment which provides authoritative guidance on the interpretation of state obligations regarding the human rights of children in the context of international migration in which it reinforced its previous critical position regarding the immigration detention of children.[215]

The Court can hardly ignore these changes, in particular, because in the past ten years it has developed its own jurisprudence related to the immigration detention of children around Rule 37 (b) of the CRC and the principle of ultimate remedy as interpreted in General Comment No 6, using it to justify limiting the detention of migrant children. With time this rule has practically turned into the sole precondition under which the immigration detention of children may still be acceptable under the Convention. Now the time has come for the Court to reconsider whether it should continue to apply the principle of 'detaining as a last resort' regardless of the call of the Committee to completely cease the detention of children on the basis of their immigration status. To take a clear stand in this regard is crucial for the development of the ECtHR's jurisprudence in relation to the immigration detention of migrant children.

[211] See section 4 of this chapter.

[212] See section 4 of this chapter.

[213] Committee on the Rights of the Child, 'General Comment No 6 on the treatment of unaccompanied and separated children outside their country of origin' (2005) UN Doc CRC/GC/2005/6. Up to now the Court has referred to General Comment No 6 only once, see *Abdullahi Elmi* (n 6), para 56.

[214] The UN Committee on the Rights of the Child, Report of the 2012 Day of General Discussion on the Rights of All Children in the Context of International Migration, paras 78 and 79.

[215] Joint General Comment No 3/22 (n 115), para III.B.32.f.

In setting out its position, the Court cannot simply ignore the fact that the Convention should be interpreted, as far as possible, in harmony with other rules of international law of which it forms a part.[216] The central international instrument for defining the best interests of the child is the CRC and the central body that provides interpretation of that instrument is the Committee on the Rights of the Child. The Court can also not ignore that following the lead of the Committee on the Rights of the Child, a growing number of international organisations, including the UN General Assembly,[217] the Committee of Migrant Workers (CMW),[218] the Parliamentary Assembly of the Council of Europe (PACE),[219] the Office of the UN High Commissioner for Human Rights (OHCHR),[220] and the Council of Europe Special Representative of the Secretary General on migrant and refugee children[221] have joined its call for the detention of migrant children to cease. The Council of Europe Strategy for the Rights of the Child (2016–2021) emphasised that the administrative detention of migrant and other children, and the conditions of deprivation of liberty, pose serious challenges to the realisation of their rights.[222] The Council of Europe Action Plan on protecting refugee and migrant children in Europe (2017–2019) proposed, *inter alia*, immediate action to avoid resorting

[216] *Hasan v United Kingdom* App no 29750/09 (ECtHR, 16 September 2014), para 77.

[217] UN General Assembly adopted on 19 September 2016 at its 71st session, New York Declaration for Refugees and Migrants, A/Res/71/1 < https://www.unhcr.org/57e39d987> accessed 20 February 2020, para 33, which recognised that detention for the purposes of determining migration status is seldom, if ever, in the best interest of the child, and pledged to work towards the ending of this practice. However, banning of the practice was ultimately omitted from the document.

[218] CMW also calls for detention of children to cease (CMW, 'Concluding observations on Belize' (26 September 2014) UN Doc CMW/C/BLZ/CO/1). It calls for expeditious and complete halt of detention of children on the basis of their or their parents' immigration status (CMW, 'Concluding observations on the initial report of Nicaragua' (11 October 2016) UN Doc CMW/C/NIC/CO/; 'Concluding observations on the second periodic report of Sri Lanka' (11 October 2016) UN Doc CMW/C/LKA/CO/2; 'Concluding observations on the initial report of Turkey' (31 May 2016) UN Doc CMW/C/TUR/CO/1; 'Concluding observations on the initial report of the Niger' (11 October 2016) UN Doc CMW/C/NER/CO/1).

[219] The CoE Parliamentary Assembly has recalled, in its Resolution 2020 on The Alternatives to Immigration Detention of Children of 3 October 2014, that unaccompanied children should never be detained and that the detention of children on the basis of their or their parents' immigration status is contrary to the best interests of the child and constitutes a child rights violation. See <https://assembly.coe.int/nw/xml/XRef/Xref-XML2HTML-en.asp?fileid=21295&lang=en> accessed 16 December 2020.

[220] See UN Human Rights Office of the High Commissioner, 'UN Child Rights Experts call for EU-wide ban on child immigration detention' (UNHR, 21 February 2018) <https://www.ohchr.org/EN/NewsEvents/Pages/DisplayNews.aspx?NewsID=22681&LangID=E> accessed 10 May 2019. According to the Committee, a number of promising practices already exist in Europe and elsewhere, which allow for effective migration management while guaranteeing the protection of the best interests of the child. These include providing children and their families with community-based placement; access to services in a protective environment, on a non-discriminatory basis, with child-friendly, clear information and support; and the appointment of guardians at the point of arrival or upon first identification of the unaccompanied child.

[221] Mr Tomáš Boček, issued a 'Thematic Report on migrant and refugee children' (SG/Inf(2017)13) in which he emphasised that immigration detention was never in the best interests of the child.

[222] CoE Strategy for the Rights of the Child (2016–2021) (Council of Europe, March 2016) para 17. For the implementation of the Strategy see, CoE Strategy for the Rights of the Child (2016–2021)—Mid-term Evaluation Report (Council of Europe, November 2019) 15, 18–19.

to the deprivation of children's liberty on the sole ground of their immigration status.[223]

Also, a growing number of Council of Europe Member States either do not apply immigration detention to children, such as Andorra, Armenia, and Iceland; or prohibit the immigration detention of children below a certain age, such as Switzerland that prohibits the detention of children below the age of fifteen, and Montenegro that prohibits the detention of children below the age of sixteen.[224]

Numerous studies consistently show that detention has a profoundly negative impact on the well-being of children. Even short periods of detention can cause serious psychological and physical harm that undermines cognitive development.[225] Furthermore, out of fear that they might be detained or deported, irregular child migrants are unable to access education and healthcare, and to assert their rights.

The Court should not disregard 'the fact that the Convention is a "living instrument which must be interpreted in the light of present-day conditions" [and] that the increasingly high standard being required in the area of the protection of human rights and fundamental liberties correspondingly and inevitably requires greater firmness in assessing breaches of the fundamental values of democratic societies'.[226] Accordingly, there is a strong incentive for the Court to rely on the interpretation of the best interests of the child under Article 37 (b) of the CRC as provided by the Committee. In a recent judgment, the Court noted that various international bodies, including the Council of Europe, are increasingly calling on states to expeditiously and completely cease or eradicate the immigration detention of children. At the same time the Court referred to the principle of 'detaining as a last resort.'[227] The Court signalled that it is aware of the above described developments, but continued to rely on existing jurisprudence.[228]

If the Court continues, in the future, to take a different position from the Committee, it should provide a reasoned and well explained justification for

[223] The Action Plan was adopted at the 127th Session of the Committee of Ministers in Nicosia, Cyprus, on 19 May 2017.

[224] See PACE, 'A study of immigration detention practices and the use of alternatives to detention of children' (October 2017), paras 19–41 <http://www.assembly.coe.int/LifeRay/MIG/EndImmigrationDetention/2017/2017-ImmigrationDetentionPracticesStudy-EN.pdf> accessed 16 December 2020.

[225] Laura CN Wood, 'Impact of punitive immigration policies, parent–child separation and child detention on the mental health and development of children' BMJ Paediatrics Open, published online 26 September 2018 <https://www.ncbi.nlm.nih.gov/pmc/articles/PMC6173255/#__ffn_sectitle> accessed 21 February 2020; Martha von Werthern, Kathy Robjant, Zoe Chui, and others, 'The impact of immigration detention on mental health: a systematic review' *BMC Psychiatry* 18, 382 (2018) https://doi.org/10.1186/s12888-018-1945-y accessed 21 February 2020. See also IOM, Child Immigration Detention is not Only Wrong, It Is Ineffective (16 September 2019) <https://www.iom.int/news/child-immigration-detention-not-only-wrong-it-ineffective> accessed 21 February 2020.

[226] *Mubilanzila Mayeka* (n 8), para 48.

[227] *G.B. and others* (n 7), paras 151, 168.

[228] The facts of the case themselves did not require the Court to pronounce itself in this regard because violation of Art 3 and Art 5 § 1 and 4 of the Convention was clearly established due to many shortcomings in the conditions of detention and procedures before domestic authorities.

doing so. In any case the Court should interpret 'the principle of last resort' as requiring states to put in place non-custodial and community-based alternatives to the detention of migrant children, and their families, and be clear that the lack of such facilities should not be used as a justification for their detention.[229] If, on the contrary, the Court does acknowledge that the detention of children on the basis of their immigration status is not acceptable anymore it would be unlawful under Article 5 § 1 to detain a migrant child solely, or primarily, on that basis.[230] Furthermore, the Court would have to rethink the consequences such a position would have, for assessing the threshold of severity under Article 3 if the liberty of migrant children was, nonetheless, limited, as well as its proportionality analysis under Article 8 of the Convention.

[229] Such interpretation would be in harmony with the Global Compact for Refugees, see (n 8) para 60 and Global Compact for Safe, Orderly and Regular Migration, UN Doc. A/RES/73/195 (19 December 2018), para 29 (f), both of which aim at realisation of the UN Sustainable Development Goals which among the targets relevant to equal opportunities identified the need to facilitate, orderly, safe, regular, and responsible migration and mobility of people, including through the implementation of planned and well managed migration policies.

[230] Of course, it would be possible to detain migrant children for some other valid reasons under Art 5 of the Convention.

6

'Handle with Care' in Strasbourg

The Effective Access of Vulnerable Undocumented Migrants to Minimum Socio-economic Rights

Francesca Ippolito and Carmen Pérez González

1. Introduction

Despite unilateral, bilateral, and multilateral efforts for managing migration,[1] irregular migratory movements[2] are common practice. Often, states accept significant numbers of immigrants staying irregularly within its borders. At the same time, an individual right to migrate, to decide one's place of residency, has not yet taken shape in international law. Quite the contrary, states retain their right to establish migration controls and, consequently, to define the conditions an individual has to meet in order to legally migrate to their territories and to expel them when those conditions are not met. Enforcing migratory laws and policies has been considered 'the last bastion of sovereignty'[3] and, consequently, international law recognizes states' 'sovereign right to enact and implement migratory and border security measures'.[4] But states' right to expel is not an unconditional right. First, it is constrained due to legal duties, derived in particular from the principle of *non-refoulement*,[5] which means that certain undocumented migrants must be allowed

[1] A 'Global Compact for Safe, Orderly and Regular Migration' set in motion by the New York Declaration adopted in September 2016 was adopted on 13 July 2018. It was endorsed on 10 December 2018 at an Intergovernmental Conference held in Marrakech and endorsed by the UN General Assembly on 19 December 2018. The final version of the Global Compact is available at <https://refugeesmigrants.un.org/migration-compact> accessed 1 November 2018.

[2] Those taking place outside the regulatory norms of the origin, transit, and destination countries.

[3] Catherine Dauvergne, *Making People Illegal: What Globalization Means for Migration and Law* (Cambridge University Press 2008) 4.

[4] See para 3 b) of UNGA Res 67/172 (3 April 2013) UN Doc A/RES/67/172. In accordance with this generally accepted principle of Public International Law, Art 1 of the International Law Commission (ILC) Draft Articles on the expulsion of aliens (adopted in 2014), establishes that 'a State has the right to expel an alien from its territory'. See also paras 64–67 of International Court of Justice Judgment of 30 November 2010: *Ahmadou Sadio Diallo (Republic of Guinea v Democratic Republic of the Congo)* [2010] ICJ Rep 639. This principle is also enshrined in the ECtHR's approach to migrants' human rights.

[5] Having acquired the status of *ius cogens*, this principle serves as a shield to protect aliens from deportation to face torture or other serious violations of their fundamental rights, including the

Francesca Ippolito and Carmen Pérez González, *'Handle with Care' in Strasbourg* In: *Migration and the European Convention on Human Rights*. Edited by: Başak Çali, Ledi Bianku, and Iulia Motoc, Oxford University Press (2021). © The Several Contributors. DOI: 10.1093/oso/9780192895196.003.0006

to stay. Second, a state's desire to enforce deportations may also face political limitations. In certain circumstances, mass deportation can be impossible or not politically desirable, resulting in states *de facto* allowing individuals to remain in their territory unlawfully, which poses important challenges to European liberal democracies.[6]

In this context, International Human Rights Law (IHRL) has identified migrants unlawfully present in the territory of destination countries as a vulnerable group and tried to progressively impose upon states' specific obligations, which seek to protect them against the consequences of that vulnerability.[7] A variety of international and European human rights instruments including the European Social Charter,[8] the International Convention on the Protection of the Rights of All Migrant Workers and Members of Their Families,[9] the United Nations Convention on the Rights of the Child (CRC),[10] and different ILO instruments,[11] require states to guarantee that all migrants have access to certain rights. Addressing and reducing migrants' vulnerability is also one of the goals of the Global Compact for Safe, Orderly and Regular Migration.[12] Along with the incorporation into international instruments of particular obligations regarding the protection of social and economic rights, international human rights protection bodies have drawn specific

protection of their life or physical integrity. In this context, obligations derived from *non-refoulment* principle have been well developed by international human rights bodies, including the ECtHR. Although the principle has not been still developed in the sense of protecting against return to socio-economic deprivation, some consequences linked to the access to health assistance have been drawn by the ECtHR (see section 3.2 of this chapter). See Michelle Foster, *International Refugee Law and Socio-Economic Rights: Refugee from Deprivation*, (Cambridge University Press 2007); and Veronika Flegar, 'Vulnerability and the Principle of Non-Refoulement in the European Court of Human Rights: Towards an Increased Scope of Protection for Persons Fleeing from Extreme Poverty?' (2016) 8 Contemporary Readings in Law and Social Justice 148.

[6] We will avoid throughout this volume the expression 'illegal migrant'. As it has been said 'the categorization of people as "illegal" has been deplored by the UN and many other institutions but remains current in the language used by numerous states': Elspeth Guild, 'Unsafe, Disorderly, and Irregular Migration? Examining the Assumptions Underlying the United Nations' New York Declaration' (2018) 50 Peace Research: The Canadian Journal of Peace and Conflict Studies 53, 68. We will refer to the unlawful presence of the migrant in the territory (see n 2) or to 'undocumented migrant' (an alien who doesn't have the right to enter or remain in the territory of a State of which he or she is not a national).

[7] Besson offers a definition of vulnerability: 'From a general point of view, we could affirm that vulnerability might be defined as the trait of an individual or a group whose interests are likely to be harmed; this is, the trait of those whose interests are threatened.' Samantha Besson, 'La vulnérabilité et la structure des droits de l'homme. L'exemple de la jurisprudence de la Cour Européenne des Droits de l'Homme' in Laurance Burgorgue-Larsen (ed), *La vulnérabilité saisie par les juges en Europe* (Pedone 2014) 59, 60. See also Alexander H E Morawa, 'Vulnerability as a Concept of International Human Rights Law' (2003) 6 Journal of International Relations and Development 139.

[8] European Social Charter (revised) ETS 35.

[9] The Convention was adopted by UNGA Res 45/158 (18 December 1990) UN Doc A/RES/45/158.

[10] Convention on the Rights of the Child (adopted 20 November 1989, entered into force 2 September 1990) 1577 UNTS 3.

[11] Available at <https://www.ilo.org/global/topics/labour-migration/lang--en/index.htm> accessed 1 November 2018.

[12] Global Compact on Migration (n 1).

obligations with regard to reducing migrant vulnerability from 'general obligations assumed by states towards all persons on their territory or under their jurisdiction, irrespective of their status'.[13]

In Europe, institutions of the Council of Europe have played a leading role in this regard. The European Committee of Social Rights (ECSR), the Parliamentary Assembly of the Council of Europe, the Commissioner for Human Rights and the European Commission against Racism and Intolerance, have adopted relevant decisions encouraging member states to ensure undocumented migrants have access to inalienable basic social rights.[14]

The European Convention on Human Rights[15] (ECHR) does not guarantee an individual right to migrate, nor has the European Court of Human Rights (ECtHR) derived such a right by way of interpretation. The right to freedom of movement is guaranteed under Article 2 Protocol No 4 ECHR,[16] which states in its second paragraph that 'everyone shall be free to leave any country, including his own'. But it does not guarantee the right to enter any country. Nevertheless, in certain cases, states have been required by the ECtHR to permit a migrant to enter or to remain in its territory.[17]

In light of this normative background, this chapter aims to explore how the ECtHR, despite the limited scope of protection for undocumented migrants enshrined in the ECHR and the Court's resistance to impose impossible or disproportionate burdens on contracting states, has contributed to the consolidation of a minimum standard of socio-economic rights for undocumented migrants.[18] In particular, this chapter focusses on Strasbourg case-law developments regarding rights to adequate housing, health care, and education, along with protections against labour exploitation and trafficking with the purpose of labour exploitation. Relevant contributions from other human rights bodies, particularly the ECSR, will be also considered in order to determine whether we can affirm the existence of minimum legal standards, a minimum core,[19] in this regard.

[13] See United Nations High Commissioner for Human Rights, *Report on the economic, social and cultural rights of migrants in host countries and State obligations in this context* (2014), para 9.

[14] See Carmen Pérez González and Francesca Ippolito, 'Eppur si muove! Nuevos cambios jurisprudenciales para la protección de los derechos sociales de los migrantes indocumentados en Europa' (2016) 53 Revista de Derecho Comunitario Europeo 79.

[15] Convention for the Protection of Human Rights and Fundamental Freedoms (European Convention on Human Rights, as amended) ETS 5.

[16] Protocol 4 to the Convention for the Protection of Human Rights and Fundamental Freedoms, securing certain rights and freedoms other than those already included in the Convention and in the first Protocol thereto ETS 46.

[17] See *Vilvarajah and others v United Kingdom* App nos 13163/87, 13164/87, 13165/87, 13447/87, and 13448/87 (ECtHR, 30 October 1991) para 102; and *Chahal v United Kingdom* [GC] App no 22414/93 (ECtHR, 15 November 1996), para 73.

[18] See Virginia Mantouvalou, 'Labour Rights in the European Convention on Human Rights: An Intellectual Justification for an Integrated Approach to Interpretation' (2013) 13 Human Rights Law Review 529.

[19] Katharine G Young, 'The Minimum Core of Economic and Social Rights: A Concept in Search of Content' (2008) 33 Yale Journal of International Law 113.

It is possible to advance that the ECtHR, and also the ECSR, have taken significant steps towards the 'humanisation' and 'dignification' of undocumented migrants. The aforementioned notion of vulnerability along with the one of human dignity will serve as core ideas for our analysis. Human dignity and vulnerability are two different but nonetheless interlinked concepts. In 2010, Anna Grear maintained—in contrast to Kantian Philosophy, according to which the essence of human dignity rests on the autonomy which is inherent in each individual[20]—that dignity might be aligned to vulnerability, as both are inherent to the human condition.[21] Along with dignity, vulnerability plays a foundational role in human rights discourse,[22] also being conceived as a source of its core values.[23] The principle of human dignity has become the key legal basis for strengthening the position of migrants who are in an irregular situation. In a direct or indirect way, human dignity has been invoked as the legal rationale for guaranteeing different social rights to both children and adult undocumented migrants. The provisions of the ECHR have been interpreted by the ECtHR in the light of this core concept to extend the protection of those provisions to migrants considered to be in an irregular administrative situation. Even if the principle of dignity is not yet perceived as independent, but as a general principle inspiring more rules and more rights, it began to be used before Courts in the supranational European context in 1995 when the ECtHR declared human dignity to be 'the very essence' of the Convention.[24]

In order to analyse the above-mentioned developments, we will first discuss ECtHR case law dealing with the recognition of the right to education of undocumented migrants (section 2). Articles 3 and 4 of the ECHR have been invoked at Strasbourg for protecting migrants unlawfully present in the states parties' territory against a range of harms—a lack of adequate housing, return to their country of origin when it could imply a risk to their health, and against labour exploitation. These 'socio-economic dimensions' of the absolute rights enshrined in those articles will be considered at section 3. Finally, some conclusions will be drawn.

[20] Immanuel Kant, *Critic of Pure Reason* (first published 1781, Macmillan 1929).

[21] Anne Grear, *Redirecting Human Rights: Facing the Challenge of Corporate Legal Humanity* (Palgrave Macmillan 2010) 196–98.

[22] ibid.

[23] Mary Neal, 'Respect for Human Dignity as 'Substantive Basic Norm' (2014) 10 International Journal of Law in Context 26, 31. See also Pawel Lukóv, 'A Difficult Legacy: Human Dignity as the Founding Value of Human Rights' (2018) 19 Human Rights Review 313.

[24] *S.W. v United Kingdom* App no 20166/92 (ECtHR, 22 November 1995), para 44. Within the European Union (EU) legal framework, the Charter of Fundamental Rights includes the right to human dignity in its first chapter, and when it mentions human dignity in art 1, it does it as the 'basis' for the other fundamental rights. Charter of Fundamental Rights of the European Union [2010] OJ C83/02. Recently, also the European Court of Justice (ECJ) case law is showing an analogous positive attitude for human dignity as regards the protection of undocumented migrants: see Francesca Ippolito, 'Migration and Asylum Cases before the Court of Justice of the European Union: Putting the EU Charter of Fundamental Rights to Test?' (2015) 17 European Journal of Migration and Law 1.

2. ECtHR Case Law Regarding Access to Education for Undocumented Migrants: *Vikulov and others v. Latvia, Georgiu v. Greece, and Ponomaryovi v. Bulgaria*

The ECHR unequivocally provides for the right to education in Protocol 1, Article 2.[25] According to this article 'no person shall be denied the right to education'. This provision should be implemented in accordance with the non-discrimination clause embedded in Article 14 and thus applied to both nationals and non-nationals who are within the territory of a contracting party unless there is an objective and reasonable justification for the differential treatment.[26] In the ECtHR view, the right to education emerges as one of the most fundamental values of the democratic societies making up the Council of Europe:[27] it is a right to which everyone is entitled.[28]

Regarding undocumented migrants, the ECtHR approach to this right also includes the situation of children faced with their parents' expulsion or their own expulsion due to an irregular entry and/or stay in the contracting state. In general, aliens cannot derive from the right to education the right to enter or remain in the territory of the contracting state.[29] If a parent is going to be expelled from a country under national immigration laws, the fact that the child (due for example to his/her age) will be obliged to accompany him/her will not amount per se to a violation of Protocol 1, Article 2.[30] Only when the timing of the return is likely to have a negative effect on the culmination of a concrete phase of the migrant child's education

[25] Protocol 1 to the European Convention for the Protection of Human Rights and Fundamental Freedoms ETS 9.

[26] Ryszard Cholewinski, *Irregular migrants: access to minimum social rights* (Council of Europe 2005) 30. See, for instance, *Case 'relating to certain aspects of the laws on the use of languages in education in Belgium' v Belgium* App nos 1474, 1677, 1691/62, 1769, 1994/63, and 2126/64 (ECtHR, 23 July 1968); *Cyprus v Turkey* App no 25781/94 (ECtHR, 10 May 2001); and *Vikulov and others v Latvia* App no 16870/03 (ECtHR 25 March 2004).

[27] *Timishev v Russia* App nos 55762/00 and 55974/00 (ECtHR, 13 December 2005) , para 64. Not without grandiloquence, the ECtHR affirms in this judgment that 'the Convention and its Protocols do not tolerate a denial of the right to education' (ibid, para 65).

[28] In general, universal human rights instruments refer to everyone's right to education. Children should be granted access to, at a minimum, primary education. Art 3(e) of the UNESCO Convention against Discrimination in Education (adopted 14 December 1960) makes a reference to the right of migrants to education by requiring state parties '[t]o give foreign nationals resident within their territory the same access to education as that given to their own nationals'. Also Art 30 of the International Convention on the Protection of the Rights of All Migrant Workers and Members of Their Families (n 9) guarantees access to education for migrant children and prohibits state parties to refuse or limit that right 'by reason of the irregular situation with respect to stay or employment of either parent or by reason of the irregularity of the child's stay in the State of employment'.

[29] In *15 Foreign students v United Kingdom* App no 7671/76 (ECtHR, 19 May 1977) the ECtHR found inadmissible an application founded in the lack of education in the countries of education of the applicants.

[30] See *Sorabjee v United Kingdom* App no 23938/94 (ECtHR, 23 October 1995); *Jaramillo v United Kingdom* App no 24865/94 (ECtHR, 23 October 1995); *Dabhi v United Kingdom* App no 28627/95 (ECtHR, 17 January 1997); and *Ajayi and others v United Kingdom* App no 27663/95 (ECtHR, 22 June 1999).

and there was no imperative need for this expulsion to take place,[31] or when the child would not be able to obtain secondary education in the country to which he/she and his/her parents were being expelled, an exception has been made by the Court to this general tendency.

The ECtHR has also addressed the cases of migrants who had been deprived of liberty and could not follow their educational courses during these periods. In *Georgiu v. Greece*[32] a Cypriot national who studied law at the University of Athens maintained that the fact that he was not entitled to prepare for, and take, the final examination for his law diploma at the University during both his pre-trial detention and his post-conviction detention constituted a violation of his right to education. The ECtHR considered that the applicant was only prevented during a short period (fourteen months) from taking an exam at the University. Since he was not otherwise deprived of access to the educational institution of his choice or of his right to an effective education, the Court found the applicant's claim manifestly ill-founded.[33] In *Vikulov and others v. Latvia*, the applicants alleged that the detention of their child, from 3rd to 17th September 2003, had also constituted a violation of his right to education. Again, the short duration of the deprivation of liberty was considered by the Court to conclude that there was no violation of the right to education.

Looking at the right to education for undocumented migrant children from another perspective, in *Ponomaryovi v. Bulgaria*[34] the ECtHR made an important clarification. The applicants were two Russian nationals who had been legally residing in Bulgaria since 1994. On attaining their majority, they applied for permanent-resident status. However, they did not pay the prescribed fee as it was beyond their and their parents' means. As a result, they became liable to pay secondary-school fees from which they would have been exempt if they had been in possession of a permanent-residence permit. They were informed that failure to pay the school fees would mean they would be barred from attending classes and would not receive a certificate confirming completion of the relevant school year.

The applicants complained, *inter alia*, that they had been prevented by unreasonably high fees from obtaining permanent-resident status and had consequently also become liable to pay substantial fees to complete their secondary-school education. They further complained of discriminatory treatment. While the ECtHR assumed that a state could have legitimate reasons for curtailing the use of resource-hungry public services (such as welfare programs, public benefits, and health care) by short-term and illegal immigrants, who, as a rule, did not contribute to their

[31] In *Vikulov and others* (n 26) the removal of the family, a Russian couple and their son, was postponed until the completion of the child's school year. For this reason, the ECtHR concluded there had not been violation of Protocol 1, Art 2.

[32] *Georgiu v Greece* App no 45138/98 (ECtHR, 13 January 2000).

[33] ibid, para 7.

[34] *Ponomaryovi v Bulgaria* App no 5335/05 (ECtHR, 21 June 2011).

funding, it emphasised that, although similar arguments applied to a certain extent in the field of education, they could not be transposed there without qualification.

In particular, while recognising that education was an activity that was complex to organise and expensive to run, and that the state had to strike a balance between the educational needs of those under its jurisdiction and its limited capacity to accommodate them,[35] the Court could not overlook the fact that, unlike some other public services, education was a right that enjoyed direct Convention protection. It is also a very particular type of public service, which not only directly benefits those using it but also serves broader societal functions and is indispensable to the furtherance of human rights.[36] Therefore, the Court's reasoning went a step further in affirming that the state's margin of appreciation in this domain increased with the level of education, in inverse proportion to the importance of that education for those concerned and for society at large. Thus, at the university level, which thus far had remained optional for many people, higher fees for aliens—and indeed fees in general—seemed to be commonplace and could, in the present circumstances, be considered fully justified. The opposite applied to primary schooling, which provided basic literacy and numeracy—as well as integration into and first experiences of society—and was compulsory in most countries.[37] Secondary education, which was at issue in the applicants' case, fell between those two extremes. However, according to the ECtHR, with more and more countries moving towards what has been described as a 'knowledge based' society:

> *Secondary education* played an ever-increasing role in *successful personal development* and in the social and professional integration of the individuals concerned. Indeed, in a modern society, having no more than basic knowledge and skills constituted a barrier to successful personal and professional development and *prevented those concerned from adjusting to their environment, with far reaching consequences for their social and economic well-being.*[38]

[35] As it has been highlighted, 'the margin of appreciation doctrine is central to the ECtHR's approach to questions raising issues of resource allocation. The Court has constantly held that states' margin of appreciation is wider in the socio-economic sphere.' Sylvie Da Lomba, 'The ECHR and the Protection of Irregular Migrants in the Social Sphere' (2015) 22 International Journal on Minority and Groups Rights 39, 54.

[36] *Ponomaryovi v Bulgaria* (n 34), para 55. As the CESCR put it in 1999, the right to education is a 'empowerment right': CESCR, 'General Comment No 13, The right to education (Art. 13)' (1999) UN Doc E/C.12/1999/10, para 1.

[37] In the American context, the Inter-American Court of Human Rights has also stressed the importance of the right to primary education for 'all children', regardless of their legal status, in *Girls Yean and Bosico v Dominican Republic*, Inter-American Court of Human Rights Series C No 130 (8 September 2005). In this case the Inter-American Court stated that:'(i)t is worth noting that, according to the child's right to special protection embodied in art 19 of the American Convention, interpreted in light of the Convention on the Rights of the Child and the Additional Protocol to the American Convention on Human Rights in the Area of Economic, Social and Cultural Rights, in relation to the obligation to ensure progressive development contained in art 26 of the American Convention, the State must provide free primary education to all children in an appropriate environment and in the conditions necessary to ensure their full intellectual development' (para 185).

[38] *Ponomaryovi* (n 34), para 57 (emphasis added).

In the ECtHR's view, the concept of 'human development' incorporates the notion of human dignity applied, in this case, to the peculiar vulnerable category of children. Consequently, a more sophisticated and advanced notion of 'human dignity', which refers to 'successful personal development' and 'social and economic well-being', is defended by the Court. As a consequence of this, when the applicants are not in the position of individuals arriving to the country unlawfully and then claiming for the use of its public services, including free schooling, but they have fallen, somewhat inadvertently, into the situation of being aliens lacking permanent residence permits and the authorities had no substantive objection to their remaining in the host state, or any serious intention of deporting them, the ECtHR considers that the requirement for the applicants to pay fees for their secondary education, on account of their nationality and immigration status, was not justified.[39] However, such a progressive approach taken by the Court would not be necessarily extended to illegal immigrants seeking to take advantage of free public services.

3. A Social Dimension of the Absolute Rights Enshrined in Articles 3 and 4 of the Convention?

3.1 A Right to Adequate Housing Derived from Article 3: *Yordanova and others v. Bulgaria*, *N v. United Kingdom*, and *Hunde v. Netherlands*

When international law and international legal instruments refer to shelter or adequate housing it means more than just a roof over one's head—an adequate standard of living should include sufficient privacy, space, and security. The International Covenant on Economic, Social and Cultural Rights[40] (ICESCR) at Article 11(1) defines adequate housing as 'the right to live somewhere in security, peace and dignity'. In analogous terms though circumscribed to the category of children, the CRC focuses on the right to an adequate standard of living in Article 27(1) and (3). According to the principles of indivisibility and universality of human rights, the right to adequate housing is guaranteed to everyone, including non-nationals. [41] However, the European Social Charter, while providing a specific

[39] ibid, para 60.

[40] International Covenant on Economic, Social and Cultural Rights (adopted 16 December 1966, entered into force 3 January 1976) 993 UNTS 3.

[41] Art 2(3) of the ICESCR has to be taken into account at this point. According to it, 'developing countries, with due regard to human rights and their national economy, may determine to what extent they would guarantee the economic rights recognized in the present Covenant to non-nationals'. As Weissbrodt and Meili highlight, the exception should be should be narrowly construed in order to 'maintain the overall thrust of the human rights protections': David Weissbrodt and Stephen Meili, 'Human Rights and Protection of Non-Citizens: Whither Universality and Indivisibility of Human Rights?' (2009) 28 Refugee Survey Quarterly 34, 38.

reference to the right to housing and adequate living conditions, expressly excludes those who are unlawfully present in the host contracting state from the Charter application.[42]

Regarding the ECHR, it must be highlighted that, though applicable to all individuals within a state's jurisdiction (Article 1), and, consequently, to undocumented migrants present on the state's territory, it does not contain a right to housing as such. However, the jurisprudence of both monitoring bodies of the Council of Europe—the ECSR and the ECtHR—have mitigated this situation. It is worth noting that neither Article 2 nor Protocol 1 Article 1 of the ECHR have played a role in this. Neither does Article 8 ECHR despite its reference to 'home' provides the strongest textual link to a right to housing in the ECHR. If Article 8 ECHR does not provide the right to a home itself,[43] merely protecting the home once the individual has established residence and has 'sufficient continuing links' with the accommodation; it is Article 3 ECHR that could serve to recognise a right to housing in the migration context. In particular, its theoretical contribution to the partial 'socialisation' and 'dignification' of undocumented migrants' (but also asylum seekers') right to housing[44]—a line of jurisprudence that is also referred to by the ECSR in its case law—is linked to the notion of vulnerability, a discursive argument which shares a universal and 'natural' profile (being an inherent and intrinsic dimension of every human being) with the notion of human dignity.

In the case of undocumented migrants it is not a vulnerability per se that has been recognised by the ECtHR as being derived from their deprivation of migration status.[45] The Court rather considered that the level of vulnerability necessary to engage Article 3 ECHR[46] accumulates from the deprivation of status and other exceptional personal elements such as administrative detention; racial, ethnic, or religious discrimination;[47] age factors; the health of applicants—ranging from psychiatric illness[48] to a fragile state of health;[49] HIV positive status (vulnerability occurs in this case not only because of the need for medical treatment but also from

[42] The Appendix to the Charter confers this right only upon lawfully residing migrants.

[43] *X. v Germany* App no 165/56 (Commission Decision, 29 September 1956).

[44] For an analysis of the case law related to the right to housing more in general see Françoise Tulkens and Sébastien Van Drooghenbroeck, 'Le droit au logement dans la Convention Européenne des droits de l'Homme: bilan et perspectives' in Nicolas Bernard and Charles Mertens (eds), *Le logement dans sa multidimensionnalité: Une grande cause régionale* (Ministère de la Région Wallone 2005).

[45] Only in *Chowdury and others v Greece* App no 21884/15 (ECtHR 30 March 2017) concerning those of them who are exploited with unfair working conditions also a per se vulnerability collective qualification seems to have been acknowledged. See section 3.3 of this chapter.

[46] *Soering v United Kingdom* App no 14038/88 (ECtHR, 7 July 1989); *Cruz Varas and others v Sweden* App no 15576/89 (ECtHR 20 March 1991); *R. v United Kingdom* App no 146/1996/767/964 (ECtHR 2 May 1997).

[47] *Cyprus v Turkey* App no 25781/94 (ECtHR, 10 May 2001).

[48] *Sufi and Elmi v United Kingdom* App nos 8319/07 and 11449/07 (ECtHR, 28 November 2011).

[49] *Aden Ahmed v. Malta* App 55352/12 (ECtHR, 27 March 2013), para 46.

the history of prejudice and stigmatisation of people infected with this disease); mental or physical disabilities;[50] and services available in the destination country.

Moving from this qualification and from the parallel recognition that 'an obligation to secure *shelter* to particularly vulnerable individuals' may flow from Article 8 of the Convention in exceptional cases;[51] the ECtHR implied, in *N. v. United Kingdom,* that—though Article 3 of the Convention does not provide undocumented migrants with an opportunity to remain in the state in order to continue to benefit from social or other forms of support[52]—such basic assistance should be attainable while they remain in the expelling state. Such an outcome is still distant from the decisions adopted instead by the ECSR in 2014 in *Conference of European Churches (C.E.C.) v. the Netherlands,*[53] and in *European Federation of National Organisations working with the Homeless (FEANTSA) v. the Netherlands,*[54] where the ESC Committee found a violation by member states in failing to provide adequate access to emergency assistance (food, clothing, and shelter) to adult migrants in an irregular situation. However, if the position of the ECtHR is different from the one of the ECSR as to a minimum right to housing, there is nonetheless a glimmer of hope in the more recent ECtHR decision in *Hunde.*[55] In this decision, the ECtHR acknowledged the conclusions of the ECSR in *FEANTSA*, although it decided that those findings did not automatically amount to a violation or Article 3 of the ECHR.

In this case, the ECtHR differentiates the status of a failed, and allegedly uncooperative, asylum seeker from that of an asylum seeker whose application is pending, as was the case in *M.S.S.* with respect to the state's correlative positive obligations under Article 3 to provide emergency social assistance.[56] Hence, though acknowledging the importance of the economic and social rights laid down in the Charter and the issues raised in the two above-mentioned decisions adopted by the ECSR, the ECtHR dismissed the applicant's argument, in the *Hunde* case, that the findings by the ECSR under the Charter should be considered to lead automatically

[50] *Stork v Germany* App no 61603/00 (ECtHR, 16 September 2005), and *Stanev v Bulgaria* App no 36760/06 (ECtHR, 17 January 2012).

[51] *Yordanova and others v Bulgaria* App no 25446/06 (ECtHR, 24 April 2012), para 130.

[52] *N. v United Kingdom* App no 26565/05 (ECtHR, 27 May 2008), para 42.

[53] *Hunde v the Netherlands* (Complaint no 90/2013) Available at https://www.coe.int/en/web/turin-european-social-charter/processed-complaints/-/asset_publisher/5GEFkJmH2bYG/content/no-90-2013-conference-of-european-churches-cec-v-the-netherlands?inheritRedirect=false accessed 1 November 2018.

[54] *European Federation of National Organisations working with the Homeless (FEANTSA) v the Netherlands* (complaint no 86/2012) Available at https://www.coe.int/en/web/turin-european-social-charter/processed-complaints/-/asset_publisher/5GEFkJmH2bYG/content/no-53-2008-european-federation-of-national-organisations-working-with-the-homeless-feantsa-v-slovenia?inheritRedirect=false&desktop=false accessed 1 November 2018.

[55] *Hunde v Netherlands* App no 17931/16 (ECtHR, 5 July 2016).

[56] *M.S.S.* judgment has been considered an example of the interrelation between human rights and of the protection of social rights through rights that are 'classically' understood as civil and political: Bernard Ryan and Virginia Mantouvalou, 'The Labour and Social Rights of Migrants in International Law' in Ruth Rubio-Marín (ed), *Human Rights and Immigration* (OUP 2014) 177, 205–06.

to a violation of Article 3 of the Convention. The applicant in the *Hunde* case was not entitled to any social assistance in the Netherlands. He referred to *M.S.S.* in arguing that the situation he found himself in was very similar to the situation in that case. However, the ECtHR underlined the crucial differences: unlike the applicant in *M.S.S.*, who was an asylum seeker, the applicant in the present case was at the material time a failed asylum seeker under a legal obligation to leave the territory of the host state. Furthermore, even though the applicant's loss of entitlement to legal residence in the host state after the rejection of his asylum claim did not automatically affect his vulnerability as a migrant, the situation in which he found himself remained significantly different from that of *M.S.S.* In the latter case, the relevant facts, which had culminated in the finding of a violation of Article 3, were the long duration in which the applicant had lived in a state of the most extreme poverty (ie lack of food, hygiene, and a place to live), and of fear of being attacked and robbed together with the fact that there had been no prospect of improvement. Additionally, that situation was linked to his status as an asylum seeker and, consequently, the applicant's suffering could have been alleviated if the Greek authorities had promptly assessed his asylum application. By failing to do so the applicant was left in a state of uncertainty. On the contrary, the ECtHR emphasised that the applicant's uncertainty in *Hunde* was inherently different from that in *M.S.S.* in that it was not linked to the national authorities' assessment of his asylum request nor to their inaction: his asylum case had already been examined and his asylum application refused, and the applicant had not advanced any complaints about this before the Court. Furthermore, after the applicant's asylum proceedings had come to an end, the applicant was afforded a four-week grace period to organise his voluntary return to his country of origin during which period he retained his entitlement to state-sponsored care and accommodation. Besides, after he had overstayed this grace period, the applicant had the possibility of applying for reception facilities at a centre where his liberty would be restricted. This was nevertheless subject to the condition that he would cooperate in organising his departure to his country of origin or that he could prove the impossibility of his return for reasons which cannot be attributed to him. In the latter situation, he even had the possibility of applying for a residence permit for persons who, through no fault of their own, are unable to leave. However, nothing in the case file showed that he had ever applied for such a residence permit, nor that he had ever contended at any stage during the domestic proceedings that he could not leave the host state.

Still, while the ECtHR in *Hunde* reiterates that there is no right to social assistance as such under the Convention,[57] at the same time, it underlines that such a right to social assistance is lacking 'to the extent that Article 3 requires states to take action in situations of the most extreme poverty—also when it concerns irregular

[57] See *Hunde* (n 55), para 59.

migrants'.[58] Then, the Court links the inadmissibility of the claim to the fact that 'it cannot be said that the Netherlands authorities have fallen short of their obligations under Article 3 by having remained inactive or indifferent'.[59] Therefore, any indifference on the part of the national legal order also in respect of a minimum level of social assistance should *a contrario* be seen as possibly amounting to a breach of Article 3 ECHR. In particular, the Court gives some guidance in terms of national practices in this regard when it underlined that 'the Netherlands authorities have already addressed this in practical terms', for instance in giving (failed asylum seekers) the possibility of applying for a 'no-fault residence permit' and/or to seek admission to a centre where their liberty would be restricted; as well as allowing undocumented migrants to seek a deferral of removal for medical reasons and to receive free medical treatment in case of emergency; and by setting up a special scheme providing basic needs for undocumented migrants living in their territory in an irregular manner.[60]

3.2 The Right to Health: *N. v. United Kingdom, and Poposhvili v. Belgium*

The position with regard to a right to health in the ECHR is similar to the right to housing just explored, in the sense that the ECHR does not provide per se for either. However, many of the ECHR's provisions have been used as a basis for arguing for a human right to health care. The most relevant Articles in this regard are 2, 3, 8, and 14 ECHR. These provisions have typically been invoked to resist the expulsion of undocumented migrants where it is believed that their health will be compromised as a result of the cessation of treatment, or due to the same treatment being unavailable, or prohibitively expensive in the expelled individual's home country. Once more, it has been due to the obvious *indignity* that this entails, that the absolute nature of Article 3 ECHR has made it a popular choice for those seeking to resist deportation on health grounds. But the ECtHR has affirmed that only in extraordinary circumstances may the denial of health care to undocumented migrants amount to an infringement of the right to be free from inhuman and degrading treatment contained in Article 3 ECHR. Although undocumented migrants who are ill may invoke Article 3 to prevent their expulsion to countries of origin or third countries with inadequate health care facilities,[61] the most recent jurisprudence of the ECtHR suggests that this principle will only apply *exceptionally*.[62] Three

[58] ibid.
[59] ibid.
[60] ibid.
[61] *D. v United Kingdom* App no 30240/96 (ECtHR, 2 May 1997).
[62] See cases *Karara v Finland* App no 40900/98(Commission decision, 29 May 1998); *S.C.C. v Sweden* App no 46553/99 (ECtHR, 15 February 2000); *Bensaid v United Kingdom* App no 44599/98 (ECtHR, 6 February 2001); *Arcila Henao v the Netherlands* App no 13669/03 (ECtHR, 24 June 2003); *Ndangoya*

established elements for the test of 'very exceptional circumstances' were introduced by the case of *N. v United Kingdom*:[63] the gravity and stage of the physical illness (the majority of the Court's case law has related to physical chronic illnesses such as AIDS/HIV,[64] chronic lymphocytic leukemia, tuberculosis,[65] and chronic kidney failure);[66] the availability of medical treatment/care; and the availability of social and familial support in the receiving country.[67] The position of states, that access to basic social rights for migrants acts as a pull factor and as 'too great a burden' on national resources has been endorsed by the ECtHR since *N.* Accordingly, to find the respondent state in breach of Article 3 would amount to requiring states 'to alleviate [unavoidable social and economic disparities between countries] disparities through the provision of free and unlimited health care to all aliens without a right to stay within its jurisdiction'.[68] The rationale is that in contrast with short-term and undocumented migrants, the applicant who was in possession of a lawful residence and work permit 'did not belong to the category of persons who, as a rule, do not contribute to the funding of public services and in relation to whom a state may have legitimate reasons for curtailing the use of resource-hungry public services such as social insurance schemes, public benefits and health care'.[69]

However, such an attitude fails to account for national immigration policies which, for instance, might be responsible for making regularised migrants fall back into an irregular situation as a result of changes in the law,[70] or for the 'gap between those [foreign nationals] liable to deportation, "deportable", and those actually deported'.[71]

Thus, it is important to put the accent on the responsibility of states in creating and perpetuating disadvantage. Undocumented migrants' vulnerability can derive from the combination of their migratory status and the health conditions of the applicants.[72] But when the ECtHR case law imposes positive conventional obligations

v Sweden App no 17868/03 (ECtHR, 22 June 2004); *Amegnigan v the Netherlands* App no 25629/04 (ECtHR, 25 November 2004); *N.* (n 52); and *Yoh-Ekale Mwanje v Belgium* App no 10486/1020 (ECtHR, 20 December 2011).

[63] *N.* (n 52), paras 50, 51, 47, and 48.
[64] *D.* (n 61); *N* (n 52); *Yoh-Ekale Mwanje* (n 61); and *S.J. v Belgium* App no 70055/10 (ECtHR, 19 March 2015).
[65] *Paposhvili v Belgium* App no 41738/10 (ECtHR, 13 December 2016), paras 124–33.
[66] *M.T. v Sweden* App no 1412/13 (ECtHR, 26 February 2015).
[67] *Bensaid* (n 62); *Tatar v Switzerland* App no 65692/12 (ECtHR, 14 April 2015), and *Kochieva and others v Sweden* App no 75203/12 (ECtHR, 30 April 2013).
[68] *N.* (n 52), para 44.
[69] *Dhahbi v Italy* App no 17120/09 (ECtHR, 8 April 2014), para 84. See also *Fawsie v Greece* App no 40080/07 (ECtHR, 16 April 2010).
[70] Ryszard Cholewinski, 'Identifying and Clarifying Concepts on "Irregular Migration"', (2006) Paper Presented at the 10th IOM Regional Conference on Migration, Singapore.
[71] Emanuela Paoletti, 'Deportation, non-deportability and ideas of membership' (2010) 65 RSC Working Papers Series 14 <https://www.rsc.ox.ac.uk/files/files-1/wp65-deportation-non-deportability-ideas-membership-2010.pdf> accessed on 15 September 2019.
[72] See, Aden (n 49) (para 46).

upon contracting states regarding the right to health of undocumented migrants, building resilience, that irregular status does not translate into a condemnation.[73]

An *N.*-type approach would therefore not be permissible in that it sets ECHR subjects' Article 3 rights against immigration control and resource considerations, as opposed to an interpretation in line with the absolute nature of the provision. Moreover, a vulnerability discourse could bring the Court to focus on preventing further *vulnerabilisation* through an assessment of how societal structures could dynamically build resilience in overcoming different forms of vulnerability. In this sense, the Court's exercise of a 'fair balance ... between the demands of the general interest of the community and the requirements of the protection of the individual's fundamental rights, "must be based on an inquiry into lived vulnerability" ',[74] which also demands that the ECtHR assesses whether states have realised their ECHR obligations to the maximum of all their resources. Thus, the Court's over-reliance on the scarce resource argument must give way to a comprehensive investigation into states' resource-based arguments, reconsidering the margin of appreciation conferred on states. This so far has been expressed within the jurisprudence of the ECtHR only by dissenting opinions. It happened as far back as the *N.* case when the Joint Dissenting Opinion of Judges Tulkens, Bonello, and Spielmann emphasised how 'the very nature of the rights guaranteed by the Convention that would be completely negated if their enjoyment were to be restricted on the basis of *policy considerations* such as budgetary constraints'.[75] In *Yoh-Ekale Mwanje v. Belgium*, six out of seven judges expressed the need for the Court to reconsider 'this extreme severity threshold—to be close to dying' as not easily reconcilable with the letter and spirit of Article 3, which guaranteed an absolute right inherent in human integrity and *dignity*.[76] More explicitly, in his partly dissenting opinion in the recent case of *Tatar*, Judge Lemmens proposed a more human approach to the expulsion of persons with a severe long-term illness. He urged a move away from the requirement of very exceptional circumstances as the high threshold required to engage Article 3 of the Convention. He called explicitly the Court to focus 'more on the specific vulnerability of these persons'.[77]

[73] This has also recently brought a partial reversal of the idea of compounded vulnerability as the only one applied to undocumented migrants in *Chowdury and others v Greece*. See section 3.3 of this chapter. See Deborah Russo, 'Lo sfruttamento del lavoro negli Stati membri del Consiglio d'Europa: una riflessione a margine del caso Chowdury' (2017) 3 Rivista di Diritto Internazionale 835.

[74] See on this point Sylvie Da Lomba, 'Irregular Migrants and the Human Right to Healthcare: A Case Study of Healthcare Provision for Irregular Migrants in France and the UK' (2011) 7 International Journal of Law in Context 357.

[75] At para 8 (emphasis added).

[76] See the Partly Concurring Opinion of Judges Tulkens, Jočienė, Popović, Karakaş, Raimondi, and Pinto De Albuquerque, para 6.

[77] See *Tatar* (n 67) Partly Dissenting Opinion of Judge Lemmens, paras 4 and 5. He argued that the mere possibility of medical treatment in other regions of Turkey was solely based on theoretical assumptions. Instead, he proposed a similar approach as in the case of *Tarakhel* (*Tarakhel v Switzerland* App no 29217/12 (ECtHR, 4 November 2014), para 121). In the case of *Tarakhel* the Court requested that the Swiss authorities first obtained sufficient assurances on the appropriate accommodation of this family before they could send them back to Italy. In this case, the Swiss authorities settled with prima

Even the majority of the Strasbourg judges seem to have partially moved from their past positions on Article 3, if we consider the judgment of the Grand Chamber in *Paposhvili*.[78] In this decision the Court stated that in assessing whether the exceptional circumstances of a case reaches the threshold of Article 3 of the Convention that the real risk of ill-treatment (including any decline in health, severe suffering, or reduction in life expectancy)[79] should be measured by looking at the 'availability in reality, not merely in theory' of the appropriate health care in the country of origin.[80] Furthermore, the third condition of the very exceptional circumstances test, ie the lack of family and social assistance, seems to have been dismissed in *Paposhvili*. In any case, the threshold required to prevent the deportation of an alien suffering from an illness remains high. However, the task of assessment is primarily for the national authorities, who must put in place adequate procedures in order to evaluate the risks run in the event of deportation. The assessment must take account both of the general situation in the receiving state (obtaining assurances that medical treatment will be available and accessible to the person concerned) and of the alien's particular case, including their vulnerability.

3.3 The Protection against Labour Exploitation, Forced Labour and Trafficking with the Purpose of Labour Exploitation: *Siliadin v. France, and Chowdury and others v. Greece*

Given that they are, by and large, excluded from the formal market, undocumented migrants are particularly vulnerable to more or less severe forms of exploitation.[81] Labour rights are considered as social rights and have been incorporated into social rights treaties. For this reason, the ECHR only refers to two labour rights: the right to form and join a trade union (Article 11), and the prohibition of slavery,

facie assurances, not taking into account the real circumstances the applicant would endure upon his return to Turkey. In other words, regarding medical expulsion cases, a state should always obtain sufficient assurances by the receiving country. See Eva Brems, 'Moving away from N v UK—Interesting tracks in a dissenting opinion (Tatar v Switzerland)' *Strasbourg Observers*, 4 May 2015) <https://strasbourgobservers.com/2015/05/04/moving-away-from-n-v-uk-interesting-tracks-in-a-dissenting-opinion-tatar-v-switzerland/> accessed 1 November 2018.

[78] *Paposhvili v Belgium* (n 65), para 182.

[79] ibid. The impact of removal on an applicant must now be assessed by considering how an applicant's condition 'would evolve after transfer to the receiving State' (ibid, para 188) so realigning with the 'preventive purpose' of Art 3 (ibid, para 186). But the temporal horizon is circumscribed to situations involving an applicant's 'rapid decline' (ibid, para 183).

[80] ibid, para 183.

[81] According to Art 5 of the 1990 International Convention on the Protection of the Rights of All Migrant Workers and Members of Their Families, migrant workers are considered as documented or in a regular situation if they are not 'authorized to enter, to stay and to engage in a remunerated activity in the State of employment pursuant to the law of that State and to international agreements to which that State is a party'.

servitude, forced and compulsory labour (Article 4). In this section, we will refer to the ECtHR case law on the latter.

Slavery and forced labour, but not explicitly trafficking in human beings,[82] are prohibited under the ECHR. According to Article 4 of the Convention 'no one shall be held in slavery or servitude' nor 'shall [they] be required to perform forced or compulsory labour'. The article hinges on the principle of equal treatment between nationals and non-nationals in respect of these rights and covers various forms of abuse: slavery, servitude, forced labour, and compulsory labour. Despite the absence of an express reference to trafficking, a number of decisions of the ECtHR[83] have progressively developed concrete obligations in this regard.[84] In particular, states are obliged to establish a legislative and administrative framework that is adequate to ensure the practical and effective protection of the rights of victims and potential victims,[85] to take operational measures for the protection of victims, and to investigate and prosecute human trafficking and other phenomena covered by Article 4.[86]

The vulnerability of applicants has been taken into account by the Court in order to conclude that a particular situation qualifies as slavery.[87] In *Siliadin* the

[82] An explicit reference is made by Art 5.3 of EU Charter of Fundamental Rights (n 24). The European Anti-trafficking Convention was adopted under the auspicious of the Council of Europe in 2005. At the universal level, the most significant instrument is still the Protocol to prevent, suppress and punish trafficking in persons especially women and children, supplementing the United Nations Convention against Transnational Organized Crime (Palermo Protocol), adopted in 2000. The ECtHR has affirmed that trafficking in human beings threatens human dignity (see *Ranstev v Cyprus* App no 25965/94 (ECtHR, 7 January 2010), para 282, and *Chowdury and others* (n 45), para 93).

[83] *Siliadin v France* App no 73316/01 (ECtHR, 26 July 2005); *Rantsev v Cyprus and Russia* App no 25965/04 (ECtHR, 7 January 2010); *C.N. v France* App no 67724/09 (ECtHR, 11 October 2012); *C.N. v United Kingdom* App no 4239/08 (ECtHR, 13 November 2012); *Chitos v Greece* App no 51637/12 (ECtHR, 4 June 2015); *L.E. v Greece* App no 71545/12 (ECtHR, 21 January 2016); *J. and others v Austria* App no 58216/12 (ECtHR, 17 January 2017); and *Chowdury and others* (n 45).

[84] See Roza Pati, 'States' Positive Obligations with Respect to Human Trafficking: The European Court of Human Rights Breaks New Ground in Ranstev v Cyprus and Russia' (2011) 29 Boston University International Law Journal 79; and Ryszard Piotrowicz, 'States' Obligations under Human Rights Law towards Victims of Trafficking in Human Beings: Positive Developments in Positive Obligations' (2012) 26 International Journal of Refugee Law 181.

[85] In *Siliadin* (n 83), the victim was a Togolese national arrived in France in 1994 whose passport had been confiscated and whose employers had reduced her 'to the status of an object'. The Court found that French criminal law in force at the time had not protected her sufficiently. In *C.N.* (n 83), the Court affirmed that the legislative provisions in force in the United Kingdom at the relevant time had been inadequate to afford practical and effective protection against treatment contrary to Art. 4.

[86] The ECtHR refers to States' obligation to put in place not also effective criminal investigations, but also labour inspections. As it has been said 'the vulnerability of migrants might also require from the national authorities to take a much more proactive approach by not only acting when the matter has come to their attention, but also establishing "useful detection and reporting mechanisms [which] are fundamental to the effective implementation of the relevant criminal laws". This implies that labour inspectors have a crucial role since they can detect abusive labour practices.': Vladislava Stoyanova, *Human Trafficking and Slavery Reconsidered. Conceptual Limits and State's Positive Obligations in European Law* (Cambridge University Press 2017) 364.

[87] In any case, vulnerability plays a key role in the definition of human trafficking. Art 3 of Palermo Protocol lists the abuse of a position of vulnerability as one of the 'means' within the definition of trafficking in persons. In this context, the United Nations Office on Drugs and Crime has noted that 'the existence of vulnerability is best assessed on a case-by-case basis, taking into consideration the personal, situational or circumstantial situation of the alleged victim': See UNODC Human Trafficking

Court considered that the applicant was held in servitude because, in addition to the fact that she was required to perform forced labour, she was a minor with no resources, *vulnerable* and isolated with no means of living elsewhere than the home where she worked.[88] In *Chowdury*, the Court noted that the fact that the applicants were undocumented workers exacerbated their vulnerability.[89] The Court positively insisted that the vulnerability caused by a precarious administrative situation be emphasised as a source of the applicants' vulnerability. The vulnerability would be exacerbated by their lack of financial means and the risk of detention or deportation they would face if they contacted the authorities, and all this would increase the risk of labour exploitation.[90] Connecting the eventual risk of forced servitude and the vulnerability of undocumented migrant workers, the *Chowdury* decision affirmed that 'today's slaves are predominantly female and usually work in private households, starting out as migrant domestic workers'.[91]

Nevertheless, with regard to protections against forced labour and trafficking for forced labour, some aspects need further clarification. On the one hand, the ECtHR does not clearly distinguish 'trafficking for forced labour' and 'forced labour' that does not entail trafficking.[92] According to ECtHR case law, forced and compulsory labour refers to: '... all work or service which is exacted from any person under the menace of any penalty and for which the said person has not offered himself voluntarily'.[93] On the other hand, some scholars have denounced the fact that the broad approach to positive obligations initially imposed by the ECtHR in *Rantsev*[94] has gradually being eroded, calling into question the human rights-based approach to trafficking driven by IHRL.

and Migrant Smuggling Section, 'Guidance Note on 'abuse of a position of vulnerability' as a means of trafficking in persons in art 3 of the Protocol to Prevent, Suppress and Punish Trafficking in Persons, Especially Women and Children, supplementing the United Nations Convention against Transnational Organized Crime' (2012), <https://www.unodc.org/documents/human-trafficking/2012/UNODC_2012_Guidance_Note_-_Abuse_of_a_Position_of_Vulnerability_E.pdf> accessed 1 November 2018.

88 *Siliadin* (n 83), para 126–27 (emphasis added).

89 See *Chowdury and others* (n 45), para 95.

90 ibid, para 97.

91 *Siliadin* (n 83), para 88.

92 Valentina Milano, 'Uncovering Labour Exploitation: Lights and Shadows on the Latest European Court of Human Rights' Case Law on Human Trafficking' (2017) 21 Spanish Yearbook of International Law 83, 114.

93 This definition was offered by Art 2 the International Labour Organization Convention on Forced Labour in 1930, <http://www.ilo.org/dyn/normlex/en/f?p=NORMLEXPUB:12100:0::NO::P12100_ILO_CODE:C029> accessed 1 November 2018. In 1983, in *van der Mussele v Belgium* App no 8919/80 (ECtHR, 23 November 1983) the Court had said that this definition could provide a starting-point for interpretation.

94 *Ranstev v Cyprus and Russia* App no 25965/04 (ECtHR, 7 January 2010). See, in particular, paragraphs 294–98 and 304–09.

Less severe forms of exploitation are not explicitly prohibited by the ECHR,[95] but they could, at least in some cases, be undeniably covered by Article 3 of the Convention.

4. Conclusions

International human rights mechanisms, both at universal and regional levels, have repeatedly affirmed that despite their sovereign right to regulate conditions of entry and stay in their territories, states assume obligations and duties under international law to respect, to protect, and to fulfil the human rights of all individuals under their jurisdiction. Being considered a particularly vulnerable group, a prevailing view in the practice of international human rights protection bodies is that the dignity of all migrants acts as the cornerstone for the protection of their rights. This chapter supports the idea that protection against vulnerability seems better suited as a 'presuppositional' core of human dignity, and so a condition for the respect of human dignity and human rights.[96]

Regarding access to socio-economic rights, however, their enjoyment by undocumented migrants have been neglected under IHRL due to two different reasons. First, due to their irregular status, states tend to assume that decisions regarding an undocumented migrant's access to social and/or economic rights depends on political choices based on governmental immigration policies. Second, undocumented migrants have serious difficulties in accessing national courts and international supervisory mechanisms for human rights. Besides that, socio-economic rights have traditionally been given a weaker legal status, as they are seen as resource-dependent and consequently 'ill-suited for adjudication'.[97]

Notwithstanding this fact, it can be affirmed that when it comes to the role played in this regard by international human rights monitoring bodies, the trend

[95] Art 31 of the Charter of Fundamental Rights of the European Union (n 24) refers to 'all workers' right to fair and just working conditions of all workers, with respect to his/her health, safety and *dignity* (emphasis added). According to para 2, fair and just working conditions would include the right to limitation of maximum working hours, to daily and weekly rest periods and to an annual period of paid leave.

[96] Aniceto Masferrer and Emilio García-Sánchez, 'Vulnerability and Human Dignity in the Age of Human Rights' in Aniceto Masferrer and Emilio García-Sánchez (eds), *Human Dignity of the Vulnerable in the Age of Rights: Interdisciplinary Perspectives* (Springer 2016) 2–5; and Roberto Andorno, 'Is Vulnerability the Foundation of Human Rights?' in ibid, 257. For a reading of vulnerability as co-foundational of human rights together with human dignity see: Debra B Bergoffen, *Contesting the Politics of Genocidal Rape: Affirming the Dignity of the Vulnerable Body* (Routledge 2011); Martha Albertson Fineman, '"Elderly" as Vulnerable: Rethinking the Nature of Individual and Societal Responsibility' (2012) 20 The Elder Law Journal 101; Anna Grear, *Redirecting Human Rights: Facing the Challenge of Corporate Legal Humanity* (Palgrave 2010) 132–33; and Bryan S Turner, *Vulnerability and Human Rights* (Penn State University Press 2006).

[97] Da Lomba (n 35), 41. In this context, the entry into force of the Optional Protocol to the ICESCR recognising the competence of the Committee to receive and consider communications submitted by or on behalf of individuals or groups of individuals.

is for closing the existing gaps between the different categories of human rights. In this context, a significant group of national and international human rights bodies, including national and international courts but also non-judicial mechanisms, including the ECtHR, are contributing to the definition of a shared global understanding of the centrality of human dignity in the quest to protect fundamental rights. And, paradoxically, fragmentation of IHRL[98] is resulting in an integrated approach to a minimum core of economic and social rights for this vulnerable group.

98 Much has been said about fragmentation of IHRL. As Brems has put it:

> As a political and ethical project, human rights are one, indivisible and universal. As law however, they are fragmented … The complex architecture of international human rights law is characterized by a multitude of highly diverse sources. These sources can be differentiated in several cross-cutting ways: by governance level (regional, world), by their material scope (general, categorical, single issue), by their personal scope (universal or specific target group), by their legal force (hard or soft law) and by the type of monitoring mechanism that accompanies them.

Eva Brems, 'We Need to Look at International Human Rights Law (Also) as a Whole' (EJIL: Talk!, 17October 2014) <https://www.ejiltalk.org/we-need-to-look-at-international-human-rights-law-also-as-a-whole/> accessed 1 November 2018.

PART III
RIGHTS OF LONG-TERM MIGRANTS

This part critically analyses the general interpretative outlook of the European Court of Human Rights on long-term migrants with a focus on their rights to remain in the host countries, alongside their religious and cultural rights.

7

The European Court of Human Rights and Removal of Long-term Migrants

Entrenched Statism with a Human Voice?

Başak Çalı and Stewart Cunningham

1. Introduction

Migration control is firmly on the European agenda. People fleeing persecution and conflict, but also those searching for better life prospects for themselves and their families, continue seeking to reach Europe, often at great risk to their lives.[1] Who should remain in destination countries, be they migrants or refugees, and on what terms, unceasingly sparks debate in liberal democracies.[2] There is much talk and action about stopping migrants arriving to Europe,[3] the migrant's duty to integrate,[4] and the states' right to expel or even strip citizenship[5] from those who disturb the public order. Conditional stay,[6] and expulsion of migrants,[7] as well as

[1] International Organization for Migration's Global Migration Data Analysis Centre, 'The Central Mediterranean Route: Deadlier than Ever', Data Briefing Series Issue No 3, June 2016.

[2] Arash Abizadeh, 'Democratic Theory and Border Coercion: No Right to Unilaterally Control your Own Borders' (2008) 36 Political Theory 37; David Miller, 'Why Immigration Controls Are not Coercive: A Reply to Arash Abizadeh' (2010) 38 Political Theory 111; Michael Blake, 'Immigration, Jurisdiction, Exclusion' (2013) 41 Philosophy & Public Affairs 103; Philip Cole, 'Taking Moral Equality Seriously: Egalıtarianism and Immigration Controls' (2012) 8 Journal of International Political Theory 121; Joseph Carens, *The Ethics of Immigration* (OUP 2013); Cathryn Costello, *Human Rights of Migrants and Refugees in European Law* (OUP 2015); Marie Benedicte Dembour, *When Humans Become Migrants: Study of the European Court of Human Rights with an Inter-American Counter Point* (OUP 2015); Bastian Vollmer, 'The Continuing Shame of Europe: Discourses on Migration Policy in Germany and the UK' (2017) 5 Migration Studies 49.

[3] *Hirsi Jamaa and others v Italy* [GC] App no 27765/09 (ECtHR, 23 February 2012); European Council, 'EU-Turkey Statement', Press Release 144/16, 18 March 2016, <http://www.consilium.europa.eu/en/press/press-releases/2016/03/18-eu-turkey-statement/> accessed 15 March 2019.

[4] Alexandra Xanthaki, 'Against Integration, for Human Rights' (2016) 20 International Journal of Human Rights 815.

[5] *K.2 v United Kingdom* (dec) App no 42387/13 (ECtHR, 7 February 2017) (stripping of UK citizenship from a UK/Sudan dual citizen due to involvement in terrorism).

[6] *Jeunesse v the Netherlands* [GC] App no 12738/10 (ECtHR, 3 October 2014).

[7] *Khan v Germany* [GC] (striking out) App no 38030/12 (ECtHR, 21 September 2016).

Başak Çalı and Stewart Cunningham, *The European Court of Human Rights and Removal of Long-term Migrants*
In: *Migration and the European Convention on Human Rights.* Edited by: Başak Çali, Ledi Bianku, and Iulia Motoc, Oxford University Press (2021). DOI: 10.1093/oso/9780192895196.003.0007

restrictions to migrants' cultural and religious rights,[8] have seen continued litigation, in particular, at the European Court of Human Rights (ECtHR).

In recent Strasbourg jurisprudence on migration, those who are seeking permission to enter or remain in Council of Europe States, on the grounds of fear of torture or inhuman and degrading treatment on return to their country of origin, have received much attention, as have reception conditions in Europe.[9] An equally important aspect of Strasbourg's migration jurisprudence, however, concerns those who legally reside in a European state over long periods but who face the risk of deportation, normally due to their criminal convictions, but without the risk of torture, inhuman or degrading treatment upon return to another country. This latter case law opens up questions about the circumstances under which long-term migrants may have a legitimate claim to equal treatment akin to citizens who violate the laws of their country. Much recent work in liberal political theory queries the compatibility of the right to deport with the duty of equal concern and respect for long-term migrants, who contribute significantly to European societies. It is argued that time spent in a country should carry normative significance and increase the case for equal treatment of long-term migrants with citizens of host states.[10] What is more, long-term migrants make up a significant proportion of Europe's population.[11] In the case of citizens, violation of domestic laws gives rise to imprisonment with accompanying rights to rehabilitation and re-integration back into society. In the case of long-term migrants, states see deportation as the default legal policy treating those who violate domestic laws as outstaying their welcome, despite the length of time spent in the host state. Against this background, this chapter seeks to critically examine the ECtHR's approach to right-of-stay cases of long-term migrants who do not face risks of torture, inhuman or degrading treatment upon return and asks whether the ECtHR is an agent that can pierce the deportation veil with respect to long-term migrants. In our analysis, we primarily focus on cases brought by long-term migrants that have lived in Europe for five years or more when they face deportation.

[8] *Osmanoglu and Kocabas v Switzerland* App no 29086/12 (ECtHR, 10 January 2017); *Ebrahimian v France* App no 64846/11 (ECtHR, 26 November 2015); *S.A.S. v France* [GC] App no 43835/11 (ECtHR, 1 July 2014).

[9] *Hirsi Jamaa* (n 3); *F.G. v Sweden* [GC] App no 43611/11 (ECtHR, 23 March 2016); *J.K. and others v Sweden* [GC] App no 59166/12 (ECtHR, 23 August 2016); *N.D. and N.T. v Spain* App nos 8675/15 and 8697/15 (ECtHR, 3 October 2017); *M.A. and others v Lithuania* App no 59793/17 (ECtHR, 11 December 2018); *Khan v France* App no 12267/16 (ECtHR, 28 February 2019). See also Chapter 1 of this volume.

[10] Cole (n 2); Carens (n 2); Gila Stopler, 'Rights in Immigration: The Veil as a Test Case' (2010) 43 Israel Law Review 183.

[11] On 1 January 2018 there were 22.3 million non-EU citizens living in the EU, which represents 4.4 per cent of the EU's population. See Eurostat, 'Migration and migration population statistics' <https://ec.europa.eu/eurostat/statistics-explained/index.php?title=Migration_and_migrant_population_statistics#Migrant_population:_22.3_million_non-EU_citizens_living_in_the_EU_on_1_January_2018> accessed 18 March 2019.

In what follows, we begin by exploring the general interpretative outlook of the ECtHR to the rights of long-term migrants facing deportation. This outlook is strongly marked by recognising the primacy of state discretion in the field of migration policy, while at the same time ensuring that long-term migrants are given access to the protection of the Convention. We then survey the case law of the ECtHR related to the deportation of long-term migrants, identifying the factors that the Court employs in balancing its dual commitment to states and long-term migrants. The central argument of the chapter is that the Court's approach to the right to stay of long-term migrants falls short of adequately recognising the unique position of long-term migrants and is unable to differentiate between those who have lived for lengthy periods in host states and any other category of alien. The Court's recent emphasis on principled deference to domestic courts in balancing the rights of long-term migrants and host states further undercuts any future progressive developments in the field of right to stay for long-term migrants. We conclude by looking at the implications of this for the protection of long-term migrants under the ECHR.

2. State Discretion and Rights of Long-term Migrants

The case law of the ECtHR treats the status of long-term migrants, already residing in a host country, as a domain of state discretion. Migrants do not have an absolute right to citizenship[12] or residency.[13] Neither do they have an absolute right not to be removed from the country,[14] or the right not to be stripped of their citizenship, which they can acquire through naturalisation.[15]

That the Convention does not provide for a right to nationality in explicit terms colours the Court's general interpretive approach to the status of long-term migrants. The Court starts with a recognition that there is neither such a right under the Convention nor can the right to citizenship be directly derived from any of the other rights it protects.[16] Long-term stay in a country cannot, in and of itself, lead to a right to citizenship. The Court, however, does take into account exceptional circumstances, such as arbitrary denial of citizenship, only when it has a serious impact on the private rights of the individual.[17] Arbitrariness in the case law of the Court includes discriminatory application of citizenship laws to individuals. [18] By the same token, the Court also recognises that migrants can be stripped of their

[12] *Ramadan v Malta* App no 76136/12 (ECtHR, 21 June 2016), para 84.
[13] *Üner v the Netherlands* [GC] App no 46410/99 (ECtHR, 18 October 2006).
[14] *Khan* (n 7).
[15] *Ramadan* (n 12); *K.2* (n 5).
[16] *Karassev v Finland* (dec) App no 31414/96 (ECtHR, 12 January 1999), para 1(b).
[17] ibid; *Savoia v Italy* (dec) App no 8407/05 (ECtHR, 11 July 2006).
[18] *Genovese v Malta* App no 53124/09 (ECtHR, 11 October 2011). The Court found that not granting citizenship to an illegitimate child of a Maltese citizen was discriminatory.

citizenship on account of non-compliance with the conditions imposed for receiving citizenship, for example, by committing fraud or being involved in activities that threaten the public interests of the community as a whole. In both of these instances, the long-term stay of the applicant in the country does not, in and of itself, compel the state to treat the migrant's citizenship as native citizenship. This has been the case even when the migrant stripped of citizenship faces the risk of statelessness.[19]

Assigning unfettered discretion to states also shapes the Court's approach to rights of residency. In a much quoted leading judgment that involved the expulsion of a young Turkish adult from the Netherlands, who had migrated there when he was twelve years old to join his guest worker father, and was deported after seventeen years of stay, the Court laid out these general principles as regards the rights of the receiving state:

> The Court reaffirms at the outset that a State is entitled, as a matter of international law and subject to its treaty obligations, to control the entry of aliens into its territory and their residence there. The Convention does not guarantee the right of an alien to enter or to reside in a particular country.[20]

Whilst the ECtHR does not recognise that long-term migrants should, at some point in the migration process, acquire stable personal status in the form of residency or citizenship rights, it also recognises that they cannot be fully excluded from the protections afforded under the ECHR with respect to rights that are not tied to status determination. In this approach, the right to private and family life protected under Article 8 of the Convention takes centre stage. For the Court, the family ties and other personal relationships that migrants have in the destination country,[21] as well as the level of social integration of the migrants in the society[22] cannot be left outside of the scope of the Convention, even if a determination of their legal status is excluded. Despite recognising that long-term migrants come within the scope of the Convention, their rights under Article 8 are rebuttable, subject to a balancing exercise.[23] This is closely connected to the Court's acceptance that migrants do not automatically qualify for citizenship status or citizen-like treatment due to their length of stay or relationships in the migrant receiving country. The right to a private and family life, therefore, does not amount to a right of stay, as migrants can continue to exercise such a right in their country of origin. Refusal of legal residency, or expulsion, from the country can be carried out so long as these decisions do not come at too high a cost to the private and family life of the

19 *Ramadan* (n 12). See also the dissenting opinion of Judge Pinto de Albuquerque.
20 *Üner* (n 13), para 54. See also *Jeunesse* (n 6), para 100.
21 *Emre v Switzerland* App no 42034/04 (ECtHR, 22 May 2008).
22 *Slivenko v Latvia* [GC] App no 48321/99 (ECtHR, 9 October 2003); *Üner* (n 13).
23 *Trabelsi v Germany* App no 41548/06 (ECtHR, 13 October 2011).

long-term migrant. This is because the Court takes it, as a given, that prevention of crime and disorder, national security, or public order are prima facie legitimate aims in the context of migration policy that do not require close scrutiny.[24] In other words, not only is refusal to afford permanent residence and nationality, by and large, outside of the purview of the Court, but states also enjoy a wide margin of appreciation with respect to the private and family life of those with temporary migration status. The Court, therefore, implicitly recognises a distinction between 'well behaving' and 'not well behaving' long-term migrants even though both categories of migrants may have spent a significant part of their lives in the migrant receiving countries. Even those who benefit from naturalisation can be denaturalised on the grounds of their lack of authentic citizenship status.[25]

3. Strasbourg Removal Case Law: Balancing Factors

The Court's way out of its double recognition that states enjoy full discretion in status determination, and that long-term migrants cannot be fully excluded from the right to private and family life, leads it to frame right-to-stay cases in terms of a fair balance between the interests of the host state and the interests of long-term migrants. In what is known as the '*Boultif* criteria', the Court asks states to consider a range of factors in striking a fair balance between states' rights in immigration policy and the human face of the rights of long-term migrants.[26] These can be summarised broadly around: (1) length of stay in the country; (2) impact of removal on family relationships, especially, children; (3) seriousness of criminal convictions, conduct since conviction, and risks of reoffending.[27] Yet, these *Boultif* factors overlap and intersect with one another and therefore are highly fluid. The post *Boultif* case law is full of attempts to fine tune the relative significance of the human realities involved in balancing the right to privacy and family life with states' discretion in deportation. Below, we review how the Court approaches the ordering and evaluation of these factors, which gives a human voice to the rights of long-term migrants in the face of concerns for public order and national security.

24 The Court is willing to scrutinise legitimate aims in other domains of qualified rights. *Bayev and others v Russia* App nos 67667/09, 44092/12, and 56717/12 (ECtHR, 20 June 2017); *SAS* (n 8).

25 *K.2* (n 5).

26 *Boultif v Switzerland* App no 54273/00 (ECtHR, 2 August 2001), para 48.

27 In *Boultif*, the Court laid out detailed criteria which includes the nature and seriousness of the offence committed by the applicant; the length of the applicant's stay in the country from which he or she is to be expelled; the time elapsed since the offence was committed and the applicant's conduct during that period; the nationalities of the various persons concerned; the applicant's family situation, such as the length of the marriage, and other factors expressing the effectiveness of a couple's family life; if there is a spouse, whether the spouse knew about the offence at the time when he or she entered into a family relationship; whether there are children of the marriage, and if so, their age; and the seriousness of the difficulties which the spouse is likely to encounter in the country to which the applicant is to be expelled. See also *Üner* (n 13), para 58.

3.1 When the Applicant Migrated as a Child

It was in *Üner* that the Court aimed to develop a more principled approach to the first of the *Boultif* factors, namely the length of the migrant's stay, in particular, in situations where the applicant migrated as a child. This case was brought by a young man who had been born in Turkey and moved to the Netherlands in 1981, when he was twelve years old, to join his father who had been living there already for ten years. Üner secured permanent residence in 1988. In 1993 he was involved in a dispute in a café, which led to him shooting and killing someone, resulting in a conviction for manslaughter and a seven-year jail term. As a result of this conviction, his permanent residence was withdrawn, he was deported to Turkey and was given a ten-year exclusion order. His case to have the exclusion order revoked took him to the Strasbourg Court. The ECtHR pointed out the importance of taking into account the long-term migrant status of applicants in cases where the applicant was born in, or moved to, the host country at an early age. However, it also made clear that length of stay is merely one consideration, out of many, in decisions concerning long-term migrants. In this case, the Court held that:

> [A]lthough the applicant in Boultif was already an adult when he entered Switzerland, the Court has held the 'Boultif criteria' to apply all the more so (à plus forte raison) to cases concerning applicants who were born in the host country or who moved there at an early age (see Mokrani v. France, no. 52206/99, § 31, 15 July 2003). *Indeed, the rationale behind making the duration of a person's stay in the host country one of the elements to be taken into account lies in the assumption that the longer a person has been residing in a particular country, the stronger his or her ties with that country and the weaker the ties with the country of his or her nationality will be. Seen against that background, it is self-evident that the Court will have regard to the special situation of aliens who have spent most, if not all, their childhood in the host country, were brought up there and received their education there.*[28]

In a subsequent case, *Maslov v Austria*,[29] the Court continued to focus on long-term migrant children and the impact that migrating as a young child has on the conduct of their balancing exercise with regard to Article 8 cases. The applicant in *Maslov* moved to Austria at the age of six (in 1990) and lived lawfully in the country from that moment on. He had a long history of juvenile crime for petty theft, burglary, and gang activity and was given two short prison sentences (one suspended on

[28] *Üner* (n 13), para 58 (emphasis added). Despite the importance of the principles laid out, the Court found no breach of Article 8. Whilst it accepted that the applicant had strong ties to the Netherlands, he had weak family relationships with his partner and son. The Court held that returning the applicant to Turkey, while it might not have been easy was not unreasonable given the seriousness of his criminal convictions.

[29] *Maslov v Austria* [GC] App no 1638/03 (ECtHR, 23 June 2008).

probation and the other for fifteen months). He committed all of his offences while he was under the age of eighteen. Austria imposed an exclusion order on him in 2001, when he was seventeen years old and he was eventually deported in 2003. In this case the Court, following the approach in *Üner*, noted that as well as the length of the applicant's residence being a key factor, that the age during which the length of residence was accrued was also an important consideration:

> [W]hen assessing the length of the applicant's stay in the country from which he or she is to be expelled and the solidity of the social, cultural and family ties with the host country, it evidently makes a difference whether the person concerned had already come to the country during his or her childhood or youth, or was even born there, or whether he or she only came as an adult.[30]

The Court went on to note that for those who migrated as children, or as youth, then only in the most serious circumstances would expulsion be justified.[31]

3.2 If the Long-term Migrant Committed a Crime as a Child

In *Maslov*, the Court not only addressed the impact of migrating as a child but also made clear that the age at which the crimes were committed was also an important factor to be balanced in these cases. As such, it is noted that the best interests of the child test must be applied 'if the person to be expelled is himself or herself a minor, or if—as in the present case—the reason for the expulsion lies in offences committed when a minor'.[32] The Court described the applicant's offences as 'acts of juvenile delinquency',[33] which were all committed before he reached the age of eighteen. After conducting the balancing exercise, the conclusion reached was that Austria's expulsion of the applicant did breach Article 8 and the Court based its decision on the 'non-violent nature of the offences committed when a minor and the State's duty to facilitate his reintegration into society, the length of the applicant's lawful residence in Austria, his family, social and linguistic ties with Austria and the lack of proven ties with his country of origin'.[34]

In *A.A. v United Kingdom*,[35] the applicant committed a serious crime (rape) when he was fifteen years old and the victim was thirteen years old. Interestingly, he had moved to the UK when he was thirteen years old so had accrued just two years of residence before his criminal offence. He was convicted and sentenced

30 ibid, para 73.
31 ibid, para 75.
32 ibid, para 82.
33 ibid, para 81.
34 ibid, para 100.
35 *A.A. v United Kingdom* App no 8000/08 (ECtHR, 20 September 2011).

to four years' imprisonment in a young offenders' institution. Even though, in this instance, the offence was extremely serious the Court took into account the fact that it was committed while the applicant was a juvenile as well as his conduct since serving his sentence. In this case, the Court describes the applicant's post-conviction behavior as 'exemplary conduct' in which he made 'commendable efforts to rehabilitate himself and to reintegrate into society over a period of seven years'.[36] As such, the Court found that his deportation would breach Article 8. The Court further noted that in situations where the crimes were committed as a minor, and even if the crimes were of a serious nature, if there is evidence that the applicant has ceased offending, and made considerable efforts to rehabilitate and re-integrate into society, then the government must provide 'further support' to demonstrate that the applicant poses a continuing risk to the public, as justification for his deportation.[37]

There are examples, however, of cases where even though the applicant committed crimes at a young age the Court still finds that removal was proportionate, thereby distinguishing these cases from the principled position set out in *Maslov* and *A.A.* An example of such an exceptional case can be found in *Mutlag v Germany*,[38] which involved a Jordanian national who was born in Germany in 1981 and spent his entire life there. He was deported to Jordan at the age of twenty-five after committing a number of serious offences involving considerable violence. In this case, the seriousness of the offences and their repeated nature were a deciding factor in the Court finding no violation of Article 8. Furthermore, while the applicant had spent his life in Germany, it was held by the Court that he had developed very few social relations outside of those with his family.

In *Yesufa v United Kingdom*,[39] the applicant had been in the UK since he was three years old. Between the ages of fourteen and nineteen he accumulated several criminal convictions for minor offences such as criminal damage, possession of cannabis, and burglary. In 2004 (at the age of twenty) he was sentenced to four years imprisonment for robbery and released in 2007 at which point he was convicted again of a further eight offences. He was deported back to Nigeria on 22 October 2008 and only after deportation did he raise grounds under Article 8 on the basis of his ten-year relationship with a British citizen, who had given birth to their child on 7 June 2009. The Court, in its decision, acknowledged his length of residence and the fact that his crimes were committed at a relatively young age but the deciding factor, in finding his removal proportionate, was the length, and extent, of his offending and the fact that his offending continued well into adulthood. The Court also noted that he continued to offend after being served the deportation

[36] ibid, para 68.
[37] ibid.
[38] *Mutlag v Germany* App no 40601/05 (ECtHR, 25 March 2010).
[39] *Yesufa v United Kingdom* (dec) App no 7347/08 (ECtHR, 26 January 2010).

order and after being released from prison on licence. In other words, there was no indication that he was addressing his offending behaviour and might continue to offend into the future.

3.3 When the Long-term Migrant Has Children

While in *Maslov* the best-interests-of-the-child test was applied to the applicant himself, it remains a weighty factor in other cases where the long-term migrant is a parent, but this often turns on the age of the children at the time of the deportation decision, as well as the quality of their relationship to the applicant. However, as with all of the factors taken into account by the Court, the best-interests-of-the-child test is not decisive and is, instead, balanced against the other aspects of the *Boultif* criteria. For example, in *M.P.E.V. and others v Switzerland*,[40] the Court found a breach of Article 8 in respect of the applicant's deportation from Switzerland, partly based on his relationship with his younger daughter and given her level of integration in Switzerland, they concluded that she should not be expected to return to Ecuador. However, this was taken into account together with the 'moderate nature of the criminal offences committed by the applicant'.[41]

Another example of how the best interests of the child is taken into account in combination with the nature of the criminal offences and applicant's subsequent conduct is provided by *Udeh v Switzerland*.[42] In this case, the applicant's criminal offence was serious (drug trafficking), albeit of an isolated nature, and the Court found that this did not demonstrate a prolonged pattern of criminal behavior. His conduct had also been beyond reproach since his release from prison. The Court attached significant weight to his relationship with his daughters, in conjunction with evidence of his post-conviction conduct:

> In view of the foregoing, and particularly having regard to the first applicant's first two children, to the genuine family relationship between them and to the fact that the first applicant committed only one serious offence and his subsequent conduct has been irreproachable, suggesting a positive evolution in the future, the Court finds that the respondent State overstepped the margin of appreciation afforded to it in the present case.[43]

[40] *M.P.E.V. and others v Switzerland* App no 3910/13 (ECtHR, 8 July 2014).
[41] ibid, para 58.
[42] *Udeh v Switzerland* App no 12020/09 (ECtHR, 16 April 2013).
[43] ibid, para 54.

The age of the children is also a relevant factor when the Court applies the best-interests-of-the-child test. For example, in *Üner*, the Court found that the applicant's children were at an adaptable age when the exclusion order was finalised (they were six and one and a half), and therefore could readjust to life in Turkey. In the case of *Adeishvili (Mazmishvili) v Russia*,[44] the Court found no breach of Article 8 on the grounds that the children were again of an adaptable age (six and three respectively) and the Court felt that the family 'could make the transition to Georgian culture and society, although ... this transition might entail a certain degree of social and economic hardship'.[45] In this case, the Court also relied upon the fact that their family life had been established in Russia at a time when the applicant's migration status was precarious.[46]

However, in another case, *Jeunesse v the Netherlands*,[47] the Court found that Article 8 would be breached in removing a woman from the Netherlands *despite* the fact that she had established her family life while her migration status was precarious. The applicant, who was a national of Suriname, had a husband with Dutch nationality as well as three Dutch national children all born in the Netherlands. Her attempts to gain a residence permit were consistently refused by authorities due to her failure to comply with national immigration rules[48]. The Court, in this case, paid due regard to multiple factors, including the fact that she was the primary caregiver to her children. This was considered alongside her level of integration into the society, the contribution of the actions of the government to her long-term stay, and her lack of a criminal record. Instead of developing the normative significance of long-term migration, however, the Court found the facts of the case exceptional in deciding that the state had failed to strike a fair balance.[49] Perhaps it is also significant in this case that there was no issue of criminal convictions.

While we have highlighted the key factors addressed by the Court when it conducts its balancing exercise between the rights of states to protect national security and public order and the rights of long-term migrants to a private and family life, it is clear that no single factor outweighs any other in the Court's eyes. Long-term stay, therefore, in and of itself, is not accepted by the Court as an isolated factor that can, or should, tip the balance in favour of the migrant in deportation cases.

[44] *Adeishvili (Mazmishvili) v Russia* App no 43553/10 (ECtHR, 16 October 2014).

[45] ibid, para 83.

[46] ibid, para 82.

[47] *Jeunesse* (n 6).

[48] ibid. She had arrived in the Netherlands on a short-term tourist visa and remained unlawfully in the country after her visa expired.

[49] ibid.

4. The Limits of the ECtHR Approach to Right of Stay Claims of Long-term Migrants

The preceding analysis shows that whilst the Court strives to inject a human voice into states' unfettered discretion in the field of migration policy through its right to private and family life case law, the counter weights developed by the Court against deportation offer either highly rebuttable or narrowly construed positions. This moves the Court away from balancing the state's discretionary powers with the right to private and family life to a logic of exceptional accumulation of facts on the part of long-term migrants.

The rebuttable position is most apparent when it comes to the consideration of the length of time spent by a migrant in a country, first emphasised in *Üner* as a weighty factor. Despite the recommendations by the Parliamentary Assembly of the Council of Europe from 1988, and the Committee of Ministers from 2000, that a right of permanent residence for migrant workers that had spent at least five years in one of the Member States should be established, the Court does not treat five years, or longer, as a significant stand-alone factor, but a rebuttable factor.[50] In particular, more time spent in the host country is not seen as capable of generating more rights, let alone equal rights with citizens. Instead, the length of stay is a criterion that is taken into account together with other criteria, in particular, in conjunction with the strength of personal and social ties that a migrant is able to develop in the time that she spends in the receiving country and the legal nature of the length of time spent. The Court, therefore, does not see *the length of time* as a sliding scale, but in competition with other considerations.[51]

Length of time matters most for those long-term migrants who arrived in a country as children, who committed criminal offences as a child, and those who are still a child when they face deportation. Yet, the Court is careful to state, as it did in *Üner*, that all these considerations are rebuttable in nature: 'These principles apply regardless of whether an alien entered the host country as an adult or at a very young age, or was perhaps even born there.'[52] What is more, the *Mutlag* and *Yesufa* cases show that whilst the Court recognises that length of time spent as a migrant in a country as a child is a factor, it is also sensitive to how this time is spent well into adulthood. The older the applicant is at the time of deportation, the less

[50] Parliamentary Assembly of the Council of Europe, Recommendation 1082 (1988) on the right of permanent residence for migrant workers and members of their families (30 June 1988) <https://assembly.coe.int/nw/xml/XRef/Xref-XML2HTML-en.asp?fileid=15116&lang=en>, accessed 18 March 2019; Committee of Ministers of the Council of Europe, Recommendation (2000) 15 Concerning the Security of Long-term Migrants (13 September 2000 <https://rm.coe.int/native/09000016804eb800> accessed 18 June 2019.

[51] On the distinctions between *jus temporis* and *jus nexis*, see Paulina Ochoa Espejo, 'Taking Place Seriously: Territorial Presence and the Rights of Immigrants' (2016) 24 Journal of Political Philosophy 67.

[52] *Üner* (n 13), para 55.

attention the Court pays to the length of time spent, and instead it focuses on their conduct in the host state, particularly the extent to which any criminal behavior continued into adulthood. The seriousness of the crime and perceived lower levels of integration of long-term migrants work against them despite the length of their lives spent in Europe. The Court also takes into account the irregular status of migrants, despite the significant amount of time the latter may spend in a country.[53]

When long-term migrants first migrated as adults it appears that the Court is more likely to find that they have retained some strength of social ties with their country of origin, which is a factor taken into account, as always, with others in finding that their deportation would not breach Article 8. For example, in *Sarkozi v Austria*,[54] the fact that the applicant migrated to Austria as an adult and maintained some cultural ties to Slovakia were key considerations in the Court reaching the decision that her removal did not breach Article 8. Yet again, these factors were considered alongside other key issues including the 'serious and repetitive nature of the criminal offences' and the fact that Slovakia was so close to Austria so as to enable her family members to visit her often as well as the fact that her exclusion order was time-limited.[55] In *Krasniqi v Austria*, yet again, the fact that the applicant migrated to Austria as an adult and 'still has cultural and linguistic ties with his home country' was a key factor taken into account with the seriousness of his offences, the fact that his family could visit him regularly in Kosovo, and the time-limited nature of his expulsion order, in the Court's finding that his expulsion would not breach Article 8.[56]

Whilst the focus on right to private and family life humanises the migrant, the Court looks less favourably on the hardships faced by long-term migrants who are not children and places the burden of integration on these long-term migrants. An adult long-term migrant must not only show that she has legal status as well as a vibrant family and social life in the receiving country. The migrant must also show that her right to private or family life is not 'transportable' elsewhere.[57] In most respects there is a high burden for the migrant to prove legal and social integration irrespective of the time they spend in the receiving country. What is more, this approach does not take into account the negative effects that precarious legal arrangements, or lack of citizenship, have in developing a vibrant private life in the host state. In other words, states' failure to help long-term migrants integrate is not relevant in the Court's assessment of the lives migrants have been able to create. The necessity of proving the existence of a legally and socially integrated private and family life in the receiving country distracts from the neutrality of the

[53] *Abuhmaid v Ukraine* App no 31183/13 (ECtHR, 12 January 2017). The applicant lived in the Ukraine for over twenty years.
[54] *Sarkozi v Austria* App no 27945/10 (ECtHR, 2 April 2015).
[55] ibid, para 74.
[56] *Krasniqi v Austria* App no 41697/12 (ECtHR, 25 April 2017), para 56.
[57] *Maslov* (n 29), para 63.

human voice in the Court's deportation case law and encourages states to characterise long-term migrants who do not fully respect domestic laws as not worthy of stay in the country.

The social and legal integration-bias of the case law aside, the ECtHR further sees states as enjoying a wide margin of appreciation when it comes to migration.[58] This margin of appreciation is both explicit and implicit and is deeply entrenched in the general approach to long-term migrants in the case law of the Court. In recent Strasbourg case law, it appears that the margin of appreciation has been significantly strengthened. In *Ndidi v United Kingdom*, the First Section delivered a judgment in which it suggested that the Court's requirement to ensure that the decision complied with Article 8 'does not mean that ... it is necessarily the Court's task to conduct the Article 8 proportionality assessment afresh'.[59] The Court referred to two recent cases (*Hamesevic v Denmark*[60] and *Alam v Denmark*[61]) noting that in these cases 'the Court declined to substitute its conclusions for those of the domestic courts' on the basis that they had conducted their own balancing exercise taking into account the criteria set out in the Strasbourg case law and 'reached conclusions which were "neither arbitrary nor manifestly unreasonable"'.[62] Later in the decision, the Court noted that the domestic decision makers 'gave thorough and careful consideration to the proportionality test required by Article 8' and that it 'sees no grounds upon which the decision of the domestic authorities can be impugned'.[63] The Court suggested that if there had been a significant change in the applicant's circumstances since the last domestic decision then this could provide it with strong reasons to substitute its own proportionality assessment but no such change was evident in this case. The Court, therefore, found that the removal would not breach Article 8.

In a dissenting opinion, Judge Turkovic challenged the majority's position noting that the Court had established in *AA v United Kingdom* that in cases where the ECtHR was reaching its decision and the applicant had not yet been expelled that the Court 'must assess the compatibility with the Convention of the applicant's actual expulsion with reference to the facts known to the ECtHR at the time of proceedings before it, but post-dating the domestic proceedings'.[64] Judge Turkovic pointed out that the majority's assertion that there was no change in the applicant's circumstances since the last domestic decision failed to take account of the fact that:

[58] *Ebrahimian* (n 8); *SAS* (n 8).
[59] *Ndidi v United Kingdom* App no 41215/14 (ECtHR, 14 September 2017), para 76.
[60] *Hamesevic v Denmark* (dec) App no 25748/15 (ECtHR, 16 May 2017).
[61] *Alam v Denmark* (dec) App no 33809/15 (ECtHR, 6 June 2017).
[62] *Ndidi* (n 59), para 76.
[63] ibid, para 81.
[64] ibid, dissenting opinion, para 2.

> [A] considerable period of time (10 years) has elapsed since the offence was committed, since the applicant was released from the Young Offenders' Institution under license (6 and a half years) and since the license expired (4 and a half years) and that during that period the applicant has not committed any further offences and has demonstrated serious efforts to rehabilitate himself and to reintegrate into society.[65]

In *AA v United Kingdom*, it was established that in cases where the applicant committed crimes as a minor and had since demonstrated willingness to cease criminal conduct and re-integrate into society that the 'Government are required to provide further support for their contention that the applicant can reasonably be expected to cause disorder or to engage in criminal activities such as to render his deportation necessary in a democratic society'.[66] Judge Turkovic indicated that the Court's findings in *Ndidi* were departing from the position set out in *AA* and 'the Court is now requiring the applicant to demonstrate that there has been some change in his or her circumstances over and above the fact that he or she did not commit further offences for a significant period of time after being released and assessed as posing a low risk of re-offending'.[67] In other words, the applicant was required to demonstrate some kind of 'exceptional' change in their circumstances for the Court to engage in the assessment of proportionality.[68] She suggested that the 'inconsistencies in application of the *Üner*, *Maslov* and *A.A.* principles ... may warrant their further clarification and/or elaboration'.[69]

With the decision in *Ndidi* the position for long-term migrants who commit crimes, even when these crimes were committed as minors, appears relatively bleak. It is arguable that the facts of the case in *Ndidi* were similar to that in *AA* in the sense that the applicant had since demonstrated significant efforts to stop offending and re-integrate into society. Despite the fact he had lived in the UK since he was two years old and the passage of ten years of crime-free conduct the Court was unwilling to interfere with the decision of the domestic authorities.

5. Conclusion

The preceding sections have shown that whilst the Court treats the rights of long-term migrants within a fair balance interpretative paradigm, the factors employed in this balance do not propose a sliding scale approach.[70] That is, the Court does

65 ibid, para 3.
66 *AA* (n 35), para 68.
67 *Ndidi* (n 59), dissenting opinion, para 4.
68 ibid, para 4.
69 ibid, para 7.
70 Stopler (n 10).

not treat the length of stay and the deep personal and social integration of long-term migrants in their host countries as weighty reasons not to deport. In particular, the more serious the criminal offence committed by the long-term migrant, and the older the long-term migrant, the less likely is the Court to attach significant weight to their length of residence. The Court's humanising approach to deportation, therefore, is built on rebuttable or narrowly construed circumstances. One set of circumstances where the Court has been more willing to defend a principled stance is with regard to children as long-term migrants or risks of harm to young children when their parents are at risk of deportation.

The interplay of the factors laid out by the Court leaves the assumptions underpinning the legitimate purposes of deportation untouched. Specifically, the Court does not scrutinise, or challenge, the positions taken by states that long-term migrants who commit criminal offences are deemed to outstay their welcome despite studies that show barriers to integration faced by long-term migrants.[71] In its recent case law, the Court has further strengthened its commitment to respecting state discretion by recognising that it will have to have very strong reasons for not respecting how domestic courts weigh the factors laid out in *Boultif* and subsequent case law.[72] Thus, it is not only that the factors are highly fluid in their application, but also that the Court is less willing to assess how these are balanced domestically.

One central objection to the characterisation of the Court as failing long-term migrants facing deportation may be that migration policy is not the Convention regime's strongest point. The word migration does not figure in the Convention and the large number of protocols that were subsequently adopted have not made the text of the Convention any stronger when it comes to rights of long-term migrants in Europe. Conversely, the Convention has seen important modifications to further entrench the subsidiary role of the Court and the importance of domestic courts in being the guardians of Convention standards across Europe in follow up to the Brighton Declaration in 2012.[73] Seen from this perspective, the Court seeking to extend some form of protection to long-term migrants by bringing them under the scope of right to private and family life may even be seen as commendable. Backlash against the Convention regime, including sensationalist headlines stating that even pets of migrants have a right to private life under the Convention,[74] points to the fact that many continue to see even these modest

[71] European Union Agency for Fundamental Rights, Together in the EU—Promoting the Participation of Migrants and their Descendants (European Union 2017).

[72] *Ndidi* (n 59).

[73] Mikael Madsen, 'Rebalancing European Human Rights: Has the Brighton Declaration Engendered a New Deal on Human Rights in Europe?' (2018) 9 Journal of International Dispute Settlement 199.

[74] 'Immigrant allowed to stay because of pet cat' *The Telegraph* (17 October 2009) <https://www.telegraph.co.uk/news/newstopics/howaboutthat/6360116/Immigrant-allowed-to-stay-because-of-pet-cat.html> accessed 18 March 2019. While this headline was written in relation to a decision, on Article 8 grounds, made by the domestic tribunal in the UK, it is worth noting that the ECtHR has concluded that

interventions in immigration policy, brought about by the Court's concern for right to private and family life of migrants, as illegitimate.

Yet, an alternative perspective is that the Court may be falling short of broader developments in piercing the veil of deportation. The Parliamentary Assembly of the Council of Europe has gone well beyond the case law of the Court in its issuing of Recommendations on the issue of long-term migrants. In addition to the Recommendations that call upon states to grant a permanent right of residence to migrants after they have completed five years of lawful residence,[75] the Parliamentary Assembly has also recommended that the practice of deporting long-term migrants on the basis of criminal convictions be stopped.[76] In its Recommendation on the expulsion of long-term migrants, the Parliamentary Assembly notes that long-term migrants, especially those who migrated as children or were born in the host state, 'are no longer humanly or sociologically foreigners' and the practices of expulsion used against them are 'disproportionate and discriminatory'.[77] Their position is that long-term migrants should only ever be deported 'in highly exceptional cases, and when it has been proven … that the person concerned represents a real danger to the state'.[78] As the case law of the ECtHR currently stands, however, the Court is one-step ahead of government policies, but a few steps behind the Recommendations of the Parliamentary Assembly on the deportation of long-term migrants.

relationships between owners and pets do constitute private life under Article 8. See *X. v Iceland* App no 6825/74 (Commission decision, 18 May 1976).

75 Parliament Assembly of the Council of Europe (n 50).

76 Parliamentary Assembly of the Council of Europe, Recommendation 1504 (2001), Non-expulsion of long-term migrants, <http://assembly.coe.int/nw/xml/XRef/Xref-XML2HTML-en.asp?fileid=16881&lang=EN> accessed 18 March 2019.

77 ibid, paras 2 and 3.

78 ibid, para 10.

8

Cultural Rights of Migrants

Living Together in Dignity?

Bianca Selejan-Gutan

1. Introduction

The growing challenges that global migration raises for contemporary states are multifarious: there are political, legal, social, economic, constitutional identity[1] and, last but not least, human rights protection challenges. In this context, one preliminary question may be asked: could there be commonalities regarding the rights of migrants, and of minorities, in terms of how human dignity is upheld in Europe? After centuries of various forms of repression against minorities (especially religious, but also ethnic cleansing-related and various types of political repression), the majority of European countries have adopted human dignity as a fundamental constitutional principle. Germany is the best-known example, where human dignity has become the foundational concept of the entire fundamental rights system,[2] but there are also other countries that recognise human dignity as an important value of the society.[3] The constitutions of post-communist countries,[4] for example, include human dignity as a supreme value. However, the very notion of human dignity does not have a single legal definition.[5] It is included in constitutions either

[1] Jürgen Bast and Liav Orgad, 'Constitutional Identity in the Age of Global Migration' (2017) 18(7) German Law Journal 1588.

[2] Art 1 of the Fundamental Law of the Federal Republic of Germany: 'Human dignity shall be inviolable. To respect and protect it shall be the duty of all state authority.'

[3] eg France (Preamble of the 1946 French Constitution, included in the *bloc de constitutionnalité* by the Conseil Constitutionnel in 1971).

[4] eg Art 1 (3) Constitution of Romania (1991): 'Romania is a democratic and social state, governed by the rule of law, in which human dignity, the citizens' rights and freedoms, the free development of human personality, justice and political pluralism represent supreme values, in the spirit of the democratic traditions of the Romanian people and the ideals of the Revolution of December 1989, and shall be guaranteed'; Preamble of the Constitution of Hungary (2011): 'We hold that human existence is based on human dignity.'; Art 30 Constitution of Poland (1997): 'The inherent and inalienable dignity of the person shall constitute a source of freedoms and rights of persons and citizens'; Preamble of the Constitution of the Czech Republic (1993): 'Resolved to build, safeguard, and develop the Czech Republic in the spirit of the sanctity of human dignity and liberty.'

[5] Michèle Finck, 'The Role of Human Dignity in Gay Rights Adjudication and Legislation: A Comparative Perspective' (2016) 14 International Journal of Constitutional Law 28. For more details regarding the definition of human dignity, see Joel Andriantsimbazovina and others, *Dictionnaire des Droits de l'Homme* (Presses Universitaires de France 2008) 287–88.

Bianca Selejan-Gutan, *Cultural Rights of Migrants* In: *Migration and the European Convention on Human Rights.*
Edited by: Başak Çali, Ledi Bianku, and Iulia Motoc, Oxford University Press (2021).
DOI: 10.1093/oso/9780192895196.003.0008

as a fundamental principle, or as a supreme value of the state. Human dignity is also a foundational concept of international systems of human rights protection, both at the UN[6] and within the Council of Europe.[7] Constitutional courts use it in their case law related to fundamental rights. For example, the French Constitutional Council referred to dignity as requiring 'the protection of the human person against any form of servitude and degradation'.[8]

In this context, it is worth mentioning that human dignity is not expressly provided for or referred to in the text of the European Convention on Human Rights (ECHR),[9] although it appears in the Universal Declaration of Human Rights (UDHR),[10] which is considered the main source of inspiration for the Convention. The first explicit inclusion of human dignity in the Convention system was made by Protocol No. 13 of 2002,[11] which prohibits the use of the death penalty in all circumstances by the ratifying states. Thus, at the normative level, one can observe that Protocol No. 13 has not only started to turn Article 2 which allows the death penalty, dead letter, it has also expressly introduced human dignity in the Convention system. However, the European Court of Human Rights (ECtHR) had started to use human dignity in its judgments even before 2002. Most of these references related to Article 3 of the Convention (*Ireland v United Kingdom*,[12] *Selmouni v France*)[13] but also Article 8 (*Goodwin v United Kingdom*).[14] The Court continued to invoke human dignity, for example, in the case of *Pretty v United Kingdom* (2002), where it stated that 'the very essence of the Convention is respect for human dignity and human freedom'.[15]

The European Court also used the concept of human dignity in cases related to the right to life,[16] the prohibition of inhuman and degrading treatment (corporal punishments,[17] conditions of detention,[18] police brutality,[19] etc), the prohibition

[6] '*Whereas* recognition of the inherent dignity and of the equal and inalienable rights of all members of the human family is the foundation of freedom, justice and peace in the world'—Preamble of the Universal Declaration of Human Rights, 10 December 1948.

[7] European Social Charter Revised (1996), Preamble & Art 26 ('The right to dignity at work'); Convention on Human Rights and Biomedicine (1997), Preamble ('recognising the importance of ensuring the dignity of the human being') & Art 1 ('Parties to this Convention shall protect the dignity and identity of all human beings and guarantee everyone, without discrimination, respect for their integrity and other rights and fundamental freedoms with regard to the application of biology and medicine.').

[8] Conseil Constitutionnel, Décision No 2015-517 QPC du 22 janvier 2016, paras 4, 10.

[9] Convention for the Protection of Human Rights and Fundamental Freedoms (European Convention on Human Rights, as amended) ETS 5. For a possible explanation of this absence, see Jean-Paul Costa, 'Human Dignity in the Jurisprudence of the European Court of Human Rights' in Christopher McCrudden (ed), *Understanding Human Dignity*, Proceedings of the British Academy vol 192 (OUP 2014), 393–94.

[10] Universal Declaration of Human Rights (adopted 10 December 1948) UNGA Res 217 A(III).

[11] Protocol 13 to the European Convention on Human Rights and Fundamental Freedoms on the Abolition of the Death Penalty in All Circumstances ETS 187.

[12] *Ireland v United Kingdom* App no 5310/71 (ECtHR, 18 January 1978).

[13] *Selmouni v France* [GC] App no 25803/94 (ECtHR, 28 July 1999).

[14] *Goodwin v United Kingdom* App no 28957/95 (ECtHR, 11 July 2002).

[15] *Pretty v United Kingdom* App no 2346/02 (ECtHR 29 April 2002), para 65.

[16] *Pretty* (n 15); *Haas v Switzerland* App no 31322/07 (ECtHR, 20 January 2011).

[17] *Tyrer v United Kingdom* App no 5856/72 (ECtHR, 25 April 1978).

[18] *Kudla v Poland* App No 30210/96 (ECtHR, 26 October 2000).

[19] *Selmouni v France* (n 13).

of forced labour,[20] and it discussed human dignity as a potential limit on the freedom of the press. Other national and international courts have used human dignity in the context of protecting socio-economic rights, anti-discrimination law, or to enhance the content of various rights.[21] In any case, as McCrudden put it, '[w]hether dignity is used as a principle with specific content, or as a right, or as an obligation, or as a justification, particular values seem particularly closely related to the judicial interpretation of the core idea of dignity'.[22] The European Court's general trend in using human dignity was 'to reinforce the reasoning leading to a violation of the Convention',[23] and only in a few cases was dignity used to dismiss cases, which tended to occur in cases where the applicant was advancing arguments, which themselves were contrary to human dignity.[24] For example, cases in which the applicants complained of being convicted for offences, which resulted in the infringement of the human dignity of others (such as *S. W.* and *C.R. v United Kingdom* (1995),[25] which dealt with marital rape). The case law in which the Court has used human dignity is seen as a 'bridge' between the international texts that enshrine human dignity expressly and the 'silence' of the European Convention in this regard.[26]

In terms of the use of human dignity by various courts, it has been argued that, although dignity has different meanings and can be used by jurisdictions for different purposes, including to restrict certain rights and freedoms, it has an important role in creating a common judicial human rights language:

> The point is not simply that the concept of dignity is vague and open to interpretation and gives judges discretion; in that it does not differ from all human rights obligations and rights. Rather, my argument is that, just as dignity played a significant role politically in smoothing over the transition to human rights in the post-Second World War period at the international level, so too dignity is playing a similar role judicially, enabling rights to be interpreted in a way that domesticates them. Its role, in practice, is to enable local context to be incorporated under the appearance of using a universal principle. Dignity, in the judicial context, not

[20] *Siliadin v France* App No 73316/01 (ECtHR, 26 October 2005); *Rantsev v Cyprus* App no 25965/04 (ECtHR, 7 January 2010)—both cases related to immigrants subjected to servitude and human trafficking, respectively.

[21] For further details, see Christopher McCrudden, 'Human Dignity and Judicial Interpretation of Human Rights' (2008) 19(4) European Journal of International Law 655, 689–93. See also Cinzia Piciocchi, 'The Role of Dignity in Constitutional Comparative Justice', in Manuel Guţan and Bianca Selejan-Guţan (eds), *Europeanization and Judicial Culture in Contemporary Democracies* (Hamangiu 2014).

[22] McCrudden, (n 21) 655.

[23] Costa (n 9) 400.

[24] ibid.

[25] *S.W. v. United Kingdom* App no 20166/92 (ECtHR, 22 November 1995) para 44: 'the abandonment of the unacceptable idea of a husband being immune against prosecution for rape of his wife was in conformity not only with a civilised concept of marriage but also, and above all, with the fundamental objectives of the Convention, the very essence of which is respect for human dignity and human freedom'.

[26] Costa (n 9) 401.

> only permits the incorporation of local contingencies in the interpretation of human rights norms; it requires it. Dignity allows each jurisdiction to develop its own practice of human rights.[27]

Dignity is also related to other concepts frequently used in human rights adjudication: liberty, equality and, more recently, identity. All of them can be included in the broader concept of personal autonomy. Within this meaning, human dignity has often acquired a justificatory function for extending the rights of persons that have previously been marginalised, like sexual minorities (lesbian, gay, bisexual, and transgender people). In this context, as Finck put it, 'human dignity is frequently encountered in the process of a transition from exclusion to inclusion'.[28]

Taking these aspects of dignity as a starting point, some other questions, related to the topic of this chapter, may arise: is human dignity a concept fit to accommodate the current migration phenomenon and the rights of migrants ? Or do national and international systems need other instruments to be introduced in order to deal with these new challenges and ensure that the fundamental rights of all members of society are protected? I will not give a definitive answer to these questions, as the matter is permanently under discussion in various legal and political arenas, but I will try to situate them within the perspective of the recent jurisprudence of the ECtHR. I argue that human dignity, with its essential core of personal autonomy in its Kantian meaning, can be used to enhance the content of the right to cultural identity, a cultural right related to minorities and migrants, the protection of which has been recognised *par ricochet* by the European Court.

2. Culture and Cultural Rights in the Case Law of the Strasbourg Court

Culture as an important element of the free development of human personality and personal autonomy has been included by the ECtHR in its reasoning, both as a multifaceted right and as a limit on the exercise of other rights. In both meanings, culture has generated a rich and interesting case law that has, at present, important implications on the protection of the rights of migrants in a multicultural European space.

Although the ECHR does not expressly protect cultural rights, instead mainly civil and political rights, the European Court has extended the Convention's realm into this category of rights, using a technique that has also been used with regard to social and economic rights or the right to a healthy environment. This is known as protection *par ricochet*, ie indirect protection, using other Convention-protected

[27] ibid, 720.
[28] Finck (n 5) 29.

rights such as the right to privacy, the right to freedom of religion, or the right to education. Another feature of this extended protection of cultural rights is that, at the beginning of their indirect inclusion in the scope of the Convention, they were related mainly to persons belonging to national minorities and therefore seen as part of the cultural identity of these persons.

The inclusion of cultural rights within the sphere of protection of the Convention system was achieved by the European Court in several ways, including: individual cultural rights as 'active rights', seen as the right to create culture, or more technically put, the right to artistic expression,[29] derived from the right to freedom of expression; individual cultural rights as 'passive rights' or rights related to accessing culture, derived especially from the right to freedom of information,[30] including access to culture for prisoners;[31] a right to the protection of national cultural heritage;[32] and the right to academic freedom.[33]

The recognition of cultural rights also has a collective dimension, with respect to a certain group's identity or to the community as a whole. Thus, the European Court stated in a judgment that 'any negative stereotyping of a group, when it reaches a certain level, it is capable of impacting on the group's sense of identity and the feelings of self-worth and self-confidence of members of the group'[34] or, in other words, on the human dignity of the members of the group. One statement of the Court, in *Munoz Diaz v Spain* (2009),[35] is particularly powerful: 'The Court takes the view that the force of collective beliefs of a community that is well-defined culturally cannot be ignored.'

The most relevant cultural rights for the purposes of this chapter's analysis are the right to cultural identity (which includes religious identity, as stated by the Court, for instance, in *Ahmet Arslan and others v Turkey* (2010),[36] and the right to education. Both of these rights are most likely to fall within the European Convention system using the tool of human dignity. These rights have been the subject of cases related to the protection of national minorities on the territory of the states parties, but they have gradually been extended towards the protection of migrants and non-nationals.

The aforementioned recognition of culture as an important tool to support the free development of the human being has led to the gradual recognition, by the Strasbourg Court, of a right to cultural identity, stemming from inherent cultural

[29] *Müller and others v Switzerland* App no 10737/84 (ECtHR, 24 May 1988); *Wingrove v United Kingdom* App no 17419/90 (ECtHR, 25 January 1996) etc.

[30] *Ahmet Yildirim v Turkey* App no 3111/10 (ECtHR, 18 December 2012); *Ashby and others v France* App no 36769/08 (ECtHR, 10 January 2013); *Akdas v Turkey* App no 41056/04 (ECtHR, 16 February 2010).

[31] *Laduna v Slovakia* App no 31827/02 (ECtHR, 13 December 2011).

[32] *Akdas v Turkey* (n 30).

[33] *Sorguç v Turkey* App no 17089/03 (ECtHR, 23 June 2009).

[34] *R.B. v Hungary* App no 64602/12 (ECtHR, 12 April 2016).

[35] *Munoz Diaz v Spain* App no 49151/07 (ECtHR, 8 December 2009).

[36] *Ahmet Arslan and others v Turkey* App no 41135/98 (ECtHR, 23 February 2010).

differences between different groups residing on the same territory and protected indirectly by means of the Convention's provisions: Article 8, Article 9, and Article 11. The right to education is closely related to the right to cultural identity and it is the only cultural right that has been expressly recognised in the Convention system, by way of Article 2 of Protocol 1.[37] In this section, I will describe, on the basis of some of the cases dealing with these rights, the trends that can be observed in the European Court's case law in relation to cultural rights.

The cultural differences between majority/minority or majority/migrants have been the subject of legal disputes in Europe long before the current migration phenomenon, partly because of previous migration waves to France, Germany, Belgium, etc. The most controversial issue from the cultural rights point of view, at the national level, has been the manifestation of religious identity through the use of religious signs, symbols, and clothes in public space. The receiving societies have implemented various solutions to respond to this, from the highest levels of tolerance to more-or-less restrictive measures, but until now no common understanding or 'European consensus' has been reached in respect of the cultural problems raised by migration. That is why, at a certain point in these national legal disputes, the Strasbourg Court was called on to intervene, with a view to finding common ground on these issues, using a 'human rights filter'. However, in my view, this common ground is far from being found, as the reasoning of the Court in *S.A.S. v France*,[38] or in the more recent *Dakir v Belgium*,[39] is seriously flawed with regard to the interpretation of the legitimate aims necessary to justify interferences with freedom of religion and the right to privacy, as I will show in the following section.

The Strasbourg Court dealt with the matter of cultural differences in the education context in cases such as *Kervanci v France*,[40] *Dogru v France*,[41] and *Sahin v Turkey*.[42] The first two cases from France related to the wearing of religious clothing in schools and the Court put forward the principle of secularism in public space, as opposed to cultural diversity in public schools: the prohibition on wearing the Islamic veil in school was justified by the necessity to respect the internal rules of the educational establishments, without any distinction whatsoever. The Court recognised that the state had a wide margin of appreciation and held that 'it belongs to national authorities to ensure with great vigilance that, while respecting the pluralism and the freedom of others, the manifestation by students of religious beliefs does not transform into an ostentatious act that would constitute a source

[37] Protocol 1 to the European Convention for the Protection of Human Rights and Fundamental Freedoms ETS 9.
[38] *S.A.S. v France* [GC] App no 43835/11 (ECtHR, 1 July 2014).
[39] *Dakir v Belgium* App no 4619/12 (ECtHR, 11 July 2017).
[40] *Kervanci v France* App no 31645/04 (ECtHR, 4 December 2008).
[41] *Dogru v France* App no 27058/05 (ECtHR, 4 December 2008).
[42] *Sahin v Turkey* [GC] App no 44774/98 (ECtHR, 10 November 2005).

of pressure and exclusion.' The position of the Court in these cases is not immune from criticism. Thus, it has been argued that, in *Sahin v Turkey*—a case concerning the ban on Islamic headscarf for university students, the Court 'oversimplified the use of headscarf in Turkey as merely an indicator of a polarizing opposition between the threat of fundamental Islamism to secularists seeking to retain a secular democracy and legal system … The Strasbourg Court equated Islam with intolerance, suggesting that the Islamic woman is under oppression.'[43] The dissenting judge in the *Sahin* case, Françoise Tulkens, also criticised the majority's view, from two points of view: that of the particular situation of the applicant and that of the situation of Muslim women in general. Related to the applicant's freedom of religion, Judge Tulkens pointed out that the Court should have taken into account the attitude and personal situation of the applicant when wearing the headscarf:

> Merely wearing the headscarf cannot be associated with fundamentalism and it is vital to distinguish between those who wear the headscarf and 'extremists' who seek to impose the headscarf as they do other religious symbols. Not all women who wear the headscarf are fundamentalists and there is nothing to suggest that the applicant held fundamentalist views.… The applicant's personal interest in exercising the right to freedom of religion and to manifest her religion by an external symbol cannot be wholly absorbed by the public interest in fighting extremism.[44]

Moreover, concerning the applicant's right to education and the situation of Muslim women in general, Judge Tulkens argued that:

> By accepting the applicant's exclusion from the university in the name of secularism and equality, the majority have accepted her exclusion from precisely the type of liberated environment in which the true meaning of these values can take shape and develop. University affords practical access to knowledge that is free and independent of all authority. Experience of this kind is far more effective a means of raising awareness of the principles of secularism and equality than an obligation that is not assumed voluntarily, but imposed. A tolerance-based dialogue between religions and cultures is an education in itself, so it is ironic that young women should be deprived of that education on account of the headscarf. Advocating freedom and equality for women cannot mean depriving them of the chance to decide on their future. Bans and exclusions echo that very fundamentalism these measures are intended to combat.[45]

[43] Hilal Elver, 'Secular Constitutionalism and Muslim Women's Rights' in Beverley Baines, Daphne Barak-Erez, Tsvi Kahana (eds), *Feminist Constitutionalism: Global Perspectives* (Cambridge University Press 2012) 413, 426, 427.

[44] *Sahin* (n 42) Dissenting Opinion of Judge Tulkens, para 10.

[45] ibid, para 19.

In the famous case of *Lautsi v Italy*,[46] the Grand Chamber made a general statement concerning the role of cultural and historical diversity in the field of human rights:

> The Court must moreover take into account the fact that Europe is marked by a great diversity between the States of which it is composed, particularly in the sphere of cultural and historical development. It emphasizes, however, that the reference to a tradition cannot relieve a Contracting State of its obligation to respect the rights and freedoms enshrined in the Convention and its Protocols.[47]

In a more recent case, *Osmanoglu v Switzerland*,[48] involving cultural differences and the right to education, the applicants, who were devout Muslims, refused to send their daughters to compulsory school swimming lessons on the grounds that their beliefs prohibited them from allowing their children to take part in mixed-sex swimming lessons. They stated that although the Koran did not instruct women to cover their bodies until puberty, their beliefs required them to prepare their daughters for the precepts that would be applied to them from that point onwards. As holders of parental responsibility for their daughters, the applicants alleged that there had been a violation of Article 9 of the Convention in their respect because the school refused to exempt their daughters from the swimming lessons, based on the local legislation, and, following their refusal to allow the girls attend the lessons, they were fined by the local education authorities. The Court admitted that there was an interference with the applicants' rights under Article 9 and decided that the interference was prescribed by law and had a legitimate aim. In evaluating whether the interference was necessary in a democratic society, the Court said, *inter alia,* that the children's interest in an all-round education, facilitating their successful social integration according to local customs and mores, takes precedence over the parents' wish to have their daughters exempted from mixed swimming lessons. For the same reason, said the Court, the applicants' argument that swimming lessons are not included in the curriculum of all schools in Switzerland had to be rejected, on the grounds that sports education, of which swimming is an integral part in the school attended by the applicants' daughters, is of special importance for children's development and health. The Court emphasised, in this respect, that a child's interest in attending those lessons lies not merely in learning to swim and taking physical exercise, but above all in participating in that activity with all the other pupils, without exceptions based on the child's origin or the parents' religious or philosophical convictions. With regard to the applicants' argument that their daughters attended

[46] *Lautsi and others v Italy* [GC] App no 30814/06 (ECtHR, 18 March 2011); see Bianca Selejan-Gutan, 'Semne şi simboluri religioase în jurisprudenţa de la Strasbourg. Cronica unei hotărâri aşteptate' (2011) 5 Pandectele române 96.

[47] *Lautsi* (n 46), para 68.

[48] *Osmanoglu v Switzerland* App no 29086/12 (ECtHR, 10 January 2017).

private swimming lessons, the Court argued that 'what was important for the children was not only taking physical exercise or learning to swim—legitimate aims in themselves—but above all the fact of *learning together* (emphasis added) and taking part in that activity collectively'.[49] The Court also stated that 'exempting children whose parents have sufficient financial resources to offer them private classes would create, in respect of those children whose parents do not have such resources, a level of inequality that is unacceptable in compulsory education'.[50] Finally, the Court stated that by giving precedence to the obligation for the children to follow the full school curriculum and their successful integration over the applicants' private interest in obtaining an exemption from mixed swimming lessons for their daughters on religious grounds, the domestic authorities did not exceed the margin of appreciation afforded to them in the present case, which concerned compulsory education. As a result, there had been no violation of Article 9 of the Convention.

The case of *Ponomaryiovi v Bulgaria*[51] concerned restrictions, on the grounds of nationality, on the cultural right to education of aliens. The imposition of fees for access to primary and secondary education for aliens in Bulgaria was considered an infringement of both Article 14 of the Convention and Article 2 of Protocol 1. The applicants were not in the position of individuals arriving in the country unlawfully and then laying claim to the use of its public services, including free schooling. According to the Court, even when the applicants found themselves, somewhat inadvertently, in the situation of aliens lacking permanent residence permits, the authorities had no substantive objection to their remaining in Bulgaria and, therefore, did not have any serious intention of deporting them. The Court emphasised the importance of secondary education for the free development of individuals and quoted the International Covenant on Economic, Social, and Cultural Rights in support of its assertions: 'in a modern society, having no more than basic knowledge and skills constitutes a barrier to successful personal and professional development. It prevents the persons concerned from adjusting to their environment and entails far-reaching consequences for their social and economic well-being.'[52] Therefore, the requirement for the applicants to pay fees for their secondary education, on account of their nationality and immigration status, was not justified and amounted to a violation of Article 14 of the Convention taken in conjunction with Article 2 of Protocol No 1.

The Court has also dealt with cases regarding cultural rights at the workplace and in education institutions, but on a case-by-case basis rather than in a general doctrinal manner. Thus, *Eweida and others v United Kingdom*[53] concerned the

[49] ibid, §100.
[50] ibid.
[51] *Ponomaryovi v Bulgaria* App no 5335/05 (ECtHR, 21 June 2011).
[52] ibid, § 57.
[53] *Eweida and others v United Kingdom* App nos 48420/10, 59842/10, 51671/10, and 36516/10 (ECtHR, 15 January 2013).

dismissal of employees, both in the private and public sector, for openly wearing the Christian cross at work and the dismissal of a registrar of births, deaths, and marriages as a result of her refusal to officiate at same-sex partnership ceremonies. The case of *Ebrahimian v France*[54] dealt with the situation of a social worker in the psychiatric department of a public hospital who was prohibited from wearing a headscarf at work. In the first case, the Court concluded that there had been a violation of Article 9 for dismissing the first applicant for visibly wearing the cross; the same conclusion was given as regards the dismissal of the registrar of births. In the second case, on the contrary, the Court found no violation of Article 9: 'the Court considers that the domestic authorities did not exceed their margin of appreciation in finding that it was impossible to reconcile the applicant's religious beliefs and the obligation not to manifest them, and subsequently in deciding to give priority to the requirement of State neutrality and impartiality'. The *Hamidovic v Bosnia and Herzegovina*[55] case concerned the refusal of the applicant to remove an object of religious clothing (a skullcap) during court proceedings. The Court conducted a comparative study of the legislation in 38 of the 47 member states and concluded that there was no blanket or general prohibition on the wearing of religious symbols in court proceedings in any of them. In some countries, however, judges may impose dress code rules in their courtroom. In the present case, the Court saw no reason to doubt that the applicant's act of wearing the skullcap was inspired by his sincere religious belief that he must wear it at all times and that the applicant had no 'hidden agenda to make a mockery of the trial, incite others to reject secular and democratic values or cause a disturbance'.[56] The Court recalled its previous general statement that pluralism, tolerance, and broadmindedness are hallmarks of a 'democratic society' and that, although individual interests must on occasion be subordinated to those of a group, democracy does not simply mean that the views of a majority must always prevail. In this respect, the Court stated that the role of the authorities is not to avoid social tensions by eliminating pluralism, but to ensure that competing groups understand the importance of tolerance. The applicant appeared before the court as summoned and stood up when requested, thereby clearly submitting to the laws and courts of the country, which the Court noted shows that there was no indication that he had a disrespectful attitude. Therefore, his punishment for contempt of court on the sole ground of his refusal to remove his skullcap was not necessary in a democratic society and, as a consequence, the Court decided that there had been a violation of Article 9 of the Convention.

Following all these cases and many others, a trend has emerged in the direction of extending, via the Strasbourg Court case law, the Convention's protection of the cultural rights of persons belonging to minorities in a broader sense

[54] *Ebrahimian v France* App no 64846/11 (ECtHR, 26 November 2015).
[55] *Hamidovic v Bosnia and Herzegovina* App no 57792/15 (ECtHR, 5 December 2017).
[56] ibid, §41.

(national minorities and migrants). However, in respect of migrants, the problems and challenges can be more difficult to solve than in the case of national minorities historically settled on a state's territory, especially in the countries that recognise specific cultural rights to persons belonging to national minorities. These difficulties can be caused by cultural differences as well as by a stronger need to integrate migrants (as opposed to persons belonging to national minorities which are either fully integrated or benefit from cultural autonomy, depending on the respective state's legislation). That is why, the use of new concepts in order to preserve the legal and cultural background of the 'receiving' societies was deemed necessary by the Strasbourg Court. However, I argue that such concepts should be used in conjunction with human dignity in order to ensure a balance between the protection of the interests at stake: societal v individual.

3. Migration and Cultural Rights

Nowadays, the 'new' migration phenomenon—a new one because of its context, not by nature, as migration is one of the oldest dynamics of human behavior in the world—raises social and economic problems in the receiving states, but also becomes a vehicle for the manifestation of other cultures, including languages, traditions, and religions. The already multicultural societies of the EU member states (some historically, due to the presence of minorities on their territories, some as an effect of decolonisation, some as a result of older waves of economic migration) are under pressure to receive and accommodate these new changes. In Europe, especially, one of the main challenges of migration is seen to centre around the idea of the so-called 'constitutional identity':

> Cultural diversity caused by immigration presents a challenge to a country's identity. Recent tensions have focused on cultural and religious accommodation in education law, labour law and family law.... How should a liberal society reconcile the self-determination of individuals belonging to immigrant and minority groups with self-determination of individuals belonging to a majority population?[57]

In this context, one can also ask whether the European Union is prepared to adopt its policies towards refugees and migrants while respecting its commitment to fundamental values and the duty to respect the constitutional identity of the member states. The same questions must be asked of the Council of Europe's human rights protection system and for the principles set forth by the case law of the ECtHR.

[57] Bast and Orgad (n 1) 1592.

International soft law documents and guidelines issued at the UN level (such as by the OHCHR—UN Office of the High Commissioner for Human Rights),[58] or at the Council of Europe level,[59] mainly refer to the social and economic rights of migrants (right to housing, right to decent working conditions, to social security, education, etc). These are the most basic rights coming after the right to life, the right to physical and moral integrity, or the right not to be subjected to slavery or forced labour. However, freedom of religion and the 'cultural identity' rights related to it should also be fully discussed.

It is important to point out that some of the issues raised by migration are similar to the ones raised by the recognition of the cultural rights of persons belonging to national minorities. National minorities are defined as national or ethnic groups historically established on the territory of a given state that has a majority population of a different ethnic or national origin.

From a legal perspective, the issue of cultural and religious diversity has already been the subject of decisions of European constitutional courts. For instance, the German Federal Constitutional Court has dealt with the Islamic headscarf issue in decisions *Headscarf I*[60] and *Headscarf II*.[61] In *Headscarf I* (2003), the Court avoided ruling on the constitutionality of the prohibition on the wearing of the Islamic headscarf by teachers in public schools, and asked the *Länder* (Germany's federal states) to create a legal basis for such prohibitions. In *Headscarf II* (2015), the Court decided that the general prohibition on wearing the Islamic headscarf in public schools in the state of North Rhine-Westphalia was unconstitutional, as it was a disproportionate means of achieving the stated aim ('peace in schools and neutrality of the State towards religion'), which was given as the legal basis for the prohibitory measure. The decisions of constitutional courts are, however, quite rare and rather divergent at the moment.[62]

Migration, and the changing multicultural contexts in Europe, have brought new challenges not only to European states, but also to case law of the ECtHR. This was emphasised in the 2014 Grand Chamber judgment of *S.A.S. v France*,[63] where the Court used two apparently convergent concepts—human dignity and 'living

[58] For example, OHCHR, 'Principles and Guidelines on the Human Rights Protection of Migrants in Vulnerable Situations' (YEAR),<http://www.ohchr.org/Documents/Issues/Migration/PrinciplesAndGuidelines.pdf> accessed October 2020.

[59] Yannis Ktistakis, *Protecting Migrants under the ECHR and the ESC* (Council of Europe Publishing 2013).

[60] BVerfG, Judgment of the Second Senate of 24 September 2003–2 BvR 1436/02.

[61] BVerfG, Order of the First Senate of 27 January 2015–1 BvR 471/10. See also, for details, Claudia E Haupt, 'The "New" German Teacher Headscarf Decision', International Journal of Constitutional Law Blog, (17 March 2015, <http://www.iconnectblog.com/2015/03/the-new-german-teacher-headscarf-decision> accessed 30 October 2020.

[62] For instance, the decision of the Belgian Constitutional Court cited in the case *Belcacemi v Belgium* App no 37798/13 (ECtHR, 11 July 2017) and *Dakir* (n 39): Arret no 145/2012, available at https://www.const-court.be/public/f/2012/2012-145f.pdf accessed 30 October 2020.

[63] *S.A.S.* (n 38).

together' and, more recently, in 2017, the Court used the same reasoning in *Dakir v Belgium*[64] and *Belcacemi v Belgium*.[65]

From the outset it must be stated that 'living together' is an entirely new concept among the various reasons used by the Court to justify restrictive measures imposed by states in the context of cultural rights. The Court thus goes beyond the margin of appreciation doctrine and creates[66] a legitimate aim not elucidated in the Convention but deduced from the wider expression 'protection of rights and freedoms of others'. The leading case, *S.A.S. v France*, regarded a complaint against the blanket ban, instituted by the French Law of 11 October 2010, of wearing the burqa (full Islamic veil) and other clothes that cover the face in public spaces. The applicant argued that this prohibition (which came with administrative and criminal penalties) violated her right to freedom of conscience and religion, her right to respect for private life and her right to be free from discrimination. The French Government, in turn, quoted from the explanatory report on the law adopted in 2010, which emphasised the fact that the ban was justified because the wearing of the full veil was considered as clearly contravening 'the principle of respect for the dignity of the person/*atteinte à la dignité de la personne*'. The explanatory report went on to state that dignity was under threat because the wearing of the full face veil equals 'a public manifestation of a conspicuous denial of equality between men and women' and, moreover, that 'it is not only about the dignity of the individual who is confined in this manner, but also the dignity of others who share the same public space and who are thus treated as individuals from whom one must be protected by the refusal of any exchange, even if only visual'.[67]

In its argumentation, the Court acknowledges the existence of an interference with the right to freedom of religion, on the grounds of Article 9(2). By reference to the legitimate aim, the Court states, on the one hand, that it is a matter of the protection of public order (although, as it was pointed out, there was no immediate general threat to this value)[68] and, on the other hand, of respect for the rights and freedoms of others. The latter legitimate aim was the one that led the Court to the principle it used to finally decide the case, by finding that 'the impugned ban can be regarded as justified in its principle solely in so far as it seeks to guarantee the conditions of "living together" '.[69]

64 *Dakir* (n 39).
65 *Belcacemi* (n 62).
66 Which is considered as 'unsettling' by certain scholars. See Hakeem Yusuf, 'SAS v France: Supporting Living Together or Forced Assimilation?' (2014) 3(2) International Human Rights Law Review 277, 288.
67 *S.A.S.* (n 38), para 25.
68 Francois-Xavier Millet, 'When the European Court of Human Rights Encounters the Face' (2015) 11 European Constitutional Law Review 415.
69 *S.A.S.* (n 38), para 142.

When analysing the proportionality of the measure by reference to the legitimate aim concerned, the Court firstly acknowledged that 'a large number of actors, both international and national, in the field of fundamental rights protection have found a blanket ban to be disproportionate'.[70] Secondly, the Court ruled in favour of a wide margin of appreciation for the state, in the absence of a European consensus on the matter, stating that:

> the respondent State is seeking to protect a principle of interaction between individuals, which in its view is essential for the expression not only of pluralism, but also of tolerance and broadmindedness without which there is no democratic society. It can thus be said that the question whether or not it should be permitted to wear the full-face veil in public places constitutes a choice of society.[71]

It is also interesting to note that the Court did not raise the argument of human dignity either in respect of the applicant or based on the government's submissions and that the full veil was treated, in line with the previous case law, as 'the expression of a cultural identity which contributes to the pluralism that is inherent in democracy'.[72] In the same context, it was underlined that, essential as it may be, the respect for personal dignity in general cannot legitimate the general ban on wearing the full veil in public space. Thus, instead of relying on human dignity as it was invoked by the government, which was not powerful enough to justify the prohibition, the principle of 'living together' became the determining factor in the case, bypassing other principles such as equality.

From the cultural rights' point of view, the problem with the concept of 'living together' is that, in order to apply it, the authorities must make value judgements of a general kind on the targeted behaviours, which could lead to an infringement of neutrality, as the Court itself emphasised: 'the State's duty of neutrality and impartiality is incompatible with any power on the State's part to assess the legitimacy of religious beliefs or the ways in which those beliefs are expressed'.[73]

Despite the cultural arguments, however, the Court concluded that, especially by taking into account the wide margin of appreciation of the state, the prohibition can be considered as proportionate to the legitimate aim pursued, notably to preserve the conditions of 'living together' as an element of the protection of the rights and freedoms of others.

This reasoning was criticised by the dissenting judges, as well as by some legal scholars. Thus, the concept of 'living together' seems an inclusive, integrative, one, but, in this case it had, as the dissenting judges said, an exclusionary effect. Judges

[70] ibid, para 147.
[71] ibid, para 153.
[72] ibid, para 120.
[73] ibid, para 127.

Nussberger and Jäderblom emphasised, in their separate opinion, that, although it used 'living together' as a legitimate aim for the limitation of fundamental rights:

> The Court's case-law is not clear as to what may constitute 'the rights and freedoms of others' outside the scope of rights protected by the Convention. The very general concept of 'living together' does not fall directly under any of the rights and freedoms guaranteed within the Convention. Even if it could arguably be regarded as touching upon several rights, such as the right to respect for private life (article 8) and the right not to be discriminated against (article 14), the concept seems far-fetched and vague.[74]

Moreover, arguing from the individuals' perspective, the dissenting judges stated that:

> [I]t can hardly be argued that an individual has a right to enter into contact with other people, in public places, against their will. Otherwise such a right would have to be accompanied by a corresponding obligation. This would be incompatible with the spirit of the Convention. While communication is admittedly essential for life in society, the right to respect for private life also comprises the right not to communicate and not to enter into contact with others in public places—the right to be an outsider.[75]

The Court's decision was also criticised by academics. Thus, it has been pointed out that:

> The Court seems to neglect the fact that individuals have the right to choose the degree of their allegiance to society provided that this does not harm others.... However, a liberal democratic regime should allow the possibility to its members to withdraw and to appreciate critically the membership in their community.... Forcing human beings to be sociable by forcing them to uncover their faces in this context is equivalent to accepting an omnipotent state, which is allowed to define a person as far as all aspects of her existence are concerned. It is equivalent to accepting a very wide interpretation of the harm principle that is threatening to the principle of self-determination. And it is contrary to the idea of equal respect that must be recognized to everyone on the basis of human dignity.[76]

74 ibid, Joint Partly Dissenting Opinion of Judges Nussberger and Jäderblom, para 5.

75 ibid, para 8.

76 Ioanna Tourkochoriti, 'The Burka Ban before the European Court of Human Rights: A Comment on SAS v France', International Journal of Constitutional Law Blog, 9 July 2014 <http://www.

Another author argued that:

> [T]he basis of the Strasbourg Court notion of 'living together' is both questionable and unsettling with wide ranging implications arguably well beyond the court's contemplation in *S.A.S* v *France*. In an era of heightened 'politics of identity', caution is particularly important in adjudicating the rights of minorities who are rendered vulnerable to forced assimilation policies.[77]

The contradictions present in the Court's reasoning were also emphasised. Thus, it was argued that 'it is even contradictory to rely, in order to save the ban, on the existence of a national margin of appreciation in religious matters and, at the same time, in the socio-ethical argument deriving from the crucial importance of showing one's face'.[78]

These critical opinions are in line with pre-*S.A.S.* criticisms of similar bans, in the fundamental rights scholarship on 'state paternalism' regarding religious symbols and clothes, especially referring to the French Law of 2004, which prohibited the wearing of visible religious symbols in state schools. Thus, Laborde considered that 'republican paternalists are wrong to think that autonomy is about emancipation from religion and culture through the exercise of secular reason. One does not need to detach oneself from one's beliefs and culture to be free'.[79] In the same vein, the prohibition on wearing the full-face veil has been compared with other types of clothing:

> The veil is a piece of fabric, and, alongside other garments made of fabric, it does not violate rights. In fact, there are no laws in Europe banning or limiting the right of women to wear any particular kind of clothing, even when, as in the case of high heels or exaggeratedly tight-fitting trousers, these may actually harm their health. In liberal societies, many women, from virtually all cultural and religious groups and social classes, undergo tremendous societal, group and/or family pressure to dress one way or another. However, with extremely limited exceptions, liberal societies do not consider articles of clothing, other than Islamic ones, a matter to be regulated judicially or legally.[80]

iconnectblog.com/2014/07/the-burka-ban-before-the-european-court-of-human-rights-a-comment-on-s-a-s-v-france> accessed 30 October 2020.

[77] Yusuf (n 66) 284.

[78] Millet (n 68) 420.

[79] Cecile Laborde, 'State Paternalism and Religious Dress Code' (2012) 2(10) International Journal of Constitutional Law 402.

[80] Susanna Mancini, 'Patriarchy as the Exclusive Domain of the Other: The Veil Controversy, False Projection and Cultural Racism' (2012) 2(10) International Journal of Constitutional Law 412.

In 2018, the UNHR Committee issued some views on a case regarding the wear of the niqab in France.[81] The Committee rejected the arguments of the government on the proportionality of the measure banning the wearing of the veil:

> Even if the State party could demonstrate the existence of a specific and significant threat to public safety and order in principle, it has failed to demonstrate that the prohibition contained in Act No. 2010-1192 is proportionate to that objective, in view of its considerable impact on the author as a woman wearing the full-face veil. Nor has it attempted to demonstrate that the ban was the least restrictive measure necessary to ensure the protection of the freedom of religion or belief.[82]

While acknowledging that the State party concerned used the concept of 'living together' to justify the measures restraining the rights protected by the Covenant, the Committee did not agree that this concept could be considered an absolute legitimate aim for this purpose:

> Even assuming that the concept of living together could be considered a 'legitimate objective' in the sense of article 18 (3), the Committee observes that the State party has failed to demonstrate that the criminal ban on certain means of covering of the face in public, which constitutes a significant restriction of the rights and freedoms of the author as a Muslim woman who wears the full-face veil, is proportionate to that aim, or that it is the least restrictive means that is protective of religion or belief.
>
> In the light of the foregoing, the Committee considers that the State party has failed to demonstrate that the limitation of the author's freedom to manifest her religion or beliefs, through the wearing of the niqab, was necessary and proportionate within the meaning of article 18 (3) of the Covenant. The Committee therefore concludes that the ban introduced by Act No. 2010-1192 and the conviction of the author under said Act for wearing the niqab violated the author's rights under article 18 of the Covenant.[83]

In its further analysis of the claim that the ban violated Article 26 of the Covenant on freedom of religion, the Committee agreed with the applicant that although the ban addressed face covering in any context, the restrictive measure mainly applies, in practice, to religious clothing, ie the full-face veil worn by Muslim women. The Committee made some interesting remarks on the potential adverse effects of the measure on this group of women: 'The Committee further considers that the

[81] Yaker v France, *Views adopted by the Committee under article 5(4) of the Optional Protocol concerning communication no 2747/2016*, adopted on 17 July 2018 and published on 7 December 2018.
[82] ibid, para 8.8.
[83] ibid, para 8.11–8.12.

prohibition, rather than protecting fully veiled women, could have the opposite effect of confining them to their homes, impeding their access to public services and exposing them to abuse and marginalization.'[84] In its concluding remarks on this aspect, the Committee found that:

> [T]he criminal ban introduced by article 1 of Act No. 2010-1192 disproportionately affects the author as a Muslim woman who chooses to wear the full-face veil, and introduces a distinction between her and other persons who may legally cover their face in public that is not necessary and proportionate to a legitimate interest, and is therefore unreasonable. The Committee hence concludes that this provision and its application to the author constitutes a form of intersectional discrimination based on gender and religion, in violation of article 26 of the Covenant.[85]

Therefore, the concept of 'living together' expresses a very limited interpretation of a legitimate aim that can be used to impose rights limitations and is certainly not universally accepted as a potential ground for the restriction of cultural rights.

In my view, the cultural dimension of the blanket ban on the full-face veil in public spaces, in the context of the cultural diversity created by the migration phenomenon, may raise certain worrying issues in contemporary multicultural societies. Such a ban may not be proportionate if it is directed, in an obvious manner, towards a certain category of persons belonging to one religion (eg Muslim women), thus affecting the human dignity of that group and its members. The prohibition on covering one's face does not apply to other types of clothing without religious connotation (sports, artistic, professional, etc). In support of my view, I would invoke again the dissenting ECtHR judges, who have also underlined that:

> [T]his idea cannot be turned around, to lead to the conclusion that human interaction is impossible if the full face is not shown. This is evidenced by examples that are perfectly rooted in European culture, such as the activities of skiing and motorcycling with full-face helmets and the wearing of costumes in carnivals. Nobody would claim that in such situations (which form part of the exceptions provided for in the French Law) the minimum requirements of life in society are not respected. People can socialize without necessarily looking into each other's eyes.[86]

[84] ibid, para 8.15.
[85] ibid, para 8.17.
[86] *S.A.S.* (n 38) Joint Partly Dissenting Opinion of Judges Nussberger and Jäderblom, para 9.

4. Conclusion

The concept of 'living together', which was used again by the Court in 2017, and which could easily be imposed on migrants, is problematic also because it is difficult to establish its actual content: it is a vague concept, without a clear definition and, consequently, its use and limits are unpredictable. Who decides what 'living together' should include? Are only the majority's practices included? In this case—which specific practices are acceptable? All of them or only some of them? Should there be a right to conscientious objection, if there was no immediate danger for other public or private values? These are questions to which neither the Court nor the politicians have yet found the answers.

The potential consequences of this kind of interpretation of the majority-vs-minority cultural issues were anticipated in the scholarship even before the debate generated by the *S.A.S.* judgment. Thus, it has been pointed out that, following the *Sahin* case, states would be more keen to impose bans on wearing religious-related clothing and this has actually happened.[87]

In the *S.A.S.* case, the Court suggested that the concept of 'living together' includes the possibility of looking into each other's eyes. However, one must place the concept in the context of the pluralism that characterises contemporary democratic societies. Thus, the dangers of using the concept of 'living together' as a new way to limit rights were emphasised more recently in the concurring opinion to the judgments *Belcacemi*[88] and *Dakir*[89] by Judges Spano and Karakas:

> [T]he essence of the principle of 'living together' is so malleable and vague that it could potentially serve as a rhetorical tool for the regulation of any interaction or of any behaviour in the society on the sole basis of a particular conception of what constitutes the 'good manner' of interacting between individuals in a democratic society. This is contradictory with the fundamental values of the personal autonomy, human dignity, tolerance and spirit of openness that form the assets of the Convention's system.[90]

In *Chapman v United Kingdom*,[91] a case about the recognition of traditional ways of living adopted by minorities, the Court held that the protection of minorities is important to uphold the 'dignity' of the whole community, by preserving its cultural diversity:

[87] Elver (n 43) 432. The author also claims that 'the ECtHR adopted an approach that allows states to violate the rights of members of specifically non-Christian religions who wish to wear clothing in public for religious reasons. The ECtHR's approach over a series of cases has failed to give proper weight to the need for states to have strong justifications for such restrictions.'

[88] *Belcacemi* (n 62).

[89] *Dakir* (n 39).

[90] *Belcacemi* (n 62) Concurring Opinion of Judges Spano and Karakas, para 6.

[91] *Chapman v United Kingdom* App no 27238/95 (ECtHR, 18 January 2001).

> [T]here may be said to be an emerging international consensus amongst the Contracting States of the Council of Europe recognising the special needs of minorities and an obligation to protect their security, identity and lifestyle (…) not only for the purpose of safeguarding the interests of the minorities themselves, but to preserve a cultural diversity of value to the whole community.[92]

Could this 'reverse' perspective of 'living together' apply, in any way, to the cultural rights of migrants? It is a difficult question as the Court's views seem to apply only to 'culturally well-defined communities', which are not very precisely defined in the case law and, as a result, the collective dimension of these rights seems to prevail over the individual rights of the members of less-culturally established communities. A possible answer could be the application of the human dignity criterion: if a state measure restricting a cultural right would seriously impair the human dignity of the person, then there might be a violation of the right in question. Certainly, the attitude of the applicant, the impact of the restricted right in public space, and the interests of the community as a whole must be taken into account, but in my view, there is no 'living together' without respecting the human dignity of the persons with whom one wants to live together.

It is equally true that states must find effective solutions to accommodate the interests at stake in the context of migration. There are the interests of the people who migrate, which are to ensure their integration into society, but also with a view to respect their individual rights, including cultural rights. Then there are the interests of the community as a whole, as the preservation of the identity of their society and the rights and interests of its members is of equal importance for states. It is, indeed, very difficult to ensure a balance between these interests. But, in my view, if one should apply an 'ideological' principle, human dignity should prevail or at least be combined with 'living together' because with the dignity dimension included, 'living together' may constitute an appropriate foundation for the respect of individual rights in a liberal society. Otherwise it risks being transformed, if misused, into an instrument of a 'majority dictatorship'.[93] The lack of any basis in the Convention for the concept of 'living together' might raise, in this context, issues related to the disregard of human dignity and should, as a consequence, be used with caution by the national authorities as well as by the Court. A margin of appreciation should still be granted to states, but it should be more carefully evaluated by the Court with respect to the justifications for restrictive measures, including by using the human dignity criterion. A narrow or absolute interpretation of the concept of

[92] ibid, para 93.

[93] 'Living together' can be considered as another expression of 'normality' in the society. However, a subjective concept of 'normality' has been used, in the past, as a tool for serious discriminations and repressions based on race, sexual orientation, political views, and even appearance (eg the ban of wearing beards and long hair by men in Romania during the communist regime).

'living together' could entail an active imposition of the majority conception on minorities (including migrants and other categories of minorities than the national/ethnic ones) and, in my view, would be hard to reconcile with the liberal concepts of respect for human dignity, tolerance, and a spirit of openness, all characteristic of the ECHR system.

9

Islamophobia and the ECtHR

A Test Case for Positive Subsidiarity for the Protection of Europe's Long-term Migrants?

Eva Brems

1. Introduction

A reflection on the human rights of migrants in Europe cannot get around the issue of racism. Resistance to immigration in Europe is fuelled to a large extent by resistance to the 'otherness' of migrants: the colour of their skin, their lifestyle and habits, their religions. This resistance is expressed openly and strongly in political and societal discourse, in which racist stereotypes abound, and in which issues regarding the integration of minorities with a migration background are linked to questions regarding the influx of new migrants. More specifically, the 'otherness' that is most central to today's debates on migration and integration in Europe is Islam. Resistance to immigration in Europe goes hand in hand with resistance to the establishment or growth of Muslim minorities in Christian/secular European societies.[1] Thus, racism is commonly expressed as Islamophobia.

Many organisations have documented the widespread nature of Islamophobia in Europe.[2] In this context, it is widely accepted that Islamophobia is not only expressed in hate speech, hate crimes, and discrimination towards migrants, but also in 'policies or legislation that indirectly target or disproportionately affect

[1] In 2016, the Muslim population in Europe (defined as the twenty-eight countries currently in the EU plus Norway and Switzerland) was estimated at 25.8 million (4.9 per cent of the overall population)—up from 19.5 million (3.8 per cent) in 2010. Pew Research Center, *Europe's Growing Muslim Population* (29 November 2017).

[2] Amongst Others: Council of Europe Commissioner for Human Rights, *Human Rights in Europe: No Grounds for Complacency* (2010) 37ff <https://rm.coe.int/human-rights-in-europe-no-grounds-for-complacency-compilation-of-viewp/16808d2513> accessed 19 November 2020; Amnesty International, *Choice and Prejudice: Discrimination Against Muslims in Europe* Report (2012); European Monitoring Centre on Racism and Xenophobia, *Muslims in the European Union: Discrimination and Islamophobia* Report (2006) <https://fra.europa.eu/sites/default/files/fra_uploads/eumc-2006-muslims-in-the-eu-discrimination-and-islamophobia_en.pdf> accessed 19 November 2020; ENAR, *Forgotten Women: the Impact of Islamophobia on Muslim Women* Report (2016) <https://www.enar-eu.org/IMG/pdf/forgottenwomenpublication_lr_final_with_latest_corrections.pdf> accessed 19 November 2020.

Eva Brems, *Islamophobia and the ECtHR* In: *Migration and the European Convention on Human Rights*. Edited by: Başak Çali, Ledi Bianku, and Iulia Motoc, Oxford University Press (2021).
DOI: 10.1093/oso/9780192895196.003.0009

Muslims, and unduly restrict their freedom of religion'.[3] Indeed, in the same vein that policies or legislation that (in)directly target women, can be called sexist, and that policies or legislation that (in)directly target LGBT individuals, can be called homophobic, policies and legislation that (in)directly target Muslims, can be called Islamophobic. In all of these examples, this is especially the case, when there are clear indications that the policies or legislation in question are driven by prejudice against the 'indirectly targeted' group.

Islamophobia is not a 'theme' in the case law of the European Court of Human Rights (ECtHR) or a sub theme in the protection of the rights of Europe's migrants. A HUDOC database search for 'Islamophobia' and 'Islamophobic' only results in a few indirect references to hate speech cases,[4] in addition to one reference in a case concerning the restriction of Islamic religious practice.[5] However, in that case, *S.A.S. v France*, the reference to Islamophobia also relates to hate speech (accompanying the legislative process leading up to the French face covering ban). It would thus seem at first sight that the ECtHR's conception of Islamophobia is limited to a matter of hate speech. This may be due, in part, to the types of cases that have come before the Court, which have not yet provided it with the opportunity to rule on any of the multiple other manifestations of Islamophobia.

In the cases of Islamophobic hate speech that have come before it, the Court has taken a firm stance against it. For example, it has dismissed free-speech-based complaints seeking to challenge the criminalisation of writings inciting hatred against Maghrebin and Islamic communities in France[6] and Belgium,[7] and the criminalisation of a man who displayed a poster stating 'Islam out of Britain'.[8] In the latter case, the Court even mobilised the abuse clause of Article 17 of the European Convention on Human Rights (ECHR),[9] holding the complaint inadmissible. Despite this firm stance the Court has not directly used the term 'Islamophobia' or 'Islamophobic' in its judgments, nor has it underlined the fact that such speech often targets long-term migrants.

[3] Open Society Foundations, 'Islamophobia in Europe' (2015) <https://www.opensocietyfoundations.org/explainers/islamophobia-europe> accessed 18 November 2018.

[4] In this context, the Court states that remarks characterised by Islamophobia, are directed against the Convention's underlying values: *Paksas v Lithuania* [GC] App no 34942/04 (ECtHR, 6 January 2011), para 88; *Perinçek v Switzerland* App no 27510/08 (ECtHR, 17 December 2013), para 47. The term Islamophobia is used here to refer to the speech at stake in previous case law, even though that term was not used in the judgment as such.

[5] *S.A.S. v France* [GC] App no 43835/11 (ECtHR, 1 July 2014), para 149: 'the Court is very concerned by the indications of some of the third-party interveners to the effect that certain Islamophobic remarks marked the debate which preceded the adoption of the Law of 11 October 2010'.

[6] *Soulas and others v France* App no 43835/11 (ECtHR, 10 July 2008); *Le Pen v France* (dec) App no 18788/09 (ECtHR, 20 April 2010).

[7] *Féret v Belgium* App no 15615/07 (ECtHR, 16 July 2009).

[8] *Norwood v United Kingdom* (dec) App no 23131/03 (ECtHR, 16 November 2004).

[9] Convention for the Protection of Human Rights and Fundamental Freedoms (European Convention on Human Rights, as amended) ETS 5.

At the same time, the Court has never applied the label 'Islamophobia' or related terms to restrictions on Islamic religious practice.[10] With the exception of the above-mentioned *S.A.S.* reference, the Court has also refrained from including Islamophobia as a relevant contextual factor in cases pursued against restrictions on Islamic religious practice, either as a driving force behind such restrictions, or as a consequence of them. What is more, the Court has not focused on the intersectionality of Islamophobia and anti-migrant sentiment.

This chapter will focus on the Court's case law concerning restrictions on Islamic practices in countries in which Muslims are a long-standing minority group with a migration background. The focus of the analysis will be on the nature of the messages the Court is sending to national authorities through this case law. Ultimately, this is an exploration of the Court's guidance and leadership in this field.

2. Analysing the ECtHR's Messages to National Authorities

In what follows, the first section (2.1) will argue for the importance of adequate guidelines to be given by the ECtHR to national authorities, as a matter of subsidiarity properly understood. The subsequent two sections will analyse the messages the Court is actually sending with regard to state restrictions on Muslim minority practices. First, what could arguably be considered the 'worst practice' in the Court's case law in this field is set off against what may be seen as 'best practice' of the Court in a different, but comparable field (section 2.2). Then the entire corpus of case law regarding restrictions on Muslim minority practices will be analysed (section 2.3).

2.1 Background: Positive Subsidiarity

The focus of the analysis in this chapter is on the messages the European Court is sending to national authorities regarding their approaches to multicultural conflicts over Islamic minority practices. This view of the Court as a sender of messages to the domestic level is to be seen in the context of what I call 'positive subsidiarity'. There is a strong consensus about the subsidiary role of the ECtHR vis-à-vis national authorities, who bear frontline responsibility for human rights protection. However, when it comes to the implications of subsidiarity for the work of the ECtHR, there tends to be a one-sided focus on what I call the negative side of subsidiarity, ie a duty of restraint on the part of the Court in light of a discretionary margin for the domestic authorities. This link is made explicit in the reference to

[10] This is of course related to the fact that the Court systematically accepts such restrictions as legitimate, as discussed in this chapter.

subsidiarity that the 15th Protocol to the ECHR will insert in the Convention's Preamble:

> Affirming that the High Contracting Parties, in accordance with the principle of subsidiarity, have the primary responsibility to secure the rights and freedoms defined in this Convention and the Protocols thereto, and that in doing so they enjoy a margin of appreciation, subject to the supervisory jurisdiction of the ECtHR established by this Convention.[11]

While acknowledging that the principle of subsidiarity requires a degree of restraint on the part of the ECtHR, I argue that this is just one face of subsidiarity as seen from the perspective of the Court: negative subsidiarity. In addition, the Court has a role to play in nudging national authorities towards taking up their responsibility for the protection of Convention rights: positive subsidiarity. I argue that this means that, while respecting a domestic margin of appreciation, the Court should set standards on *how* to secure Convention rights and freedoms that function as binding guidelines to domestic authorities, and act as limits to their margin of appreciation. This role for the Court in offering a framework for the exercise of domestic discretion is the concretisation of the reference to the 'supervisory jurisdiction' of the Court (Protocol 15, Article 1). It is argued that such practice is most effective within a logic of positive subsidiarity when the Court's messages are formulated in terms that offer guidance not only to the defendant state, but also to the authorities in other states parties that may be confronted with similar issues. Finally, it is argued that there are at least three relevant dimensions to the guidance that may be offered by the Court in a positive subsidiarity framework. In the first place there is *substantive* guidance: even when there are grounds to grant a wide margin of appreciation, states parties cannot interpret Convention rights in any way they like. Some guidance by the Court concerning the scope of rights provisions, and the limits on rights restrictions, is at the heart of the enterprise of joint European human rights protection that the Convention embodies. As soon as a matter falls within the scope of the Convention, a degree of substantive guidance by the Court is needed—without that, there would be no added value to the Convention, and the matter might as well have fallen outside its scope. In addition, *procedural* guidance is a very useful companion to the margin of appreciation. The principle of subsidiarity relies on the untested assumption that domestic authorities are able and willing to control the compatibility of rights-restrictive measures with the Convention. In order to guarantee that this assumption is not a false one, it is helpful if the Court offers some guidance on the quality of procedural requirements expected as part of human rights scrutiny. Finally, I identify

[11] Protocol No 15 amending the Convention for the Protection of Human Rights and Fundamental Freedoms ETS 213, Art 1.

a category of *discursive* guidance, which concerns the way of talking and writing about certain human-rights-related topics. This category is particularly relevant in cases concerning long-term migrants as new minorities, where discourse (in particular discriminatory stereotypes) is often a component of the human rights violation. It is important for the Court to avoid using problematic discourse in its own rulings, and to lead the way in naming and deconstructing discriminatory stereotypes perpetuating distinctions between 'authentic' citizens and migrant citizens or residents.

In what follows, I shall examine the substantive, procedural, and discursive messages the Court is sending to national authorities in cases regarding Islamic minority practices. In light of both the extensively documented context of Islamophobia in Europe, and the continuous contestation regarding Islamic minority practices in several states parties, it is argued that this is a field in which it is highly relevant for the Court to offer guidance to national authorities with a view to strengthening and optimising the protection of Convention rights. The Court's case law in this field has been strongly criticised by scholars as well as human rights activists. It is indeed remarkable that the Court has, to date, dismissed nearly all cases regarding the accommodation of Muslim minority practices,[12] while obliging states to accommodate some practices of other minority religions, despite the presence of sizeable established Islamic migrant communities in Europe.[13] The defence of the Court's case law argues that these findings of no violation are simply the result of a wide margin of appreciation, which in turn is justified by a wide divergence, across the states parties, of historical and constitutional contexts in which Church-State relations and religious freedoms have taken shape. This chapter will argue, however, that, even if one accepts a wide margin of appreciation in this field, the Court's case law is problematic from a subsidiarity perspective. This is because in several of its key judgments, the Court is sending problematic messages to national authorities. As the chapter will demonstrate, this affects the three dimensions of the Court's positive subsidiarity role that were distinguished above.

[12] Defined as religion-based practices of Muslims in countries in which Muslims are a minority. The one exception is *Lachiri v Belgium* App no 3413/09 (ECtHR, 18 September 2018). In addition, the Court has rejected most cases about the accommodation of Muslim practices in Turkey.

[13] eg *Eweida and others v United Kingdom* App nos 48420/10, 59842/10, 51671/10, and 36516/10 (ECtHR, 15 January 2013) (employee in private sector should be allowed to wear Christian cross); *Jakóbski v Poland* App no 18429/06 (ECtHR, 7 December 2010) (Buddhist prisoner should get meat-free diet).

2.2 Comparing Messages in Different Fields: Face Veils vs 'Gay Propaganda'

What better way to show the range of messages the Court may choose to send, than by comparing extreme examples? In this section, I shall compare a line of case law in which the Court has been strongly criticised for abandoning a persecuted minority, to another line of case law in which the Court has taken a firm stance in defence of another persecuted minority. The first is the case law on face covering bans in France and Belgium.[14] The other is the case law on the so-called 'gay propaganda' legislation in Russia.[15] While the first line of case law addresses mainly Article 9 ECHR and the second is concerned with Articles 10 and 11 ECHR, both sets of cases are ultimately about discrimination/exclusion/ marginalisation of unpopular minorities, visibly orthodox Muslims in Belgium and France in the former and openly gay people in Russia in the latter. In both cases, government measures restricting the rights of the minority focus on the visible presence of these minorities in the public sphere. And in both cases, these measures enjoy very broad support within the relevant society. In terms of outcomes, the Court upheld the face covering bans, and found the 'gay propaganda' legislation to be in violation of the Convention. It is relevant for comparative purposes to note that these strands of case law coexist in the same time frame, with the most recent judgments in each area issued in June and July of 2017, respectively. Niqab wearers in Belgium and France consist mostly of individuals with a long-term migration background, whereas the 'out and proud' gay people targeted in Russia mostly do not. It is possible that a distinction drawn between the rights of 'authentic' citizens and migrants is an explanatory factor for the radical difference in the Court's approach to the two types of cases. But this chapter does not set out to explain that difference. The presentation of this comparison serves two more modest aims. In the first place, the choices made in the Court's current approach to (arguably) Islamophobic rights restrictions become clearer when set off against the different choices made in its case law on (arguably) homophobic rights restrictions. In addition, the latter offers a realistic alternative to the Court's current approach to its position on the full face veil bans, should it choose to alter its course.

The comparison focuses on five salient points in the Court's legal reasoning that will be successively addressed: the Court's approach to the 'legitimate aim' requirement (subsection 2.2.1), its approach to the issue of evidence (subsection 2.2.2), the Court's more or less critical attitude towards majority sentiments (subsection 2.2.3), its attitude to any negative impact of the restrictive measure on such

[14] S.A.S. (n 5); *Belcacemi v Belgium* App no 37798/13 (ECtHR, 11 July 2017); *Dakir v Belgium* App no 4619/12 (ECtHR, 11 July 2017).

[15] *Alekseyev v Russia* App nos 4916/07, 25924/08, and 14599/09 (ECtHR, 21 October 2010); *Bayev and others v Russia* App nos 4916/07, 25924/08, and 14599/09 (ECtHR, 20 June 2017).

sentiments (subsection 2.2.4), and finally its use of the 'European consensus' argument (subsection 2.2.5).

2.2.1 Deconstructing the invoked 'legitimate aim'

A first striking difference between these two sets of cases concerns the Court's approach to the interests that are invoked by the defendant state as the 'legitimate aims' of the restrictive measures. In *Bayev*, the most recent 'gay propaganda' case, the Court made an exceptional statement by finding that the Russian legal provisions do not serve to advance any 'legitimate aim' under the Convention. The Court argued that the measures served neither the protection of morals, nor the protection of health or the rights of others.[16]

In the face veil cases, the Court started off by deconstructing the invoked 'legitimate aims' and as a result rejected the relevance of gender equality as a valid ground for the restriction in this context.[17] Yet it upheld the bans in the name of the novel ground of 'living together', which does not, as such, figure in the Convention, but was linked by the Court to the protection of the 'rights and freedoms of others'.[18] As the dissenters in *S.A.S.* point out, however, the Court does not explain which concrete rights of others could be inferred from this abstract principle of 'living together'.[19]

It is submitted that in cases addressing measures that target long-term migrant minorities, the willingness to deconstruct and if necessary reject the invoked 'legitimate aims' is crucial to an effective human rights analysis. While the discriminatory intent of a restrictive measure is, of course, unlikely to ever be admitted by a defendant state, it can in many cases be uncovered by analysing the surrounding discourse. As will be shown below (subsection 2.2.3), the Court engaged in such deconstructive analysis in the 'gay propaganda' cases, but did not show the same critical rigour in the face veil cases.

2.2.2 Evidence

An important tool in the critical deconstruction of the government's intentions in the 'gay propaganda' cases is the Court's use of the requirement of evidence. One of the Russian Government's arguments was that that the ban was needed to protect minors 'against their conversion to a "homosexual lifestyle" which would be detrimental to their development and make them vulnerable to abuse'.[20] Both in *Alekseyev* and in *Bayev*, the Court treated these claims as arguments that would

[16] *Bayev* (n 15), para 83.

[17] The Court ruled that 'a State Party cannot invoke gender equality in order to ban a practice that is defended by women—such as the applicant—in the context of the exercise of the rights enshrined in those provisions, unless it were to be understood that individuals could be protected on that basis from the exercise of their own fundamental rights and freedoms': *S.A.S.* (n 5), para 119.

[18] ibid, para 121.

[19] ibid, Joint Partly Dissenting Opinion of Judges Nussberger and Jäderblom, para 10.

[20] *Bayev* (n 15), para 74.

require objective justification, in the form of 'scientific evidence or sociological data'.[21] It dismissed the government's allegations as 'lacking any evidentiary basis'.[22]

However, the claims that face covering 'fundamentally call(s) into question the possibility of open interpersonal relationships'[23] and that the face veil is a 'barrier raised against others breaching the right of others to live in a space of socialisation'[24] are not submitted to the same test of objective truth. They are instead explicitly presented as subjective claims, by the use of the words 'view' and 'perceived'.[25] These subjective claims of the authorities are not for the Court to verify, but to 'understand' and 'accept'.[26]

Uncovering anti-minority and migrant community bias may be relatively easy if such bias is not widespread, and in particular when it is absent from the environment in which those doing the uncovering (ie the judges of the ECtHR) live. However, when anti-minority bias pervades all layers and spheres of society, those who are doing the uncovering may themselves—subconsciously—also be affected by it. That is why the law requires solid, objective tools to uncover bias. It is submitted that evidence requirements are a natural legal response to this challenge, and that any arguments advanced by governments in defence of measures that directly or indirectly target migrant minorities should be rejected unless they are supported by evidence.

2.2.3 Majoritarian bias or choice of society

The acceptance of a rights restriction on a subjective ground forms the basis for treating the face veil bans as a legitimate 'choice of society'.[27] This leads the Court to the far-reaching conclusion that it should exercise restraint in the face of 'a balance (sic) that has been struck by means of a democratic process within the society in question'.[28] The possibility that 'society', ie the dominant majority, might be biased against a migrant community characterised as an unpopular minority, and whether the domestic process offered any guarantees against such bias, are not at

[21] *Alekseyev* (n 15), para 86, cited in *Bayev* (n 15), para 77.

[22] *Bayev* (n 15), para 78.

[23] *S.A.S.* (n 5), para 122.

[24] ibid.

[25] ibid: '[The Court] … *can understand the view* that individuals who are present in places open to all may not wish to see practices or attitudes developing there which would fundamentally call into question the possibility of open interpersonal relationships … The Court is therefore *able to accept* that the barrier raised against others by a veil concealing the face *is perceived* by the respondent State as breaching the right of others to live in a space of socialisation which makes living together easier.' (emphasis added).

[26] ibid.

[27] *Belcacemi* (n 14), para 53.

[28] *S.A.S.* (n 5), para 154. For a thorough critique of the quality of this process, see Saïla Ouald Chaib and Eva Brems, 'Doing Minority Justice through Procedural Fairness: Face Veil Bans in Europe'(2013) 2 (1) Journal of Muslims in Europe 1–26. In the Belgian cases, the Court explicitly defies the argument that the Belgian human rights scrutiny was even less serious than the French process, by referring to a 'large debate in the Chamber of representatives and a substantive and complete examination of all interests at play by the Constitutional Court', *Belcacemi* (n 14), para 54.

all reflected in the judgment. Yet these questions were on the table, as demonstrated in the concurring opinion in the Belgian cases, which emphasises that '"living together" finds an ideological foundation in a certain type of societal consensus, or majoritarian morality',[29] and that 'history has amply shown that democratic societies contain the risk that majoritarian sentiments' threaten fundamental rights.[30] The concurring judges conclude that it is therefore the role of the Court to research and try to detect whether legally imposed measures might be 'motivated by hostility or intolerance towards any particular idea, opinion, or religious creed'.[31] In other words, by not following this suggestion offered in the separate opinion, the Court rejects the idea that it has a role to play in uncovering majoritarian bias that discriminates against a migrant community's ways of living.[32]

This stands in stark contrast with the Court's approach to the 'gay propaganda' cases. The Court makes it very clear that there can be no legitimate choice of Russian society to uphold a concept of morals and family values that denigrates homosexuality. Already in *Alekseyev* in 2010, the Court stated that 'it would be incompatible with the underlying values of the Convention if the exercise of Convention rights by a minority group were made conditional on its being accepted by the majority. Were this so, a minority group's rights to freedom of religion, expression and assembly would become merely theoretical rather than practical and effective as required by the Convention.'[33] And yet, the fact that the majority of French and Belgian society found the face veil disturbing was considered sufficient for upholding the bans as a choice of society. In contrast, in the case of *Bayev*, the Court states in an exceptionally explicit manner that the contested Russian legislation is an expression of 'predisposed bias'.[34] To this end, it refers to contextual elements, including government quotes that deny the 'social equivalence of traditional and non-traditional sexual relationships' and instances in which homosexuality and paedophilia are mentioned together.[35] Similar scrutiny of the discourse surrounding the adoption of the French and Belgian face covering bans, would have uncovered multiple instances of stigmatising discourse about Islam and about Muslims as a long-term migrant community in Europe, as well as instances in which the religious lifestyle of a community is conflated with

[29] ibid, concurring opinion Judges Spano and Karakas, para 7 (translation from French EB).
[30] ibid, para 9.
[31] ibid.
[32] Many authors have argued that the 'living together' argument is a cover-up for majority bias: see Eoin Daly, 'Fraternalism as a Limitation on Religious Freedom: The Case of S.A.S. v France' (2016) 11(2) Religion and Human Rights 140–65; Teresa Sanader, 'S.A.S. v France—the French principle of "living together" and the limits of individual human rights' (LSE Human Rights Blog, 14 July 2014) <http://blogs.lse.ac.uk/humanrights/2014/07/14/s-a-s-v-france> accessed 18 November 2019; Hardik Singh, 'Case Analysis of S.A.S. v France' [2015] NLUJ Law Review 175; Hakeem Yusuf, 'S.A.S. v France: Supporting "Living Together" or Forced Assimilation' [2014] IHLR 277.
[33] *Alekseyev* (n 15), para 81, cited in *Bayev* (n 15), para 70.
[34] .*Bayev* (n 15), para 69.
[35] ibid.

anti-democratic attitudes and even terrorism.[36] And yet, in the face veil cases the Court was not interested in uncovering the anti-minority and anti-migrant bias.

2.2.4 The ban as an accelerator of intolerance

After deconstructing and attacking in a thorough manner all the arguments of the Russian Government, the Court's reasoning under Article 10 in the *Bayev* case concludes: 'Above all, by adopting such laws the authorities reinforce stigma and prejudice and encourage homophobia, which is incompatible with the notions of equality, pluralism and tolerance in a democratic society.'[37] This is immediately followed by the statement that the Russian authorities have overstepped their margin of appreciation and hence violated the Convention. This is a very important recognition by the Court of both the expressive harm[38] that is caused by discriminatory legislation, and of the risk of it having an accelerator effect on intolerance and discrimination against the targeted minority in society at large.

Both effects have been documented in the case of the French and Belgian face veil bans.[39] What is more, the Court stated in the face veil cases that 'a State which enters into a legislative process of this kind takes the risk of contributing to the consolidation of stereotypes which affect certain categories of the population and of encouraging the expression of intolerance, when it has a duty, on the contrary, to promote tolerance.'[40] In other words, the Court made the same analysis in both lines of case law, but while in the face veil cases, this was just a free-standing remark, in the 'gay propaganda' case law it is the cornerstone of the analysis that leads the Court to conclude that the legislation is unacceptable.

2.2.5 The European consensus

The light scrutiny in the face veil cases and the stricter scrutiny in the 'gay propaganda' cases are also reflected in the Court's application of the margin of appreciation doctrine in these lines of case law. In the face veil cases, the Court justifies a

[36] Eva Brems, Jogchum Vrielink, and Saïla Ouald Chaib, 'Uncovering French and Belgian Face Covering Bans' (2013) JLRS 69, 82–89 (analysis of parliamentary debates).

[37] *Bayev* (n 15), para 83.

[38] As defined by Anderson and Pildes, 'a person suffers expressive harm when she is treated according to principles that express negative or inappropriate attitudes toward her'. Elizabeth Anderson and Richard Pildes, 'Expressive Theories of Law: A General Restatement' (2000) 148 (5) University of Pennsylvania Law Review 1504–1575, at 1527.

[39] Open Society Justice Initiative, 'After the Ban: The Experiences of 35 Women of the Full-Face Veil in France, Research Report (2013) <https://www.opensocietyfoundations.org/sites/default/files/after-the-ban-experience-full-face-veil-france-20140210.pdf> accessed 18 November 2019; Eva Brems and others, 'Wearing the Face Veil in Belgium; Views and Experiences of 27 Women Living in Belgium concerning the Islamic Full Face Veil and the Belgian Ban on Face Covering Research Report (2012) <https://www.google.com/url?sa=t&rct=j&q=&esrc=s&source=web&cd=&ved=2ahUKEwi6iYeH2u3sAhUO3aQKHVbzCuIQFjAAegQIAhAC&url=http%3A%2F%2Fwww.hrc.ugent.be%2Fwp-content%2Fuploads%2F2015%2F10%2Fface-veil-report-hrc.pdf&usg=AOvVaw3jSbAFeLar-bVpEIVx1TI6 > accessed 18 November 2019.

[40] *S.A.S.* (n 5), para 149; *Belcacemi* (n 14), para 52.

'very large margin of appreciation'[41] by reference to the lack of a European consensus in this field. This is surprising, given the fact that, at the time of the *S.A.S.* judgment, only France and Belgium had nationwide bans in place.[42]

At the same time, in the 'gay propaganda' cases, the Court ruled that 'there is a clear European consensus about the recognition of individuals' right to openly identify themselves as gay, lesbian or any other sexual minority, and to promote their own rights and freedoms'.[43] It found this consensus, that restricted the margin of appreciation,[44] despite the fact that in addition to Russia, Lithuania also had 'gay propaganda' legislation in place, and that it was being proposed in Moldova as well.[45] The presence or absence of 'consensus' thus seems to be a matter of 'alternative truths'...

2.2.6 More questions than answers

What to make of these findings that show radically different approaches by the Court to two situations that, as explained above, nevertheless have a lot in common? Is there an explanation for the divergence? Are we to conclude that France and Belgium are allowed more leeway with their unpopular migrant minorities than Russia is with its 'authentic' minority? Or should we instead conclude that in the eyes of the Court the one 'indigenous' unpopular minority deserves more protection than the other unpopular minority that is composed largely of long-term migrants? Many would say that radical Muslims, or even Muslims *tout court*, are an unpopular minority in the eyes of the Court.[46] Indeed, while the ECtHR is taking a very clear and strong stance against homophobia, the same cannot be said about Islamophobia and the associated religious and cultural rights of long-term Muslim migrants in Europe. In fact, the case could even be made that the Court's case law shows traces of Islamophobia. Such an argument might refer to the fact that the Court consistently dismisses claims from Muslim migrant minority claimants seeking accommodation for religious/cultural practices, while upholding

[41] *Belcacemi* (n 14), para 55.

[42] In addition, there were some local bans in place, and several countries had discussed the possible adoption of a ban. In the eyes of the Court, such discussions seemed to disrupt the consensus: *S.A.S.* (n 5), para 156.

[43] *Alekseyev* (n 15), para 84; *Bayev* (n 15), para 66.

[44] *Alekseyev* (n 15), para 85.

[45] ILGA-Europe, 'Annual Review of the Human Rights Situation of Lesbian, Gay, Bisexual, Trans and Intersex People in Europe' (2017) <https://www.ilga-europe.org/sites/default/files/Attachments/annual_review_2017_online.pdf> accessed 18 November 2019.

[46] Several scholars have noted the use of negative stereotypes about Muslims and Islam in the ECtHR case law; eg Carolyn Evans, 'The "Islamic Scarf" in the European Court of Human Rights' (2006) 7(1) Melbourne Journal of International Law 52–73; Benjamin Bleiberg, 'Unveiling the Real Issue: Evaluating the European Court of Human Rights' Decision to Enforce the Turkish Headscarf Ban in Leyla Sahin v Turkey' (2005) 91 Cornell Law Review 129; Susanna Mancini, 'Patriarchy as the Exclusive Domain of the Other: The Veil Controversy, False Projection and Cultural Racism' (2012) 10(2) I-CON 411; Jill Marshall, 'Freedom of Religious Expression and Gender Equality: Sahin v Turkey' [2006] 69 (3) The Modern Law Review 452.

equivalent claims of other religious minorities (cf above). As will be shown below (section 2.3), one could also refer, in this regard, to some of the Court's rhetoric on Islam and Islamic practices.

The next section will extend the corpus of case law, to look further into the Court's messages to national authorities in cases concerning restrictions on Islamic practices.

2.3 Messages on Measures Restricting Muslim Minority Practices

The Court's case law regarding restrictions on Muslim minority practices is neither very extensive, nor very diverse. It includes fourteen judgments and decisions against four different countries (France, Belgium, Switzerland, and the Former Yugoslav Republic of Macedonia).[47] The sole Grand Chamber case in the corpus is *S.A.S. v France*,[48] the face veil case. Among the Chamber judgments on the merits, are the two Belgian face veil cases,[49] two French cases on headscarf bans during sports classes,[50] a French case concerning a ban on religious symbols for employees in a public hospital (as applied to a headscarf),[51] a Macedonian case on leave of absence of a private sector employee for attending a religious holiday,[52] and a Swiss case concerning mandatory participation in co-ed swimming classes.[53] Finally, the inadmissibility decisions[54] include a series of cases concerning the application of the French ban on the wearing of religious symbols in public schools (as applied to headscarves),[55] a Swiss case concerning dismissal of a teacher for wearing a headscarf,[56] and a French case about the mandatory removal of a headscarf for an identity check in a consulate.[57]

The next sections will analyse this corpus from the perspective of the substantive (subsection 2.3.1), procedural (subsection 2.3.2), and discursive (subsection 2.3.3) guidance that is offered by the ECtHR to national authorities.

[47] This case law study was conducted in 2017.

[48] *S.A.S.* (n 5).

[49] *Belcacemi* (n 14); *Dakir* (n 14).

[50] *Kervanci v France* App no 31645/04 (ECtHR, 4 December 2008); and *Dogru v France* App no 27058/05 (ECtHR, 4 December 2008).

[51] *Ebrahimian v France* App no 64846/11 (ECtHR, 26 November 2015).

[52] *Kosteski v FYROM* App no 55170/00 (ECtHR, 13 April 2006).

[53] *Osmanoğlu v Switzerland* App no 29086/12 (ECtHR, 10 January 2017).

[54] Only the inadmissibility decisions were included that were decided on grounds of the application being 'manifestly ill-founded'.

[55] *Aktas v France* (dec) App no 43563/08 (ECtHR, 30 June 2009); *Bayrak v France* (dec) App no 14308/08 (ECtHR, 30 June 2009); *Gamaleddyn v France* (dec) App no 18527/08 (ECtHR, 30 June 2009); *Gazal v France* App no 29134/08 (ECtHR, 30 June 2009).

[56] *Dahlab v Switzerland* (dec) App no 42393/98 (ECtHR, 15 January 2001).

[57] *El Morsli v France* (dec) App no 15585/06 (ECtHR, 4 March 2008).

2.3.1 Substantive guidance

The positive face of subsidiarity requires in the first place a degree of substantive guidance by the Court, regardless of the margin of appreciation. The margin may be wide—even very wide—but it is never unlimited. Hence, it is important that the Court should give an indication of the limits of states' margin of appreciation in the field under consideration. Such a message obviously comes across most clearly in a judgment finding a violation;[58] yet this does not do away with the possibility—and the need—to indicate the limits of the margin in 'no violation' judgments. At the time of this study (2017) *all* ECtHR rulings on claims for the accommodation of Islamic practices in states in which Islam is a minority religion, were 'no violation' judgments. Arguably issuing guidance on the limits to state discretion is particularly crucial in 'no violation' judgments; lest the judgment be interpreted by the national authority as a license to restrict minority rights.

This type of substantive guidance is extremely rare in this particular corpus of jurisprudence. The single exception appears to be the *S.A.S.* judgment, in which the Court discredited the paternalistic use of a gender equality argument in support of the restrictions on Islamic dress that women freely choose to wear.[59] In the same case, the Court also ruled that public safety justifications only allow for rights restrictions that are proportionate to an existing threat to safety. Thus, in the absence of a general threat to public safety, a blanket ban on face covering is not justified by the safety argument.[60] Yet given that the Court in the same judgment upheld a blanket ban on the ground of 'living together', these examples of substantive guidance do not have any concrete implications for face veil bans, except in indicating to governments how they should justify or support such bans.

More effective substantive guidance would indicate that, in some situations, it is simply not possible to provide justification for restricting a Muslim religious practice that would pass the Court's scrutiny. I submit that such guidance is particularly needed with regard to bans on Islamic headscarves. In light of the Court's judgments, which always allow bans on religious minority dress (including for teachers, pupils, and employees in the public sector; for undergoing identity and security checks; and for issuing identity documents),[61] and in the absence of any indication in the Court's case law that there might be a limit to state discretion in this field, headscarf bans are expanding like an oil spill in national and local contexts.

[58] Indeed, the media, political actors, and the public at large rarely pick up any limitations to state discretion to be found in a 'no violation' judgment. But legal actors can be expected to pick up such messages.

[59] *S.A.S.* (n 5), para 119.

[60] ibid, para 139.

[61] In addition to the Islamic cases, see also the Sikh turban cases regarding pupils in French public schools *Jasvir Singh v France* (dec) App no 25463/08 (ECtHR, 30 June 2009), and *Ranjit Singh v France* (dec) App no 27561/08(ECtHR, 30 June 2009); security checks at airports (*Phull v France* (dec) App no 35753/03 (ECtHR, 11 January 2005)); the photograph on a driver's licence (*Mann Singh v France* (dec) App no 4479/07 (ECtHR, 13 November 2008)); and the mandatory wearing of a motor helmet (*X. v United Kingdom* (dec) (1978) 14 DR 31.

In Belgium, for example, they are imposed, amongst others, against private sector employees, against witnesses and members of the audience in court rooms, and against users of private services, including users of a bowling alley and clients of an ice cream parlour.[62] It is my hypothesis, however, that at least this last type of headscarf ban would not be acceptable in the eyes of the ECtHR. Yet in the absence of guidance in the Court's case law, I cannot be certain of this, and national courts may rule differently (as a Belgian court indeed did on the ice cream parlour case).[63] Stopping this 'oil spill' will require a clear statement by the Court indicating the limits of rights restriction—and hence the limits of the margin of appreciation—in this field.

To conclude, in terms of substance, the message of the ECtHR to national authorities with respect to their treatment of their long-term migrant communities is close to a blank check. From a perspective of positive subsidiarity, this is highly problematic.

2.3.2 Procedural guidance

If positive subsidiarity is taken seriously, I argue that a wide margin of appreciation should be granted only in cases where the Court is satisfied that a sufficient quality control process of ensuring Convention compatibility has taken place at the domestic level. The subsidiarity principle, and its instrument, the margin of appreciation, do not single out any zone that is free from this process, but rather stipulates a division of labour with regard to such control between the national and the supranational levels. Serious control over Convention compatibility has to happen in any case. Yet, it is self-evident that the standard of what constitutes a serious and high-quality control process can only be set by the ECtHR. Hence it is part of the Court's responsibilities, in a framework of positive subsidiarity, to give procedural guidance to states regarding their assessment of the conformity of (planned) rights-restrictive measures with the ECHR.

In its developing practice of quality control of domestic procedure,[64] the Court resorts to different models, including a procedural review that is strictly focused on the formal aspects of procedure, as well as what I have called 'substance-flavoured procedural review',[65] giving binding guidance for the substance of domestic quality control on compatibility, for example, by highlighting which elements should

[62] Eva Brems and others, 'Head-Covering Bans in Belgian Courtrooms and Beyond: Headscarf Persecution and the Complicity of Supranational Courts' (2017) 39(4) Human Rights Quarterly 882.

[63] Court of first instance found no violation, Rb. Veurne, 2-07-2014. This was overruled by Court of Appeal of Ghent, Gent, 8-10-2015. However, the Court of Appeal did not impose a fine. In August 2016, we found that the ice cream parlour still advertised internal rules that ban headgear worn by clients 'except for medical reasons'.

[64] Janneke Gerards and Eva Brems, *Procedural Review in European Fundamental Rights Cases* (Cambridge University Press 2017).

[65] Eva Brems, 'The "Logics" of Procedural-Type Review by the European Court of Human Rights', in Gerards and Brems (n 64) 17.

be taken into account in the proportionality assessment.[66] In my previous work, I have argued that the logic of positive subsidiarity sits most comfortably with a procedural review of this nature that results in supranational oversight of domestic human rights scrutiny.[67] In the context of minority rights protection, this is of particular importance. When procedural review is limited to formal aspects of procedure, it may be impossible to detect the absence of a rigorous assessment of Convention compatibility. It is, therefore, regretful that the references to procedural review in the face veil cases are of a purely formal nature. The *S.A.S.* judgment has been highlighted by ECtHR judges, as well as in the literature, as one of the key cases signalling the turn to procedural-type review, even though the reference to domestic process in the judgment is vague and brief.[68]

Essentially, ECtHR restraint in scrutinising the face veil ban is justified by reference to the fact that it results from 'a democratic process within the society in question'.[69] Admittedly, the process running up to the French ban was a very elaborate one, involving, amongst others, the advice of the Council of State, and extensive hearings by a commission of inquiry.[70] Yet this process has also been widely criticised, amongst others, for disregarding the (negative) advice of the Council of State and for failing to include face veil wearers among the persons called to testify before the commission.[71] More importantly though, the reference to a 'democratic process' is not sufficient to conclude that decision makers have duly taken into account the Convention rights of their citizens with a migration background or, of long-term resident migrants who permanently live in Europe but are not naturalised. In *Belcacemi*, the reference to the domestic process leading up to the Belgian face veil ban is somewhat more elaborate, with the Court stating that 'the decisional process ... lasted several years and was characterized by an extensive debate in the Chamber of representatives as well as an extensive and complete examination of all interests at stake by the Constitutional Court'.[72] This statement

66 cf the 'checklist' approach in defamation cases: *Axel Springer A.G. v Germany* [GC] App no 39954/08 (ECtHR, 7 February 2012); *Von Hannover v Germany (No 2)* [GC] App nos 40660/08 and 60641/08 (ECtHR, 7 February 2012).

67 Brems, 'The "Logics" of Procedural-Type Review' (n 65).

68 Robert Spano, 'The European Court of Human Rights and National Courts: A Constructive Conversation or a Dialogue of Disrespect?'(2014) The Torkel Opsahl Memorial Lecture, 28 November 2014, para 20; Angelika Nussberger, 'Procedural Review by the ECHR: A View from the Court', in Janneke Gerards and Eva Brems (n 64) 161, 163; Matthew Saul, 'The ECtHR's Margin of Appreciation and the Processes of National Parliaments' (2015) 15 (4) *Human Rights Law Review* 745–774.

69 *S.A.S.* (n 5), para 154.

70 Brems, Vrielink, and Ouald Chaib (n 36).

71 The so-called 'Gérin commission' heard evidence from 211 persons, and produced a 658-page report. Yet it heard only one face-veil wearer—upon her own strong insistence. During her hearing, summarized in ten lines in the report, Kenza Drider had to uncover her face: Open Society Justice Initiative, 'Unveiling the truth; why 32 Muslim women wear the full-face veil in France' (2011) 20 <https://www.opensocietyfoundations.org/publications/unveiling-truth-why-32-muslim-women-wear-full-face-veil-france> accessed 18 November 2019; André Gérin, 'Rapport d'information fait en application de l'article 145 du règlement au nom de la mission d'information sur la pratique du port du voile integral sur le territoire national' (26 January 2010).

72 *Belcacemi* (n 14), para 54.

reveals the substantive emptiness of this type of ultra-formal procedural review. Indeed, the process lasted several years because it had to be re-started after early elections. The 'extensive debate' in the Chamber was characterised by the absence of human rights considerations and all measures that could have been employed to provide more thorough discussion (expert hearings, advice of the Council of State, re-examination by the Senate) were rejected in this case.[73] In my opinion,[74] the claim cannot in any way be upheld that the Belgian parliament in this process undertook any kind of assessment of compatibility with the Convention.[75] The Constitutional Court did engage in a fundamental rights analysis, yet it has been criticised for blindly accepting all (three) arguments advanced by the government, two of which were later discredited by the *S.A.S.* judgment.[76] Hence, I claim that both cases are bad examples of procedural review, because this type of procedural review does not check whether any domestic control of Convention compatibility has taken place, let alone set any standards for such control.

As for which standards of domestic human rights scrutiny could or should be advanced by the Court, there is one that seems particularly important in the context of minority rights protection, in particular in the context of long-term migrant communities. This is the matter of evidence. In order to make the crucial distinction between rights restrictions that are legitimately required for the protection of a general interest, and arbitrary restrictions driven by anti-majority bias, the Court must critically unpack the arguments made by national authorities in support of restrictive measures. Evidential requirements are a natural way for a court to do this. As highlighted above, good practice in this respect can be found, amongst others, in the 'gay propaganda' line of case law.[77] Even when a wide margin of appreciation is granted, the Court should not be content simply with finding that a plausible general interest (such as 'neutrality', 'pressure on others', or 'living together') was invoked by the state, but should also require evidence that such an interest is at stake in the concrete context of the case. This is exactly what the Court did in *S.A.S.* when it dismissed the pursuit of gender equality as a legitimate aim supporting a general face-covering ban.[78] The Court's reasoning that it is not sufficient for a minority practice to touch upon an important general interest (in this

[73] Ouald Chaib and Brems (n 28).

[74] The reader should know that I was a member of the federal parliament when the bill was adopted, and that I participated in the debates, both in the commission and in the plenary. As a matter of fact, I was the only MP criticising the ban and voting against it. I brought up human rights arguments, so these were on the table. However no other members engaged with these arguments.

[75] A prominent commentator, who analysed this parliamentary process in detail, stated that it was 'a merely formal respect of the requirement of democratic debate' (le respect purement formel de l'exigence de débat démocratique) and a 'refusal of all debate' (le refus de toute discussion): Xavier Delgrange, 'La loi "anti-burqa" comme symptôme' (2012) 74 Politique—revue des débats 42.

[76] Jogchum Vrielink, 'De Grondwet aan het gezicht onttrokken. Het Grondwettelijk Hof en het "boerkaverbod"' (2013) 4 Tijdschrift voor Bestuurswetenschappen en Publiekrecht 250.

[77] *Alekseyev* (n 15), para 86; *Bayev* (n 15), paras 77–78.

[78] *S.A.S.* (n 5), para 119.

case gender equality) simply according to majority opinion,[79] but that it should instead be shown concretely that this interest is in fact at stake, can and should be applied across the board. Yet this is not what is happening in practice.

It was explained above that the Court in *S.A.S.* did not see the threat to 'living together' as an objective element requiring evidence and verification, but instead as a subjective viewpoint that the Court can choose to 'understand'. In *Belcacemi* the Court demonstrates a similar 'understanding' by quoting directly from the (exceptionally woolly) language of the Belgian Constitutional Court. The Court finds in this manner that the Belgian state, through the face veil ban 'intended to respond to a practice that it considered incompatible in Belgian society with the modalities of social communication and more generally the establishment of human relations that are indispensable to social life' and to 'protect a modality of interaction among individuals that is, for the State, essential to the functioning of a democratic society'.[80] This is then taken as evidence of a 'choice of society' that necessitates restraint on behalf of the Court.

It should be emphasised that the Court had been presented with evidence demonstrating that—to the extent that these claims are verifiable—the perspective advanced by the Belgian Court is contradicted by empirical reality.[81] In a somewhat comparable vein, a difference of opinion concerning abstract versus concrete conceptions of the neutrality of public service, led to the (partly) dissenting opinion of Judge O'Leary in *Ebrahimian*.[82] The majority accepted the principled and abstract ideological interpretation of neutrality that was advanced by the French government to justify a ban on headscarves worn by staff in a public hospital, which was beyond the realm of empiricism. According to this conception, every headscarf is automatically problematic, being labelled (presumably because of its visibility) as 'ostentatious'. The dissenting judge, however, would have been able to accept the applicant's dismissal if it could be found through a more 'concrete' proportionality test that she violated the obligation of neutrality. The existence of this separate opinion is evidence of the majority having rejected the idea of a concrete and empirically verifiable test. The same approach characterises the ECtHR case law on the hijab ban in French schools, in the name of the abstract principle of *laïcité*—with the Court even accepting without any critical examination the argument that a bonnet worn in replacement of a hijab is an ostentatious religious symbol.[83] Earlier, the perfectly verifiable claim that a ban that was limited to sports classes, was necessary for reasons of health and safety, was not subjected to any evidential

[79] cf Restatement of para 119 of *S.A.S.* by the Belgian Council of State in its recent breakthrough judgment on headscarves at school: Council of State, department of administrative jurisprudence, judgment no 228.752 of 14 October 2014, *Gadghgadhi ao v Gemeenschapsonderwijs*, para 37.2.

[80] *Belcacemi* (n 14), para 53.

[81] See the third party intervention by the Human Rights Centre at Ghent University in *Dakir*, available at < https://hrc.ugent.be/clinic/third-party-interventions-before-ecthr/accessed 18 November 2019.

[82] *Ebrahimian v France* (n 51) Concurring and Partly Dissenting Opinion of Judge O'Leary, 36–38.

[83] *Gamaleddyn v France* (dec) App no 18527/08 (ECtHR, 30 June 2009), p. 9.

requirement. The Court simply stated that this position was 'not unreasonable'.[84] Other verifiable claims that were accepted without any evidence or critical scrutiny include the claim that a headscarf worn by a teacher might interfere with the freedom of conscience of her pupils,[85] and the claim that the removal of a headscarf is necessary to conduct a security check.[86] On the other hand, an applicant who claimed that the wearing of a burkini, in the context of his daughters' mandatory participation in mixed swimming classes, was stigmatising, saw his argument rejected for failure to support it with evidence.[87] Similarly, the Court accepted that an employer could require an employee to give evidence of his Muslim faith in order to justify his absence from work on a Muslim holiday.[88] The inconsistent practice of the Court in the matter of evidential requirements thus seems to lean rather unfortunately towards creating a double standard.

To conclude, in terms of the requirements of domestic human rights scrutiny, the Court's message to national authorities appears to be that any parliamentary discussion of a rights-restrictive measure will suffice, regardless of the presence or absence of actual scrutiny, and that for domestic judicial procedures it is sufficient to formally address conformity with the Convention. No standards apply with regard to the substantive or procedural criteria applied in this analysis. From a perspective of positive subsidiarity, this is highly problematic.

2.3.3 Discursive guidance

In addition to substance and procedure, I have identified a third field in which the Court can be expected to nudge national authorities in the right direction, which is discourse. Harmful stereotypes are a prominent factor in the marginalisation of minorities, whether they have migrant or non-migrant backgrounds. When these harmful stereotypes amount to hate speech, they can be human rights violations in their own right. In other situations, they may be a contributing or aggravating factor as part of a human rights violation.

In the first place, the Court should be mindful not to use harmful stereotypes or other problematic language in its own reasoning. This is important because any problematic language in ECtHR judgments can be expected to 'trickle down' into the language of the national authorities that consult these judgments for guidance. Avoiding minority stereotypes requires a process of learning and reflection by the Court, as much as for any other actor in society. The cultural change that is necessary for the realisation of minority rights, and for the equal treatment of the cultural and religious practices of long-term migrants, requires a change of mindset as well as a change of discourse. Statements that are considered truisms at one point

[84] *Dogru* (n 50), para 73.
[85] *Dahlab* (n 56), para 13.
[86] *El Morsli* (n 57), paras 3–4.
[87] *Osmanoğlu* (n 53), para 101.
[88] *Kosteski v FYROM* App no 29086/12 (ECtHR, 13 April 2006), para 39.

in time are, at a later point, deconstructed as expressions of anti-minority and anti-migrant prejudice. In this dynamic, even the Court may at some point be guilty of using language that entrenches harmful stereotypes. A good example can be found in the language of the Commission in the first gay rights case that reached Strasbourg in 1975:[89] it found that a criminal provision targeting specifically male homosexuality could not violate human rights, because:

> [Studies] have led to convincing conclusions as to the existence of a specific social danger in the case of masculine homosexuality. This danger results from the fact that masculine homosexuals often constitute a distinct socio-cultural group with a clear tendency to proselytise adolescents and that the social isolation in which it involves the latter is particularly marked.

Just how much the Strasbourg position has evolved in this regard, is shown clearly in the Court's attack on homophobic stereotypes in the course of its deconstruction of anti-minority bias in the 'gay propaganda' cases (cf subsection 2.2.3). Once the Court has cleared up its own language, the next step is for it to name harmful stereotypes and other problematic language in its analysis of human rights violations.

In the context of widespread Islamophobia and anti-migration sentiment in Europe (cf above), it is not surprising that harmful stereotypes about Muslims, both as a religious group and migrant outsiders, abound. In addition to stereotypes about Muslims in general, there are many stereotypes about orthodox Muslims, about young Muslim men, and about Muslim women and girls. Anti-Muslim prejudice is, moreover, expressed in the form of distorted representations of aspects of Islamic belief and Islamic practices. In some of its case law, the Court has, unfortunately, contributed to entrenching such stereotypes and prejudice. This applies particularly to the Court's equation of an Islamic headscarf with a message or attitude that opposes gender equality:

> [The headscarf] appears to be imposed on women by a precept which is laid down in the Koran and which, as the Federal Court noted, is hard to square with the principle of gender equality. It therefore appears difficult to reconcile the wearing of an Islamic headscarf with the message of tolerance, respect for others and, above all, equality and non-discrimination that all teachers in a democratic society must convey to their pupils.[90]

[89] *X. v Germany* App no 5935/72 (Commission Decision, 30 September 1975). Other example: the Commission's 1983 dismissal of a claim against the ban of homosexuals in the army, stating that 'homosexual conduct by members of the armed forces may pose a particular risk to order within the forces which would not arise in civilian life' (*B. v United Kingdom* App no 9237/81 (Commission Decision, 12 October 1983)).

[90] *Dahlab* (n 56).

This statement appeared for the first time in the *Dahlab* case (2001), and received its strongest confirmation in the 2005 Grand Chamber case of *Şahin*.[91] However, it has disappeared in more recent case law and has been implicitly discredited with the above-mentioned statement in *S.A.S.* on gender equality as a suspect ground for banning the face veil. The Court though has yet to take the next step towards uncovering harmful stereotypes and anti-minority and migrant prejudice in the discourse of domestic authorities (cf subsections 2.2.3 and 2.2.4).

To conclude, in terms of discursive guidance, the Court has in the past sent the wrong message to national authorities, by expressing harmful stereotypes of Muslim women in its rulings. The change in the Court's discourse away from such problematic language is a positive first step. However, the Court has yet to embark on active discursive guidance, which would require it to name harmful stereotypes in the discourse of domestic authorities and in the broader context of legal and policy measures. Furthermore, it must take these into account in its reasoning when it considers cases related to the recognition of the rights of long term migrants and their religious and cultural rights.

3. Conclusion

In the field under examination, it is very hard to identify any examples of the Court nudging state authorities towards appropriate human rights scrutiny, either in terms of substance, procedure, or discourse. On the contrary, it is relatively easy to identify examples of problematic messages sent by the Court, in the sense that they have allowed states to get away with problematic practices on all three levels. Set against the subsidiary framework that is proposed in this chapter, this signals a manifest failure at the level of positive subsidiarity. The result is that subsidiarity in this field, as expressed through a wide margin of appreciation, and ECtHR restraint, can mean in practice that no human rights scrutiny—or a highly deficient type of human rights scrutiny—is applied to rights-restrictive rules or policies. Subsidiarity that is merely negative signals an abdication of ECtHR responsibility.

This is not an across-the-board phenomenon, however, which is demonstrated in the comparison with the so-called 'gay propaganda' cases. In these judgments, which likewise concern restrictions imposed on expressions of the otherness of a minority that is unpopular in the domestic context, the Court is sending out very powerful messages to national authorities and providing binding guidance at the levels of substance, procedure, and discourse.

[91] *Şahin v Turkey* [GC] App no 44774/98 (ECtHR, 10 November 2005), para 111.

Technically—in terms of its competences and its legal toolkit—the Court can act against Islamophobia and rights-restrictive measures targeting Muslims in the same way that it acts against homophobia and rights-restrictive measures targeting LGB individuals. That it does not do so, must therefore be considered a matter of choice. The reasons underlying this choice are a subject that merits further research.

PART IV

STAGES OF MIGRATION AND THE EUROPEAN COURT OF HUMAN RIGHTS

This part offers a guide to the European Court of Human Rights (ECtHR) case law pertaining to migration. The cases are organised in thematic blocks, which in turn appear in the order in which they pertain to the different temporal stages of migration, starting from entering the destination country to the right to remain of long-term migrants and the cultural and religious rights of long-term migrants.

10

Stages of Migration and the European Convention on Human Rights

A Case List

Kristina Hatas

Introduction

This case list offers a comprehensive and holistic guide to the migration case law of the European Court of Human Rights (ECtHR) by organising the cases with respect to the stages of migration they address. The list, which includes cases delivered by the Court until March 2020, starts with the initial stage of migration covering entering the destination country, *non-refoulement* and the asylum procedure. This is followed by case law speaking to the treatment of migrants once present in the territory of a state, including asylum detention and family reunification, as well as the legal rules applicable to their expulsion. Lastly, cases follow which address the rights of migrants once forming part of the destination state, such as their access to social, economic, and cultural rights as well as freedom of religion, and considerations applicable to the removal of long-term residents. Under each section, the case list is organised under thematic blocks, in which key cases and holdings are listed. The cases are organized into three main stages of migration, which are further narrowed down to specific issues or Convention rights. Case citations are accompanied by a short description as to their relevance under the relevant migration stage. The case list is organised as follows:

Stage I: Entering the Destination Country includes case law on the right to leave a country and freedom of movement, and entering the destination country/jurisdiction. This is followed by cases on *refoulement* under the ECHR, 'Dublin' regulation cases, collective expulsions, and cases regarding the asylum procedure.

Stage II: Treatment of Migrants once Present in the Territory of a State begins with case law on the vulnerability of certain groups, which affects the application of the substantive convention rights. The case list then presents cases on asylum detention, and cases with children as migrants, and the conditions applicable to their detention. This is followed by the right to family life, and the applicable standards to the removal of migrants.

Kristina Hatas, *Stages of Migration and the European Convention on Human Rights* In: *Migration and the European Convention on Human Rights*. Edited by: Başak Çali, Ledi Bianku, and Iulia Motoc, Oxford University Press (2021). DOI: 10.1093/oso/9780192895196.003.0010

Stage III: Treatment of Long-term Migrants includes the access to social and economic rights, such as residence permits and the access to social security, education, housing, and health care, as well as protections against exploitation. Next, this section offers case law on the discrimination of migrants, their cultural and religious rights. Last, the pertinent case law on the removal of long-term migrants is presented.

Stage I: Entering the Destination Country, *Non-refoulement* and the Asylum Procedure

Right to Leave Country and Freedom of Movement

M v. Germany App no 10307/83 (ECtHR, 6 March 1984); *Schmid v. Austria* App no 10670/83 (ECtHR, 9 July 1985); *Napijalo v. Croatia* App no 66485/01 (ECtHR, 13 November 2003); *Ignatov v. Bulgaria* App no 50/02 (ECtHR, 2 July 2009); *Dzhaksybergenov v. Ukraine* App no 12343/10 (ECtHR, 10 February 2011) (denial or seizure of a passport, the confiscation of travel documents, or a ban on exit as direct interferences with the right to leave)

Streletz v. Germany App nos 34044/96, 35532/97, and 44801/98 (ECtHR, 22 March 2001) (general prohibitions from leaving also impermissible)

Baumann v. France App no 33592/96 (ECtHR, 22 May 2001); *Battista v. Italy* App no 43978/09 (ECtHR, 2 December 2014) (Art 2 Protocol 4 ECHR entails a right to leave for such country of the person's choice 'to which he may be admitted' (limitation with no textual support in the Convention))

Luordo v. Italy App no 32190/96 (ECtHR, 17 July 2003) (restriction of movement of a bankrupt person beyond the period necessary to secure assets for creditors)

Ivanov v. Ukraine App no 15007/02 (ECtHR, 7 December 2006) (restrictions on freedom of movement pending lengthy criminal proceedings deemed disproportionate)

Federov v. Russia App no 31008/02 (ECtHR, 13 October 2005) (charge of fraud without prosecution for a prolonged period during which the applicants' freedom of movement was restricted)

Riener v. Bulgaria App no 46343/99 (ECtHR, 23 May 2006); *Bartik v. Russia* App no 55565/00 (ECtHR, 21 December 2006) (legality, legitimacy, and proportionality of existing restriction must be measured on a case-by-case basis

Sissanis v. Romania App no 23468/02 (ECtHR, 25 January 2007) (indirect restriction on right to leave)

Bessenyei v. Hungary App no 37509/06 (ECtHR, 31 October 2008); Hajlik *v.* Hungary App no 41463/02 (ECtHR, 31 October 2006); A.E. *v.* Poland App no 14480/04 (ECtHR, 31 March 2009) (interferences with the right to leave one's country must remain justified and proportionate throughout its duration)

Gochev v. Bulgaria App no 34383/03 (ECtHR, 26 November 2009) (automatic and *de facto* unlimited ban breach the Convention)

Nalbantski v. Bulgaria App no 30943/04 (ECtHR, 10 February 2011); *Hajibeyli v. Azerbaijan* App no 16528/05 (ECtHR, 10 July 2008) (there must be concrete elements indicative of continued existence of the specific risk)

Miażdżyk v. Poland App no 23592/07 (ECtHR, 24 January 2012) (right to leave applies to any Contracting Party, not only to the country of which the applicant may be a national)

Nada v. Switzerland [GC] App no 10593/08 (ECtHR, 12 September 2012) (travel ban implementing UN Security Council resolution in violation of Arts 8 and 13 ECHR)

Stamose v. Bulgaria App no 29713/05 (ECtHR, 27 November 2012) (measures without any regard to the individual circumstances of the person concerned cannot be characterised as necessary in a democratic society)

Entering Destination Country/Jurisdiction

Soering v. United Kingdom App no 14038/88 (ECtHR, 7 July 1989) (extradition; no means of requiring the contracting states to impose Convention standards on other states)

Vilvarajah and others v. United Kingdom App nos 13163/87, 13164/87, 13165/87, 13447/87, and 13448/87 (ECtHR, 30 October 1991) (no right to migrate to or obtain asylum in another country)

Amuur v. France App no 19776/92 (ECtHR, 25 June 1996) ('international' zones at airports do not have extraterritorial status)

Xhavara v. Italy (dec) App no 39473/98 (ECtHR, 11 January 2001) (first case arguing that extraterritorial measures of immigration control may violate the right to leave; found inadmissible)

Banković v. Belgium and other 16 States [GC] App no 52207/99 (ECtHR, 12 December 2001) (non-migration; jurisdictional competence of a state is primarily territorial; other bases of jurisdiction exceptional)

Saadi v. United Kingdom [GC] App no 13229/03 (ECtHR, 29 January 2008) (states enjoy the right to control equally an alien's entry into and residence in their country)

Hirsi Jamaa and others v. Italy [GC] App no 27765/09 (ECtHR, 23 February 2012) (Italy could not circumvent its jurisdiction by describing the events at issue as rescue operations)

Naït-Liman v. Switzerland [GC] App no 51357/07 (ECtHR, 15 March 2018) (no breach of Art 6(1) ECHR where Swiss courts had rejected jurisdiction over torture which had taken place in the applicant's home state—his later ties to Switzerland were insufficient to give rise to a sufficient connection to Switzerland)

Rackete and others v. Italy App no 32969/19 (dec) (ECtHR, 25 June 2019) (denial of interim measure requested by applicants to be allowed to disembark in Italy from *Sea-Watch 3*; Court indicated to Italy that it was relying on the Italian authorities to continue to provide all necessary assistance to those persons on board *Sea-Watch 3* who were in a vulnerable situation on account of their age or state of health)

Non-refoulement/Deportation/Arts 2 and 3

Refoulement under the Convention

T.I. v. United Kingdom (dec) App no 43844/98 (ECtHR, 7 March 2000) (deportation a third country needs reliable assessment of available guarantees, especially protection against *refoulement*; case found inadmissible as no risk established that Germany would expel applicant to country of origin if sent there by UK)

Mamatkulov v. Turkey [GC] App nos 46827/99 and 46951/99 (ECtHR, 4 February 2005) (responsibility of state engaged by exposing individuals to risk, not only if the risk materialises)

Bader v. Sweden App no 13284/04 (ECtHR, 8 November 2005) (Arts 2 and 3 ECHR engaged where deportation would result in a flagrant denial of fair trial resulting in the death penalty)

Sharifi and others v. Italy App no 16643/09 (ECtHR, 21 October 2014) (need for effective opportunity to submit an application for international protection; protection against 'automatic' *refoulement*)

F.G. v. Sweden [GC] App no 43611/11 (ECtHR, 23 March 2016) (Arts 2 and 3 ECHR are breached if expelled person faces real risk contrary to those provisions, triggering an assessment requirement on part of authorities)

Babajanov v. Turkey App no 49867/08 (ECtHR, 10 May 2016) (the authorities were obliged to conduct a close and independent review of the claim that the applicant would face treatment contrary to Art 3 ECHR if the deportation risked *refoulement* from the third country to the country of origin)

J.K. and others v. Sweden [GC] App no 59166/12 (ECtHR, 23 August 2016) (lists set of general principles to be applied in asylum cases; assessment of real risk)

Khlaifia and others v. Italy [GC] App no 16483/12 (ECtHR, 15 December 2016) (irreversible harm as a violation of Arts 2 or 3 ECHR)

M.A. and others v. Lithuania App no 59793/17 (ECtHR, 11 December 2018) (states fully responsible for indirect refoulement and under duty to ensure that a third or intermediary country provides sufficient safeguards)

Ilias v. Hungary [GC] App no 47287/15 (ECtHR, 21 November 2019) (violation of Art 3 on account of the applicants' expulsion to Serbia due to the risk of denial of access to asylum proceedings)

States may be required by the ECtHR to permit a migrant to enter or to remain in its territory:

Cruz Varas and others v. Sweden App no 15576/89 (ECtHR, 20 March 1991) (principles laid down in *Soering* apply also to expulsion cases)

Chahal v. United Kingdom [GC] App no 22414/93 (ECtHR, 15 November 1996) (expulsion may engage the responsibility of a member state under Art 3 ECHR)

Salah Sheekh v. the Netherlands App no 1948/04 (ECtHR, 11 January 2007) (Art 3 ECHR prohibits expelling individual to a country where there is a substantial risk of treatment contrary to Art 3 ECHR)

Saadi v. United Kingdom [GC] App no 13229/03 (ECtHR, 29 January 2008) (when substantial grounds exist that person faces a real risk of treatment contrary to Art 3 if deported, implies obligation not to deport the person to that country)

Severity threshold of Art 3 ECHR

Soering v. United Kingdom App no 14038/88 (ECtHR, 7 July 1989) (extradition; conditions on death row reach severity of Art 3 ECHR)

Cruz Varas and others v. Sweden App no 15576/89 (ECtHR 20 March 1991) (ill-treatment must attain a minimum level of severity if it is to fall within the scope of Art 3 ECHR)

N. v. United Kingdom [GC] App no 26565/05 (ECtHR, 27 May 2008) (Art 3 not breached by deporting HIV-positive applicant to Uganda)

Al-Saadoon v. United Kingdom App no 61498/08 (ECtHR, 2 March 2010) (inhuman or degrading treatment or punishment includes the death penalty (subsuming Art 2 risks into Art 3 ECHR))

Harkins v. United Kingdom App nos 9146/07 and 32650/07 (ECtHR, 17 January 2012); and *Harkins v. United Kingdom* [GC] (dec) App no 71537/14 (ECtHR, 15 June 2017) (extradition: no real risk of Art 3 severity through mandatory life sentence in US)

S.K. v. Russia App no 52722/15 (ECtHR, 14 February 2017) (removing applicant to Syria would violate Arts 2 and 3 because of the security and humanitarian situation, as well as the type and extent of hostilities and violence in the country)

Absolute nature of Arts 2 and 3 ECHR

Vilvarajah and others v. United Kingdom App nos 13163/87, 13164/87, 13165/87, 13447/87, and 13448/87 (ECtHR, 30 October 1991)

Chahal v. United Kingdom [GC] App no 22414/93 (ECtHR, 15 November 1996)

Assenov and others v. Bulgaria App no 90/1997/874/1086 (ECtHR, 28 October 1998)

Selmouni v. France [GC] App no 25803/94 (ECtHR, 28 July 1999)

Labita v. Italy [GC] App no 26772/95 (ECtHR, 6 April 2000)

Salah Sheekh v. the Netherlands App no 1948/04 (ECtHR, 11 January 2007)

Saadi v. Italy [GC] App no 37201/06 (ECtHR, 28 February 2008)

Svinarenko v. Russia [GC] App nos 32541/08 and 43441/08 (ECtHR, 17 July 2014)

Muršić v. Croatia [GC] App no 7334/13 (ECtHR, 20 October 2016)

Assessing real risk

Vilvarajah and others v. United Kingdom App nos 13163/87, 13164/87, 13165/87, 13447/87, and 13448/87 (ECtHR, 30 October 1991) (mere possibility of ill-treatment is not sufficient to give rise to a breach of Art 3 ECHR; applicants found to be no more at risk than similarly situated persons)

Müslim v. Turkey App no 53566/99 (ECtHR, 26 April 2005) (mere possibility of ill-treatment as a result of temporary instability in the country did not in itself entail a breach of Art 3)

Salah Sheekh v. the Netherlands App no 1948/04 (ECtHR, 11 January 2007) (immaterial whether danger emanates from state agents or non-state actors)

Saadi v. United Kingdom [GC] App no 13229/03 (ECtHR, 29 January 2008); *N.A. v. United Kingdom* App no 25904/07 (ECtHR, 17 July 2008) (exceptionally, where a group is exposed to a systematic practice of ill-treatment, membership of that group may be enough to establish real risk)

N. v. Sweden App no 23505/09 (ECtHR, 20 July 2010) (returning separated woman to Afghanistan would likely lead to 'quasi-detention')

Sufi and Elmi v. United Kingdom App nos 8319/07 and 11449/07 (ECtHR, 28 June 2011) (exceptionally, situations of widespread general violence can suffice for assumption that person would be subject to ill-treatment if returned)

R.B.A.B. and others v. the Netherlands App no 7211/06 (ECtHR, 7 June 2016) (no sufficiently established risk of female genital mutilation if returned to Sudan)

D.L. v. Austria App no 34999/16 (ECtHR, 7 December 2017) (assessment must focus on the foreseeable consequences of the applicant's removal to the country of destination, in the light of the general situation there and of his or her personal circumstances; extradition of Serbian national to Kosovo would be no violation of Arts 2 or 3 ECHR)

I.K. v. Switzerland App no 21417/17 (ECtHR, 19 December 2017) (person facing persecution due to their sexual orientation cannot be asked to conceal it)

A. v. Switzerland App no 60342/16 (ECtHR, 19 December 2017) (Iranian asylum seeker converting to Christianity as such not sufficient to establish risk of Art 2 or 3 ECHR breach if retuned)

Evidence and authorities' assessment

Ahmed v. Austria App no 25964/94 (ECtHR, 17 December 1996) (decisive point in time for assessing risk is the Court's consideration of the case)

N. v. Finland App no 38885/02 (ECtHR, 26/ July 2005) (standard of proof as sufficient evidence to establish substantial grounds for believing that the applicant would be exposed to a real risk of treatment contrary to Art 3)

Saadi v. Italy [GC] App no 37201/06 (ECtHR, 28 February 2008) (in principle for the applicant to adduce evidence that they would be exposed to a real risk of being subjected to treatment contrary to Art 3 ECHR; where such evidence is adduced, it is for the Government to dispel any doubts about it)

A.A. and others v. Sweden App no 14499/09 (ECtHR, 28 June 2012) (no sufficient evidence to establish risk of forced marriage upon return contrary to Art 3 ECHR)

R.C. v. Sweden 41827/07 (ECtHR, 9 March 2010) (as the applicant had substantiated that he had been tortured in the past, the Court found the burden to be on the state authorities to dispel doubts that he may be subjected to ill-treatment upon return)

M.G. v. Bulgaria App no 59297/12 (ECtHR, 25 March 2014) (extradition of Chechen man to Russia would constitute violation of Art 3 ECHR)

M.A. v. Switzerland App no 52589/13 (ECtHR, 18 November 2014) (violation in event of deportation of Iran; applicant should be given benefit of the doubt concerning certain inconsistencies)

R.H. v. Sweden App no 4601/14 (ECtHR, 10 September 2015) (no plausible evidence giving rise to Art 3 violation if applicant returned to Somalia)

A.G.R. v. the Netherlands App no 13442/08 (ECtHR, 12 January 2016); *A.W.Q. and D.H. v. the Netherlands* App no 25077/06 (ECtHR, 12 January 2016); *M.R.A. and others v. the Netherlands* App no 46856/07 (ECtHR, 12 January 2016); *S.D.M. and others v. the Nether*lands App no 8161/07 (ECtHR, 12 January 2016); *S.S. v. the Nether*lands App no 39575/06 (ECtHR, 12 January 2016) (expulsion of Afghan asylum seekers, most of whom had been more or less high ranking officers in the former Afghan army or intelligence service; no violation found by Court who saw no substantiated real risk of ill-treatment if removed to Afghanistan)

M.D. v. Belgium App no 58689/12 (ECtHR, 19 January 2016) (removal of Russian couple of Chechen origin would violate Art 3 if authorities did not first re-examine risk faced in the light of the documents submitted in support of new asylum request)

X. v. Switzerland App no 16744/14 (ECtHR, 26 January 2017) (violation of Art 3 as Swiss authorities had failed to properly assess evidence of prior ill-treatment and future risk and had deported applicant to Sri Lanka, where he had been subjected to further ill-treatment)

N.A. v. Switzerland App no 50364/14 (ECtHR, 30 May 2017) (no violation of Arts 2 or 3 as risk deemed sufficiently low, since applicant's political activities abroad were not reasonably liable to attract the attention of the intelligence service)

A.I. v. Switzerland App no 23378/15 (ECtHR, 30 May 2017) (violation of Arts 2 and 3 ECHR on account of applicant's political activities in exile, which made it likely he would suffer ill-treatment upon return to Sudan)

M.O. v. Switzerland App no 41282/16 (ECtHR, 20 June 2017) (no violation as applicant would not be at risk if removed; domestic authorities had made reasoned decisions which the Court would not substitute)

K.I. v. Russia App no 58182/14 (ECtHR, 7 November 2017) (violation of Art ECHR 3 if applicant were removed to Tajikistan, authorities had not sufficiently considered evidence)

X. v. Germany (dec) App no 54646/17 (ECtHR, 30 November 2017) (inadmissible as decision to deport applicant would not constitute real risk contrary to Art 3 ECHR and domestic courts had made comprehensive assessment)

I.K. v. Switzerland (dec) App no 21417/17 (ECtHR, 18 January 2018) (claim by applicant that he was homosexual and was at risk of ill-treatment if returned to Sierra Leone declared inadmissible due to lack of credibility)

Amerkhanov v. Turkey App no 16026/12 (ECtHR, 5 June 2018); *Batyrkhairov v. Turkey* App no 69929/12 (ECtHR, 5 June 2018) (violation of Art 3 as applicant deported without examination by the national authorities of claim that he would face a real risk of ill-treatment)

B.U. and others v. Russia App nos 59609/17, 74677/17, and 76379/17 (ECtHR, 22 January 2019) (consideration of independent international sources for assessing situation in country)

M.A. v. France App no 9373/15 (ECtHR, 1 February 2018) (having been convicted of terrorist activities in France put applicant at serious risk of ill-treatment in Algeria)

A.M. v. France App no 12148/18 (ECtHR, 29 April 2019) (no risk of ill-treatment as report indicated improvement of the situation in Algeria with regard to torture of alleged terrorists)

Diplomatic assurances

Chahal v. United Kingdom [GC] App no 22414/93 (ECtHR, 15 November 1996) (assurances need to provide, in practice, sufficient guarantees against the risk of treatment contrary to the convention; good faith of promising state is insufficient if circumstances are out of its control)

T.I. v. United Kingdom (dec) App no 43844/98 (ECtHR, 7 March 2000) (court satisfied by Germany's assurances that the applicant would not be immediately or summarily removed)

Mamatkulov v. Turkey [GC] App nos 46827/99 and 46951/99 (ECtHR, 4 February 2005) (assurances given found to negate any real risk)

Saadi v. Italy [GC] App no 37201/06 (ECtHR, 28 February 2008) (weight to be given to assurances depends on the circumstances prevailing at the material time in each case)

Ismoilov v. Russia App no 2947/06 (ECtHR, 24 April 2008) (assurances found unpersuasive in light of general and expert knowledge about torture practices in Uzbekistan)

M.S.S. v. Belgium App no 30696/09 [GC] (ECtHR, 21 January 2011) (assurances deemed insufficient as they were phrased in generic terms and did not refer specifically to the applicant)

Tarakhel v. Switzerland [GC] App no 29217/12 (ECtHR, 4 November 2014) (Court requested that the Swiss authorities first obtained sufficient assurances on the appropriate accommodation of family before sending them back to Italy)

Collective Expulsion/Push-backs

Andric v. Sweden (dec) App no 45917/99 (ECtHR, 23 February 1999) (collective expulsion to be understood as measure compelling aliens, as a group, to leave a country, except where such a measure is taken on the basis of a reasonable and objective examination of the particular case of each individual alien of the group)

Čonka v. Belgium App no 51564/99 (ECtHR, 5 February 2002) (violation of Art 4 Protocol 4 as expulsion procedure had not afforded sufficient guarantees taking into account personal circumstances of each of those concerned)

Berisha v. former Yugoslav Republic of Macedonia (dec) App no 18670/03 (ECtHR, 16 June 2005) (no violation of Art 4 Protocol 4 as the applicants, spouses, had pursued a joint asylum procedure and thus received a single common decision)

Sultani v. France App no 45223/05 (ECtHR, 20 September 2007) (collective flight through which applicant was to be deported did not constitute a violation of Art 4 Protocol 4 as there had been assessment of the applicant's individual claim and situation)

Dritsas v. Italy (dec) App no 2344/02 (ECtHR, 1 February 2011) (no violation of Art 4 Protocol 4 as applicants had refused to show their identity papers to the police who then had been unable to issue individual expulsion orders)

Hirsi Jamaa and others v. Italy [GC] App no 27765/09 (ECtHR, 23 February 2012) (prohibition of collective expulsion applies also extraterritorially (*effet utile*))

M.A. v. Cyprus App no 41872/10 (ECtHR, 23 July 2013) (no violation of Art 4 Protocol 4 as every case concerning deportation was looked at individually and decided on its own particular facts)

Sharifi and others v. Italy App no 16643/09 (ECtHR, 21 October 2014) (violation of Art 4 Protocol 4 by the Italian authorities who immediately returned the applicants to Greece)

Khlaifia and others v. Italy [GC] App no 16483/12 (ECtHR, 15 December 2016) (no violation as each person had been identified individually and allowed to raise any personal objections)

Berdzenishvili and others v. Russia App nos 14594/07 and six others (ECtHR, 26 March 2019) (violation found of Convention rights of Georgian citizens subjected to administrative practice of arrest, detention, and expulsion)

N.D. and N.T. v. Spain App nos 8675/15 and 8697/15 (ECtHR, 13 February 2020) (immediate return of migrants who had attempted to enter Spain illegally not in violation of Art 4 of Protocol 4 alone or in conjunction with Art 13)

Asady and others v. Slovakia App no 24917/15 (ECtHR, 24 March 2020) (removal of group of migrants not in breach of Convention or Protocol as applicants were given short interviews and informed of their rights)

Returning Migrants under the EU Dublin Regulation

T.I. v. United Kingdom (dec) App no 43844/98 (ECtHR, 7 March 2000) (inadmissible as no risk established if sent back to Germany under Dublin system)

K.R.S. v. United Kingdom App no 32733/08 (ECtHR, 2 Dec 2008) (transfer of an asylum seeker to Greece could not be presumed to be against the Convention; overturned by *M.S.S.*)

M.S.S. v. Belgium App no 30696/09 [GC] (ECtHR, 21 January 2011) (violation of Art 3 due to conditions and deficiencies in asylum procedure in Greece)

Mohammed Hussein v. the Netherlands (dec) App no 27725/10 (ECtHR, 2 April 2013) (no sufficiently real and imminent risk of hardship severe enough to fall within the scope of Art 3 if applicant and children returned to Italy)

Mohammed v. Austria App no 2283/12 (ECtHR, 6 June 2013) (no violation of Art 3, but violation of Art 13 in conjunction with Art 3 due to lack of protection against forced transfer during asylum proceedings which had arguable claim that applicant's Convention rights would be violated if transferred)

Sharifi v. Austria App no 60104/08 (ECtHR, 5 December 2013) (transfer from Austria to Greece under Dublin II did not violate Art 3 as Austrian authorities must have been aware of serious deficiencies in the Greek asylum procedure and living and detention conditions, but did not know that those deficiencies reached Art 3 threshold)

Sharifi and others v. Italy App no 16643/09 (ECtHR, 21 October 2014) (violation of Art 3 alone and combined with Art 13 ECHR due to the immediate return to Greece, due to the lack of access to an asylum procedure in Italy and the shortcomings in the Greek asylum process)

Tarakhel v. Switzerland [GC] App no 29217/12 (ECtHR, 4 November 2014) (Court requested that the Swiss authorities first obtained sufficient assurances on the appropriate accommodation of family before sending them back to Italy)

A.S. v. Switzerland App no 39350/13 (ECtHR, 30 June 2015) (return to Italy would not breach Art 3 or Art 8 ECHR)

Asylum Procedure

Amuur v. France App no 19776/92 (ECtHR, 25 June 1996) (legitimate concern enforce immigration restrictions must not deprive asylum-seekers of the protection afforded by international conventions; right to gain effective access to the procedure for determining refugee status)

Maaouia v. France [GC] App no 39652/98 (ECtHR, 5 October 2000) (Art 6 fair trial guarantees does not apply to immigration proceedings)

Hilal v. United Kingdom 45276/99 (ECtHR, 6 March 2001) (government had not provided sufficient evidence for doubting the authenticity of the applicant's materials and documents)

Salah Sheekh v. the Netherlands App no 1948/04 (ECtHR, 11 January 2007) (authorities required to make a decision sufficiently supported by domestic materials and materials originating from other reliable and objective sources)

Abdolkhani v. Turkey App no 30471/08 (ECtHR, 22 September 2009) (denial of access to asylum procedure constitutes violation of Art 13 ECHR)

Rahimi v. Greece App no 8687/08 (ECtHR, 5 July 2011) (minors must be able in practice to contact a lawyer; interviews need to be conducted in native language in order for them to have effective access to their rights)

Popov v. France App nos 39472/07 and 39474/07 (ECtHR, 19 January 2012) (violation of Art 5(4) ECHR as domestic courts had issued removal/detention orders only against parents and not children who thereby had no legal order they could challenge in the court)

M.S.S. v. Belgium [GC] App no 30696/09 (ECtHR, 21 January 2011) (effective remedy must be available both in law and in practice; authority conducting review, though not necessarily judicial, must be independent and conduct thorough assessment)

I.M. v. France App no 9152/09 (ECtHR, 2 February 2012) (Court confines itself to verifying that domestic procedures are effective and safeguard human rights; violation of Art 13 owing to shortcomings of fast-track asylum procedure rendering remedy ineffective)

Singh v. Belgium App no 33210/11 (ECtHR, 2 October 2012) (failure to carefully examine documents submitted in breach of effective remedy obligation)

Naibzay v. the Netherlands (dec) App no 68564/12 (ECtHR, 22 October 2012) (complaint relating to status exclusion under Art 1 F Geneva Refugee Convention found incompatible *ratione materiae*)

De Souza Ribeiro v. France [GC] App no 22689/07 (ECtHR, 13 December 2012) (effectiveness of remedy undermined if duration excessive)

Kebe and others v. Ukraine App no 12552/12 (ECtHR, 12 January 2017) (violation of Art 13 in conjunction with Art 3 ECHR as applicant had been allowed to disembark ship only due to Court's order and therefore liable to be removed at any time)

R.T. v. Greece App no 5124/11 (ECtHR, 11 February 2016) (violation of Art 13 in conjunction with Art 3 ECHR due to shortcomings in asylum procedure)

A.M. v. the Netherlands App no 29094/09)(ECtHR, 5 July 2016 (an examination of domestic remedies for the purposes of Art 35(1) ECHR in expulsion cases follows the same parameters as an examination of Art 13 in conjunction with Art 3 ECHR)

A.M. v. France App no 56324/13 (ECtHR, 12 July 2016) (a legal challenge to the administrative detention pending deportation does not need to have suspensive effect on the deportation order)

J.K. and others v. Sweden [GC] App no 59166/12 (ECtHR, 23 August 2016) (burden of proof is a shared duty of the authorities and the asylum seeker to establish all relevant circumstances)

K.I. v. Russia App no 58182/14 (ECtHR, 7 November 2017) (violation of Art 5(4) due to failure to ensure diligent and speedy conduct of appeal proceedings)

Bencheref v. Sweden (dec) App no 9602/15 (ECtHR, 11 January 2018) (applicant had disclosed false nationality to both domestic authorities and Court; declared inadmissible as an abuse of the right of individual application)

J.R. and others v. Greece App no 22696/16 (ECtHR, 25 January 2018) (found breach of Art 5(2) ECHR as information brochure handed out was not sufficiently comprehensible as regarded the legal and factual reasons for the applicants' detention)

Kaak and others v. Greece App no 34215/16 (ECtHR, 3 October 2019) (violation of Art 5(4) ECHR as the applicants who did not have legal assistance and did not understand content of information brochure and unable to understand appeal possibilities available under domestic law)

Art 13 in conjunction with Art 3 ECHR

Čonka v. Belgium App no 51564/99 (ECtHR, 5 February 2002); *Gebremedhin [Geberamadhien] v. France* App no 25389/05 (ECtHR, 26 April 2007) (not having access to remedy with automatic suspensive effect in violation of Art 13 in conjunction with Art 3 ECHR; even if single remedy does not satisfy Art 13, aggregate of remedies available may)

R.U. v. Greece App no 2237/08 (ECtHR, 7 June 2011) (violation of Art 13 ECHR alone due to inability to complain about detention conditions, and Art 13 in conjunction with Art 3 ECHR due to deportation without proper examination of asylum application)

M.A. v. Cyprus App no 41872/10 (ECtHR, 23 July 2013) (Art 13 in conjunction with both Arts 2 and 3 ECHR breached; deportation order against applicant issued despite asylum application being under review, with no effective remedy)

Kholmurodov v. Russia App no 58923/14 (ECtHR, 1 March 2016) (violation of Arts 3 and 13 in conjunction with Art 3 ECHR as authorities had not afforded applicant a rigorous scrutiny and examination of his claims)

A.E.A. v. Greece App no 39034/12 (the inability to lodge an asylum request in practice in violation of Art 13 in conjunction with Art 3)

M.A. and others v. Lithuania App no 59793/17 (ECtHR, 11 December 2018) (applicants refused right to make asylum applications at border; violation of Arts 3 and 13)

Stage II: Treatment of Migrants once Present in the Territory of a State, Including Asylum Detention and Family Reunification

Vulnerability and Vulnerability of Certain Groups

Aksoy v. Turkey App no 21987/93 (ECtHR, 18 December 1996) (victims of torture)

T. v. United Kingdom [GC] App no 24724/94 (ECtHR, 16 December 1999) (children tried under criminal court)

Cyprus v. Turkey App no 25781/94 (ECtHR, 10 May 2001) (racial, ethnic, or religious discrimination)

Chapman v. United Kingdom [GC] App no 27238/95 (ECtHR, 18 January 2001); *Connors v. United Kingdom* App no 66746/01 (ECtHR, 27 May 2004); *D.H. and others v. Czech Republic* [GC] App no 57325/00 (ECtHR, 13 November 2007); *Oršuš and others v. Croatia* App no 15766/03 (ECtHR, 16 March 2010); *V.C. v. Slovakia* App no 18968/07 (ECtHR, 8 November 2011); *Winterstein and others v. France* App no 27013/07 (ECtHR, 17 October 2013) (Roma)

Anguelova v. Bulgaria App no 38361/97 (ECtHR, 13 June 2002); *Zeynep A.V.C.I. v. Turkey* App no 37021/97 (ECtHR, 3 February 2003) (persons in custody)

M.C. v. Bulgaria App no 39272/98 (ECtHR, 4 December 2003); *M. v. Croatia* App no 10161/13 (ECtHR, 3 September 2005); *Okkali v. Turkey* App no 52067/99 (ECtHR, 17 October 2006) *Juppala v. Finland* App no 18620/03 (ECtHR, 2 December 2008) (children)

Bati and others v. Turkey App nos 33097/96 and 57834/00 (ECtHR, 3 June 2004) (pregnant women)

Stork v. Germany App no 61603/00 (ECtHR, 16 September 2005) (mental or physical disabilities)

Bączkowski and others v. Poland App no 1543/06 (ECtHR, 3 May 2007); *Alekseyev v. Russia* App no 4916/07, 25924/08, and 14599/09 (ECtHR, 21 October 2010) (people with unpopular views)

N. v. United Kingdom [GC] App no 26565/05 (ECtHR, 27 May 2008) (HIV positive status)

Renolde v. France App no 5608/05 (ECtHR, 16 October 2008); *Alajos Kiss v. Hungary* App no 38832/06 (ECtHR, 20 May 2010) (persons with mental disabilities)

Salduz v. Turkey App no 36391/02 (ECtHR, 27 November 2008); *Paskal v. Ukraine* App no 24652/04 (ECtHR, 15 September 2011) (criminal defendants)

Rupa v. Romania (no 1) App no 58478/00 (ECtHR, 16 December 2008); *Salman v. Turkey* App no 21986/93 (ECtHR, 27 June 2000) (detainees)

Opuz v. Turkey App no 33401/02 (ECtHR, 9 June 2009) (women)

Kiyutin v. Russia App no 2700/10 (ECtHR, 10 March 2011); *I.B. v. Greece* App no 552/10 (ECtHR, 3 October 2013) (persons with HIV/AIDS)

M.B. v. Romania App no 43982/06 (ECtHR, 3 November 2011); *Keenan v. United Kingdom* App no 27229/95 (ECtHR, 4 March 2001) (people with disabilities)

Sufi and Elmi v. United Kingdom App nos 8319/07 and 11449/07 (ECtHR, 28 November 2011) (psychiatric illness)

Yordanova and others v. Bulgaria App no 25446/06 (ECtHR, 24 April 2012) (women affected by domestic violence)

M.S. v. United Kingdom App no 24527/08 (ECtHR, 3 May 2012) (state of great vulnerability can diminish human dignity)

Đorđević v. Croatia App no 41526/10 (ECtHR, 24 July 2012); *Stanev v. Bulgaria* [GC] App no 36760/06 (ECtHR, 17 January 2012) (persons with mental disorders)

M.S. v. Croatia (no 2) App no 75450/12 (ECtHR, 19 February 2015) (inferiority and powerlessness)

Bataliny v. Russia App no 10060/07 (ECtHR, 23 July 2015) (being under the control of the authorities)

O.M. v. Hungary App no 9912/15 (ECtHR, 5 July 2016) (sexual orientation)

Carvalho Pinto De Sousa Morais v. Portugal App no 17484/15 (ECtHR, 25 July 2017) (groups subject to stereotyping)

Sava Terentyev v. Russia App no 10692/09 (ECtHR, 28 August 2018) (groups that have 'a history of oppression or inequality, or that face deep-rooted prejudices, hostility, and discrimination)

Volodina v. Russia App no 41261/16, (ECtHR, 9 July 2019) (victims of domestic violence)

Margin of appreciation narrower if restriction applies to a particularly vulnerable group in society

Abdulaziz v. United Kingdom App nos 9214/80, 9473/81, and 9474/81 (ECtHR, 28 May 1985); *Burghartz v. Switzerland* App no 16213/90 (ECtHR, 22 February 1994) (sex)

Smith v. United Kingdom App nos 33985/96 and 33986/96 (ECtHR, 27 September 1999); *Schalk v. Austria* App no 30141/04 (ECtHR, 24 June 2010) (sexual orientation)

D.H. and others v. Czech Republic [GC] App no 57325/00 (ECtHR, 13 November 2007); *Timishev v. Russia* App nos 55762/00 and 55974/00 (ECtHR, 13 December 2005) (race or ethnicity)

Shtukaturov v. Russia App no 44009/05 (ECtHR, 27 March 2008) (mental facility)

Glor v. Switzerland App no 13444/04 (ECtHR, 30 April 2009) (disability)

Kiyutin v. Russia App no 2700/10 (ECtHR, 10 March 2011) (HIV-status)

Gravity of substantive provision influenced by vulnerability

Soering v. United Kingdom App no 14038/88 (ECtHR, 7 July 1989); *Cruz Varas and others v. Sweden* App no 15576/89 (ECtHR 20 March 1991) (minimum level of severity dependent on circumstances, including for example the sex, age, and state of health of the victim)

D. v. United Kingdom App no 30240/96 (ECtHR 2 May 1997) (Art 3 ECHR in light of the applicant's medical condition)

A. v. United Kingdom App no 25599/94 (ECtHR, 23 September 1998); *Z. and others v. United Kingdom* [GC] App no 29392/95 (ECtHR, 10 May 2001) (children in the context of Art 3)

Üner v. the Netherlands [GC] App no 46410/99 (ECtHR, 18 October 2006); *Kiyutin v. Russia* App no 2700/10 (ECtHR, 10 March 2011); *Gül v. Switzerland* App no 23218/94 (ECtHR, 19 February 1996) (test of gravity of Art 8 ECHR)

K.U. v. Finland App no 2872/02 (ECtHR, 2 March 2009); *Fernández Martínez v. Spain* [GC] App no 56030/07 (ECtHR, 12 June 2014); (children in the context of Art 8)

M. & C. v. Romania App no 29032/04 (ECtHR, 27 September 2011) (procedural obligations towards vulnerable persons who are entitled to effective protection)

V.M. and others v. Belgium [GC] (striking out) App no 60125/11 (ECtHR, 7 July 2016) (extreme vulnerability requires a greater duty of protection)

S.S. v. Slovenia App no 40938/16 (ECtHR, 30 October 2018) (in the case of vulnerable persons, the authorities must show particular vigilance and afford increased protection)

Fortalnov and others v. Russia App no 35973/07 etc (ECtHR 26 June 2018); *Hakim Aka v. Turkey* App no 62077/08 (ECtHR, 6 November 2018) (particularly vulnerable individuals may need special and heightened protection of the state for the equal and effective enjoyment of their human rights)

Vulnerability of asylum seekers

M.S.S. v. Belgium [GC] App no 30696/09 (ECtHR, 21 January 2011) (not having experienced persecution or other serious harm in country of origin categorically excludes vulnerability and entitlement to special protection)

Mahmundi and others v. Greece App no 14902/2010 (ECtHR, 31 July 2012) (family with children and a pregnant woman)

S.H.H. v. United Kingdom App no 60367/10 (ECtHR, 29 January 2013) (disability)

Aden Ahmed v. Malta App no 55352/12 (ECtHR, 23 July 2013) (fragile state of health)

Tarakhel v. Switzerland [GC] App no 29217/12 (ECtHR, 4 November 2014) (family with children)

A.S. v. Switzerland App no 39350/13 (ECtHR, 30 June 2015) (mental illness)

Jama v. Malta App no 10290/13 (ECtHR, 26 November 2015) (despite traumatic experiences, not considered more vulnerable than other adult asylum seekers)

Shioshvili and others v. Russia App no 19356/07 (ECtHR, 20 December 2016) (highly pregnant woman and young children)

Khlaifia and others v. Italy [GC] App no 16483/12 (ECtHR, 15 December 2016) (non-asylum-seeking migrants do not have specific vulnerability inherent in asylum seeker status)

Asylum Detention

Amuur v. France App no 19776/92 (ECtHR, 25 June 1996) (holding applicants in transit zone equivalent in practice to a deprivation of liberty, violation of Art 5(1) ECHR)

Chahal v. United Kingdom [GC] App no 22414/93 (ECtHR, 15 November 1996) (principle of proportionality applies to detention under Art 5(1)(f) only to the extent that the detention should not continue for an unreasonable length of time)

Shamsa v. Poland App nos 45355/99 and 45357/99 (ECtHR, 27 November 2003) (several days' detention not been ordered by court, judge, or any other person authorised by law to exercise judicial power cannot be considered lawful)

Riad v. Belgium App nos 29787/03 and 29810/03 (ECtHR, 24 January 2008) (ten-day confinement in airport transit zone amounted to violation of Art 3 ECHR)

Saadi v. United Kingdom [GC] App no 13229/03 (ECtHR, 29 January 2008) (lists conditions in order for detention of foreigner not be arbitrary, including good faith; detaining an asylum seeker for the sole purpose of administrative convenience acceptable under Art 5 ECHR)

Sadaykov v. Bulgaria App no 75157/01 (ECtHR, 22 May 2008) (not 'necessary' in the sense of Art 5(1)(f) ECHR that the detention is reasonably necessary, so long as it is with a view to deportation)

A. and others v. United Kingdom [GC] App no 3455/05 (ECtHR, 19 February 2009) (anti-terrorism; criteria for detention under Art 5(1)(f): must be carried out in good faith; closely connected to ground of detention; place and conditions of detention should be appropriate; length of the detention should not exceed that reasonably required for the purpose pursued)

S.D. v. Greece App no 53541/07 (ECtHR, 11 June 2009) (asylum detention not permitted until asylum application has been decided on as there was thus no basis for detention, which also made it impossible to have detention reviewed)

Abdolkhani v. Turkey App no 30471/08 (ECtHR, 22 September 2009) (person in detention needs to be informed of reason under Art 5(2) ECHR)

Mikolenko v. Estonia App no 10664/05 (ECtHR, 8 October 2009) (detention ceases to be lawful once removal is no longer realistic)

Louled Massoud v. Malta App no 24340/08 (ECtHR, 27 July 2010) (removal must be a realistic prospect in order for detention to be considered as being taken with a view to deportation and thereby lawful)

M. and others v. Bulgaria App no 41416/08 (ECtHR, 26 July 2011) (immaterial for Art 5(1)(f) ECHR whether expulsion order justifiable under national or Convention law)

Auad v. Bulgaria App no 46390/10 (ECtHR, 11 October 2011) (as Art 5(1)(f) ECHR contains no maximum time limits, the length of deportation proceedings and detention must be assessed on a case-by-case basis)

Yoh-Ekale Mwanje v. Belgium App no 10486/1020 (ECtHR, 20 December 2011) (in case of vulnerable persons, authorities must consider alternatives to detention)

Horshill v. Greece App no 70427/11 (ECtHR, 1 August 2013); *E.A. v. Greece* App no 74308/10 (ECtHR, 30 July 2015) (Art 3 violation found, but no Art 5(1) violation)

Nabil and others v. Hungary App no 62116/12 (ECtHR, 22 September 2015) (detention unlawful if courts fail to examine whether the legal conditions for detention under national law are met)

H.A. v. Greece App no 58424/11 (ECtHR, 21 January 2016) (applicant held at border police station pending his expulsion; violation of Arts 5(1) and 5(4) due the lack of effective remedy)

Amadou v. Greece App no 37991/11 (ECtHR, 4 February 2016) (violation of Art 5(4) ECHR) due to inability to have lawfulness of detention reviewed)

J.N. v. United Kingdom App no 37289/12 (ECtHR, 19 May 2016) ('quality-of-law' which forms basis for deprivation of liberty must be sufficiently accessible, precise, and foreseeable in its application; absence of fixed time-limits and automatic judicial review did not in itself breach the requirements of Art 5 ECHR)

O.M. v. Hungary App no 9912/15 (ECtHR, 5 July 2016) (no legal basis for asylum detention in violation of Art 5(1) ECHR)

V.M. v. United Kingdom App no 49734/12 (ECtHR, 1 September 2016) (the six-month delay in procedure was significant in view of overall length of detention and the applicant's deteriorating mental health; failure of the authorities conduct proceedings with due diligence and violation of 5(1) ECHR)

Khlaifia and others v. Italy [GC] App no 16483/12 (ECtHR, 15 December 2016) (legal basis for detention not public or known to applicants cannot satisfy criteria of Art 5(1) ECHR; if person not informed of ground for detention, possibility of appeal rendered ineffective)

Ahmed v. United Kingdom App no 59727/13 (ECtHR, 2 March 2017) (five- and seven-month appeal procedures, under which detention continued, not considered lack of due diligence and no violation of Art 5(1)(f) ECHR)

S.M.M. v. United Kingdom App no 77450/12 (ECtHR, 22 June 2017) (absence of fixed time-limits and automatic judicial review does not breach the 'quality-of-law' requirements of Art 5(1)(f))

K.I. v. Russia App no 58182/14 (ECtHR, 7 November 2017) (no violation of Art 5(1) regarding applicant's detention pending extradition)

K.G. v. Belgium App no 52548/15 (ECtHR, 6 November 2018) (thirteen-month detention of asylum-seeker for security reasons not in breach of ECHR, as public interest considerations weighed heavily and no evidence of arbitrariness)

O.S.A. and others v. Greece App no 39065/16 (ECtHR, 21 March 2019) (violation of Art 5(4) as applicants who understood only Farsi and had no legal assistance were only issued documents in Greek which did not specified which administrative court had jurisdiction)

Kaak and others v. Greece App no 34215/16 (ECtHR, 3 October 2019) (detention in hotspots Vial and Souda not violation of Art 5(1), but in violation of Art 5(4) ECHR)

S.Z. v. Greece App no 66702/13 (ECtHR, 21 June 2018) (whether deportation is realistically feasible, and detention thereby lawful, evaluated against the general situation in the country of origin)

Z.A. and others v. Russia [GC] App nos 61411/15, 61420/15, 61427/15, and 3028/16 (ECtHR, 21 November 2019) (violation on account of the applicants' confinement in a transit zone, the living conditions in that zone, and the treatment to which they were subjected)

Ilias v. Hungary [GC] App no 47287/15 (ECtHR, 21 November 2019) (violation of Art 5(1) and (4); no violation of Art 3 due to detention conditions but violation of Art 13 due to lack of effective remedy)

Detention Conditions

Dougoz v. Greece App no 40907/98 (ECtHR, 6 June 2001) (conditions of detention, in particular serious overcrowding and absence of sleeping facilities, combined with length of detention, amounted to degrading treatment contrary to Art 3 ECHR)

Aliev v. Ukraine App no 41220/98 (29 April 2003) (non-migration; lack of resources cannot justify prison conditions which are so poor as to reach the threshold of Art 3 ECHR)

Palushi v. Austria App no 27900/04 (ECtHR, 22 December 2009) (refusing access to doctor during detention violates Art 3 ECHR)

R.U. v. Greece App no 2237/08 (ECtHR, 7 June 2011) (violation of Art 3 ECHR due to conditions, in detention centres and violation of Art 13 ECHR due to inability to complain about the detention conditions)
H.A. v. Greece App no 58424/11 (ECtHR, 21 January 2016) (applicant held at border police station pending his expulsion; violation of Art 3 ECHR due to detention)
Amadou v. Greece App no 37991/11 (ECtHR, 4 February 2016) (conditions in detention and after release violated Art 3)
R.T. v. Greece App no 5124/11 (ECtHR, 11 February 2016) (violation of Art 3 as concerning detention conditions at Tychero border post)
Sakir v. Greece App no 48475/09 (ECtHR, 24 March 2016) (violation of Arts 3 and 13 ECHR with regard conditions of detention in a police station and the failure to take into account applicant's vulnerability due to his medical condition, and a violation of Art 3 due to conduct of investigation carried out following an assault on the applicant)
Khlaifia and others v. Italy [GC] App no 16483/12 (ECtHR, 15 December 2016) (no violation of Art 3 ECHR due to conditions on ships)
Thimothawes v. Belgium App no 39061/11 (ECtHR, 4 April 2017) (detention can be justified despite mental health problems, also due to psychological support adapted to mental health situation)
J.R. and others v. Greece App no 22696/16 (ECtHR, 25 January 2018) (one month's detention not found in breach of Art 5(1) and not considered excessive for Art 3 ECHR severity threshold to be met)
Batyrkhairov v. Turkey App no 69929/12 (ECtHR, 5 June 2018); *Amerkhanov v. Turkey* App no 16026/12 (ECtHR, 5 June 2018) (violation of Art 3 ECHR due to conditions at detention centre)
O.S.A. and others v. Greece App no 39065/16 (ECtHR, 21 March 2019) (detention conditions in Vial centre not severe enough to meet Art 3 ECHR threshold)
Kaak and others v. Greece App no 34215/16 (ECtHR, 3 October 2019) (detention conditions in the 'hotspots' of Vial and Souda not in violation of Art 3 ECHR)
Ilias v. Hungary [GC] App no 47287/15 (ECtHR, 21 November 2019) (no Art 3 ECHR violation as regards the living conditions in the Röszke transit zone)

Children as Migrants

Hokkanen v. Finland App no 19823/92 (ECtHR, 23 September 1994); *Kutzner v. Germany* App no 46544/99 (ECtHR, 26 February 2002) (non-migration; authorities have margin of appreciation in assessing best interest, depending on issues at stake)
Siliadin v. France App no 73316/01 (ECtHR, 26 July 2005) (applicant, who was a minor, subjected to domestic servitude)

Muskhadzhiyeva and others v. Belgium App no 41442/07 (ECtHR, 19 January 2010) (children being accompanied by mother does not free authorities from protecting the children)

Rahimi v. Greece App no 8687/08 (ECtHR, 5 July 2011) (access to justice, effective remedies to challenge conditions of detention)

Y.C. v. United Kingdom App no 4547/10 (ECtHR, 13 March 2012) (list of factors which may be decisive for vulnerability not exhaustive and depends on circumstances of each case)

Ahmade v. Greece App no 50520/09 (ECtHR, 25 September 2012) (applicant's refusal to submit to a radiological examination to be interpreted that he had reason revealing a reality which did not correspond to the ages he had indicated to the authorities)

Mohamad v. Greece App no 70586/11 (ECtHR, 11 December 2014) (no regard had been paid to the applicant's status as an unaccompanied minor)

Tarakhel v. Switzerland [GC] App no 29217/12 (ECtHR, 4 November 2015) (deportation of family/children)

Mahamed Jama v. Malta App no 10290/13 (ECtHR, 26 November 2015) (no special vulnerability found)

Abdi Mahamud v. Malta App no 56796/13 (ECtHR, 03 May 2016) (vulnerability in and of itself not ground for exemption from detention; in present case, lack of information on and excessive length of vulnerability determination in breach of Art 5(1) ECHR)

A.B. and others v. France App no 11593/12 (ECtHR, 12 July 2016) (absence of a particular risk of absconding the administrative detention of eighteen days disproportionate to the aim pursued)

Abdullahi Elmi v. Malta App nos 25794/13 and 28151/13 (ECtHR, 22 February 2017) (delays in the procedure, including age assessment, lack of support, as well as prolonged detention in unsuitable conditions)

S.F. and others v. Bulgaria App no 8138/16 (ECtHR, 7 December 2017) (ill treatment of minors while in detention; migrant minors' extreme vulnerability is the decisive factor that takes precedence over considerations relating to the status of illegal immigrant; conditions of applicants so bad that Court found violation even where detention lasted for only thirty-two or forty-one hours)

H.A. and others v. Greece App no 19951/16 (ECtHR, 28 February 2019) (compounded vulnerability of unaccompanied minor migrants)

Khan v. France App no 12267/16 (ECtHR, 28 February 2019) (authorities have to do all reasonably expected of them to fulfil the obligation of protection and care for an unaccompanied foreign minor)

Detention of minors

Muskhadzhiyeva and others v. Belgium App no 41442/07 (ECtHR, 19 January 2010 (detention conditions in closed centre designed for adults unsuitable for children, even when accompanied by their mother)

Popov v. France App nos 39472/07 and 39474/07 (ECtHR, 19 January 2012) (fifteen-day detention in a closed centre with unsuitable living conditions disproportionate in case at hand; also part of finding Art violation was the conditions' unsuitability for children, like lack of play areas or activities for children, and instances of danger for children)

Kanagaratnam v. Belgium App no 15297/09 (ECtHR, 13 March 2012) (detention in view of expulsion; placing migrant children accompanied by their mother in a closed centre for four months exposed them to feelings of anxiety and inferiority, risking compromising their development))

Mahmundi and others v. Greece App no 14902/2010 (ECtHR, 31 July 2012) (family with children and a pregnant woman)

A.B. and others v. France App no 11593/12 (ECtHR, 12 July 2016) (if necessity of detention of minor is not satisfied, detention is arbitrary and unlawful under Art 5(1)(f))

R.K. and others v. France App no 68264/14 (ECtHR, 12 July 2016) (detention of families with children in absence of flight risk incompatible with Art 8)

A.M. and others v. France App no 24587/12 (ECtHR, 12 July 2016); *R.C. v. France* App no 76491/14 (ECtHR, 12 July 2016) (Court did not find a violation of Art 5(1) ECHR as domestic authorities had effectively sought to establish whether the placement of the families in administrative detention was a measure of last resort)

R.M. and others v. France App no 33201/11 (ECtHR, 12 July 2016) (material conditions in the detention facilities deemed unproblematic)

Muzamba Oyaw v. Belgium (dec) App no 23707/15 ECtHR, 4 April 2017) (inadmissible as administrative detention of applicant while his partner, a Belgian national, had been pregnant was not in breach of Arts 5 (1)(f) and 8 ECHR as an adequate assessment had taken place)

S.F. and others v. Bulgaria App no 8136/16 (ECtHR, 7 December 2017) (conditions of administrative detention for accompanied underage migrants)

Bistieva and others v. Poland App no 75157/14 (ECtHR, 10 April 2018) (administrative detention only measure of last resort; failure to take into account the best interests of children; authorities must act with great speed and diligence when dealing with minors in such situations)

Guliyev v. Russia App no 29790/14 (ECtHR, 17 April 2018) (domestic courts did not respect best interests of children and did not assess the proportionality of the measure with regard to applicant's family life)

G.B. and others v. Turkey App no 4633/15 (ECtHR, 17 October 2019) (detention conditions unsuited for children amounting to an Art 3 ECHR violation)

Bilalova v. Poland App no 23685/14 (ECtHR, 26 March 2020) (violation of Art 5(1)(f) ECHR concerning the detention of five children, aged between four and ten years, in a closed centre together with their mother)

Unaccompanied minors

Mubilanzila Mayeka v. Belgium App no 13178/03 (ECtHR, 12 October 2006) (minor was separated from uncle through detention and became unaccompanied, authorities did not work towards reunification with family)

Mohamad v. Greece App no 70586/11 (ECtHR, 11 December 2014) (detention conditions had amounted to inhuman and degrading treatment)

Abdullahi Elmi v. Malta App nos 25794/13 and 28151/13 (ECtHR, 22 February 2017) (cumulative effect of detention conditions complained of and length of detention, aggravated by applicants' vulnerability, amounted to degrading treatment contrary to Art 3 ECHR)

H.A. and others v. Greece App no 19951/16 (ECtHR, 28 February 2019) (compounded vulnerability of unaccompanied minor migrants)

Sh. D. and others v. Greece, Austria, Croatia, Hungary, North Macedonia, Serbia, and Slovenia App no 14165/16 (ECtHR, 13 June 2019) (case admissible only re Greece; violations of Arts 3 and 5(1) ECHR due to unaccompanied minors being placed in police stations and due to the conditions in Idomeni camp)

Right to Family Life

Marckx v. Belgium App no 6833/74 (ECtHR, 13 June 1979) (non-migration; Art 8 ECHR obliges states to act in a manner calculated to allow those concerned to lead a normal family life)

Abdulaziz v. United Kingdom App nos 9214/80, 9473/81, and 9474/81 (ECtHR, 28 May 1985) (inability of women to have their husbands join them from abroad not in violation of Art 8 ECHR alone, but only in conjunction with Art 14 ECHR and account of sex discrimination)

Berrehab v. the Netherlands App no 10730/84 (ECtHR, 21 June 1988) (expulsion of father who could not see daughter in violation of Art 8 ECHR)

Sorabjee v. United Kingdom App no 23938/94 (Commission Decision, 23 October 1995) (despite young age and British nationality of child, could leave the UK to live with mother being sent back to Kenya)

Gül v. Switzerland App no 23218/94 (ECtHR, 19 February 1996) (no obstacles for family to develop family life in Turkey)

Ahmut v. the Netherlands App no 21702/93 (ECtHR, 28 November 1996) (underage children living in their home countries can develop a family life with their parents there)

Boultif v. Switzerland App no 54273/00 (ECtHR, 2 August 2001) (practical impossibility to form family life outside Switzerland rendered non-renewal of residence permit disproportionate)

Şen v. the Netherlands App no 31465/96 (ECtHR, 21 December 2001) (failure to strike fair balance between the interests of the applicants and the state's objective of immigration control)

Tuquabo-Tekle and others v. the Netherlands App no 60655/00 (ECtHR, 1 December 2005) (despite somewhat older minor and ties to country of origin, the applicant being taken out of school and threatened to be married off made court consider the balancing of rights as with a younger minor)

Mugenzi v. France App no 52701/09 (ECtHR, 10 July 2014); *Tanda-Muzinga v. France* App no 2260/10 (ECtHR, 10 July 2014) (where children are involved, the national authorities must, in their assessment of proportionality for the purposes of the Convention, ensure their best interests; reunification procedure must be flexible, prompt, and effective)

Jeunesse v. the Netherlands [GC] App no 12738/10 (ECtHR, 3 October 2014) (domestic authorities did not consider convenience, feasibility, and proportionality in regard of best interests of children)

Z.H. and R.H. v. Switzerland App no 60119/12 (ECtHR, 8 December 2015) (no violation of Art 8 ECHR when Swiss authorities refused to recognize the marriage between a fourteen-year-old and an eighteen-year-old)

I.A.A. and others v. United Kingdom (dec) App no 25960/13 (ECtHR, 8 March 2016) (lists principles applicable in Art 8 determinations in immigration contexts; complaint regarding authorities' refusal to grant adult and teenage children entry to be reunited with mother declared inadmissible as fair balance had been struck between applicants' and state's interest in controlling immigration)

Biao v. Denmark [GC] App no 38590/10 (ECtHR, 24 May 2016) (national immigration policy measure regulating family reunification had an indirect discriminatory effect based on ethnicity and nationality, in violation of Art 14 of the Convention)

El Ghatet v. Switzerland App no 56971/10 (ECtHR, 8 November 2016) (consideration for best interest of the child must be sufficiently reflected in authorities' decision)

Muzamba Oyaw v. Belgium (dec) App no 23707/15 ECtHR, 4 April 2017) (inadmissible as administrative detention of applicant while his partner, a Belgian national, had been pregnant was not in breach of Arts 5 (1)(f) and 8 ECHR as an adequate assessment had taken place)

I.M. v. Switzerland App no 23887/16 (ECtHR, 9 April 2019) (violation of Art 8 where national authorities had failed to take account of applicant's dependence on his adult children and the low risk of reoffending due to disability)

Abokar v. Sweden (dec) App no 23270/16) (ECtHR, 6 June 2019) (application under Art 8 inadmissible as authorities had struck a fair balance between applicant's interests the effective implementation of immigration policy)

Removal of Migrants

N. v. United Kingdom [GC] App no 26565/05 (ECtHR, 27 May 2008) (Art 3 ECHR engaged when deporting a seriously ill person only in 'very exceptional cases' when humanitarian considerations prevail over other interests)

Butt v. Norway App no 47017/09 (ECtHR, 4 December 2012) (persons illegally residing in a member state cannot be considered 'settled migrants' in the sense of the Court's case law on removals)

Hasanbasic v. Switzerland App no 52166/09 (ECtHR, 11 June 2013) (removal based on economic considerations deemed disproportionate when weighed against the circumstances of the applicant)

Ustinova v. Russia App no 7994/14 (ECtHR, 8 November 2016) (violation of Art 8 of the Convention as authorities did not explain why the applicant represented a 'real' danger due to HIV infection)

Paposhvili v. Belgium App no 41738/10 [GC] (ECtHR, 13 December 2016) (Art 3 implied if ill person, although under no imminent risk of death, would face, because of the lack of adequate treatment or access to treatment in the country of destination, a real risk of being exposed to a serious, rapid, and irreversible decline in his state of health leading to severe suffering or decrease in life expectancy)

Abuhmaid v. Ukraine App no 31183/17 (ECtHR, 12 January 2017) (no breach of the positive obligation to provide an effective and accessible procedure)

Gaspar v. Russia App no 23038/15 (ECtHR, 12 June 2018); Zezev v. Russia App no 47781/10 (ECtHR, 12 June 2018) (procedural deficiency where applicants were unable to challenge the reasons underlying the decision prejudicial to them)

Respect for family life with removal (when deciding on removal order, applicant's family situation must be taken into account)

Moustaquim v. Belgium App no 12313/86 (ECtHR, 18 February 1991) (separating applicant who had arrived in country at a very young age from all close relatives a disproportionate interference with family life)

Üner v. the Netherlands [GC] App no 46410/99 (ECtHR, 18 October 2006) (decision had balanced applicant's and state's interests in light of gravity of crime and time limitation of exclusion order)

Maslov v. Austria [GC] App no 1638/03 (ECtHR, 23 June 2008) (expulsion measures against a juvenile carries obligation to take the best interests of the child into account and facilitate their reintegration)

Darren Omoregie and others v. Norway App no 265/07 (ECtHR, 31 July 2008) (removing applicant to Nigeria despite having a wife and child in Norway not considered in breach of Art 8 ECHR as applicant had strong ties with home country)

Bajsultanov v. Austria App no 54131/10 (ECtHR, 12 June 2012) (no violation of Art 8 ECHR due to gravity of crimes, links to country of origin, and possibility to form family life there)

Khan v. Germany App no 38030/12 (ECtHR, 23 April 2015) (authorities acted within margin of appreciation when weighing the impact on the applicant's private life against the danger she posed to public safety); *Khan v. Germany* [GC] (striking out) App no 38030/12 (ECtHR, 21 September 2016)

Kolonja v. Greece App no 49441/12 (ECtHR, 19 May 2016) (life-long expulsion which would likely result in his son growing up separated from his father, against child's best interest)

Salem v. Denmark App no 77036/11 (ECtHR, 1 December 2016) (separation of the applicant from his family if deported did not represent a serious obstacle for his family, especially considering his serious criminal record)

Paposhvili v. Belgium App no 41738/10 [GC] (ECtHR, 13 December 2016) (failed consideration of the effect on family if state of health deteriorated due to deportation)

Kamenov v. Russia App no 17570/15 (ECtHR, 7 March 2017) (failure by domestic authorities to analyse the applicant's family ties)

Krasniki v. Austria App no 41697/12 (ECtHR, 25 April 2017) (applicant and wife had sufficient social and linguistic ties with country of origin, so that removal order would not separate the family)

Külekci v. Austria App no 30441/09 (ECtHR, 1 June 2017) (despite lack of social ties to Turkey, cultural and linguistic ties as well as the time limitation of the exclusion order rendered the decision of the authorities within margin of appreciation)

Ndidi v. United Kingdom App no 41215/14 (ECtHR, 14 September 2017) (when balancing has taken place, only serious reasons could lead the Court to reassess it)

Ejimson v. Germany App no 58681/12 (ECtHR, 1 March 2018) (no violation as relationship with adult daughter could exist via electronic means, and agreement allowing applicant to return to Germany had been proposed)

Stage III: Treatment of Long-term Migrants
Access to Civil, Social and Economic Rights

Residence permit and citizenship

Right to residency (permit)

Gaygusuz v. Austria App no 17371/90 (ECtHR, 16 September 1996) (denying the applicant a social security benefit solely on basis of nationality breaches Art 14 ECHR)

Teshome Goraga Bonger v. the Netherlands (dec) App no 10154/04 (ECtHR, 15 September 2005) (applicant caught in legal 'limbo' of neither having residence or work permit but unable to return to country of origin; ruled falling outside of scope of Art 3 or other provision and therefore inadmissible)

Üner v. the Netherlands [GC] App no 46410/99 (ECtHR, 18 October 2006) (no absolute right to residency; ECHR does not guarantee the right of an alien to enter or to reside in a particular country)

Sisojeva and others v. Latvia [GC] (striking out) App no 60654/00 (ECtHR, 15 January 2007) (Latvians of Russian origin, considered now resolved by GC)

N. v. United Kingdom [GC] App no 26565/05 (ECtHR, 27 May 2008) (Art 3 does not provide opportunity to remain in the state in order to benefit from social support)

Ibrahim Mohamed v. the Netherlands (striking out) App no 1872/04 (ECtHR, 10 March 2009); *Said Botan v. the Netherlands* (striking out) App no 1869/04 (ECtHR, 10 March 2009 (where applicant was granted residence status as a refugee rather than the family residence permit sought, the court nevertheless regards the issue as resolved and would not judge on what type of legal status should be accorded to applicants)

I. v. the Netherlands (dec) App no 24147/11 (partial decision as to admissibility) (ECtHR, 18 October 2011); final decision as to admissibility (ECtHR, 10 July 2012) (applicant's wife was penalised for having been harbouring an 'illegal alien')

Aristimuno Mendizabal v. France App no 51431/99 (ECtHR, 3 November 2011) (continuous renewal of temporary residence permit over years, instead of a permanent one, disproportionate and in violation of Art 8 ECHR)

Kiyutin v. Russia App no 2700/10 (ECtHR, 10 March 2011); *Novruk and others v. Russia* App nos 31039/11 and four others (ECtHR, 15 March 2016) (denying applicants access to residence permit due to being HIV positive contrary to Art 14 ECHR)

G.R. v. the Netherlands App no 22251/07 (ECtHR, 10 January 2012) (the administrative charge for a residence permit application in view of the applicant's low income deprived him of access to the procedure in violation of Art 13 ECHR)

Jeunesse v. the Netherlands [GC] App no 12738/10 (ECtHR, 3 October 2014) (refusal of residence permit without fair balance towards applicant's family life in violation of Art 8 ECHR)

B.A.C. v. Greece App no 11981/15 ECtHR, 13 October 2016) (violation of Art 8 both alone and in conjunction with Art 13 ECHR, as Turkish political dissident lived in with uncertain status for years due to application being neither accepted nor rejected)

Abuhmaid v. Ukraine App no 31183/17 (ECtHR, 12 January 2017) (uncertainty due to inability to regularise status not in violation of Art 13 taken in conjunction with Art 8 ECHR)

Hoti v. Croatia App no 63311/14 (ECtHR, 26 April 2018) (violation of Art 8 due to the impossibility in which the stateless applicant had been to regularise his residence status; however emphasises the 'complex and very specific factual and legal situation' which arose following the break-up of the Socialist Federal Republic of Yugoslavia)

Right to citizenship

Karassev v. Finland (dec) App no 31414/96 (ECtHR, 12 January 1999) (no right to citizenship to be directly derived from any of the rights protected in ECHR)

Slivenko v. Latvia [GC] App no 48321/99 (ECtHR, 9 October 2003) (while no right to acquire citizenship as such, arbitrary denial in breach of Art 8 ECHR impact on private life)

Savoia v. Italy (dec) App no 8407/05 (ECtHR, 11 July 2006) (exceptional circumstances of arbitrary denial of citizenship considered only when it has a serious impact on the private rights of the individual)

Genovese v. Malta App no 53124/09 (ECtHR, 11 October 2011) (not granting citizenship to an illegitimate child of a citizen discriminatory)

Ramadan v. Malta App no 76136/12 (ECtHR, 21 June 2016) (no absolute right to citizenship; long-term stay of applicant in country does not compel the state to treat the migrant's citizenship as native citizenship—even when faced with risk of statelessness)

K.2. v. United Kingdom (dec) App no 42387/13 (ECtHR, 7 February 2017) (stripping of UK citizenship from a UK/Sudan dual citizen due to involvement in terrorism)

Ljatifi v. former Yugoslav Republic of Macedonia App no 19017/16 (ECtHR, 17 May 2018) (violation of Art 1 of Protocol No 7 as claim that applicant was threat to national security not scrutinized by domestic courts)

Right to education

Case 'relating to certain aspects of the laws on the use of languages in education in Belgium' v. Belgium App nos 1474/62, 1677/62, 1691/62, 1769/63, 1994/63, and 2126/64 (ECtHR, 23 July 1968); *Cyprus v. Turkey* App no 25781/94 (ECtHR, 10 May 2001) (right to education without discrimination between nationals and non-nationals absent objective and reasonable justification)

15 Foreign Students v. United Kingdom App no 7671/76 (ECtHR, 19 May 1977) (expulsion of a foreign student does not, in principle, interfere with his right to education)

Sorabjee v. United Kingdom App no 23938/94 (ECtHR, 23 October 1995); *Jaramillo v. United Kingdom* App no 24865/94 (ECtHR, 23 October 1995); *Dabhi v. United Kingdom* App no 28627/95 (ECtHR, 17 January 1997); *Ajayi and others v. United Kingdom* App no 27663/95 (ECtHR, 22 June 1999) (if a parent is going to be expelled, fact that child will have to accompany them will not amount per se to a violation of Art 2 Protocol 1)

Georgiu v. Greece App no 45138/98 (ECtHR, 13 January 2000) (pre-trial detention and detention after conviction does not constitute a violation of right to education)

Vikulov and others v. Latvia App no 16870/03 (ECtHR 25 March 2004) (no violation of Art 2 Protocol 1 as removal of family postponed until the completion of the child's school year; through short duration of deprivation of liberty also no violation of the right to education)

Timishev v. Russia App nos 55762/00 and 55974/00 (ECtHR, 13 December 2005) (Convention and Protocols prohibit a denial of the right to education)

Ponomaryovi v. Bulgaria App no 5335/05 (ECtHR, 21 June 2011) (requirement to pay fees for secondary education on account of foreign nationality and immigration status not justified under Art 14 ECHR)

Right to housing

X. v. Germany App no 165/56 (Commission Decision, 29 September 1956) (Art 8 ECHR does not provide the right to a home itself)

Van Volsem v. Belgium (dec) App no 1464/89 (Commission decision, 9 May 1990) (non-migration; state housing situation which left applicant without heat or power inadmissible)

Chapman v. United Kingdom [GC] App no 27238/95 (ECtHR, 18 January 2001) (Art 8 ECHR does not impose a duty on states to guarantee everyone within their jurisdiction the right to be provided with a home)

O'Rourke v. United Kingdom App no 39022/97 (ECtHR, 26 June 2001) (non-migration; fourteen months on the streets to the detriment of the applicant's health did not reach level of severity to engage Art 3)

Müslim v. Turkey App no 53566 (ECtHR, 26 April 2005) (Art 8 does not impose a general obligation to assist refugees in order to ensure them a certain standard of living; no right to work provided in ECHR)

Moreno Gómez v. Spain App no 4143/02 (ECtHR, 16 November 2004); *Öneryildiz v. Turkey* App no 48939/99 (ECtHR, 30 November 2004); *Fadeyeva v. Russia* App no 55723/00 (ECtHR, 9 June 2007); *Budayeva v. Russia* App no 15339/02 (ECtHR, 20 March 2008) (duty to provide alternative shelter under Art 8 ECHR where housing deprivation is state-caused or -aggravated)

Rahimi v. Greece App no 8687/08 (ECtHR, 5 July 2011) (not helping unaccompanied child in finding accommodation breach of Art 3 ECHR)

Bah v. United Kingdom App no 56328/07 (ECtHR, 27 September 2011) (differential treatment in allocation of housing based on immigration status justified)

Ndikumana v. the Netherlands App no 4714/06 (ECtHR, 6 May 2014) (applicant spending two days on the streets in front of the reception centre before he was provided with accommodation, found manifestly ill-founded)

Yordanova and others v. Bulgaria App no 25446/06 (ECtHR, 24 April 2012) (obligation to secure shelter to particularly vulnerable individuals may flow from Art 8 in exceptional cases)

Tarakhel v. Switzerland [GC] App no 29217/12 (ECtHR, 4 November 2014) (Art 3 does not contain a general obligation to guarantee financial assistance or standard of living)

Hunde v. the Netherlands (dec) App no 17931/16 (ECtHR, 5 July 2016) (ECtHR differentiates the status of a failed and pending asylum seeker as to the positive obligations under Art 3 to provide emergency social assistance)

N.T.P. and others v. France App no 68862/13 ECtHR, 24 May 2018) (accommodation arrangements for family with young children while waiting to submit asylum application not in violation of Art 3 ECHR; night-time accommodation in a hostel, nursery school, and publicly-funded medical care had led applicants to be able to attend to most basic needs and authorities had not been indifferent to their fate)

Right to health care

D. v. United Kingdom App no 30240/96 (ECtHR, 2 May 1997) (ill migrants may invoke Art 3 ECHR to prevent their expulsion to countries with inadequate health care facilities in exceptional circumstances; gravity and stage of illness decisive)

Karara v. Finland App no. 40900/98 (Commission decision, 29 May 1998) (applicant's HIV deemed to be at a stage where a deportation would not be contrary to Art 3 ECHR)

Wasilewski v. Poland App no 32734/96 (ECtHR, 20 April 1999) (Convention does not guarantee the right to any particular standard of medical services or the right to access to medical treatment in any particular country)

S.C.C. v. Sweden (dec) App no 46553/99 (ECtHR, 15 February 2000) (inadmissible as the applicant's state of health would not make her removal to Zambia treatment contrary to Art 3)

Bensaid v. United Kingdom App no 44599/98 (ECtHR, 6 February 2001) (deportation of a schizophrenic patient would not breach Arts 3 or 8 ECHR despite risk of deterioration of mental health in other country)

Pretty v. United Kingdom App no 2346/02 (ECtHR, 29 April 2002) (non-migration; threshold for Art 3 ECHR to be met due to health is very high)

Arcila Henao v. the Netherlands (dec) App no 13669/03 (ECtHR, 24 June 2003) (removal permissible as applicant's illness had not reached an advanced or terminal stage there was a prospect of medical care and family support in his country of origin)

Amegnigan v. the Netherlands (dec) App no 25629/04 (ECtHR, 25 November 2004) (declared manifestly ill-founded, on the grounds that the applicant had not reached the stage of full-blown Aids and was not suffering from any HIV-related illness)

Ndangoya v. Sweden (dec) App no 17868/03 (ECtHR, 22 June 2004) (found inadmissible as applicant's illness had not reached an advanced or terminal stage and adequate treatment was to be found in Tanzania, albeit at considerable cost and with limited availability)

Hukić v. Sweden (dec) App no 17416/05 (ECtHR, 27 September 2005) (inadmissible; deportation of child with Down's syndrome to state where he would receive treatment at a lower standard not contrary to Art 3 ECHR)

N. v. United Kingdom [GC] App no 26565/05 (ECtHR, 27 May 2008) (Art 3 ECHR not breached by deporting HIV-positive applicant to Uganda)

Yoh-Ekale Mwanje v. Belgium App no 10486/1020 (ECtHR, 20 December 2011) (delay of authorities in protecting the applicants' health in violation of her dignity and hence Art 3 ECHR; applicant's health decisive also in determining whether less drastic measures to detention were available or appropriate under Art 5(1)(f) ECHR)

Kochieva and others v. Sweden (dec) App no 75203/12 (ECtHR, 30 April 2013) (physical and mental health of applicants not considered grave enough to fall within the scope of Art 3 ECHR)

Dhahbi v. Italy App no 17120/09 (ECtHR, 8 April 2014) (while short-term residents not contributing to resource intensive public services such as health care may be legitimately limited in their access to such services, this is not justified for long-term legal residents)

M.T. v. Sweden App no 1412/13 (ECtHR, 26 February 2015) (expulsion of patient with kidney failure would not meet the high threshold of Art 3 ECHR and the 'exceptional circumstances' set out in *D. v. United Kingdom*)

S.J. v. Belgium (striking out) [GC] App no 70055/10 (ECtHR, 19 March 2015) (friendly settlement, applicant granted permission to stay for humanitarian decisions based on her HIV positive status)

Tatar v. Switzerland App no 65692/12 (ECtHR, 14 April 2015) (proposed removal of a mentally-ill person at risk of severe self-harm would not constitute a violation of Arts 2 or 3 ECHR)

Paposhvili v. Belgium App no 41738/10 [GC] (ECtHR, 13 December 2016) (deportation of applicant suffering from serious illness in face of doubts as to the availability of appropriate medical treatment there would be in breach of Art 3 ECHR)

Protection against labour exploitation, forced labour, and trafficking with the purpose of labour exploitation

van der Mussele v. Belgium App no 8919/80 (ECHR, 23 November 1983) (non-migration; on forced labour)

Siliadin v. France App no 73316/01 (ECtHR, 26 October 2005) (applicant subjected to domestic slavery, violation of Art 4 ECHR positive obligation)

Rantsev v. Cyprus App no 25965/04 (ECtHR, 7 January 2010) (applicant subjected to human trafficking and sexual exploitation)

V.F. v. France (dec) App no 7196/10 (ECtHR, 29 November 2011) (risk of forced prostitution if deported to Nigeria not substantiated; inadmissible)

M. and others v. Italy App no 40020/03 (ECtHR, 31 July 2012) (violation of Art 3 ECHR procedural limb for failing to effectively investigate allegations of mistreatment, but evidence found insufficient to prove servitude or forced labour)

C.N. v. France App no 67724/09 (ECtHR, 11 October 2012) (applicants subjected to servitude)

C.N. v. United Kingdom App no 4239/08 (ECtHR, 13 November 2012) (applicant subjected to servitude)

L.E. v. Greece App no 71545/12 (ECtHR, 21 January 2016) (violation of Arts 4, 6(1) and 13 ECHR where applicant was a victim of human trafficking, forced into prostitution, and Greece failed to comply with its procedural obligations)

J. and others v. Austria App no 58216/12 (ECtHR, 17 January 2017) (authorities complied with their duty to protect the applicants as potential victims of human trafficking when finding that they had no jurisdiction over crimes committed abroad)

Chowdury and others v. Greece App no 21884/15 (ECtHR 30 March 2017) (qualification of undocumented migrants as vulnerable because of their deprivation of a status when exploited with unfair working conditions)

T.I. and others v. Greece App no 40311/10 (ECtHR, 18 July 2019) (victims of human trafficking; violation of Art 4 ECHR)

Discrimination against Migrants

Abdulaziz v. United Kingdom App nos 9214/80, 9473/81, and 9474/81(ECtHR, 28 May 1985) (Art 14 discrimination found solely on basis of gender of applicants)

Gaygusuz v. Austria App no 17371/90 (ECtHR, 16 September 1996) (denying the applicant a social security benefit on the sole ground that he had not been a national of the state where he had worked legally for over ten years breaches Art 14 ECHR)

Niedzwiecki v. Germany 58453/00 (ECtHR, 25 October 2005) (refusing child benefits to children of aliens with a stable residence permit in violation of Art 14 in conjunction with Art 8 ECHR)

Luczak v. Poland App no 77782/01 (ECtHR, 27 November 2007) (excluding non-national from social security scheme not justified under the given circumstances)

Andrejeva v. Latvia [GC] App no 55707/00 (ECtHR, 18 February 2009) (inability of applicant to receive pension solely on account of her citizenship violates Art 14 in conjunction with Article 1 Protocol 1)

Weller v. Hungary 44399/05 (ECtHR, 31 March 2009) (denying child benefits based on parents' foreign nationality in violation of Art 14 in conjunction with Art 8 ECHR)

Bigaeva v. Greece App no 26713/05 (ECtHR, 28 May 2009) (excluding foreigners from law profession as such not a violation of Art 14 ECHR, however the incoherent approach of authorities with respect to the applicant's professional life found in violation of Art 8 ECHR)

Fawsie v. Greece App no 40080/07 (ECtHR, 16 April 2010) (refusal of the authorities to award a large family allowance to the applicants had not been reasonably justified)

Saidoun v. Greece App no 40083/07 (ECtHR, 28 October 2010) (denying applicant family benefits based on her nationality in violation of Art 14 in conjunction with Art 8 ECHR)

Kiyutin v. Russia App no 2700/10 (ECtHR, 10 March 2011); *Novruk and others v. Russia* App nos 31039/11 and four others (ECtHR, 15 March 2016) (denying applicants access to residence permit due to being HIV positive contrary to Art 14 ECHR)

Bah v. United Kingdom App no 56328/07 (ECtHR, 27 September 2011) (differential treatment in allocation of housing based on immigration status justified)

Dhahbi v. Italy App no 17120/09 (ECtHR, 8 April 2014) (while short-term residents not contributing to resource intensive public services such as health care may be legitimately limited in their access to such services, this is not justified for long-term legal residents)

Pajic v. Croatia App no 68453/13 (ECtHR, 23 February 2016) (discrimination of homosexual couples based on distinction which only granted heterosexual couples access to a residence permit for family reunification)

Novruk and others v. Russia App nos 31039/11 and four others (ECtHR, 15 March 2016) (Russia had not justified the differential treatment of HIV positive migrants who were therefore victims of discrimination based on their state of health)

Biao v. Denmark [GC] App no 38590/10 (ECtHR, 24 May 2016) (national immigration policy measure regulating family reunification had an indirect discriminatory effect based on ethnicity and nationality, in violation of Art 14 of the Convention)

Tadeucci v. Italy App no 51362/09 (ECtHR, 30 June 2016) (discrimination of homosexual couple based on sexual orientation by refusing a residence permit where obtaining legal recognition of their relationship was not possible)

Deportation of Long-term Migrants

Moustaquim v. Belgium App no 12313/86 (ECtHR, 18 February 1991) (separating applicant who had arrived in country at a very young age from all close relatives a disproportionate interference with family life)

Boultif v. Switzerland App no 54273/00 (ECtHR, 2 August 2001) ('Boultif criteria': range of factors in striking a fair balance between states' rights in immigration policy and the human face of the rights of long-term migrants)

Slivenko v. Latvia [GC] App no 48321/99 (ECtHR, 9 October 2003) (social integration of applicants decisive)

Üner v. the Netherlands [GC] App no 46410/99 (ECtHR, 18 October 2006) (despite the applicant having migrated to the Netherlands as a child, the Court considered his ties to Turkey strong enough)

Kaya v. Germany App no 31753/02 (ECtHR, 28 June 2007) (fact that applicant was born and has since lived in a certain country does not bar them from being expelled)

Emre v. Switzerland App no 42034/04 (ECtHR, 22 May 2008) (family ties and other personal relationships that migrants have in receiving country relevant and engage the Convention)

Trabelsi v. Germany App no 41548/06 (ECtHR, 13 October 2011) (seriousness of crimes, committed as adult, and little social ties to Germany outside his own family rendered expulsion no violation of Art 8 ECHR)

Sarkozi v. Austria App no 27945/10 (ECtHR, 2 April 2015) (no breach of Art 8 found, among other judges on migration as adult and retained ties to country of origin)

Kolonja v. Greece App no 49441/12 (ECtHR, 19 May 2016) (permanent nature of exclusion order, combined with the long period that the applicant had lived in Greece and unlikeliness of reoffending, made entry ban violation of Art 8 ECHR)

Khan v. Germany App no 38030/12 (ECtHR, 23 April 2015) (authorities acted within margin of appreciation when weighing the impact on the applicant's private life against the danger she posed to public safety); *Khan v. Germany* [GC] (striking out) App no 38030/12 (ECtHR, 21 September 2016)

Salem v. Denmark App no 77036/11 (ECtHR, 1 December 2016) (no breach through life-long ban, while applicant had children in Denmark, offences were of a serious nature and he still had extensive ties to Lebanon)

Abuhmaid v. Ukraine App no 31183/13 (ECtHR, 12 January 2017) (irregular status of migrants taken into account, regardless of amount of time spent in receiving country)

Krasniqi v. Austria App no 41697/12 (ECtHR, 25 April 2017) (migration as adult, ties to origin country)

Hamesevic v. Denmark (dec) App no 25748/15 (ECtHR, 16 May 2017); *Alam v. Denmark* (dec) App no 33809/15 (ECtHR, 6 June 2017) (no need to make new balancing test where authorities' decision was neither arbitrary nor manifestly unreasonable)

Ndidi v. United Kingdom App no 41215/14 (ECtHR, 14 September 2017) (requirement to ensure compliance of decision with Art 8 does not mean that it is necessary to conduct Art 8 proportionality assessment anew)

Ejimson v. Germany App no 58681/12 (ECtHR, 1 March 2018) (where a long time has lapsed between denial of residence permit and deportation, developments within this time may be taken into account)

Levakovic v. Denmark App no 7841/14 (ECtHR, 23 October 2018) (there must be weighty reasons for expelling a person who has spent most of their life in a state)

Crimes committed by minors

Maslov v. Austria [GC] App no 1638/03 (ECtHR, 23 June 2008) (expulsion measures against a juvenile carries obligation to take the best interests of the child into account and facilitate their reintegration)

Mutlag v. Germany App no 40601/05 (ECtHR, 25 March 2010) (seriousness of the offences and their repeated nature were a deciding factor in the Court finding no violation of Art 8)

Yesufa v. United Kingdom (dec) App no 7347/08 (ECtHR, 26 January 2010) (deciding factor in finding removal proportionate was the length and extent of his offending and the fact that his offending continued well into adulthood)

A.A. v. United Kingdom App no 8000/08 (ECtHR, 20 September 2011) (crimes committed by minors, even if serious, if there is evidence that the applicant has ceased offending and made considerable efforts to rehabilitate and re-integrate into society then the government must provide 'further support' to demonstrate that the applicant poses a continuing risk to the public as justification for his deportation)

Long-term migrant has children

Udeh v. Switzerland App no 12020/09 (ECtHR, 16 April 2013) (relationship with children along with one-time nature of serious offence)

M.P.E.V. and others v. Switzerland App no 3910/13 (ECtHR, 8 July 2014) (integration of daughter together with moderate seriousness of crimes)

Adeishvili (Mazmishvili) v. Russia App no 43553/10 (ECtHR, 16 October 2014) (no Art 8 ECHR breach as children's ages adaptable)

Üner v. the Netherlands [GC] App no 46410/99 (ECtHR, 18 October 2006) (adaptable age)

Jeunesse v. the Netherlands [GC] App no 12738/10 (ECtHR, 3 October 2014) (applicant primary caregiver, high integration level, lack of criminal record)

Cultural and Religious Rights of Migrants

Minority and cultural rights

Chapman v. United Kingdom [GC] App no 27238/95 (ECtHR, 18 January 2001) (protection of minorities is important to the dignity of the whole community)

Khurshid Mustafa v. Sweden App no 23883/06 (ECtHR, 16 December 2008) (immigrant family has a right to receive television broadcasts from abroad under Art 10 ECHR)

Senger v. Germany (dec) App no 32524/05 (ECtHR, 3 February 2009) (preventing prisoner from writing letters to relatives in Russian, as opposed to German, in accordance with the law)

Ciubotaru v. Moldova App no 27138/04 (ECtHR, 27 April 2010) (an individual's ethnic identity constitutes an essential aspect of his or her private life and identity)

Aksu v. Turkey [GC] App nos 4149/04 and 41029/04 (ECtHR, 15 March 2012) (ethnic identity forms part of an individual's private life within the sense of Art 8 ECHR)

Z.H. and R.H. v. Switzerland App no 60119/12 (ECtHR, 8 December 2015) (no violation of Art 8 ECHR when Swiss authorities refused to recognize the marriage between a fourteen-year-old and an eighteen-year-old)

Protection of minorities

Soulas and others v. France App no 43835/11 (ECtHR, 10 July 2008); *Le Pen v. France* (dec) App no 18788/09 (ECtHR, 20 April 2010); and *Féret v. Belgium* App no 15615/07 (ECtHR, 16 July 2009) (free speech-based complaints against the criminalisation of writings inciting hatred against Maghrebin and Islamic communities)

Norwood v. United Kingdom (dec) App no 23131/03 (ECtHR, 16 November 2004) (inadmissibility of a case involving a display of Islamophobia)

Paksas v. Lithuania [GC] App no 34942/04 (ECtHR, 6 January 2011); and *Perinçek v. Switzerland* App no 27510/08 (ECtHR, 17 December 2013) (remarks characterized by Islamophobia are directed against the Convention's underlying values)

R.B. v. Hungary App no 64602/12 (ECtHR, 12 April 2016) (negative stereotyping of a group is capable of impacting on the human dignity of its members)

Religious rights

X. v. United Kingdom App no 7992/77 (Commission decision, 12 July 1978) (mandatory wearing of a motorcycle helmet)

Cha'are Shalom Ve Tsedek v. France [GC] App no 27417/ (ECtHR, 27 June 2000) (access to kosher meat falls within the ambit of Art 9 ECHR)

Dahlab v. Switzerland (dec) App no 42393/98 (ECtHR, 15 January 2001) (Swiss case concerning dismissal of a teacher for wearing a headscarf)

Phull v. France (dec) App no 35753/03 (ECtHR, 11 January 2005) (requirement to remove turban in airport security checks within state's margin of appreciation)

Şahin v. Turkey [GC] App no 44774/98 (ECtHR, 10 November 2005) (student challenging headscarf ban at universities)

Kosteski v. former Yugoslav Republic of Macedonia App no 55170/00 (ECtHR, 13 April 2006) (leave of absence of a private sector employee for attending a religious holiday)

El Morsli v. France (dec) App no 15585/06 (ECtHR, 4 March 2008) (mandatory removal of a headscarf for an identity check in a consulate)

Mann Singh v. France (dec) App no 4479/07 (ECtHR, 13 November 2008) (the photograph on a driver's licence)

Kervanci v. France App no 31645/04 (ECtHR, 4 December 2008); *Dogru v. France* App no 27058/05 (ECtHR, 4 December 2008) (headscarf bans during sports classes)

Jasvir Singh v. France (dec) App no 25463/08 (ECtHR, 30 June 2009); *Ranjit Singh v. France* (dec) App no 27561/08 (ECtHR, 30 June 2009); *Aktas v. France* (dec) App no 43563/08 (ECtHR, 30 June 2009); *Bayrak v. France* (dec) App no 14308/08 (ECtHR, 30 June 2009); *Gamaleddyn v. France* (dec) App no 18527/08 (ECtHR, 30 June 2009); *Gazal v. France* App no 29134/08 (ECtHR, 30 June 2009) (French ban on the wearing of religious symbols in public schools)

Jakóbski v. Poland App no 18429/06 (ECtHR, 7 December 2010) (Buddhist prisoner should get meat-free diet)

Lautsi and others v. Italy [GC] App no 30814/06 (ECtHR, 18 March 2011) (crucifix in classrooms within state's margin of appreciation)

Eweida and others v. United Kingdom App nos 48420/10, 59842/10, 51671/10, and 36516/10 (ECtHR, 15 January 2013) (religion in the workplace: prohibiting wearing of a Christian cross disproportionate in private firm, but not in hospital; no violation of applicants' rights in requiring them to provide services to homosexual couples against their religious convictions)

S.A.S. v. France [GC] App no 43835/11 (ECtHR, 1 July 2014) (French niqab ban within margin of appreciation)

Ebrahimian v. France App no 64846/11 (ECtHR, 26 November 2015) (ban on religious symbols for employees in a public hospital)

Osmanoğlu v. Switzerland App no 29086/12 (ECtHR, 10 January 2017) (mandatory participation in co-ed swimming classes)

Belkacemi v. Belgium App no 37798/13 (ECtHR, 11 July 2017); *Dakir v. Belgium* App no 4619/12 (ECtHR, 11 July 2017) (Belgian face covering ban)

Hamidović v. Bosnia and Herzegovina App no 57792/15 (ECtHR, 5 December 2017) (holding witness in contempt of Court for refusing to remove skullcap in violation of Art 9 ECHR)

Lachiri v. Belgium App no 3413/09 (ECtHR, 18 September 2018) (exclusion from a courtroom for refusing to remove hijab violates Art 9 ECHR)

Index

For the benefit of digital users, indexed terms that span two pages (e.g., 52–53) may, on occasion, appear on only one of those pages.